GEORGE W. SAUNDERS
President and organizer of the Old Time Trail Drivers' Association

# The Gruene Cowboy

"When we reached the end of our trip, we found cattle were selling very cheap, and we had to sell on credit. The party to whom I sold went broke and I lost all that was due me. This was my last trip. After a year at home I married and settled at Goodwin, my present home, where, with much hard labor, in which my wife bore more than her part, we have prospered and are living very contented.

"Our place is better known as Gruene's, and any time any of my old friends come this way I will appreciate a visit."

— H.D. Gruene

# The Gruene Cowboy

Originally compiled and edited
by J. Marvin Hunter

Safari Multimedia, LLC

THE GRUENE COWBOY

Interesting sketches of early cowboys and their experiences on the range and on the trail during the days that tried men's souls – true narratives related by real cowpunchers and men who fathered the cattle industry in Texas.

The original manuscript, *The Trail Drivers of Texas*, was compiled and edited by J. Marvin Hunter and published under the direction of George W. Saunders, President of the Old Time Trail Drivers' Association

Published by Safari Multimedia, LLC.

Copyright 1924 by George W. Saunders
Copyright 1925 by Lamar & Barton, Agents
Copyright © 2015 by Safari Multimedia, LLC

This abridged edition is taken from the second edition of *The Trail Drivers of Texas*, published in 1925 by Cokesbury Press.

No part of this book may be reproduced or transmitted in any form or by any means, electronic or mechanical, including photocopying, recording, or by any information storage-and-retrieval system, without permission in writing from the publisher, except where permitted by law.

For information: contact@safarimultimedia.com

www.thegruenecowboy.com

ISBN-13: 978-0692509647
ISBN-10: 069250964X

Cover photo by Lynette Smith (Dreamstime)
Book design by Safari Multimedia, LLC - v9.9_r15

This book is dedicated to the memory of Texan
George W. Saunders, Feb. 12, 1854 – July 3, 1933

# Table of Contents

Introduction ................................................................................................. 13
The Trail Drivers of Texas ........................................................................... 15
Origin of the Old Chisholm Trail ................................................................ 19
Made a Long Trip to Wyoming ................................................................... 22
More About the Chisholm Trail ................................................................. 24
Cowboy Life in West Texas ........................................................................ 27
Killing of 'Billy the Kid' .............................................................................. 34
Coming Up the Trail in 1882 ..................................................................... 38
The Pumphrey Brothers' Experience on the Trail .................................... 48
Dodging Indians near Packsaddle Mountain ........................................... 50
Cyclones, Blizzards, Stampedes and Indians on the Trail ....................... 54
A Thorny Experience .................................................................................. 57
Drove a Herd over the Trail to California ................................................. 58
Parents Settled in the Republic of Texas .................................................. 61
A Girl on the Trail Masquerades as a Cowboy for Four Months ............ 63
A Trying Trip Alone Through the Wilderness ......................................... 68
Killing and Capturing Buffalo in Kansas .................................................. 78
On the Trail to Nebraska ............................................................................ 85
Echoes of the Cattle Trail ........................................................................... 87
Reminiscences of Old Trail Driving ........................................................... 92
Got 'Wild and Woolly' on the Chisholm Trail .......................................... 95
With Herds to Colorado and New Mexico ................................................ 97
Recollections of the Old Trail Days ........................................................... 99
High-Heeled Boots and Striped Breeches ............................................... 101
Sixty Years in Texas .................................................................................. 102
Courage and Hardihood on the Old Texas Cattle Trail ......................... 105
Lived on the Frontier during Indian Times ............................................ 110
Played Pranks on the Tenderfoot ............................................................. 113
When a Man's Word was as Good as a Gilt-Edged Note ....................... 115
My Experience on the Cow Trail .............................................................. 117
Punching Cattle on the Trail to Kansas .................................................. 122
Exciting Experiences on the Frontier and on the Trail ......................... 126
Observations and Experiences of Bygone Days ..................................... 132
Met Quanah Parker on the Trail .............................................................. 135
Texas Cowboys at a Circus in Minneapolis ............................................. 141
The Remarkable Career of Col. Ike T. Pryor .......................................... 145
Habits and Customs of Early Texans ....................................................... 152
Hit the Trail in High Places ..................................................................... 157

| | |
|---|---|
| The Men Who Made the Trail | 163 |
| A Few Thrilling Incidents in My Experience on the Trail | 170 |
| Memories of the Old Cow Trail | 174 |
| Trail Driving to Kansas and Elsewhere | 179 |
| When Lightning Set the Grass on Fire | 183 |
| Experiences 'Tenderfeet' Could Not Survive | 189 |
| His Father Made Fine 'Bowie' Knives | 200 |
| Scouting and Routing in the Good Old Days | 204 |
| An Indian Battle near the Leona River | 207 |
| A Woman Trail Driver | 210 |
| The Experience of an Old Trail Driver | 217 |
| Days Gone By | 226 |
| When George Saunders Made a Bluff 'Stick' | 244 |
| Reminiscences of the Trail | 249 |
| An Old Frontiersman Tells His Experience | 253 |
| Reflections of the Trail | 258 |
| Some Things I Saw Long Ago | 280 |
| Spent a Hard Winter Near Red Cloud | 285 |
| Experiences of the Trail and Otherwise | 287 |
| Sixty-Eight Years in Texas | 292 |
| My First Five-Dollar Bill | 297 |
| Some Thrilling Experiences of an Old Trailer | 301 |
| Had Plenty of Fun | 306 |
| Thrilling Experiences | 309 |
| Lost Many Thousands of Dollars | 311 |
| The Latch String Is On the Outside | 314 |
| A Faithful Negro Servant | 320 |
| Grazed on Many Ranges | 321 |
| An Eventful Career | 325 |
| No Room in the Tent for Polecats | 327 |
| Harrowing Experience with Jayhawkers | 332 |
| Reminiscences of the Old Trails | 335 |
| Why I Am a Prohibitionist | 340 |
| Played the Fiddle on Herd at Night | 344 |
| Packsaddle Mountain Fight | 347 |
| Where They Put the Trail Boss in a Jail | 353 |
| Relates Incidents of Many Drives | 362 |
| The Killing of Oliver Loving | 368 |
| W.J. Wilson's Narrative | 374 |
| On the Fort Worth and Dodge City Trail | 378 |

| | |
|---|---|
| Character Impersonation | 382 |
| A Log of the Trails | 385 |
| Experiences of a Ranger and Scout | 391 |
| The Poet of the Range | 401 |
| One Trip Up the Trail | 408 |
| A Trip to Kansas in 1870 | 412 |
| Andrew G. Jones | 415 |
| In Conclusion | 418 |
| Index | 421 |

# Introduction

IN 1915, GEORGE W. SAUNDERS, a self-described "old-time" cowboy, organized and founded the now legendary Old Time Trail Drivers' Association. Worried that other old-timers would soon die, taking their colorful accounts of the Wild West with them to their graves, Saunders urged his group to gather the accounts of aging Texans who as young men and women "went up the trail with cattle or horses between 1865 and 1896."

The result was the 1924 masterpiece, *The Trail Drivers of Texas,* from which *The Gruene Cowboy* is excerpted. The original book was hastily assembled by journalist J. Marvin Hunter, who had but three months to organize, edit and proof an early 1920 edition.

Wrote Saunders: "It is our purpose to write a history dealing strictly with trail and ranch life and the early cattle industry. This book will consist of letters written by trail drivers only, giving the minutest details of their experiences of bygone days at home and on the trail, and will contain facts and be full of thrills. Such a book has never been written; all the books published on this subject have been by some author who spent a few months on some ranch, then attempted to write a book, understanding very little about stock or the stock business, and consequently having them pulling off stunts that have never been pulled off anywhere else but in the fertile imagination of some fiction writer."

One of the elder gentlemen who answered Saunders' plea for first-hand accounts of these bygone early cowboy years was H.D. Gruene. The second son of Ernst Gruene, who arrived in New Braunfels from Germany in 1845, lost everything during a second trip up the trail in 1871. Nonetheless, as every visitor to modern-day Gruene can see, this cowboy's last trail ride ended well.

The second edition of *The Trail Drivers of Texas* in 1925 was more than 1,000 pages long. We heavily edited this version to make *The Gruene Cowboy's* length and weight more amenable to tourists strolling past the Gruene Mansion Inn, which H.D. Gruene built as his home and surrounded with cotton farms following his last trip as a Texas trail driver.

This new version includes only the more colorful stories. We've also corrected antiquated spellings and eliminated old-school hyphenations that might distract modern readers from the trail drivers' visceral storytelling. Long paragraphs were broken apart to enhance readability.

Modern readers will find offensive many of the cowboys' disparaging descriptions "Indians" and "Negroes." However, they are a matter of historical record and play an integral role in these retellings of actual events.

We hope you will appreciate this fascinating historical record, and will enjoy Mr. Saunders' Texas keepsake for many years to come.

Stephanie Lieber-Johnson, Editor
*The Gruene Cowboy*

# The Trail Drivers of Texas

*by J.R. Blocker*
*President, Old Time Trail Drivers' Association*

BEFORE THE ADVENT OF RAILROADS, the marketing of cattle was a problem that confronted the man who undertook the raising of cattle in Texas. The great expanse of unsettled domain was ideal for the business. No wire fences were here to limit the range, grass was knee high, and cattle roamed freely over the hills, valleys and prairies of Texas. The longhorn was in the hey-day of his glory. The limitless range, broken by no barrier, extending from the Gulf to Kansas, offered ample opportunities for the man with nerve and determination in this great out-of-doors. There being no fences he allowed his cattle to scatter over the range, but at times he would round them up and throw them back in the vicinity of the home ranch when they strayed too far away.

In the spring the big "roundups" usually took place, when all of the cowmen of each section would participate, coming together at a stated time, gathering all of the cattle on the range, and branding what was rightfully theirs. Be it said to their credit, those early cowmen seldom claimed animals that belonged to a neighbor. If a cow was found unbranded, and there was any evidence that she belonged to some cowman not present, or who lived over in the "next neighborhood," the owner was notified and usually got his cow.

There was a noticeable absence of greed in those days in the cattle business, for the men who chose that means of livelihood were of that whole-souled, big-hearted type that established a rule of "live and let live" and, if a man was suspected of being a thief he was watched, and, if the suspicions were realized, the man found that particular neighborhood to be a mighty unhealthy place to live.

Being sparsely settled in those early days, the ranches being from ten to fifty miles apart, counties unorganized and courts very few, every man in a way was a "law unto himself," so that speedy justice was meted out to offenders whose deeds were calculated to encourage lawlessness.

Gradually the country began to settle up with people, some coming from other states to establish homes in the great Lone Star State, and in the course of time the cattle industry became the leading industry in this region. Farming was not thought of, more than to raise a little corn for bread. Beef was to be had for the asking, or wild game for the killing. Mustangs furnished mounts for the cowman, and these horses proved their value as an aid to the development of the cattle industry. A good rider could break a mustang to the saddle in a very short time, and for endurance these Spanish ponies had no equal.

Then loomed the problem of finding a market for the ever-increasing herds of cattle that were being produced in south and southwest Texas. In this state there was no demand for the beef and hides of the longhorn, but in other states where the population was greater the beeves were needed. Then it was that some far-seeing cowman conceived the idea of getting his cattle to where the demand existed, so it was that trail-driving started. A few herds were driven to Abilene, Kansas, on the Atchison, Topeka and Santa Fe Railroad, and the venture proved so successful financially that before a great while everybody began to send their cattle "up the trail." These drives were not unattended by many dangers, as a great portion of the route was through a region infested by hostile Indians, and many times the redskins carried off the scalps of venturesome cowboys.

For many years the trail-driving continued, or until those great arteries of commerce, the railroads, began to penetrate the stock-raising region, and then gradually the cowpuncher, whose delight was to ride his pony "up the trail," was deprived of that privilege, and now instead he goes along with a trainload to "tail 'em up" when the cattle get down in a stock car.

With the passing of the trail came a better breed of cattle, the longhorn gave place to the short-horn white face Hereford, less vicious and unruly. The free range passed away, wire fences came as a new era set in, with the encroachment of civilization. The Texas cowmen formed an association with regular annual conventions, where ways and means for the improvement and betterment of their business were devised.

These gatherings are a source of much pleasure to the old-time stockmen, and it was at one of these conventions a few years ago that George W. Saunders suggested that an auxiliary association of old-time trail drivers be formed, to be composed of men who "went up the trail" in those early days.

But inasmuch as such an association would detract from the usual business transacted at the meetings of the parent association, it was eventually decided to form a separate association with a different time for its meetings, and thus the Old Trail Drivers' Association sprang into existence, and met with popular favor, so much so that within a year from its organization it had a membership of over 500.

The ranks of the old trail drivers are becoming thinner each year, but there still remain many who knew the pleasures and hardships of a six- and eight-months' trip to market with from 1,500 to 3,000 head of cattle. They are scattered from Texas to the Canadian border and from California to New York. Many are rated in Dun and Bradstreet's in the seven-figure column, while others are not so well-off financially. The stories some of these old fellows could tell would make your hair stand on end, stories of stampedes and Indian raids, stories with dangers and pleasures intermingled and of fortunes made and lost; they made history, which the world does not know a thing about.

To perpetuate the memory of these old trail drivers, who blazed the trail to greater achievement, is the aim of every native-born Texan who knows what has been so unselfishly accomplished. To stimulate it, and keep it alive in the hearts of our Texan youth, will inspire a spirit of reverence and gratitude to their heroic fathers for the liberty, which they have given them – for the free institutions, which are the result of their daring.

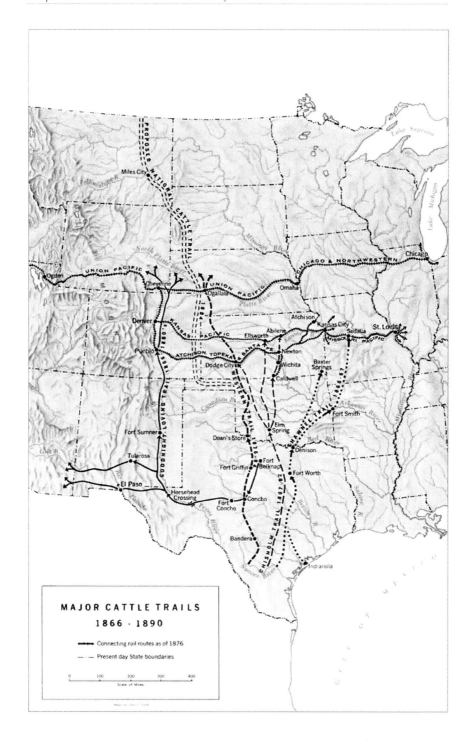

# Origin of the Old Chisholm Trail

### by W.P. Anderson

*(addressed to Mr. Luther A. Lawhon, Secretary,
Old Time Trail Drivers' Association, San Antonio, Texas)*

Dear Sir -

YOUR LETTER OF APRIL 13 came to hand after following me through the Cattle Convention to the Northwest and was finally received at El Paso, Texas, last week on my way here from San Antonio.

In reference to the Old Chisholm Trail I notice that you spell the name "Chism." Another version is "Chissum," but probably the correct one is "Chisholm." As I understand the history of these trails, the original Chisholm Trail was named after John Chisholm, who was a Cherokee cattle trader, who supplied the government frontier posts with their cattle supply in the early part of the occupation of frontier posts and during the Civil War.

Among the first herds that started north from Texas was that of Smith and Elliot, and their guide was a gentleman who was formerly a soldier with Robert E. Lee, who had to do with the civilized tribes of the Indian Territory and used the old military trails, which were supposed to run from Texas to Sedalia, Missouri, and crossed the Red River at Colbert's Ferry, and who afterward was a citizen of San Antonio and whose children reside here now. The name I do not recall at present.

The first diversion from this trail was where the trail left the Sedalia trail for Baxter Springs. It was originally used by this same John Chisholm, the Cherokee Indian cattle trader, to supply Fort Scott, Kansas.

The basic ground for the commencement of this trail was probably about the mouth of the Grand River where it emptied into the Arkansas.

The most prominent branch of this trail runs directly up the Arkansas River as far as Fort Zarah, which was about a mile east of where Great

Bend, Kansas, now stands. From along this trail there were diversions made by these cattle that went into the army supply at Fort Riley; Fort Harker, near Ellsworth; Fort Hays, near Hays City; Fort Wallace, now Wallace, Kansas; the main base being in the Arkansas bottom on what is now called Chisholm Creek near the present city of Wichita, the trail continuing on west as far as Fort Bend and Fort Lyon in Colorado, for the delivery of these cattle. Hence, all cattle trailed from Texas across the Arkansas River would, perforce, strike at some point the old Chisholm Trail, and hence practically all cattle, whether by Colbert's Ferry, Red River Crossing or Doan's Store or elsewhere intermediate, would naturally use some part of the original Cherokee Indian Chisholm Trail on some part of its journey to western Kansas.

In about the late sixties or early seventies, Mr. Charles Goodnight went the western route up the Pecos into the Colorado country, establishing what was known as the Goodnight or the Goodnight & Loving Trail, afterward trailing the "Jingle Bobs" or the John Chissum cattle north, laying the old Tascosa route out to Dodge City, Kansas, which became famous as the Chissum Trail and naturally produced the confusion as to the identity of the original Chisholm cattle trail. Nominally every man that came up the trail felt as though he had traversed the old Chisholm Trail. The facts hardly establish the original of either the New Mexican John Chissum Trail or the John Chisholm Cherokee Trail leading to western frontier army posts as originating in Texas.

In reference to Mr. Goodnight's allusion to my "blazing" the trail for the Joe McCoy herd, my recollection of the first herd that came to Abilene, Kansas, was that of J.J. Meyers, one of the trail drivers of that herd now living at Panhandle, Texas. A Mr. Gibbs, I think, will ascertain further on the subject. The first cattle shipped out of Abilene, that I recollect, was by C.C. Slaughter of Dallas, and while loaded at Abilene, Kansas, the billing was made from memorandum slips at Junction City, Kansas.

The original chapters of Joe McCoy's book were published in a paper called *The Cattle Trail*, edited by H.M. Dixon, whose address is now the Auditorium Building, Chicago. It was my connection with this publication that has probably led Mr. Goodnight into the belief that I helped blaze the trail with McCoy's cattle herd. This was the first paper I know of that published maps of the trails from different cattle-shipping points in Kansas to the intersection of the original Chisholm Trail, one from Coffeyville, Kansas, the first, however, from Baxter Springs, then from Abilene, Newton, then Wichita and Great Bend, Dodge City becoming so famous obviated the necessity for further attention in this direction.

There are many interesting incidents that could still be made a matter of record connected with the old cattle trails that I could enumerate, but I will reserve them for another time.

# Made a Long Trip to Wyoming

### by H.D. Gruene, Goodwin, Texas

IN THE SPRING OF 1870 William Murchison, who was living on the Colorado River, told me that William Green of Llano and Col. Myers of Lockhart were getting ready to take a herd of cattle to Kansas, and asked me to go along as he had hired to them.

I secured the consent of my father, as I was only nineteen years old at that time, and Bill and I pulled out for Llano, where I was engaged by Mr. Green at thirty dollars a month.

After several days gathering the cattle we started on our trip with two wagons carrying grub and luggage, going by way of Burnett and Belton, where we had an awful rain one night and all of our cattle got away. We finally succeeded in getting them together without loss of a single head.

When we reached Fort Worth, the Trinity River was on a rise, and we were compelled to drive our cattle some distance up the river to swim them across. From there we had good going and crossed Red River at Red River Station into the Indian Territory. In the Territory during the rainy nights we had several stampedes, and they came so often we soon got used to them.

When we reached Abilene, Kansas, where we were to deliver the cattle, we held the herd for several weeks and were surprised to learn that the cattle would have to be driven to Cheyenne, Wyoming.

All of the Texas boys quit the herd and returned home, with the exception of four, myself being one of the number who consented to remain with the outfit. Brace Lincecum of Lockhart was the boss of the bunch that was to take the cattle to Cheyenne. After many days hard driving we reached our destination.

There the cattle were sold to another party who wanted them delivered at Bear River, 110 miles above Salt Lake City, Utah, and our boss, Mr. Lincecum, employed to take them there. I went along on condition that I was to receive sixty dollars per month and that I would not have to work at the rear of the herd. John Riggs of Lockhart was my companion on this drive.

We had to take the cattle through the Rocky Mountains, and we found the nights so cold we had to burn sagebrush to keep warm. After the cattle were delivered all of the boys were paid off, and I received my wages in twenty-dollar gold pieces.

We boarded a train to Ogden, where we stopped off and went to Salt Lake City. There we bought some new clothes and had a general "cleaning-up," for we were pretty well inhabited by body lice, the greatest pest encountered on the trail.

The next day we took the train for Abilene, Kansas, and there we each bought a horse and rode as far as Baxter Springs, Missouri, where we met up with some people named Wilks, who were living at Mountain City, Hays County, Texas. They were returning to Texas, and as they had four wagons, we made arrangements to travel with them.

For our passage and board we agreed to do the cooking for the crowd. We finally reached home after a trip that covered nine months.

The following year (1871) I made another trip, but went only as far as Kansas City. I had 335 head of cattle, which I put in with a bunch belonging to William Green. When we reached the end of our trip we found cattle were selling very cheap, and we had to sell on credit. The party to whom I sold went broke and I lost all that was due me.

This was my last trip. After a year at home I married and settled at Goodwin, my present home, where, with much hard labor, in which my wife bore more than her part, we have prospered and are living very contented.

I am in the mercantile business and handle lumber and implements as well, besides having a cotton gin, and own some good farms. We have four children, two boys and two girls, and they are all right here with me helping to conduct my business. Our place is better known as Gruene's, and any time any of my old friends come this way I will appreciate a visit.

# More About the Chisholm Trail

*by Charles Goodnight, Goodnight*

I DO NOT LOOK AT A TRAIL as being an honor or a dishonor to anyone, but I see no reason why they should be named for people who did not make them.

(In) the first volume of this book is given an article by Fred Sutton of Oklahoma City, in which appears this statement: "This trail was started in 1868 by John Chisholm (Chisum), who drove the first bunch of cows from San Antonio to Abilene, Kansas, and for whom the trail was named."

Now, the facts are, John Chisholm (Chisum) followed the Goodnight & Loving Trail up the Pecos in 1866, reaching Bosque Grande on the Pecos about December, wintering right below Bosque Grande, with 600 Jingle Bob steers.

We wintered about eight miles apart. In the spring of 1867 he disposed of those steers to government contractors, and returned to his Colorado and Concho Ranch and began moving his cattle west.

In 1860 I formed a partnership with him on the following basis: He was to deliver to me all cattle he could handle at Bosque Grande on the Pecos River, I allowing him one-dollar per head profit over Texas prices for his risk. During this contract or agreement, he lost two herds by the Indians.

I handled the rest of his drives from Bosque Grande west, disposing of them in Colorado and Wyoming. This continued for three years, and I divided profits equally with him. These profits enabled him to buy the 60,000 head he once held on the Pecos.

Chisholm (Chisum) never drove a herd north, and never claimed to have done so. He did drive two herds to Little Rock at the end of the Civil War, less than 1,000 steers in all.

John McCoy conceived the idea of the Texas cattle trades going to Abilene, and sent scouts down to meet the herds and drive them through the country after they had passed Red River, at the place known as Red River Crossing.

Chisholm (Chisum) moved the herds before spoken of en route to Little Rock by what was well known as the Colbert Crossing, following the old U.S. Road the entire distance.

In conversation with me he said one Chisholm, in no way related to him, did pilot 600 steers from the Texas frontier to old Fort Cobb, and he presumed that this was the origin of the name of the trail, although no trail was opened.

Chisholm (Chisum) was a good trail man, and the best counter I have ever known. He was the only man I have ever seen who could count three grades accurately as they went by. I have seen him do this many times.

I estimate that he delivered to me 15,000 or 16,000 cattle in the three years mentioned. I drove the last of his cattle in 1875, being two herds of big steers, and I took them over what is known as the New Goodnight Trail, leaving the Pecos River above old Fort Sumner to Granada, Colorado.

I think W.J. Wilson, known as "One Armed Bill Wilson," will remember Chisholm's reaching the Pecos in the winter of 1866. As I remember it, he had passed up to the Colorado in 1866 with Mr. Loving with the stock cattle of our first drive, and he and Mr. Loving met me at Bosque Grande on the Pecos, I think, in February 1867.

As above stated I positively know no trail north was made by Chisholm (Chisum) but the first herd driven north out of northwest Texas was driven in 1858 by Oliver Loving, leaving Palo Pinto and Jack counties, thence north to Red River, crossing Red River in the neighborhood of Red River Crossing, and striking the Arkansas River near old Fort Zarah, then up the Arkansas to just above where Pueblo now stands.

There he wintered the herd. In 1859 (spring) he moved them to the Platte River near Denver and peddled them out.

He remained there until the Civil War broke out and had much difficulty in getting back home, but through the assistance of Maxwell, Kit Carson and Dick Wootan, he was given a passport and afterward delivered beef to the Confederacy during the war, which completely broke him up.

He joined me in 1866 on the Western trail, and followed this until his death. Part of these facts were given me by Mr. Loving himself.

CHARLES GOODNIGHT (ca. 1880) was a legendary rancher and cattleman who created the modern livestock industry and became known as the "father of the Texas Panhandle."

# Cowboy Life in West Texas

*by J. Marvin Hunter*

A FEW YEARS AGO JOHN J. LOMAX, the author of several books bearing on the life of the cowboys and cattlemen of Texas, made an address before a folklore society meeting at San Marcos.

While it is true that there are many changes in the cattle country – as witness the introduction and general use of the automobile where a few years ago the big camp meetings or neighborhood gatherings saw the "ambulances," or "buggies" or "buckboards" – sufficient of the picturesque old life remains in Southwest and West Texas to give a vivid idea of how it was in the days of the trail. He drew this picture of the Texas cowboy, his speech and mode of living:

"Prior to taking a herd of cattle up the trail from Texas to Montana or the Dakotas, occurred the spring roundup, which might include a range of country 100 miles in diameter.

"Of course, in such a stretch of land there would be a number of cattle owners. These would all join forces, and after days of hard riding would bring together in a single herd all the cattle running on this range. On this roundup ground the cattle are worked – that is, the calves following their mothers are branded and marked with the decorations employed by their owners, or they are cut into groups either for purposes of sale or for further identification.

"Those cut out are called the 'cut,' the specially trained horses used for this work, so intelligent that you can remove the bridle after the animal to be cut is indicated, and the horse will separate the cow from the bunch with unerring instinct, are called 'cutting horses,' 'carving horses' or 'chopping horses.'

"When fences became more common the calves were cut out through a cutting chute or 'dodged out' so they could be counted. Some cattlemen now employ a branding chute, where an arrangement for holding the cattle while they are being branded is called a 'squeezer' or 'snappin' turtle.'

"In branding cattle, a cowboy, after the rope has dragged the animal near the fire, throws him by 'tailing' or 'flanking.' 'Flanking' consists in seizing the animal by the skin of the flank opposite the cowboy, with his arm thrown over the animal's back. When the animal jumps with all four feet off the ground, the cowboy, by a jerk, throws it on its side; or he 'bulldogs' them by twisting the neck, or 'tails' him by giving a sudden jerk on the tail when some of the animal's feet are off the ground. I once saw a cowboy 'flank' a calf in such a fashion that he threw him completely on his back with all four feet in the air. 'See him sun his moccasins,' said another cowboy who stood near.

"When the flanker and assistants have the animals stretched on the ground they call out 'hot iron' or 'sharp knife,' the brander responding, 'Right here with the goods.'

"Ordinarily the brand is put on by stamping with an iron stamp carrying one, two or three letters, and the different brands and marks employed, like 'Flying U' and the 'Lazy S,' are so various as to require a separate paper to give them adequate description.

"A 'running iron' is a branding iron made of a straight piece of iron with a curve at one end. This end is heated red hot and the branding artist is thus enabled to 'run' any letter he wishes to put on the side of the animal.

"Some of the terms used in marking are 'crop,' 'under bit,' 'over bit,' 'half crop,' 'split,' 'over slope,' 'under slope,' etc. A 'jingle bob' is to split the ear to the head and let the pieces flap. A jug-handled 'dewlap' is a cut in the fleshy part of the throat, also used sometimes as a mark of distinction. Roping a cow is sometimes referred to as 'putting your string on her. ' If a cowboy ropes a cow without hitching the rope to the saddle, 'he takes a dolly welter,' evidently a corruption of Spanish.

"To 'fair ground' is to rope an animal by the head, throw the rope over the back while still running and then throw the animal violently to the ground, where it will usually lay until 'hog tied,' tying three feet together, 'side lined,' tying two feet together on the same side, or 'hoppled,' both hind legs tied together. To tell the age of an animal, the cowboy 'tooths' him, meaning to make an examination of the teeth, as is commonly done in the case of horses, which gives fairly accurate indication of their ages.

"In a cattle outfit the owner is called the 'big boss,' the leader of any particular bunch of men is called the 'boss,' his first lieutenant is called the 'straw boss,' or right-hand man, sometimes called the 'top screw' or 'top waddy.'

"The chief of any group of line riders is a 'line boss,' while the boss of a herd on the trail is the 'trail boss.' Ordinarily, a cowboy is a 'waddy' or 'screw' or 'buckaroo.'

"A green cow hand is called a 'lent,' and his greenness is expressed by the word 'lenty.' He is also sometimes called 'Arbuckle,' on the assumption that the boss sent off Arbuckle premium stamps to pay for the extraordinary services of the greenhorn.

"The 'stray man' is the cowboy's name for one who goes to the neighboring ranches after stray cattle. The 'fence rider,' also called the 'line rider,' is employed to ride fences and repair them.

"Before the day of fences, line riding was following an imaginary line between two ranches and turning the cattle back. The 'line rider' has charge of a 'line camp.'

"In addition to the 'chuck wagon,' a second wagon for carrying the extra beds and bringing wood and water into camps sometimes goes along. This equipage is called the hoodlum wagon and the man who drives it is 'the hood.'

"The cabin where the bachelor cowboys sometimes sleep in very bad weather is called a 'hooden.' A 'bog rider' is the cowboy who 'tails' up the poor cows, which get stuck in the mud.

"The 'chuck wagon' is the cowboy's home! The chuck box is his store; the chuck box lid his table. After a meal, if a luckless cowboy happens to put his tin plate and cup on the chuck box lid instead of the 'round pan' (a tin tub for dishes), this constitutes a 'leggins case;' that is, he is laid over a barrel and treated to a dose of leggins in the hands of the most athletic cowboy.

"The chief man about the camp is the cook, his pay usually equaling that of any of the men, and his expertness in preparing food remarkable when one considers his cook-stove, a hole in the ground, and his cooking utensils, skillets and pots. Naturally, the cook, his pay usually equaling that of any of the men, 'sheffi,' 'dough roller,' 'dinero,' 'coocy' and 'biscuit shooter.' His invariable cry when calling the men to a meal is 'Come and git it!'

"I think I may claim that these few samples of cowboy lingo are characterized by simplicity, strength and directness, and, it may be added, accuracy. I knew a saloon once in the West known as 'The Wolf', another that was aptly named with a big flaring sign on the outside, 'The Road to

Ruin.'

"Out in Arizona there is a town called Tombstone, and the leading paper of that town has named itself the *Tombstone Epitaph*. Let me add a few of his miscellaneous expressions. Of a tall man he does not like, the cowboy says, 'He's just as long as a snake and he drags the ground when he walks.' Of a fool he says, 'He has no more sense than a little nigger with a big navel,' or 'He don't know dung from wild honey.'

"Although a cow is one of the most stupid of animals, when a cowboy says that a man has good 'cow sense' he means to pay him a high compliment. When he means a thing is easy, he says, 'It's just as easy as gutting a slut;' of washing his face, 'bathing out your countenance' or 'washing the profile;' of bathing, 'washing out your canyon;' of vomiting, 'airing the paunch;' an 'eye-bailer' is a person who pokes himself into other people's business; going courting is 'goin' gallin',' 'sitting the bag,' 'sittin' her.'

"'Cutting a rusty' means doing your best; moving fast is 'faggin,' 'leffin' here' or 'sailing away,' 'dragging his navel in the sand'; 'goin' like the heel flies are after him.'

"A very small town is a wide place in the road. A 'two-gun man' is a man who uses a gun in each hand, often at the same time. A man quick to retort is said to have a 'good come-back.' 'Telling a windy' means telling a boastful story; a 'goosy' man is a man physically nervous. When a man plays the deuce spot in a card game, he is said to be 'laying down his character.' To 'fork a horse' is to ride him; when a man is without information on a subject, he tells you, 'I ain't got any medicine;' 'anti-godlin' means going diagonally or in a roundabout way.

"The 'roustabout' is a man of all work about a camp. 'Sweating a game' means doing nothing but sitting around looking at a card game. 'Tie your hats to the saddle and let's ride' means to go on a long hurry-up roundup. The boss' house is referred to as the 'White House.' When a fellow makes a night of it, he is said to have 'stayed out with the dry cattle.' When a delicate situation arises there is said to be 'hair in the butter.'

"The water on the plains is sometimes so muddy that the cowboy says 'he has to chew it before he can swallow it.' When he has gained a little more experience on a proposition, he says he 'has taken a little more hair off the dog.' When there is room for doubt about his knowledge he is said to know as much about it as 'a hog does about a side saddle.'

"A man who is good at roping is said to 'sling the catgut well.' Damp, freezing weather is characterized as cold as 'a well digger in Montana.'

Riding on a freight train in place of paying regular fare on a passenger train is said to be 'saving money for the bartender.' Ordinary stealing is 'yamping. ' 'Plumb locoed' is quite crazy. A very black Negro is characterized as a 'headlight to a snowstorm.'

"Living in isolated groups, visiting but little except among these groups, rarely going to town, shy and timid as a result of long days of solitude, the cowboy develops his own form of speech. Cowboy words, phrases and customs therefore easily become community property – his language a dialect of his own.

"In closing this paper I cannot refrain from giving you one or two cowboy graces repeated indiscriminately either before or during a meal, and I shall end finally with some of his most characteristic dance calls.

"On some future occasion, if I am invited, and if I am provided with just the right kind of an audience, I engage myself to read a paper on cowboy profanity. There is a certain wholesome strength, cleanliness and variety in his profanity, and even his vulgarity, that I do not believe is equaled by any other race of men.

"The rhyme dance calls are supplementary to his spoken directions to the dancers, and add almost as much interest and loveliness of the dance as does the music. Here are two cowboy graces:

> *Eat the meat and leave the skin;*
> *Turn up your plate and let's begin.*
> *Yes, we'll come to the table*
> *As long as we're able,*
> *And eat every damn thing*
> *That looks sorter stable.*

The rhymed dance calls are chanted between the shorter calls and are supplementary to them.

> *Swing your partners round and round;*
> *Pocket full of rocks to hold me down;*
> *Ducks in the river going to ford,*
> *Coffee in a little rag; sugar in the gourd.*
> *Swing 'em early, swing 'em late;*
> *Swing 'em round Mr. Meadow's gate.*
> *Ladies to the center, how do you do;*
> *Right hands cross, and how are you!*

*Two little ladies, do si do,*
*Two little gents you orter know.*
*Swing six when you all get fixed,*
*Do si, ladies like picking up sticks.*
*Chicken in the bread tray kicking up dough;*
*"Granny, will your dog bite?" "No, No, by Joe."*
*Swing corners all,*
*Now your pardners and promenade the hall.*
*You swing me, and I'll swing you;*
*All go to heaven in the same old shoe.*
*Same old road, same old boy,*
*Dance six weeks in Arkansaw.*
*Walk the huckleberry shuffle and Chinese cling.*
*Elbow twist and double L swing.*

THE CHUCK WAGON, invented by Charles Goodnight to carry food and cooking equipment, was the cowboy's home for months at a time while on the trail. The term "chuck wagon" comes from "chuck," a slang term for food which, on the trail, typically included easy-to-preserve items like beans and salted meats, coffee and sourdough biscuits.

# Killing of 'Billy the Kid'

### by Fred E. Sutton of Oklahoma City, Oklahoma

I RECEIVED A LETTER FROM YOUR PRESIDENT, Mr. George W. Saunders, asking for a little story of the most exciting incident that I can recall, which occurred during our cowboy days.

As I was at an excitable age and working out of Dodge City, Kansas, which, to put it mildly, was an exciting town, it is a little hard to decide which particular incident to tell about.

But one that was indeed interesting to me I believe will be of some interest to you and your readers. It took place in the fall of '81, when fifty other punchers and myself were rounding up some 30,000 head of cattle for Jesse Evans, in New Mexico, during which we had considerable trouble with a bunch of outlaws and cattle rustlers headed and controlled by the notorious "Billy the Kid."

For those who are not familiar with his history, I will say that his name was William H. Bonney. He was born in New York City on July 9, 1859, and at the age of twelve he killed a boy companion with a pocket-knife, after which he escaped and went to Kansas, stopping near Atchison (where the writer then lived), where he worked on a farm for a year and a half.

Leaving there he went to New Mexico and went to work on a ranch. He stayed until the fall of '79, when, after a fancied slight, he fell out with a rancher, whom he killed, and from that day on he was an Ishmaelite – his hand against every man and every man's hand against him.

After killing the rancher he surrounded himself with a bunch of the toughest characters to be found on the frontier. His stronghold was the Pecos Valley, where he drank, gambled, stole cattle and murdered all that he fell out with until, at the age of twenty-two, his victims numbered the same as his years.

In the latter part of 1880, a then noted frontier officer by the name of

Pat Garrett was detailed to bring "The Kid" in, dead or alive, and as he knew our boys had been bothered a great deal and had lost several cattle, he came to our camp for help. I was detailed as one of the posse to go with Garrett, and we finally located the outlaw in a ranch house about forty miles from White Oaks.

After surrounding them a halt was called for a parley, during which "Billy the Kid" sent out word by a Mexican outlaw by the name of Jose Martinez, one of his leaders, that if Garrett would send the writer, who was known as "The Crooked S Kid," and Jimmy Carlyle, a young cowboy, to the house he would try and come to some kind of an agreement.

Garrett readily consented to this, as he knew his men and those of "The Kid," and he knew a battle meant death to many. Leaving our guns behind, Jimmy and I went to the house, where we found as tough a bunch of outlaws, gunfighters, and cattle thieves as ever infested a country, or were ever congregated in a space of that size.

After an hour spent in propositions and counter-propositions, we agreed to disagree, and started back to our own crowd with the promise of not being fired on until we reached them.

But we had only traversed about three-fourths of the distance when there was an avalanche of lead sent in our direction, and poor Jimmy, Sheriff William Bradley, and a ranchman by the name of George Hindman, were instantly killed.

Our posse then withdrew.

The killing inflamed the whole Southwest, as all of the dead men were fine men and, with the exception of Jimmy, all had families.

After a few days of rest, Garrett started out with the avowed intention of staying on the trail until he got "The Kid" either dead or alive, and in the summer of 1882 he located him at Sumner, New Mexico, and killed him first and read the warrant to him afterward.

Pat Garrett was one of the bravest of frontier officers, and one who never took advantage of an enemy, no matter what the circumstances or provocation. A short time later he was killed by an outlaw by the name of Wayne Brazel, at Las Cruces, New Mexico, where his grave is now marked by a monument erected by the people of that state who knew and loved him.

I do not know of a more exciting time for yours truly than when "Billy the Kid" and his grand aggregation of murderers and cow thieves opened fire on poor Jimmy Carlyle and me, and do not know why I was not killed, but such is the case, and in a few weeks we were on our way to

Dodge City by way of the Chisholm Trail with 30,000 head of cattle rounded up in New Mexico and Texas.

If this little story comes to the eye of any of the old-time boys who were on this drive with me, I would certainly be glad to have them drop me a line.

This Upham tintype of William Bonney aka 'Billy the Kid' is the only surviving picture of the famous outlaw. One of Billy's old girlfriends said a traveling photographer took the tintype outside Beaver Smith's saloon in Fort Sumner, New Mexico, in 1879 or 1880.

# Coming Up the Trail in 1882

*by Jack Potter, Kenton, Oklahoma*

IN THE SPRING OF 1882, the New England Livestock Co. bought 3,000 short horns in Southwest Texas, cut them into four herds and started them on the trail to Colorado with King Hennant of Corpus Christi in charge of the first herd, Asa Clark of Legarta the second herd, Billie Burke the third herd, and John Smith of San Antonio in charge of the fourth.

When they reached a point near San Antonio, Smith asked me to go with the herd at thirty dollars a month and transportation back. Now, friends, it will not take long to tell my experiences going up the trail, but it will require several pages to recount what I had to endure coming back home.

There was no excitement whatever on this drive. It was to me very much like a summer's outing in the Rocky Mountains.

We went out by way of Fredericksburg, Mason and Brady City, and entered the Western trail at Cow Gap, going through Albany near Fort Griffin, where we left the Western trail and selected a route through to Trinidad, Colorado, via Double Mountain Fork of the Brazos, Wichita and Pease Rivers to the Charles Goodnight Ranch on the Staked Plains.

We had several stampedes while crossing the plains.

En route we saw thousands of antelope crossing the trail in front of the herd. We crossed the Canadian at Tuscosa. This was a typical cowboy town, and at this time a general roundup was in progress, and I believe there were 150 cow-punchers in the place.

They had taken a day off to celebrate, and as there were only seven saloons in Tuscosa they were all doing a flourishing business. We had trouble in crossing the river with our herd, as those fellows were riding up and down the streets yelling and shooting.

Our next point was over the Dim Trail and freight road to Trinidad, Colorado, where we arrived the tenth of July. Here the manager met us and relieved two of the outfits, saying the country up to the South Platte was easy driving and that they would drift the horses along with two outfits instead of four.

The manager and King Hennant made some medicine and called for the entire crews of John Smith and Asa Clark, and told Billie Burke to turn his crew over to Hennant, who was to take charge of the whole drive. I was disappointed, for I did not want to spoil the summer with a two months' drive.

They called the men up one at a time and gave them their checks. However, King Hennant arranged with the manager for me to remain with them, and then it was agreed to send me with some of the cow ponies to the company's cattle ranch in the Big Horn Basin later on.

The drive up the South Platte was fine. We traveled for 300 miles along the foothills of the Rockies, where we were never out of sight of the snowy ranges.

We went out by way of La Junta, Colorado, on the Santa Fe, and then to Deer Trail. We would throw our two herds together at night and the next morning again cut them into two herds for the trail. We arrived at the South Platte River near Greeley, Colorado, about the 10th of August.

The itch or ronia had broken out on the trail and in those days people did not know how to treat it successfully. Our manager sent us a wagon load of kerosene and sulphur with which to fight the disease.

When we reached Cow Creek we turned the herds loose and began building what is known as the Crow Ranch. I worked here thirty days and it seemed like thirty years.

One day the manager came out and gave instructions to shape up a herd of 150 select cow ponies to be taken to the Big Horn Ranch, and I was chosen to go with the outfit.

This was the first time I had seen an outfit fixed up in the North. I supposed we would get a pack horse and fit up a little outfit and two of us hike out with them. It required two days to get started.

The outfit consisted of a wagon loaded with chuck, a big wall tent, cots to sleep on, a stove, and a number one cook. We hit the trail, and it was another outing for me, for this time we were traveling in new fields.

After leaving Cheyenne we pulled out for Powder River and then up to Sheridan. The weather was getting cold and I began to get homesick. When we reached the Indian country I was told that it was only one day's drive to Custer's battleground.

I was agreeably surprised the next morning as we came down a long slope into the Little Big Horn Valley to the battleground.

I was under the impression that Sitting Bull had hemmed Custer up in a box canyon and came up from behind and massacred his entire army. But that was a mistake, as Sitting Bull with his warriors was camped in the beautiful valley when Custer attacked him in the open.

It seems that the Indians retreated slowly up a gradual slope to the east and Custer's men followed. The main fight took place at the top of the rise, as there is a headstone where every soldier fell, and a monument where Custer was killed.

The balance of that day we passed thousands of Indians who were going the same direction we were traveling. When they go to the agency to get their monthly allowance they take along everything with them, each family driving their horses in a separate bunch.

When we arrived at the Crow Agency the boss received a letter from the manager instructing him to send me back to Texas, as the company were contracting for cattle for spring delivery, and I would be needed in the trail drives.

The next morning I roped my favorite horse and said to the boys: "Goodbye, fellows, I am drifting south where the climate suits my clothes."

That day I overtook an outfit on the way to Ogallala and traveled with them several days, and then cut out from them and hiked across the prairie 150 miles to the Crow Ranch, where I sold my two horses and hired a party to take me and my saddle to Greeley, where I set out for home.

*Coming Off the Trail*

Now, reader, here I was, a boy not yet seventeen years old, 2,000 miles from home. I had never been on a railroad train, had never slept in a hotel, never taken a bath in a bath house, and from babyhood I had heard terrible stories about ticket thieves, money-changers, pickpockets, three-card monte, and other robbing schemes, and I had horrors about this, my first railroad trip.

The first thing I did was to make my money safe by tying it up in my shirt tail. I had a draft for $150 and some currency. I purchased a second-hand trunk and about 200 feet of rope with which to tie it. The contents of the trunk were one apple-horn saddle, a pair of chaps, a Colt .45, one sugan, a hen-skin blanket, and a change of dirty clothes. You will see later that this trunk and its contents caused me no end of trouble.

My cowboy friends kindly assisted me in getting ready for the journey. The company had agreed to provide me with transportation, and they purchased a local ticket to Denver for me and gave me a letter to deliver to the general ticket agent at this point, instructing him to sell me a reduced ticket to Dodge City, Kansas, and enable me to secure a cowboy ticket from there to San Antonio for twenty-five dollars.

Dodge City was the largest delivering point in the Northwest, and by the combined efforts of several prominent stockmen a cheap rate to San Antonio had been perfected for the convenience of the hundreds of cowboys returning home after the drives.

About 4 p.m. the Union Pacific train came pulling into Greeley. Then it was a hasty handshake with the boys. One of them handed me my trunk check, saying, "Your baggage is loaded. Good-bye, write me when you get home," and the train pulled out. It took several minutes for me to collect myself, and then the conductor came through and called for the tickets.

When I handed him my ticket he punched a hole in it, and then pulled out a red slip, punched it, too, and slipped it into my hatband. I jumped to my feet and said, "You can't put that on me. Give me back my ticket." But he passed out of hearing and, as I had not yet learned how to walk on a moving train, I could not follow him.

When I had become fairly settled in my seat again the train crossed a bridge, and as it went by I thought the thing was going to hit me on the head. I dodged those bridges all the way up to Denver. When I reached there I got off at the Union Station and walked down to the baggage car, and saw them unloading my trunk. I stepped up and said: "I will take my trunk."

A man said, "No, we are handling this baggage." "But," said I, "that is my trunk, and has my saddle and gun in it." They paid no attention to me and wheeled the trunk off to the baggage room, but I followed right along, determined that they were not going to put anything over me.

Seeing that I was so insistent one of the men asked me for the check. It was wrapped up in my shirt tail, and I went after it, and produced the draft I had been given as wages. He looked at it and said, "This is not your trunk check. Where is your metal check with numbers on it?"

Then it began to dawn on me what the darn thing was, and when I produced it and handed it to him, he asked me where I was going. I told him to San Antonio, Texas, if I could get there. I then showed him my letter to the general ticket agent, and he said : "Now, boy, you leave this trunk right here and we will recheck it and you need not bother about it." That sounded bully to me.

I followed the crowd down Sixteenth and Curtiss Streets and rambled around looking for a quiet place to stop. I found the St. Charles Hotel and made arrangements to stay all night.

Then I went off to a barber shop to get my hair cut and clean up a bit. When the barber finished with me he asked if I wanted a bath, and when I said yes, a Negro porter took me down the hallway and into a side room. He turned on the water, tossed me a couple of towels and disappeared.

I commenced undressing hurriedly, fearing the tub would fill up before I could get ready. The water was within a few inches of the top of the tub when I plunged in. Then I gave a yell like a Comanche Indian, for the water was boiling hot! I came out of the tub on all fours, but when I landed on the marble floor it was so slick that I slipped and fell backwards with my head down. I scrambled around promiscuously, and finally got my footing with a chair for a brace.

I thought: "Jack Potter, you are scalded after the fashion of a hog." I caught a lock of my hair to see if it would "slip," at the same time fanning myself with my big Stetson hat. I next examined my toe nails, for they had received a little more dipping than my hair, but I found them in fairly good shape, turning a bit dark, but still hanging on.

That night I went to the Tabor Opera House and saw a fine play. There I found a cowboy chum, and we took in the sights until midnight, when I returned to the St. Charles. The porter showed me up to my room and turned on the gas.

When he had gone I undressed to go to bed, and stepped up to blow out the light. I blew and blew until I was out of breath, and then tried to fan the flame out with my hat, but I had to go to bed and leave the gas burning. It was fortunate that I did not succeed, for at that time the papers were full of accounts of people gassed just that way.

The next morning I started out to find the Santa Fe ticket office, where I presented my letter to the head man there.

He was a nice appearing gentleman, and when he had looked over the letter he said, "So you are a genuine cowboy? Where is your gun and how many notches have you on its handle? I suppose you carry plenty of salt with you on the trail for emergency? I was just reading in a magazine a few days ago about a large herd that stampeded, and one of the punchers mounted a swift horse and ran up in front of the leaders and began throwing out salt, and stopped the herd just in time to keep them from running off a high precipice."

I laughed heartily when he told me this and said, "My friend, you can't learn the cow business out of books. That yarn was hatched in the brain of some fiction writer who probably never saw a cow in his life. But I am pleased to find a railroad man who will talk, for I always heard that a railroad man only used two words, 'yes' and 'no.'"

Then we had quite a pleasant conversation. He asked me if I was ever in Albert's Buckhorn saloon in San Antonio and saw the collection of fine horns there. Then he gave me an emigrant cowboy ticket to Dodge City and a letter to the agent at that place stating that I was eligible for a cowboy ticket to San Antonio.

As it was near train time I hunted up the baggage crew and told them I was ready to make another start. I showed them my ticket and asked them about my trunk.

They examined it, put on a new check and gave me one with several numbers on it. I wanted to take the trunk out and put it on the train, but they told me to rest easy and they would put it on. I stood right there until I saw them put it on the train, then I climbed aboard.

This being my second day out, I thought my troubles should be over, but not so, for I couldn't face those bridges. They kept me dodging and fighting my head.

An old gentleman who sat near me said, "Young man, I see by your dress that you are a typical cowboy, and no doubt you can master the worst bronco or rope and tie a steer in less than a minute, but in riding on a railway train you seem to be a novice. Sit down on this seat with your back to the front and those bridges will not bother you." And sure enough it was just as he said.

We arrived at Coolidge, Kansas, one of the old landmarks of the Santa Fe trail days, about dark. That night at twelve o'clock we reached Dodge City, where I had to lay over for twenty-four hours.

I thought everything would be quiet in the town at that hour of the night, but I soon found out that they never slept in Dodge. They had a big dance hall there, which was to Dodge City what Jack Harris' Theater was to San Antonio. I arrived at the hall in time to see a gambler and a cowboy mix up in a six-shooter duel.

Lots of smoke, a stampede, but no one killed. I secured a room and retired. When morning came I arose and fared forth to see Dodge City by daylight. It seemed to me that the town was full of cowboys and cattle owners.

The first acquaintance I met here was George W. Saunders, now the president and chief remudero of the Old Trail Drivers. I also found Jesse Pressnall and Slim Johnson there, as well as several others whom I knew down in Texas. Pressnall said to me: "Jack, you will have lots of company on your way home.

"Old 'Dog Face' Smith is up here from Cotulla and he and his whole bunch are going back tonight. Old 'Dog Face' is one of the best trail men that ever drove a cow, but he is all worked up about having to go back on a train. I wish you would help them along down the line in changing cars."

That afternoon I saw a couple of chuck wagons coming in loaded with punchers, who had on the same clothing they wore on the trail, their pants stuck in their boots and their spurs on. They were bound for San Antonio.

Old "Dog Face" Smith was a typical Texan, about thirty years of age, with long hair and three months' growth of whiskers. He wore a blue shirt and a red cotton handkerchief around his neck. He had a bright, intelligent face that bore the appearance of a good trail hound, which no doubt was the cause of people calling him "Dog Face."

It seemed a long time that night to wait for the train and we put in time visiting every saloon in the town. There was a big stud poker game going on in one place, and I saw one Texas fellow, whose name I will not mention, lose a herd of cattle at the game. But he might have won the herd back before daylight.

I will never forget seeing that train come into Dodge City that night. Old "Dog Face" and his bunch were pretty badly frightened and we had considerable difficulty in getting them aboard. It was about 12:30 when the train pulled out. The conductor came around and I gave him my cowboy ticket. It was almost as long as your arm, and as he tore off a chunk of it.

I said: "What authority have you to tear up a man's ticket?" He laughed and said, "You are on my division. I simply tore off one coupon and each conductor between here and San Antonio will tear off one for each division." That sounded all right, but I wondered if that ticket would hold out all the way down.

Everyone seemed to be tired and worn out, and the bunch began bedding down. Old "Dog Face" was out of humor, and was the last one to bed down. At about three o'clock our train was sidetracked to let the westbound train pass.

This little stop caused the boys to sleep the sounder. Just then the westbound train sped by traveling at the rate of about forty miles an hour, and just as it passed our coach the engineer blew the whistle. Talk about your stampedes! That bunch of sleeping cowboys arose as one man, and started on the run with Old "Dog Face" Smith in the lead. I was a little slow in getting off, but fell in with the drags.

I had not yet woke up, but thinking I was in a genuine cattle stampede, yelled out, "Circle your leaders and keep up the drags."

Just then the leaders circled and ran into the drags, knocking some of us down. They circled again and the news butcher crawled out from under foot and jumped through the window like a frog. Before they could circle back the next time, the train crew pushed in the door and caught old "Dog Face" and soon the bunch quieted down.

The conductor was pretty angry and threatened to have us transferred to the freight department and loaded into a stock car.

We had breakfast at Hutchinson, and after eating and were again on our way, speeding through the beautiful farms and thriving towns of Kansas, we organized a kangaroo court and tried the engineer of that westbound train for disturbing the peace of passengers on the east-bound train.

We heard testimony all morning, and called in some of the train crew to testify. One of the brake-men said it was an old trick for that engineer to blow the whistle at that particular siding and that he was undoubtedly the cause of a great many stampedes.

The jury brought in a verdict of guilty and assessed the death penalty. It was ordered that he be captured, taken to some place on the western trail, there to be hog-tied like a steer, and then have the road brand applied with a good hot iron and a herd of not less than 5,000 longhorn Texas steers made to stampede and trample him to death.

We had several hours layover at Emporia, Kansas, where we took the MK&T for Parsons, getting on the main line through Indian Territory to Denison, Texas. There was a large crowd of punchers on the through train who were returning from Ogallala by way of Kansas City and Omaha.

As we were traveling through the Territory, Old "Dog Face" said to me: "Potter, I expect it was me that started that stampede up there in Kansas, but I just couldn't help it. You see, I took on a scare once and since that time I have been on the hair-trigger when suddenly awakened. In the year 1875 me and Wild Horse Jerry were camped at a water hole out west of the Nueces River, where we were snaring mustangs. One evening a couple of peloncias pitched camp nearby, and the next morning our remuda was missing, all except our night horses.

"I told Wild Horse Jerry to hold down the camp and watch the snares, and I hit the trail of those peloncias, which headed for the Rio Grande. I followed it for about forty miles and then lost all signs. It was nightfall, so I made camp, prepared supper and rolled up in my blanket and went to sleep. I don't know how long I slept, but I was awakened by a low voice saying: *"Dejarle descansar bien por que en un rato el va a comenzar su viaje por el otro mundro."* (Let him rest well, as he will soon start on his journey to the other world.)

"It was the two Mexican horse thieves huddled around my campfire smoking their cigarettes and taking it easy, as they thought they had the drop on me.

"As I came out of my bed two bullets whizzed near my head, but about that time my old Colt .45 began talking, and the janitor down in Hades had two more peloncias on his hands.

"Ever since that night, if I am awakened suddenly I generally come out on my all fours roaring like a buffalo bull. I never sleep on a bedstead, for it would not be safe for me, as I might break my darn neck, so I always spread down on the floor."

It was a long ride through the Territory, and we spent the balance of the day singing songs and making merry. I kept thinking about my trunk, and felt grateful that the railroad people had sent along a messenger to look out for it.

At Denison we met up with some emigrant families going to Uvalde, and soon became acquainted with some fine girls in the party. They entertained us all the way down to Taylor , where we changed cars.

As we told them goodbye one asked me to write a line in her autograph album. Now I was sure enough "up a tree." I had been in some pretty tight places, and had had to solve some pretty hard problems, but this was a new one for me. You see, the American people go crazy over some new fad about once a year, and in 1882 it was the autograph fad.

I begged the young lady to excuse me, but she insisted, so I took the album and began writing down all the road brands that I was familiar with. But she told me to write a verse of some kind.

I happened to think of a recitation I had learned at school when I was a little boy, so I wrote as follows : "It's tiresome work says lazy Ned, to climb the hill in my new sled, and beat the other boys. Signed, Your Bulliest Friend, JACK POTTER."

We then boarded the I. & G.N. for San Antonio, and at Austin a lively bunch joined us, including Hal Gosling, United States Marshal, Capt. Joe Sheeley and Sheriff Quigley of Castroville. Pretty soon the porter called out "San "Antonio, Santonnie-o," and that was music to my ears. My first move on getting off the train was to look for my trunk and found it had arrived. I said to myself, "Jack Potter, you're a lucky dog. Ticket held out all right, toe nails all healed up, and trunk came through in good shape."

After registering at the Central Hotel, I wrote to that general ticket agent at Denver as follows:

San Antonio, Texas, Oct. 5, 1882
Gen. Ticket Agt. A.T. & S.F.,
1415 Lamar St., Denver, Colorado

DEAR SIR – I landed in San Antonio this afternoon all OK. My trunk also came through without a scratch. I want to thank you very much for the man you sent along to look after my trunk. He was very accommodating, and would not allow me to assist him in loading it on at Denver. No doubt he will want to see some of the sights of San Antonio, for it is a great place, and noted for its chili con carne. When he takes a fill of this food, as every visitor does, you can expect him back in Denver on very short notice, as he will be seeking a cooler climate. Did you ever eat any chili con carne? I will send you a dozen cans soon, but tell your wife to keep it in the refrigerator as it might set the house on fire. Thank you again for past favors.

Your Bulliest Friend,
JACK POTTER.

> *EDITOR'S NOTE: The foregoing will be read with much interest by the old cowboys who worked the range and traveled the trail with Jack Potter. Mr. Potter is now a prosperous stockman, owning large ranch interests in Oklahoma and New Mexico. He is the son of Rev. Jack Potter, the "Fighting Parson," who was known to all the early settlers of West Texas. The above article is characteristic of the humor and wit of this rip-roaring, hell-raising cow-puncher, who, George W. Saunders says, and other friends concur in the assertion, was considered to be the most cheerful liar on the face of the earth. But he was always the life of the outfit in camp or on the trail.*

# The Pumphrey Brothers' Experience on the Trail

### by J.B. Pumphrey, Taylor, Texas

I AM GLAD THAT THE OLD TRAIL DRIVERS' ASSOCIATION is making up a collection of letters and stories of the "Boys Who Rode the Trail," and it will be fine to read them and recall the old days. I am pleased to hand you a brief sketch of myself and some of my experiences.

My mother was a Boyce, one of the old pioneer families of Texas, and my father came from Ohio as a surgeon with Gen. Taylor during the war between the United States and Mexico, and afterward settled in Texas. My oldest uncle, Jim Boyce, was killed and scalped by Indians on the bank of Gilleland's Creek, near Austin.

I was born at old Round Rock on the 10th of November, 1852, and had the usual schooling of that time, when the "Blue Back Speller" and "Dog-wood Switch" were considered the principal necessities for the boy's education.

All of my life I have been engaged in the cow business, taking my first job in 1869 at fifteen dollars a month, for eighteen hours a day if necessary, with horses furnished.

In February, 1872, I made my first trip on the long trail helping to gather a herd at the old Morrow Ranch, about two miles from Taylor, and from there we went through to Kansas, and then rode back, making about a four months' trip in all, and then I felt like I was a real graduated cowboy.

I would like to see this ride in '72 compared with the longest ride that was ever made. My wages on the trail were sixty dollars per month, I furnishing six head of cow ponies.

This trip was made while working for Cul Juvanel, who was from Indiana and had a lot of Indiana boys with him, whom we called "Short Horns." Myself and two others, Beal Pumphrey, my brother, and Taylor

Penick, were the only Texans in the bunch.

When we reached the South Fork of the Arkansas River it was night, and about five o'clock in the morning, after waking the cook, I was on my way back to the herd when I saw our horses were being hustled, and was afraid they would stampede the herd, when just then the cook yelled "Indians," and sure enough they had rounded up our horses and were going away with them.

A heavy rain was falling and the boss said, "You Texas boys follow the Indians and get those horses."

The two others and myself rode one day and night, having to swim rivers and creeks with our clothing fastened on our shoulders to keep them dry, making the hardest ride of my life, but we did not overtake the Indians, and I am now glad that we did not. We were left with but one horse each, with this herd, but had another herd nearby and, throwing the two together, making about 6,000 head, we took them through to Kansas.

I remember one trip later in the year with Dave Pryor and Ike Pryor, when we were working for Bill Arnold of Llano County. We got back home on the night of Dec. 24, and rolling up in our blankets, slept in the yard, where the folks found us in the morning.

In 1873 I made another trip to Kansas with Bill Murchison of Llano County, and in later years took two other herds through to Kansas.

I have handled cattle in Mexico, South and Central Texas, Oklahoma, and once had a herd in Wyoming. I was director and vice president of the Taylor National Bank for twenty-four years, president of the McCulloch County Land & Cattle Company about twenty-five years, and now have ranches in McCulloch and Stonewall Counties.

I have never forgotten the feel of the saddle after a long day, the weight and pull of the old six-shooter, and what a blessing to cowmen was the old yellow slicker.

Those were the days when men depended upon themselves first, but could rely on their friends to help, if necessary. Days of hard work but good health; plain fare but strong appetites, when people expected to work for their living and short hours and big pay was unknown.

# Dodging Indians near Packsaddle Mountain

*by E.A. (Berry) Robuck, Lockhart, Texas*

I WAS BORN IN CALDWELL COUNTY, TEXAS, Sept. 3, 1857, and was in my sixteenth year when I entered the trail life. My father came to this state from Mississippi in 1854, when he was sixteen years old. He enlisted in the Confederate Army and died in 1863 of pneumonia while in the service.

I was the oldest of three brothers, one of them being Terrell (Tully) Robuck, who went to North Dakota with Col. Jim Ellison's outfit in 1876. He was then sixteen years old. Emmet Robuck, who was assassinated at Brownsville in 1902 while serving as a state ranger, was my son.

I made my first trip up the trail to Utah territory with old man Coleman Jones, who was boss for a herd belonging to Col. Jack Meyers. This herd was put up at the Smith & Wimberly Ranch in Gillespie County.

I gained wonderful experience on this trip in the stampede, high water, hailstorms, thunder and lightning, which played on the horns of the cattle and on my horse's ears.

We suffered from cold and hunger and often slept on wet blankets and wore wet clothing for several days and nights at a time, but it was all in the game, and we were compensated for the unpleasant things by the sport of roping buffalo and seeing sights we had never seen before.

On one occasion my boss sent me from the Wimberly Ranch to another ranch twenty miles away to get some bacon. At the foot of Packsaddle Mountain, in Llano County, I passed about fifty Indians who had killed a beef and were eating their breakfast, but I failed to see them as I passed.

When I reached my destination a man came and reported the presence of the Indians. I had to return over the same route I had come, so I took the best horse I had for my saddle horse and put the packsaddle and bacon on another horse, for I was determined to go back without being handicapped by that bacon. I dodged the Indians and got back to the Wimberly Ranch in safety.

On one of my trail trips we had a trying experience between Red River and the Great Bend of the Arkansas River on the Western trail, when we had to go without water for twenty-four hours. When we finally reached water about 600 head of the cattle bogged in the mud and we worked all night pulling them out.

At another time I was on the Smoky River in Kansas when 2,800 beeves stampeded. I found myself in the middle of the herd, while a cyclone and hailstorm made the frightened brutes run pell-mell. The lightning played all over the horns of the cattle and the ears of my horse, and the hail almost pounded the brim of my hat off.

I stuck to the cattle all night all alone, and was out only one hundred head the next morning. Another time I ran all night, lost my hat in the stampede, and went through the rain bareheaded.

On one trip myself and a Negro, Emanuel Jones, ran into a herd of buffalo in the Indian Territory, and roped two of them. The one I lassoed got me down and trampled my shirt off, but I tied him down with a hobble I had around my waist.

One day my boss told me we were going to make a buffalo run, and asked me to ride my best horse. The horse I rode was a red roan belonging to George Hill, who was afterward assassinated at Cotulla, Texas. Myself and Wash Murray rode together, and when we got into the chase I caught a five-year-old cow.

My horse was "Katy on the spot" in a case of that kind, and helped me to win the championship on that occasion. I was the only man in the party that succeeded in roping a buffalo.

I met Mac Stewart, Noah Ellis, Bill Campbell and several other old Caldwell County boys in Ellsworth, Kansas, on one of my trips. Stewart served three years in the Confederate Army, after which he took to trail life and followed that for several years, then going to Mexico, where he became involved in a difficulty with an officer and killed him.

He was in prison for over ten years with the death sentence hanging over him, but through the influence of friends in this country, he was finally released and returned to Texas, dying shortly afterward.

After meeting this bunch in Ellsworth, a number of us returned home together with the saddle horses. We came back the old Chisholm Trail. While returning through the Indian Territory we were caught in a cyclone and hailstorm one night while I was on guard. The wind was so strong at times it nearly blew me out of the saddle, and the hail pelted me so hard great knots were raised on my head.

Next morning I found myself alone in a strange land with the horses, for I had drifted with the storm. Picking up the back trail, I started for camp, and before long in the distance I saw some people coming toward me. I thought they might be Indians, but it turned out to be Mac Stewart and others who had started out to search for me. The horse I was riding that night was raised by Black Bill Montgomery, and had been taken up the trail that year by Mark Withers.

Three days later we reached Red River, which was on a big rise. We were out of grub, but had to remain there for three days waiting for the river to run down, but it kept getting higher, so we decided to attempt the crossing. We put into the stream, and with great difficulty got the horses across.

Mac Stewart's horse refused to swim, and as Mac could not swim, I went to his rescue. The horse floated down the river, and Mac told me he had $300 in money and his watch tied on his saddle. Sam Henry and I then swam to the horse and took the saddle off, and came out under a bluff. We had a pretty close call, but reached the bank, where we had a big reunion and something to eat.

There is one incident, which I feel I ought to add, as perhaps it did not fall to the lot of many of the boys to have a similar one. I am the chap who caught the blue mustang mare.

This was while we were range herding cattle in Kansas on the Smoky River, near the King Hills, about fifteen miles from old Fort Hays. This blue mustang would come to our saddle horses at night, and also to the river for water.

The boys were all anxious to get her, had set snares made of ropes at the watering places, hoping to get her by the feet, but she always managed to avoid this danger.

One day the boys found her with the horses and, on seeing them, she stampeded. I was on the range about the foot of the hills, saw her coming and made for her with my rope ready. To get back to her herd she had to go through a gap in the hills.

I was riding a good sorrel horse, an E P horse, raised by Ed Persons of Caldwell County. I made for the gap, getting there just in time and as she started to enter, running at breakneck speed, just in the nick of time I threw my rope; it went true and fell securely around her neck.

When the rope tightened, she jerked my horse fully thirty feet, and both animals went down together, not more than ten feet apart. I scrambled to my feet, getting out of the mix-up, but I had my mustang. Manuel Jones and Dan Sheppard, two of the cowboys on the range, coming up about this time, helped me to further secure her and we got her safely back to camp.

In time she responded to good treatment, made a fine saddle animal, and, with her long black mane and tail, she was a beauty of which I was justly proud. Good saddle horses could be had cheap at that time, but I sold her near Red River for sixty-five dollars.

# Cyclones, Blizzards, Stampedes and Indians on the Trail

### by G.H. Mohle, Lockhart, Texas

IN APRIL, 1869, I WAS EMPLOYED BY Black Bill Mongomery to go with a herd of 4,500 head of stock cattle on the drive to Abilene, Kansas. We started from Lockhart and crossed the Colorado River below Austin, out by way of Georgetown, Waxahachie and on to Red River, which we found very high.

We were several days getting the herd across this stream. The first day I crossed over with about 1,000 head and came back and worked the rest of the day in the water, but could not get any more of the cattle across on account of the wind and waves.

Two of the boys and myself went across with grub enough for supper and breakfast, but the next day the weather was so bad the others could not cross to bring us something to eat and we were compelled to go hungry for forty-eight hours.

The next night about twelve o'clock we heard yelling and shouting, but thinking it might be Indians, we remained quiet and did not know until noon the next day that it was some of the boys of our outfit who had brought us some grub, which we found hanging in a tree.

The third day the balance of the herd was crossed over without further trouble. Flies and mosquitoes were very bad, and kept us engaged in fighting them off.

When we reached the North Fork of the Canadian River it was also pretty high, on account of heavy rains. The water was level with the bank on this side, but on the far side the bank was about six feet above the water and the going out place being only about twenty feet wide. We had trouble getting the cattle into the water, and when they did get started they crowded in so that they could not get out on the other side, and began milling, and we lost 116 head and three horses.

When we arrived at the Arkansas River we found it out of its banks and we were compelled to wait several days for it to run down. We were out of provisions, and tried to purchase some from a government train, which was camped at this point.

This wagon train was loaded with flour and bacon, en route to Fort Sill. The man in charge refused to sell us anything, so when the guard was absent we "borrowed" enough grub to last us until we could get some more.

When the flood stage had passed we crossed the river and reached Abilene, Kansas, the latter part of June, camping there a month, and finally sold the cattle to Mr. Evans of California for twenty-five dollars per head, with the understanding that Black Bill Montgomery, Bill Henderson, myself and Gov, the Negro cook, were to go along with the cattle. Mr. Evans also bought the horses.

About the first of August we started for California.

When we reached the Republican River a cyclone struck us, turned our wagon over, and scattered things generally. Mr. Evans had a large tent. It went up in the air and we saw it no more.

We next reached the Platte River, where we camped for several days to allow the cattle to graze and rest. On account of quicksand in the river we had to go up the stream about twenty-five miles to make a crossing.

At Platte City we purchased a supply of provisions, and went on up the northwest side of the river about a hundred miles, to where about 500 soldiers were camped.

We camped about a quarter of a mile above the soldiers' camp, and thought we were pretty safe from Indian attack, but one night about three o'clock we were awakened by an awful noise.

We thought it was a passing railroad train, but instead it was our horses being driven off by Indians right along near our camp.

As they passed us the Indians fired several shots in our direction, but no one was hit. We had sixty-three horses and the red rascals captured all of them except five head.

Mr. Evans sent one of the hands to notify the soldiers of our loss and get them on the trail of the Indians. It was nine o'clock the next morning before the soldiers passed our camp in pursuit, and as the Indians had such a good start, they were never overtaken.

We remained there all day, and the next morning we started out afoot. For about a week we felt pretty sore from walking, as we were not used to this kind of herding. When we reached Cheyenne we secured mounts and laid in a supply of grub and traveled up Crow Creek to Cheyenne Pass, where we had our first blizzard and snow.

The next morning the snow was six inches deep and the weather was bitterly cold. Our next town was Fort Laramie, and from there we went on to Elk Mountain on the Overland Immigrant Trail to California, where we stopped for three days because of the heavy snow. We had very little trouble until we reached Bitter Creek, called Barrel Springs on account of many barrels having been placed in the ground and served as water springs.

Here we cut out 500 of the cattle because they were not able to keep up. Five of us were left to bring them on, and we traveled down the creek for a distance of about twenty miles.

One day at noon we camped and some of the cattle drank water in the creek, and within twenty minutes they died.

I drank from a spring on the side of the mountain, thinking the water was good, and in a short while I thought I was going to die too. An Irishman came along and I told him I was sick from drinking the water, and he informed me that it was very poisonous.

He carried me to a store and bought me some whiskey, and pretty soon I was able to travel.

We went up Green River and crossed it at the mouth of Hamsford, and then crossed the divide between Wyoming and Utah. The temperature was down to zero, and when we reached the little town of Clarksville, Utah, we remained there two weeks.

Mr. Evans sent the cattle up into the mountains, and we took stage for Corrine, just north of Salt Lake City, where we boarded the train for home.

# A Thorny Experience

### by S.B. Brite, Pleasanton, Texas

LIKE MOST OF THE BOYS OF THE EARLY DAYS, I had to sow my wild oats, and I regret to say that I also sowed all of the money I made right along with the oats.

I went up the trail in 1882 with a herd belonging to Jim Ellison of Caldwell County, delivering the cattle at Caldwell, Kansas. I went again in 1884 with Mark Withers, starting from the Tigre Ranch in LaSalle County, where Mr. J.M. Dobie now lives.

When we reached the Canadian River it was on a rise, and we drowned a horse, which was hitched to the chuck wagon. While making this crossing a Negro's horse sank in the middle of the river and left the rider standing on a sandbar.

After we crossed the cattle over I swam my horse out and allowed the Negro to swing to his tail, and thus ferried him across. The Negro thanked me and said that horse's tail was just like the "hand of Providence."

We delivered the cattle on the Platte River and I returned to the Tigre Ranch, where I worked for seven years. While on this ranch one day Gus Withers, the boss, picked out a fine bay horse and told me that if I could ride him I could use him for a saddle horse.

I managed to mount him, but after I got up there I had to "choke the horn and claw leather," but to no avail, for he dumped me off in the middle of a big prickly pear bush.

When the boys pulled me out of that bush they found that my jacket was nailed to my back as securely as if the job had been done with six-penny nails.

I went up the trail twice, and drove the drag both times, did all the hard work, got all the "cussin'," but had the good luck never to get "fired."

# Drove a Herd over the Trail to California

### by W.E. Cureton, Meridian, Texas

I WAS BORN IN THE OZARK MOUNTAINS OF ARKANSAS, in 1848, came to Texas with my father, Capt. Jack Cureton, in the winter of 1854–55; settled on or near the Brazos River below old Fort Belknap in what is now Palo Pinto County, and began raising cattle. The county was organized in 1857.

In 1867 we (my father and John C. Cureton) drove a herd of grown steers from Jim Ned, a tributary of the Colorado of Texas, now in Coleman County, up the Concho at a time when the Coffees and Tankersleys were the only inhabitants there.

That year the government began the building of Fort Concho, which is now a part of the thrifty little city of San Angelo. The Indians killed a Dutchman and scalped and partly skinned him a little ahead of us, and Capt. Snively, with a gold hunting outfit, had quite a skirmish along the Concho with them.

From the head waters on the Concho we made a ninety-six-mile drive to Horsehead Crossing on the Pecos River without giving the cattle a good watering.

Our trail was the old military stage route used by the government before the Civil War. The Indians had killed a man and wounded a woman ahead of us at the old adobe walls at Horsehead Crossing on the Pecos, and captured a herd of cattle belonging to John Gamel and Isaac W. Cox of Mason, Texas.

A few miles above Horsehead Crossing the Indians stole eleven head of our horses one night; only having two horses to the man, we felt the loss of half our mounts very severely. A little further up the river the Indians wounded Uncle Oliver Loving, the father of J.C. and George B. of the noted Loving family of the upper Brazos country, and the founder of the great Texas Cattle Raisers' Association.

The old man died at Fort Sumner of his wounds. They also killed Billy Corley, one of Lynch & Cooper's men, from Shackleford County, the same drive.

We left the Pecos near where now stands the town of Roswell, and traveled up the Hondo out by Fort Stanton over the divide to San Augustine Springs, near the Rio Grande, and wintered the cattle and sold them in the spring of 1868 to Hinds & Hooker, who were the United States contractors to feed the soldiers and Indians, as they were pretending to subdue and keep the Indians on reservations, but in reality were equipping them so they could depredate more efficiently on the drovers and emigrants.

In the summer of 1869 I sold a bunch of grown steers in Palo Pinto County, Texas, to Dr. D.B. Warren of Missouri, and we trailed them to Baxter Springs, Kansas.

We swam Red River at the old Preston Ferry. We camped near the river the night before and tried to cross early in the morning. The river was very full of muddy water, and the cattle refused to take the water. After all hands had about exhausted themselves Dr. Warren, who was his own boss, said to me: "William, what will we do about it?"

I answered him that we had better back out and graze the cattle until the sun got up so they could see the other bank, and they would want water and go across. "You should know that you can't swim cattle across as big a stream as this going east in the morning or going west late of an evening with the sun in their faces."

About 1 p.m. we put them back on the trail and by the time the drags got near the river the leaders were climbing the east bank. The doctor looked at me and said, "Well, I'll be damned – every man to his profession."

In the spring of 1870 my father took his family along, and turned over more than 1,000 cattle to us boys, John C. and J.W., to drive to California.

We went out over the old Concho Trail to the Rio Pecos, up the river to the Hondo, out by the Gallina Mountains, crossing the Rio Grande at Old Albuquerque, over to and down the Little Colorado of the West, through New Mexico into Arizona, by where Flagstaff is now, on the Santa Fe Railroad, parallel to the Grand Canyon on the south side of the Colorado, crossed the Colorado at Hardyville above the Needles, crossed over the California desert, climbed over the Sierra Nevadas and wintered the cattle between San Bernardino and Los Angeles in California, a 1,500-mile drive.

In the spring of 1871 we drove the cattle back across the Sierras, north up the east side of the mountains to the head of Owens River, where we fattened them on the luxurious California meadows; then drove them to Reno, Nevada, 500 miles from our wintering grounds, and sold them, and Miller & Lux, the millionaire butchers of San Francisco, shipped them to their slaughtering plant in San Francisco, California – and, by the way, the firm still controls the California market there.

We paid ten dollars for grown steers in Texas; got thirty dollars after driving them 2,000 miles and consuming two years on the trip. After all, I honor the old longhorn; he was able to furnish his own transportation to all the markets before the advent of railroads.

I made many other trips, but think these will give a fair idea of the hardships of the pioneers I have been interested in cattle raising for sixty years, ranching in Texas, New Mexico, Arizona and California during that time, but always claimed Texas as home.

# Parents Settled in the Republic of Texas

*by Joseph S. Cruze, Sr., San Antonio, Texas*

MY PARENTS, WILLIAM AND ISABELLA CRUZE, came to the Republic of Texas in 1840 and located on the Brazos River in Washington County. There I was born July 27, 1845, and when I was three months old father placed a buffalo hair pillow on the horn of his saddle, placed me thereon, mounted his horse and was ready to emigrate west with his family.

He settled on Onion Creek, nine miles south of Austin, near the Colorado River, where he remained for several years, then in 1854 we moved to the central part of Hays County, where father died in 1856.

I enlisted in the Confederate Army in 1862, received my discharge in 1865, and returned home to my widowed mother. On July 24, 1865, I was married to Miss Mary Kate Cox of Hays County.

In the years 1870 and 1871 I drove cattle to Kansas over the old Chisholm Trail. I remember the killing of Pete Owens, who was with the same herd I was with. We had reached the Cross Timbers of Texas, and passed a ranch where booze was sold. There was a row and Pete was shot and killed.

He was a good friend to me, we had been soldier comrades for nearly three years, worked cattle together, and I loved him as a brother. Billie Owens, known to many of the old trail drivers, was his brother. The Owens boys were good soldiers, upright, honest and brave men.

In those days the cowmen underwent many hardships, survived many hairbreadth escapes and dangers while blazing our way through the wilderness. My comrades yet living have not forgotten what we had to endure. Everything was then tough, wild and woolly, and it was dangerous to be safe.

In September 1866, I settled on Loneman Creek, in Hays County, near the Blanco River, and established the Cruze Ranch, which I sold to my son, S.J. Cruze, in 1917, and moved to San Antonio with my wife and two daughters, Margaret and Addie, and my grandson, Forest Harlan. I have a nice little home in Los Angeles Heights, and would be glad to hear from any of my old friends at any time.

My address is Route 10, Box 101a, Los Angeles Heights, San Antonio.

# A Girl on the Trail Masquerades as a Cowboy for Four Months

*by Samuel Dunn Houston, San Antonio, Texas*

NOW I AM GOING TO WRITE A SKETCH OF A TRIP I made while I was with the Holt Live Stock Company of New Mexico, in the spring, 1888.

I was hiring men for the spring drive and they were not very plentiful in that country, but as luck was on my side, I heard that there were four men at Seven Rivers who had come up from Texas and wanted work. I got in my chuck wagon, went to Seven Rivers and found what I was looking for, so that completed my outfit.

In a few days I went up the Pecos to the spring roundup and took charge of the steer herd of 2,500 three's and up. George Wilcox, the ranch boss, counted them out to me and said, "Sam, they are yours."

I lined up my men, drifted over toward Roswell, and did fine the first night. We passed around town the next morning, and camped that night on Salt Creek. I picked the wrong place to bed the herd, so about nine o'clock they broke, and we didn't get them stopped until four o'clock in the morning. I told the boys we had lost half of the herd.

Just as soon as daylight came I had everything in the saddle to move the herd off the bed ground. I counted them and I was out 635 head of steers. I left four men with the herd and cut for sign.

I found where they had struck the Pecos River and went down that stream. We struck a gallop and found the entire bunch, six miles down the river. They showed they had been in a stampede for they were as green as the grass itself.

When I got back to camp I found the cause of the stampede. I had failed to go over the bed ground the evening before and I found I had bedded the herd on high ground and on the worst gopher holes I could have found in that country. I was out only four or five head and they were close to the range.

I had a boy with me by the name of Gus Votaw. He was about twenty years old, and was the son of Billie Votaw, who all the old-timers knew in San Antonio. Gus made a good hand.

That day while drifting along up the Pecos River I went ahead to hunt a watering place and when I rode up on a gyp hill overlooking the herd I saw six or seven men in a bunch. I went down to the herd to know the cause and hand out a few orders.

When I got to them I found the four men I had secured at Seven Rivers were gunmen and had been playing pranks on Gus Votaw. I told them they would have to cut that out and they didn't say yes or no, so I kept my eyes open from there on.

In a few days I caught one of them at the same thing and I read the law to him and when I got them all in camp I told them that I was going to run the outfit and such things as that must be cut out right now. I also told Gus that if they worried him any more to let me know.

I will leave off now from here to Fort Sumner, New Mexico, which was less than a month.

I arrived at Fort Sumner in less than a month and had to stop and write some letters, so I told the cook and horse rustler to take the wagon and camp it up the river and for the cook to have dinner early, for I would be there about ten o'clock.

I finished my job at the post office, mounted my horse and pulled out for camp. When I got up within 200 yards of camp I looked up and saw what I thought, every man in camp and only one man with the herd. When I rode up every man had a gun in his hand but Gus Votaw. I got off my horse and, of course, knew the cause. The cook said, "Boss, there is going to be hell here. I am glad you came."

I went to the front of the wagon, got my gun off of the water barrel and told the men that I would play my trump card, that I had to have every gun in camp. I didn't expect to live to get the last one, but I did. I got six of them, knocked the loads out, threw them in the wagon, got out my time and checkbooks and gave the four men their time.

I told the cook and horse rustler to hitch up the mules and we would move camp. I left the four bad men sitting on their saddles under a cottonwood tree and felt that I had done the right thing. I went up the river about two miles and camped.

After all this occurred, right here my troubles began. I had to leave the Pecos River and drive across the Staked Plains, ninety miles without water. The next water was the Canadian River. Being short handed, I had to put my horses in the herd, put the horse rustler with the herd and made a hand myself.

I held the herd over that day and rested, raised the men's wages five dollars, and made my plans. The next day we had dinner early, filled my water barrel and left the old Pecos at eleven o'clock for a long, dry drive.

That evening at sundown we reached the top of the mesa, fifteen miles up hill all the way. We rounded up the herd on the trail, got a bite to eat, changed horses and drove until daybreak, bedded on the trail again and had lunch.

The cattle were getting very dry and men were worn out. We kept this up until we reached the Canadian River, which was fifty-two hours from the time we left the Pecos River. I didn't lose a steer.

I could not let the herd string out in making the trip. If I had we would have lost cattle. I kept them in a bunch and when I reached the Canadian River I laid over three days to let the men, horses and cattle rest. I would run off the range cattle in the evening and turn everything loose at night except one horse for each man.

It was only a few miles to Clayton, New Mexico, a small railroad town ahead, so I struck camp, left the boys with the herd and I went to town to see if I could get two or three trail men.

When I got there I found there were no men in town, but I met an old friend of mine and he told me that there was a kid of a boy around town that wanted to get with a herd and go up the trail, but he had not seen him for an hour or so.

I put out to hunt that kid and found him over at the livery stable. I hired him and took him to camp, and put him with the horses and put my rustler with the cattle.

I got along fine for three or four months. The kid would get up the darkest stormy nights and stay with the cattle until the storm was over. He was good natured, very modest, didn't use any cuss words or tobacco, and always pleasant.

His name was Willie Matthews, was nineteen years old and weighed 125 pounds. His home was in Caldwell, Kansas, and I was so pleased with him that I wished many times that I could find two or three more like him.

Everything went fine until I got to Hugo, Colorado, a little town on the old K.P. Railroad, near the Colorado and Wyoming line. There was good grass and water close to town, so I pulled up about a half a mile that noon and struck camp. After dinner the kid come to where I was sitting and asked me if he could quit. He insisted, said he was homesick, and I had to let him go.

About sundown we were all sitting around camp and the old herd was coming in on the bed ground. I looked up toward town and saw a lady, all dressed up, coming toward camp, walking. I told the boys we were going to have company. I couldn't imagine why a woman would be coming on foot to a cow camp, but she kept right on coming, and when within fifty feet of camp I got up to be ready to receive my guest.

Our eyes were all set on her, and every man holding his breath. When she got up within about twenty feet of me, she began to laugh, hand said, "Mr. Houston, you don't know me, do you?"

Well, for one minute I couldn't speak. She reached her hand out to me, to shake hands, and I said, "Kid, is it possible that you are a lady?" That was one time that I could not think of anything to say, for everything that had been said on the old cow trail in the last three or four days entered my mind at that moment.

In a little while we all crowded around the girl and shook her hand, but we were so dumbfounded we could hardly think of anything to say. I told the cook to get one of the tomato boxes for a chair. The kid sat down and I said, "Now I want you to explain yourself."

"Well," she said, "I will tell you all about it, Mr. Houston. My papa is an old-time trail driver from Southern Texas. He drove from Texas to Caldwell, Kansas, in the '70's. He liked the country around Caldwell very much, so the last trip he made he went to work on a ranch up there and never returned to Texas any more.

"In two or three years he and my mother were married. After I was ten or twelve years old, I used to hear papa talk so much about the old cow trail and I made up my mind that when I was grown I was going up the trail if I had to run off.

"I had a pony of my own and read in the paper of the big herds passing Clayton, New Mexico, so I said, now is my chance to get on the trail. Not being far over to Clayton, I saddled my pony and told brother I was going out in the country, and I might be gone for a week, but for him to tell papa not to worry about me, I would be back.

"I had on a suit of my brother's clothes and a pair of his boots. In three or four days I was in Clayton looking for a job and I found one. Now, Mr. Houston, I am glad I found you to make the trip with, for I have enjoyed it. I am going just as straight home as I can and that old train can't run too fast for me, when I get on it."

The train left Hugo at 11:20 in the evening. I left one man with the herd and took the kid and every man to town to see the little girl off. I suppose she was the only girl that ever made such a trip as that. She was a perfect lady.

After I got through and returned to the ranch on the Pecos River, I had many letters from the little girl and her father also, thanking me for the kindness toward Willie and begging me to visit them.

# A Trying Trip Alone Through the Wilderness

*by Samuel Dunn Houston, San Antonio, Texas*

IN 1879 I WENT THROUGH SOUTHERN TEXAS with a big herd of cattle to the Northern market, Ogallala, Nebraska. This herd belonged to Head & Bishop.

We reached Ogallala Aug. 10, 1879, and there we met R.G. Head, who gave the boss, John Sanders, orders to cross the South Platte the next morning and proceed to the North Platte. He said he would see us over there and would tell us where to take the herd.

On Aug. 11 we crossed the South Platte and went over on North River about ten miles and camped. Dick Head came over to camp for dinner and told our boss to take the herd up to Tusler's Ranch on Pumpkin Creek and Mr. Tusler would be there to receive the cattle. He said it was about one hundred miles up the Platte.

After dinner we strung the herd out and drove them up there. We rushed them up because we were anxious to get back to Ogallala to see all of our old cowboy friends get in from the long drive from Texas.

We reached the Tusler Ranch on Aug. 19 and on the 20th we counted the old herd over to the ranch boss and started back to Ogallala, making the return trip in four days.

The next morning as we were going through town, I met an old trail boss, and he wanted me to go with him to Red Cloud Agency, Dakota, with 4,000 big Texas steers that belonged to D.R. Fant. They were Indian contracted cattle, so I told the boss I was ready to make the trip. Tom Moore was the foreman's name and he was a man that knew how to handle a big herd.

I went to camp with Tom that night and he got all the outfit together and on Aug. 28 we took charge of the big herd. They were one of the old King herds, which had come in by way of Dodge City, Kansas, from the old coast country down in Southern Texas.

They wanted to walk, so we strung them out and headed for the old South Platte. When the lead cattle got to the bank of the river the boss said, "Now, Sam, don't let them turn back on you, and we won't have any trouble." We landed on the other side all OK and went through the valley and on through the town.

Everybody in town was out to see the big King herd go through. I threw my hat back on my head and I felt as though the whole herd belonged to me.

When the lead cattle struck the foothills I looked back and could see the tail end coming in the river, and I told my partner, the right-hand pointer, that we were headed for the North Pole. We raised our hats and bid Ogallala good-bye.

When the lead cattle got to North River it was an hour and ten minutes before the tail end got to the top of the hills. My partner and I threw the range cattle out of the flats and we had it easy until the chuck wagon came over and struck camp for noon, then four of us boys went to camp.

We had a highball train from there on. We didn't cross the North Platte until we got to Fort Laramie, Wyoming. The snow was melting in the mountains and the river was muddy and no bottom to the quicksand. I was looking every night for a stampede, but we were lucky.

The night we camped close to the Court House Rock, they made a jump off the bed ground, but that didn't count. I think they got wind of the old Negro cook. This herd had come from the old King Ranch, away down in Texas with a Mexican cook. I told the boss that the next morning and he said he was almost sure that was the cause.

The North Platte River in places is more than a mile wide and it seemed to me when we reached the place we were to cross, it was two miles wide. The range cattle on the other side looked like little calves standing along the bank.

When we reached Fort Laramie we made ready to cross. I pulled my saddle off and then my clothes. Tom came up and said, "Sam, you are doing the right thing."

I told him I had crossed that river before and that I had a good old friend who once started to cross that river and he was lost in the quicksand. His name was Theodore Luce of Lockhart, Texas. He was lost just above the old Seven Crook Ranch above Ogallala. Tom told all the boys to pull off their saddles before going across. When everything was ready we strung the herd back on the hill and headed for the crossing. Men and steers were up and under all the way across.

We landed over all safe and sound, got the sand out of our hair, counted the boys to see if they were all there and pulled out to the foothills to strike camp.

About ten o'clock that night the first guards came in to wake my partner and I to stand second guard. I got up, pulled on my boots, untied my horse and then the herd broke. The two first guards had to ride until Tom and the other men got there. Three of us caught the leaders and threw them back to the tail end, then ran them in a mill, until they broke again. We kept that up until three o'clock in the morning, when we got them quieted.

We held them there until daylight, then strung them toward the wagon and counted them. We were out fifty-five head, but we had the missing ones back by eight o'clock. We were two miles from the grub wagon when the run was over. The first guards said that a big black wolf got up too close to the herd and that was the cause of the trouble.

Our next water was the Nebraska River, which was thirty miles across the Laramie Plains. We passed over that in fine shape. From there our next water was White River. The drive through that country was bad, because the trail was so crooked with such deep canyons. We reached White River, crossed over and camped.

About the time we turned the mules loose, up rode about thirty bucks and squaws, all ready for supper. They stood around till supper was ready and the old Negro cook began to get crazy and they couldn't stay any longer. They got on their horses and left.

An Indian won't stay where there is a crazy person. They say he is the devil.

The next morning the horse rustler was short ten head of horses. He hunted them until time to move camp and never found them, so Tom told me that I could stay there and look them up, and he would take the herd eight or ten miles up the trail and wait for me. I roped out my best horse, got my Winchester and six-shooter and started out looking for the horses. I rode that country out and out, but could not find them, so I just decided the Indians drove them off during the night to get a reward or a beef.

I thought I would go down to the mouth of White River, on the Missouri River in the bottom where the Indians were camped. When I got down in the bottom I saw horse signs, so I was sure from the tracks they were our horses. I rode and rode until I found them. There was no one around them, so I started back with the bunch.

When I had covered three or four miles, I looked back and saw a big dust on the hill out of White River. Then I rode for my life, because I knew it was a bunch of Indians and they were after me. I could see the herd ahead of me, and never let up. I beat them to camp about a half mile.

When they rode up and pointed to the horses, one Indian said, "Them my horses. This man steal 'em! Him no good!" We had an old squaw humper along with us, and he got them down to a talk and Tom told them he would give them a beef. Tom went with them out to the herd and cut out a big beef and they ran it off a short distance and killed it, cut it up, packed it on their ponies and went back toward White River.

If those Indians had overtaken me I am sure my bones would be bleaching in that country today. The Indians were almost on the warpath at that time and we were lucky in that we did not have any more trouble with them.

A week longer put us at the Agency. Tom went ahead of the herd and reported to the agent. We camped about four miles this side that night and the next morning we strung the old herd off the bed ground and went into the pens at Red Cloud Agency, Dakota. There I saw more Indians than I ever expected to see. The agent said there were about 10,000 on the ground.

It took us all day to weigh the herd out, ten steers on the scales at one time. We weighed them and let them out one side and the agent would call the Indians by name and each family would fall in behind his beef and off to the flats they would go.

After we got the herd all weighed out the agent told us to camp there close and he would show us around. He said the Indians were going to kill a fat dog that night and after they had feasted they would lay the carcass on the ground and have a war dance.

All the boys wanted to stay and see them dance. A few of the bucks rode through the crowd several times with their paint on. In a little while a buck came up with a table on his head and set it down in the crowd and then came another with big butcher knives in his hand and a third came with a big fat dog on his shoulder, all cleaned like a hog.

He placed it on the table, then every Indian on the ground made some kind of a pow-wow that could be heard for miles, after which the old chief made a speech and the feast began. Every Indian on the ground had a bite of that dog.

They wanted us to go up and have some, but we were not hungry, so we stood back and looked on. "Heap good," said the chief, "heap fat." About ten o'clock they had finished eating and two squaws took the carcass off the table and put it on the ground and the dance began. Every Indian was painted in some bright color. That was a wonderful dance.

The next morning we started back over our old trail to Ogallala. It was about Oct. 16 and some cooler and all of the boys were delighted to head south. Seven days' drive with the outfit brought us back to the Niobrara River and we struck camp at the Dillon Ranch.

The Dillon Ranch worked a number of half-breed Indians. I was talking with one about going back to Ogallala, as I was very anxious to get on the trail road and go down in Texas to see my best girl.

He told me he could tell me a route that could cut off 200 or 300 miles going to Ogallala. So I wrote it all down. He told me to go over the old Indian trail across the Laramie Plains, saying his father had often told him how to go and the trail was wide and plain and it was only 175 or 200 miles.

Right there I made up my mind that I would go that way and all alone. There were only two watering places and they were about forty miles apart. The first lake was sixty-five or seventy miles.

I had the best horse that ever crossed the Platte River and if I could cut off that much I would be in Texas by the time the outfit reached Ogallala.

I asked Tom to pay me off, saying that I was going back to Texas over the old Indian trail across the Laramie Plains. I knew if an Indian crossed that country I could also.

He said, "You are an old fool. You can't make that trip, not knowing where the fresh water is, you will starve to death." I told him that I could risk it anyway, and I knew I could make it.

Next morning I was in my saddle by daylight, bade the boys good-bye and told them if they heard of a dead man or horse on the old Indian trail, across the plains, for some of them the next year to come and pick me up, but I was sure I could make the trip across.

The first day's ride I was sure I had covered sixty-five or seventy miles. I was getting very thirsty that evening, so I began to look on both sides of the trail for the fresh water lake, but was disappointed. I was not worried. Just as the sun went down I went into a deep basin just off the trail where there was a very large alkali lake.

I had a pair of blankets, my slicker and saddle blankets, so I made my bed down and went to bed. I was tired and old Red Bird (my horse) was also jaded. I lay awake for some time thinking and wondering if I was on the wrong trail.

The next morning I got up, after a good rest, ate the rest of my lunch, and pulled down the trail looking on both sides of the trail for the fresh water lake, but failed to find it. I then decided that the half-breed either lied or had put me "up a tree."

Anyway, I would not turn back. I had plenty of money, but that was no good out there. I could see big alkali lakes everywhere, but I knew there would be a dead cowboy out there if I should take a drink of that kind of water.

I rode until noon, but found nothing. The country was full of deer, antelope, elk and lobo wolves, but they were too far off to take a shot at. When I struck camp for noon I took the saddle off my horse and lay down for a rest. Got up about one-thirty and hit the trail.

That was my second day's ride and my tongue was very badly swelled. I could not spit anymore, so I began to use my brain and a little judgment and look out for "old Sam" and that horse.

About the middle of the afternoon I looked off to my left and saw a large lobo wolf about one hundred yards away and he seemed to be going my route. I would look in his direction quite often. He was going my gait and seemed to have me spotted. I took a shot at him every little while, but I kept on going and so did he. I rode on until sundown and looked out for my wolf, but did not see him.

The trail turned to the right and went down into a deep alkali basin. I rode down into it and decided that I would pull into camp for the night, as I was very much worn out. I went down to the edge of the lake, pulled off my saddle and made my bed down on my stake rope so I would not lose my horse. The moon was just coming up over the hill.

I threw a load in my gun and placed it by my side, with my head on my saddle, and dropped off to sleep. About nine o'clock the old wolf's howls woke me up. I looked up and saw him sitting about twenty feet from my head just between me and the moon.

I turned over right easy, slipped my gun over the cantle of my saddle and let him have one ball. He never kicked. I grabbed my rope, went to him, cut him open and used my hands for a cup and drank his old blood.

It helped me in a way, but did not satisfy as water would. I went down to the lake and washed up, went back to bed and thought I would get a good sleep and rest that night, but found later I had no rest coming.

I was nearly asleep when something awakened me. I raised up and grabbed my gun, and saw that it was a herd of elk, so I took a shot or two at them. As soon as I shot they stampeded and ran off, but kept coming back. About twelve o'clock I got up, put my saddle on my horse and rode until daylight. I was so tired, I thought I would lay down and sleep awhile.

Riding that night I must have passed the second water lake. After sleeping a little while I got up and broke camp and rode until twelve o'clock, when I stopped for noon that day.

That being my third day out, I thought I would walk around, and the first thing I saw was an old dead horse's bones. I wondered what a dead horse's bones were doing away out there, so I began to look around some more and what should I see but the bones of a man.

I was sure then that some man had undertaken to cross the plains and had perished, so I told old Red Bird (my horse) that we had better go down the trail and we pulled out.

That evening about four o'clock, as I was walking and leading my horse, I saw a very high sand hill right on the edge of the old trail. I walked on to the top of the sand hill and there I could see cottonwood trees just ahead of me.

I sat down under my horse about a half an hour. I could see cattle everywhere in the valley, and I saw a bunch of horses about a mile from me. I looked down toward the trees about four miles and saw a man headed for the bunch of horses.

I didn't know whether he was an Indian or not. He was in a gallop and as he came nearer to the horses I pulled my gun and shot one time. He stopped a bit and started off again. Then I made two shots and he stopped again a few minutes.

By that time he had begun to round up the horses, so I shot three times. He quit his horses and came to me in a run. When he got up within thirty or forty feet of me he spoke to me and called me by my name and said, "Sam you are the biggest fool I ever saw."

I couldn't say a word for my mouth was so full of tongue, but I knew him. He shook hands and told me to get up behind him and we would go to camp. He took his rope and tied it around my waist to keep me from falling off, for I was very weak.

Then he struck a gallop and we were at camp in a very few minutes. He tied his horse and said, "Now, Sam, we will go down to the spring and get a drink of water."

Just under the hill about twenty steps was the finest sight I ever saw in my life. He took down his old tin cup and said, "Now, Sam, I am going to be the doctor."

I was trying all the time to get in the spring, but was so weak he could hold me back with one hand. He would dip up just a teaspoonful of the water in the cup and say, "Throw your head back," and he poured it on my tongue. After a while he increased it until I got my fill and my tongue went down. When I got enough water then I was hungry. I could have eaten a piece of that fat dog if I'd had it.

My friend's name was Jack Woods, an old cowboy that worked on the Bosler Ranch. Jack and I had been up the trail from Ogallala to the Dakotas many times before that.

Jack said, "Now, Sam, we will go up to the house and get something to eat. I killed a fat heifer calf yesterday and have plenty of bread cooked, so you come in and lay down and I will start a fire quickly and cook some steak and we will eat some supper."

Before he could get it cooked, I could stand it no longer, so I slipped out, went around behind the house where he had the calf hanging, took out my pocket knife and went to work eating the raw meat, trying to satisfy my appetite.

After fifteen or twenty minutes Jack came around hunting me and said, "Sam, I always thought you were crazy, now I know it. Come on to supper." I went in the house and ate a hearty supper.

After finishing supper, I never was so sleepy in my life. Jack said, "Sam, lay down on my bed and go to sleep and I will go out and get your horse and treat him to water and oats." He got on his horse and struck a gallop for the sand hills, where my poor old horse was standing starving to death.

Next morning Jack told me that a man by the name of Lumm once undertook to cross those plains from the Niobrara River to the head of the Little Blue over that same Indian trail. Jack said, "He and his horse's bones are laying out on the plains now. Perhaps you saw them as you came along."

I told him I saw the bones of a man and the horse, but didn't remember how far back it was. It seemed about twenty-five miles.

I remained there five days and every morning while I was there, Jack and I would get on our horses and go out in the valley and round up the horses he was taking care of, rope out the worst outlaw horse he had in the bunch and take the kink out of his back. The five days I was there I rode four and five horses every day.

On October 29 I saddled my horse and told Jack I was going to Texas. He gave me a little lunch, and I bid him good-bye and headed for the North Platte. I reached Bosler's Ranch at 12:20 p.m., had dinner, gave the boss a note from Jack Woods, fed my horse, rested one hour, saddled up, bade the boys good-bye and headed for Ogallala on the South Platte, forty miles below.

I reached Ogallala that night at 9:30, put my horse in the livery stable, went up to the Leach Hotel and there I met Mr. Dillon, the owner of the Niobrara Ranch, sold my horse to him for eighty dollars, purchased a new suit, got a shave and haircut, bought my ticket to Texas, and left that night at 11:30 for Kansas City.

On Nov. 6 I landed in Austin, Texas, thirty miles from my home, and took the stage the next morning for Lockhart. That was where my best girl lived, and when I got there I was happy.

This was the end of a perfect trip from Nebraska on the South Platte to Red Cloud Agency, North Dakota.

The Gruene Cowboy | 77

THE COWBOY, from the John C. H. Grabill Collection, Library of Congress, 1888

# Killing and Capturing Buffalo in Kansas

### By M.A. Withers, Lockhart, Texas

I WAS BORN IN MONROE COUNTY, MISSOURI, Sept. 23, 1846. I came to Texas with my parents and settled in Caldwell County in November 1852 or 1853, and have lived in the same county ever since.

In 1859, when I was only thirteen years old, I made my first trip on the trail. I went with a herd of cows and calves from Lockhart to Fredericksburg. The cattle were sold to Tom and Sam Johnson by George Haynes at three dollars per head.

My next trip, in 1862, was from Lockhart, Texas, to M.A. Withers, Shreveport, Louisiana, with a herd of steers for the Confederate States government. George Haynes was the contractor and S.H. Whitaker was the boss.

After arriving at Shreveport a herd of steers, too poor for Confederate soldiers to eat, was delivered to us to be driven to the Brazos River and turned loose on the range. I rode one horse on this entire trip. I was to get two dollars per day and board. I got the board, consisting of cornbread, bacon, and sometimes coffee, but I never got the two dollars per day promised me.

On my return to Lockhart I joined the Confederate Cavalry and served to the end of the war in Company I, 36th Texas Cavalry.

I left Lockhart, Texas, April 1, 1868, with a herd of 600 big wild steers. The most of them belonged to my father, brothers and myself. I bought some of them at ten dollars per head to be paid for when I returned from the drive. I had eight hands and a cook, all of whom are dead except myself.

We crossed the Colorado River at Austin, the Brazos River at Waco, the Trinity River where Fort Worth now is. Only one or two stores were there then. We crossed the Red River where Denison now is, and the Arkansas River at Fort Gibson, then traveled up the north side of the Arkansas River to Wichita, Kansas, which then consisted of a log house used for a store.

Before we reached Wichita I went several miles ahead of the herd and stopped at a large lake to get a drink of water and water my horse.

Suddenly my horse became restless and when I looked up I saw seven Osage Indians coming helter-skelter straight for me. Maybe you think I wasn't scared, but I surely was. I could not run for the lake was on one side and the Indians on the other.

I thought my time had come. They ran their horses up to me and stopped. All had guns, and I thought they were the largest ones I had ever seen. There I was with my back to the lake and with only my horse between me and the Indians, who were looking at me.

After looking at me for a few minutes, the big chief held out his hand and said "How," and then asked for tobacco.

I did not give my hand, but I gave him all the tobacco I had. It was a great relief to me when I saw them whirl their horses and leave in as big a hurry as they came.

A few days later we killed and barbecued a beef. Early the next morning one of the boys, who was with the herd, came running into camp and shouting, "Indians! Indians!"

We looked up and saw about thirty Osage Indians coming as fast as their horses could run straight for our camp. Each Indian gave the customary greeting, "How," and all placed their guns around a tree. They made short work of our barbecued meat, and then began to pick up the things scattered about the wagon.

They asked us to give them a beef and we gladly gave them a "stray." They butchered it and immediately began to eat it. While they were thus engaged we moved the herd away as quickly as possible.

We continued our journey to Abilene, Kansas, reaching there about July 1, 1868. Between Wichita and Abilene we found the skull of a man with a bullet hole in the forehead. Whose skull it was we never knew.

After reaching Abilene we established our summer camp on the Chatman Creek, twelve miles north of Abilene, Kansas.

We discharged four hands and kept the others to range herd the cattle until fall, when I sold the steers to W.K. McCoy & Bros. of Champagne, Illinois, for twenty-eight dollars per head. The cattle were worth from eight to ten dollars per head in Texas and the expenses were about four dollars per head. The steers were not road-branded and we reached there with a full count.

I received $1,000 in cash and the remainder in drafts on Donald Lawson & Co., of New York City, signed by W.K. McCoy & Bros. One of these drafts for a small amount was never paid and I still have it in my safe. I would like to collect it now with compound interest.

On our trip from Lockhart, Texas, to Abilene, Kansas, we found plenty of grass and water. The cattle arrived in Abilene in fine condition and were rolling fat when sold.

After selling out we bought new wagons and harness and made work horses out of our cow ponies. We sent the boys through Arkansas and loaded the wagons with red apples.

After reaching Texas they placed an apple on a twig on the front end of the wagon and began to peddle them. They received a fine price for those that they did not eat or give away to the girls along the road.

I went from Abilene, Kansas, to St. Louis, Missouri, and took the last steamer down the Mississippi River, which would reach New Orleans before Christmas. It took eleven days to make the trip, for the boat stopped at every landing and added chickens, turkeys, ducks, etc., to her cargo. There was a dance on deck each night except Sunday night.

I came from New Orleans to Galveston, Texas, by steamer, from Galveston to Columbus by train, and from Columbus to Lockhart by stage, and arrived at home on Christmas day, 1868.

In the summer of 1868 I was chosen to go with Joe G. McCoy and a party to Fossil Creek Siding on the Kansas Pacific Railway for the purpose of roping buffalo bulls to be sent east as an advertisement.

It had been found that by advertising a large semi-monthly public sale of stock cattle to take place at the shipping yards at Abilene, Kansas, a ready market had been found for the stock cattle. Buyers were also needed for grown cattle.

The plan adopted to call attention to the fact was to send east a carload of wild buffaloes, covering the side of the car with advertisements of the cattle. But how to get the buffaloes was the next point to be considered.

The slats of an ordinary stock car were greatly strengthened by bolting thick planks parallel with the floor and about three feet above it to the side of the car. One-half dozen horses, well trained to the lasso, were placed in one car and in the other were six men with supplies. Both cars departed for the buffalo region.

In the party chosen were four Texas cowboys, Jake Carroll, Tom Johnson, Billy Campbell and myself, also two California Spaniards, all experts with the rope.

On the afternoon of our arrival on the buffalo range we started out to capture our first buffalo. After riding for a short while, we saw a moving object in the distance, which we supposed was the desired game. We followed and saw that it was a man after an animal. We thought it was an Indian after a buffalo.

All of us, with the exception of Tom Johnson, who rode away to the right, started in pursuit of the desired game. We soon discovered what we supposed was an Indian and a buffalo was a white man driving a milch cow to the section house.

He ran to the section house and told them that the Indians had chased him and were coming straight to the house. He said that one long-legged Indian riding a white horse tried to spear him.

The supposed Indian on the white horse was none other than Tom Johnson, who was about 400 yards away from the man. When we reached the section house, the men had barricaded themselves in the dugout awaiting the arrival of the Indians.

They supposed we were Indians until we were close enough for them to tell we were white men. They came out and told us what the frightened man had told them.

During our hunt we had to guard our horses at night from the savages. We saw three small parties of Indians, and one bunch gave some of us a little chase over the prairie.

The next morning after our arrival we spied seven buffalo bulls on the north side of the Saline River and preparations were made to capture them. Two of them refused to cross the river, and when I attempted to force one to cross he began to fight and I shot him with my Navy six-shooter. This was the first buffalo I ever killed.

The others were started in the direction of the railway and when in several hundred yards of it two of them were captured. The two Spaniards roped one and Billy Campbell and I roped the other one.

The buffalo charged first at one and then the other of us. He would drop his head, stiffen his neck, and await for us to come near him, then chase one of his captors until there was no hope of catching him, then turn and go after the other.

When he was near the track a third rope was placed around his hind legs and in a moment he was laying stretched out on the ground. Our well-trained horses watched his movements and kept the ropes tight. After he ceased to struggle his legs were tied together with short pieces of rope, then the lariats were taken off and the buffalo was lifted into the car by means of a block and tackle.

One end was fastened to the buffalo's head and the other to the top of the car on the opposite side. After his head was securely bound to a part of the car frame his feet were untied. Sometimes the buffalo would sulk for hours after being loaded and show no desire to fight.

In about a week we captured twenty-four buffalo bulls. Some of them died from heat and anger caused by capture, others became sullen and laid down before they were gotten near the cars, and only twelve were successfully loaded and started on the road to Chicago.

It was very interesting to see how well trained were the horses. They seemed to know what movements to make to counteract those of the captured animal. It was almost impossible to entangle them in the rope, for they knew by experience the consequences of being entangled.

After hanging upon each side of the cars an advertisement of the cattle near Abilene, they were sent to Chicago via St. Louis, causing much newspaper comment. Upon reaching Chicago the buffalo were sent to the fairgrounds, where the two Spaniards, Billie Campbell and I roped them again to show the people how it was done.

This advertisement feat was followed by an excursion of Illinois cattlemen to the West. The people were taken to the prairie near Abilene and shown the many fine herds of cattle.

Several people invested in these cattle, and in a short time the market at Abilene assumed its usual life and activity. The year of 1868 closed with Abilene's success as a cattle market of note. Soon Texas cattle became in great demand for packing purposes.

Later in the fall of the same year, 1868, I went on a hunt with a party about seventy-five miles south of Abilene to the valley between the Big and Little Arkansas Rivers, where we saw countless numbers of buffalo.

As far as we could see the level prairies were black with buffaloes. The grass was eaten off as smooth as a floor behind these thousands of animals. We killed all we wanted in a very short time.

In 1872 on the Smoky River near Hays City, Kansas, while with a herd of cattle we had a big stampede. While running in the lead of the steers I saw by a flash of lightning that I was on the edge of a big bluff of the river.

There was nothing left for me to do but jump, so I spurred my horse and landed in the river, which had three or four feet of water in it. Neither my horse nor I was hurt, although some of the steers were killed and many crippled.

While riding that same horse that fall in Nevada, he fell into a prospector's hole full of snow, and both of us had to be pulled out.

On this same trip between Fort Steele on the North Platte River and Independence Rock on the Sweetwater, we crossed a desert, which was seventy miles across. There was no grass or water except some alkali lakes, which were not good for man or beast.

On the banks of one of these lakes I found what I thought were pretty rocks. I picked up a few and later showed them to a jeweler, who told me that they were moss agates and that they made fine sets for rings or pins and were very valuable.

Soon after crossing the desert two of our men quit, and as we were far from any human habitation and in an Indian country, I have often wondered what became of them.

We found game of all kinds, fine grass and water on this trip. The Indians made two attempts to get our horses, but they did not succeed. I sold this herd of 3,400 two-year-old steers and heifers to Tabor & Rodabush at twenty dollars per head, delivered at Humbolt Wells, Nevada. I also sold the horses to them at the same price. Our horses gave out and we walked most of the last 500 miles. Bart Kelso of Pleasanton, Texas, was with me on this trip.

While following the trail I was in a number of storms. During a storm in 1882, while I was delivering cattle to Gus Johnson, he was killed by lightning. G.B. Withers, Johnson and I were riding together when the lightning struck.

It set Johnson's undershirt on fire and his gold shirt stud, which was set with a diamond, was melted and the diamond was never found. His hat was torn to pieces and mine had all the plush burned off of the top. I was not seriously hurt, but G.B. Withers lost one eye by the same stroke that killed Johnson.

I followed the trail from 1868 to 1887. I bought cattle in Texas and New Mexico and drove them to Kansas, Colorado, Nebraska, North and South Dakota, Montana, Oregon, Wyoming, Utah, Idaho and Nevada. My first herd numbered 600 Texas steers. The largest herd I ever drove from Texas was 4,500 steers, which I drove from Fort Griffin, Texas, to Dobie Walls in what was then known as "No Man's Land." These cattle were sold to Gus Johnson.

At different times while driving cattle to Northern markets I had as partners Bill Montgomery, George Hill, Dr. John G. Blanks, Dick Head and Jesse Presnall. Some years we had five or six herds, each herd numbering from 2,000 to 3,000 steers. At first we could buy cattle in Texas on time and sell them in Kansas and the territories for cash, but the last few years I drove we had to pay cash for cattle and sell to Northern buyers on credit, and then I quit the trail.

I had a number of flattering offers to remain North in the cattle business, but I loved Texas so well that I always returned after each drive.

# On the Trail to Nebraska

*by Jeff D. Farris, Bryan, Texas*

I WAS BORN IN 1861 ON A FARM IN MADISON COUNTY, TEXAS. My parents had moved to the country from Walker County in 1858. They originally came from Tennessee to Texas in 1850.

When my father located in Madison County there were only seven white men in the neighborhood where he located. My wife's father hauled the first load of iron that was put on the ground to build up our state penitentiary, which now covers twenty acres of ground.

As I grew up I remained on the small farm we cultivated, and in the spring I gathered wild horses and helped brand cattle until 1881, when I went to Bryan with a bunch of cattle, where I found an outfit going to Kansas with a herd belonging to Col. Jim Ellison of San Marcos.

Tom Taylor was the boss and I decided to go along with this outfit and see some of the country that I had heard so much about. I have been told that Tom still lives at Uvalde.

We had 2,500 head to drive and a force of ten men, some of whose names I can't recall. One was named Hamby, and a one-armed boy named Hugh Strong. We went north from Bryan to Cleburne and Fort Worth, and crossed the Red River in Montague County. Just below old Fort Sill we struck the trail for Fort Dodge, Kansas, and passed through the Indian Territory.

There was no Oklahoma in those days. When we reached Fort Dodge we continued north until we came to the South Platte River, and from there to Ogallala, Nebraska, on the north side of the river, where I quit the outfit and came home. Ogallala was the town where Sam Bass, the noted outlaw, made his headquarters after holding up the Union Pacific. He later came to Texas and was killed by the Rangers at Round Rock.

I remained at home until the spring of 1883, when I went to Hearne, Texas, and struck out with an outfit going to San Angelo, in Tom Green

County. We left Hearne about the 10th of May and reached San Angelo the later part of July.

In 1885 I married the sweetest woman in all the country and to our union were born five boys and three girls, all of whom are living except one. I am living within half a mile of where I was born.

# Echoes of the Cattle Trail

*by Jerry M. Nance, Kyle, Texas*

I LEFT HAYS COUNTY, TEXAS, ON APRIL 15, 1877, bound for Cheyenne, Wyoming, with 2,100 cattle, forty head of ponies and two yoke of oxen with the chuck wagon.

The country was open, no fences to bother us. We crossed the Colorado about four miles below Austin, and went through Belton. We camped one night near Belton, and while there it came a heavy rain. From here we moved out several miles the next morning to where there was grass, and where we stopped for breakfast.

After we had been there about an hour I saw a man ride up and begin looking over the herd. After he had looked through closely he came over to the camp and I asked him if he found any of his cattle in the herd. He said no.

I asked him to get down and have breakfast with us, explaining that our breakfast was late on account of leaving Belton so early that morning to get out where there was grazing for the cattle.

He said he lived where we had camped the night before, and when we got up the next morning he did not see his small bunch of cattle and thought we had driven them off with our herd. He probably found them when he returned home.

We crossed the Brazos above Waco. The river was on a rise and it was so wide that all of the cattle were in the river swimming at the same time, and it looked as if I had no cattle at all, for all we could see was the horns. A boat helped us get the chuck wagon across.

One of the boys was taken sick the next day, and went back home. When we reached Fort Worth, then a small village, we bought enough supplies from York Draper to carry us through to Dodge City, Kansas.

We crossed the Red River at Red River Station, into the Indian Territory. After leaving this point we saw no more white people, except those with herds, until we reached Dodge City. When we reached the Washita River it was up and hard to cross. There I met Joel Collins of Goliad. He had just crossed and had made a raft of three big logs tied together with ropes. I exchanged some of my ropes for his raft and used it in ferrying my stuff across.

The next day I put the cattle to swimming the river, which had a very swift current. At first they would not take the water, but I cut off bunches of about seventy-five to a hundred and put them to moving Indian fashion and shoved them right off into the water.

Some of them would turn and try to come back, but the swift current had carried them down to where the steep banks on this side kept them from coming out, and they had to go across. I crossed the whole herd in this manner.

We had but little trouble in getting the horses across. One of the boys had a mule in the outfit, which had a pair of hopples tied around his neck, and in swimming the mule passed near a willow limb that had been broken off by the cattle, and this limb had caught the hopples on the mule's neck and held him there swimming in the water.

I told the man who owned the mule that unless the hopples were cut loose the animal would drown. It was a dangerous undertaking, but he plunged in and cut the hopples, and the mule swam across. From here we made the trip all right until we reached the North Canadian, which was also on a rise and all over the bottom-lands.

We waited for several days for the floodwaters to subside, but all to no use. I decided to make a raft and go across. The cattle were started across and were going fine, when it came up a terrific hailstorm, which interrupted the proceedings.

One man was across on the other side of the river, naked, with his horse and saddle and about half of the herd and the balance of us were on this side with the other half of the herd and all the supplies.

There was no timber on our side of the river, and when the hail began pelting the boys and myself made a break for the wagon for shelter.

We were all naked, and the hail came down so furiously that within a short time it was about two inches deep on the ground. It must have hailed considerably up the river, for the water was so cold we could not get any more of the herd across that day. We were much concerned about getting help to the man across the river.

We tried all evening to get one of the boys over, to carry the fellow some clothes and help look after the cattle, but failed in each attempt. We could not see him nor the cattle on account of the heavy timber on the other side, and the whole bottom was covered with water so that it was impossible for him to come near enough to hear us when we called him.

The water was so cold that horse nor man could endure it, and in trying to cross over several of them came near drowning and were forced to turn back, so the man on the other side had to stay over there all night alone and naked. I was afraid the Indians would run the cattle off, but they did not molest them.

Next morning everything was lovely and our absent man swam back to us after he had put the cattle in shape. He had a good saddle blanket, which he said had kept him comfortable enough during the night. While we were getting the balance of the cattle across one of my Mexican hands suffered three broken ribs and a fractured collar bone by his horse falling with him.

Some movers who were waiting for the river to fall, agreed to convey the Mexican to Fort Reno, twenty miles away, for me. At Fort Reno an army surgeon patched him up, and he remained there until the following September, when he came back home.

On the 8th of June, while we were on the Salt Fork, a cold norther blew up, accompanied by rain, and it soon became so cold we had to stop driving about three o'clock in the afternoon and gather wood for the night. We undertook to hold our cattle that night in the open, but it was so cold that we finally drifted them close to the river where there was a little protection, and kept a man on guard to look after them.

About daybreak they stampeded, but we soon caught them without loss of a single head. Eight ponies belonging to other herds near us froze to death that night.

We crossed the Arkansas River at Dodge, but stopped there one day only, for supplies. At this place we saw a number of Texas cattlemen who were waiting for their herds.

We crossed the Platte River at Ogallala, Nebraska, and still had a long stretch to cover to reach Cheyenne. Near Julesburg we came to a stone dam across a little creek. There was no sign of a habitation near this dam, and why it was placed there, and who constructed it, was beyond my comprehension.

We reached Cheyenne sometime in July, after having been on the trip for about three months. We sold our cattle and ponies and took the railroad for home.

I also drove another herd of 2,000 head of cattle from Hays County in

1880 to Dodge City, Kansas. We crossed the Colorado at Webbersville, and after crossing Brushy Creek near Taylor, we struck camp.

Just before sundown two men drove up in a wagon, and one of them, who had been drinking, ordered us to move on, saying we could not camp there. I told him he had arrived too late, for we were going to remain right there.

He said he would get the sheriff to come and move us, and as he was standing up in the back end of his wagon he fell out when the driver started the team. He turned a complete somersault and fell hard upon the ground. If he had been sober I am sure he would have broken his neck. Picking himself up, he clambered back into his wagon and drove on amid the yells and whoops of my boys. That was the last we saw of him.

After we crossed Gabriel, the other side of Taylor, we turned west and went by Lampasas, and quit the trail on account of water. We passed through Comanche and struck the trail again in Brown County. When we reached Fort Griffin we purchased supplies to last us until we reached Dodge, Kansas.

We crossed the Brazos high up where there was not much water in it, and the water it did contain was so salty our cattle would not drink it. At Doan's Store we crossed Red River when it was very low, and I was glad of it. We drove on through the Territory until we reached Dodge. We were bothered some by Indians on this trip.

In 1881, I sold a herd of 2,000 head of cattle to be delivered at Ogallala, Nebraska, on the Platte River. I did not go up the trail with this herd that year.

In 1883 I became part owner in a ranch in Jeff Davis County. I shipped my cattle out there and ranched them ten years with the Toyah Land & Cattle Company.

In 1885 I drove 3,000 steer yearlings out there, which I bought at Columbus, Texas. We went by way of Blanco, Fredericksburg, Mason, San Angelo, up the Main Concho and across the plains to Fort Stockton. We also had ninety ponies along.

That was too many cattle to have in one herd, and they did not do well. Water was scarce and, being late in the season, one sixty-mile drive from the head of the Concho to the Pecos River without water, was a pretty hard trip, worse than going to Kansas.

In 1887 we shipped 2,000 head from the ranch to Big Springs, and drove them across to Coolidge, Kansas, where we sold them out. Part of them were shipped west to Pueblo, Colorado, and part of them were driven back to Fort Sill in the Indian Territory, and delivered there.

In 1888 we drove 2,000 head to Panhandle City. We sold some of them to be delivered above Amarillo, and the remainder were driven on to Kiowa and sold there. In driving this herd across the plains from the Pecos River to Warfield, a station ten miles west of Midland, I had made arrangements with a ranchman at Warfield to have enough water pumped up for 2,000 head of cattle. He had a windmill and troughs for watering and charged five cents per head.

We could water only about 150 head at a time, so it took some time to water them all. When we had the last bunch in the pen late that evening a heavy hailstorm and rain came up and scattered our herd. Everybody stayed with the herd, which began to drift with the storm's course. Some of the boys used blankets and heavy gloves to protect their heads.

We had one bald-headed man in the outfit, and when the hail storm was over he was a sight to behold. He had welts and bruises all over, and lots of hide had been peeled off.

The hail had beaten the grass into the ground and killed lots of jackrabbits in the vicinity. We lost about a hundred head of cattle during the storm, and they were the last ones to water in the pen. We found them the next day several miles away.

In the fall of 1888, we shipped about 2,000 head to Colorado City and Sweetwater to winter on account of no grass at the ranch, and in the spring of 1889 we gathered them to ship out.

Those at Colorado City were put in a small five-section pasture for a few days before shipping them north. While they were in this little pasture a cyclone came along and killed about 150, two- to five-year-old steers and crippled about a hundred others for us.

The cyclone was only about one hundred yards wide and went through about a mile of pasture, leaving everything trimmed clean in its path. Even the mesquite switches had all the bark pulled off. Deer, rabbits, owls, snakes and many other animals were to be found in its wake.

# Reminiscences of Old Trail Driving

### by J.M. Hankins, San Antonio, Texas

I WAS BORN IN 1851 NEAR PRAIRIE LEA, in Caldwell County, Texas, and remember when the Civil War began and the many hard trials experienced during that period.

It was in 1868 that I recall the first herd of cattle driven from Prairie Lea "up the trail," though possibly Col. Jack Myers and others at Lockhart had driven earlier. That year Baker & Duke, merchants, bought some steers and exchanged merchandise for them.

Father and others put in a few head, and I put in a five-year-old steer, for which I received a pair of shoes, a straw hat and a linen coat, the value of all being about ten dollars, but I was fully rigged out for Sunday wear, and was satisfied with the deal.

After 1868 the drives became general and large herds could be seen on the Lockhart trail from March to August. I very often helped local buyers get up bunches of Kansas cattle, as they were called, and in 1871 I was employed by Smith Brothers at Prairie Lea to go "up the trail."

I furnished my own mounts, three corn-fed horses, which they agreed to feed until grass came.

We left Prairie Lea the latter part of February for San Miguel Creek, went to San Antonio, and expected to be absent about thirty days. We failed to gather the cattle we expected to on the San Miguel, so we were ordered to move on to the Nueces River, where Jim and Tobe Long and others put up a herd for them.

We got back to the San Marcos River about the 15th of May, without having had a bushel of corn for our horses after leaving San Antonio. The country was very dry, no water from one river to the other, no grass nearer than three miles out.

Those who worked soon got afoot. Between the Cibolo and Guadalupe Rivers I swapped horses twice in one day, the last time with a Negro, and got a small pony, which seemed to be fat. That was all I saw until he took his saddle off, when a foot of hide stuck to the blanket. The boys set up a big laugh, but I "scaffold" up, threw my "hull" on and galloped around the herd. It beat walking and punching the "dogies" at the rear. I was promoted right then to the flank.

That night I experienced the first stampede. Early in the night it had rained, and I was on the watch. The herd began drifting, and the boss and several others came out to help with the cattle, and after the rain ceased we got them stopped, when Rany Fentress, a Negro who had been in stampedes before, came to where I was in the lead and told me to move further away.

About that time some of the boys struck a match to light a pipe, and the flare frightened the big steers and they began to run. I was knocked down three times, but managed to stay with the pony, and came out with the drags, which I stayed with until daylight.

After we crossed the San Marcos River the boys began leaving for home, but I remained until the boss said I could not go until the others returned. At this I rebelled, "cut my bedding," rounded up my "crow bait" and pulled out for home, where I stayed two days.

Father insisted that I go back. I told him I had nearly killed three horses, which they never fed as they agreed to. But I went back with a fresh mount and got "fired" just as the herd was ready to start on the trail. Smith Bros. went "busted" that year.

In 1874 I left home again in February with Ellison & Dewees, with young Jim Ellison as boss. We went to San Antonio, where we received a bunch of cow ponies, and then established camp near the Cibolo, where the Lowe cattle were received and started.

Our camp was the catch and cut-out for all the other bosses. Young Jim Ellison took the first herd with all Negro hands about the 9th of March. Jim Rowden took the second herd, and so on, until all the Lowe cattle were received and started. Our outfit then went to Burnet County and received our herd from Oatman, mostly wild mountain steers.

When we were nearing Red River we threw in with Peter Smith, making one large herd, with which I stayed until we arrived at Dodge City, Kansas. Our trip was like most others, sometimes good, and at other times pretty tough, especially when the cattle stampeded during stormy nights and mixed with other herds, causing no end of worry and trouble and often forcing us to go without our breakfast until ten or eleven o'clock the next day. But as soon as we were filled with frijoles and black coffee, and the sun shone clear, we were jolly and happy again.

One little incident during a run on a stormy night was amusing. The cattle had been running most of the night, but at last they had quieted down.

We saw a light a short distance away swinging around, and heard a voice calling out to us. We supposed it was the cook, and the boss said some ugly words about the cook screaming at us, and sent a man into the herd to find out what he wanted.

It turned out to be a man standing on the top of his dugout, and he was in great distress. The cattle had crushed in the roof of his domicile and one had fallen through his bedroom and disturbed his peaceful slumbers.

The country was wild and unsettled then, and from the Red River to the Kansas line was known as the Indian Territory. Montague was the last town I saw until we reached Great Bend, Kansas.

I might add incidents, but as short sketches for this book are expected, will say to all the old cow-punchers and trail drivers of Texas that I will be glad to meet any of you and talk about the old times and the pioneers of Texas.

# Got 'Wild and Woolly' on the Chisholm Trail

*by J.N. Byler, Dallas, Texas*

I WAS RAISED IN EAST TEXAS and worked cattle back in the piney woods and canebrakes of that region. Went west after the Civil War and worked cattle there.

The range was at that time somewhat overstocked with beef cattle and bulls. A great many of the old bulls were shipped over to Cuba, and supplied the natives there with beef. In getting them ready to ship the cowboys would rope them on the range, throw them down, and chop the points of their horns off with an axe to keep them from hurting each other on the boats. In those days beef cattle on the range were worth about ten dollars per head. A few were driven to Louisiana.

In 1866 Monroe Choate and B.A. Borroum drove a herd to Iowa to find a market. They crossed Red River at Colbert's Ferry, went by way of Boggy Depot, crossed the Arkansas at Fort Gibson, and then struck west of the settlements of Kansas.

In 1867 Butler, Baylor & Rose drove a herd to Abilene, Kansas, as did also Pucket & Rogers. In 1868 the drives were pretty heavy, but further west, crossing Red River at Gainesville.

In 1869 and 1870 they were heavier still, most of the herds crossing at Red River Station, passing east of old Fort Sill and west of the Indian and Negro settlements, over which route water and grass were plentiful. This was known as the old Chisholm Trail.

When we reached Kansas we usually found plenty of buffalo. When these animals were disturbed they would begin to travel northward. That is where the expression "wild and woolly" originated.

When the boys reached Abilene or some other Kansas town, they were usually long-haired and needing a barber's attention, as there were no barbers on the trail. Upon being asked how they got there, they would sing out: "Come the Chisholm trail with the buffalo wild and woolly."

# With Herds to Colorado and New Mexico

*by G.W. Scott, Uvalde, Texas*

I WAS BORN AT COMFORT, TEXAS, SEPT. 3, 1871, and was raised on a ranch. In 1876 my father moved to Coleman County, but in 1877 he moved to Frio County and bought a farm. In 1888 I came to Uvalde, and in the spring of 1890 I hired to Paul Handy of Colorado to drive a herd to that state.

We left the Plank Pens on the Leona Ranch south of Uvalde on March 10 with our herd, numbering 2,221 two-year-old steers, sixty-four horses and eleven men, including the cook.

We crossed the Nueces and camped the first night in the Moore & Allen pasture. After six or eight days our herd was easily controlled, especially at night. Grass and water were plentiful, and we had an easy time until we reached Fort McKavett, where I accidentally caused the cattle to stampede one moonlit night.

From here we drove to San Angelo and stopped one night near that town, which at that time was a wide-open place. Several of the boys went in to see the sights and have a good time. We drove our herd across the plains to Quanah, where we were quarantined for several weeks on account of Texas fever.

While we were here holding our cattle it came up a severe rainstorm one night and we had another stampede, the steers going in all directions, running over wire fences and going across creeks that happened to be in their course.

We had thirteen steers killed by lightning that night. When daylight came I was about four miles from camp with 400 head of the steers. We held these steers at Quanah for seven weeks before being allowed to proceed on to Colorado.

In 1881 I went with a herd to White Lake, New Mexico, for James Dalrymple, starting from the Leona Ranch. Most of the boys in this outfit were from the Frio Canyon, and I recall the names of Sam Everts, George Leakey, Tobe Edwards, James Crutchfield, Os Brown, Allison Davis and Tip Davis. We drove 2,178 two-year-old steers this trip, crossing the Nueces River at Eagle Pass crossing. We headed north toward Devil's River, which we crossed above Paint Cave.

At this time the range was dry and water scarce, and many of our cattle gave out and had to be left on the trail. We reached the Pecos River, at the mouth of Live Oak, where we rested for a few days.

We were in the Seven D Range at this time, and Taylor Stevenson was foreman of the Seven D Ranch, and he brought his outfit and helped us work up the Pecos from the mouth of Live Oak to Horse Head Crossing, where we left the thinnest of our cattle and proceeded on our journey.

Our next point was Midland, where we found plenty of fine grass and water. After leaving Midland we again found a dry range with no grass. When we reached the Colorado River that stream was very low. Here I saw my first buffalo, but it was a tame animal and was branded a long S on each side.

After a great deal of hard luck and trouble we reached Yellow Horse Draw about ten miles from Lubbock, where we encountered a heavy hailstorm.

We had lost a great many of our cattle on the trip, and the sudden change chilled a number of others to death as well as five saddle horses. We left camp at this point with only 1,072 head. We reached White Lake, New Mexico, on June 21, and delivered to Mr. Handy. Here we found Ham Bee and his outfit and accompanied them back to Midland, where we took the train for Uvalde.

# Recollections of the Old Trail Days

*by B.A. Borroum, Del Rio, Texas*

MY FIRST EXPERIENCE ON THE TRAIL was in the year 1870.

About the first of April of that year I started from Monroe Choate's Ranch in Karnes County with a herd of cattle belonging to Choate & Bennett. E.B. Rutledge was the boss and part owner. Among the hands were Jesse McCarty, Drew Lamb, George Blackburn, John Strait, and one or two others whose names I have forgotten.

Going north all the time, we crossed the Guadalupe at Gonzales, the Colorado at Austin, the Brazos at Old Fort Graham, the Trinity at Fort Worth, Red River at Red River Station, the Washita at Dr. Stearn's, the Red Fork near Turkey Creek Stage Stand in Kaw Reservation, the Salt Fork at Cow Creek Station, the Arkansas at Wichita, the Smoky at Abilene, Kansas, which was our destination, and where we arrived about July 1.

Like many others, when I had work for the time being I did not think I would ever make another trip up the trail, but also like many others, when the next drive came I was rarin' to go. In the spring of 1871 I again went up with a herd belonging to Choate & Bennett, with Jack Scroggin as boss and part owner. The hands on this trip were W.M. Choate, John Paschal, Monroe Stewart, Joe Copeland, John Ferrier, myself and John Sumner, the cook.

We started from Rock Creek, Atascosa County, about the first of April and traveled the same trail after coming into it at Gonzales through to Abilene. We went into the Chisholm Trail about three miles below Red River Station, and just as soon as we crossed Red River all our stock seemed to go wild, especially our horses, although we did not come into contact with any buffalo until we reached a point between the Red Fork and the Salt Fork of the Arkansas River.

Several herds lost heavily at that time by cattle and horses getting into the buffalo drifts, which were at that season drifting northward.

These animals were in countless numbers; in fact, the whole face of the earth seemed to be literally covered with them, all going in the same direction. The drovers were compelled to send men on ahead to keep them from stampeding their herds.

On a plain about halfway between the Red Fork and the Salt Fork we had to stop our herds until the buffalo passed. Buffalo, horses, elk, deer, antelope, wolves, and some cattle were all mixed together, and it took several hours for them to pass, with our assistance, so that we could proceed on our journey. I think there were more buffalo in that herd than I ever saw of any living thing, unless it was an army of grasshoppers in Kansas in July, 1874.

Just after we crossed the Red Fork I went on ahead of the herd to the Trinity Creek Stage Stand, a distance of about six miles, and at this place I found the present president of the Old Trail Drivers' Association, George W. Saunders, surrounded by a big bunch of Kaw Indians.

George was mounted on a little gray bob-tailed pony, his saddle had no horn, and one stirrup leather was made of rawhide and the other was a grass-hopple. He was trying his best to trade those Indians out of a buffalo gun, as he was in the buffalo range. And he made the deal.

I never saw him again until after we reached Kansas, when the drovers made up an outfit to bring their horses back to Texas. George and I were in this outfit and we came back the trail we had gone up, except we crossed Red River at Gainesville instead of at Red River Station.

I went up the trail again in 1874, starting from Druce Rachel's ranch on the Nueces Bay in San Patricio County, March 25. This herd also belonged to Choate & Bennett, with D.C. Choate as boss. We followed the same trail as previously mentioned. After crossing Red River we stopped on the Ninnesquaw for the summer, and shipped out in the fall from Great Bend.

The Osage Indians being on the warpath, we had to detour our horses in bringing them back to Texas, crossing the Arkansas River near Coffeyville into the Cerokee, Creek, Choctaw and Chickasaw nations, crossing Red River at Colbert's Ferry near Sherman into Texas.

In the eighties I drove several herds up the western trail to Dodge City, Kansas, for the firm of Borroum & Choate. I think everyone of the boys that went up with the herds mentioned above have passed beyond the Divide from which no mortal returns, except Brown (A.B.), Paschal and myself.

# High-Heeled Boots and Striped Breeches

### by G.O. Burrows, Del Rio, Texas

I HAD MY SHARE OF THE UPS AND DOWNS – principally downs – on the old cattle trail. Some of my experiences were going hungry, getting wet and cold, riding sore-backed horses, going to sleep on herd and losing cattle, getting "cussed" by the boss, scouting for "gray-backs," trying the "sick racket" now and then to get a night's sleep, and other things too numerous to mention in this volume.

But all of these were forgotten when we delivered our herd and started back to grand old Texas. Have often stopped a few days in Chicago, St. Louis and Kansas City, but always had the "big time" when I arrived in good old Santone rigged out with a pair of high-heeled boots and striped breeches, and about $6.30 worth of other clothes.

Along about sundown you could find me at Jack Harris' show occupying a front seat and clamoring for the next performance.

This "big time" would last but a few days, however, for I would soon be "busted" and would have to borrow money to get out to the ranch, where I would put in the fall and winter telling about the big things I had seen up North.

The next spring I would have the same old trip, the same old things would happen in the same old way, and with the same old wind-up. I put in eighteen or twenty years on the trail, and all I had in the final outcome was the high-heeled boots, the striped pants and about $4.80 worth of other clothes, so there you are.

# Sixty Years in Texas

### by William J. Bennett, Pearsall, Texas

MY FATHER MOVED TO TEXAS IN 1848 from Randolph County, Missouri, and settled on the Trinity River about five miles from Fort Worth, which was at that time an Indian reservation with Lt. Worth in command of the post. There was only one store there then.

The Indians often came to my father's house and were friendly to the few white settlers there. Game was plentiful, deer, turkey, buffalo and prairie chickens, as well as the fiercer animals.

We lived near Fort Worth four or five years, until father sold out to a man named Parker, and we moved above Fort Worth some twenty miles to Newark.

After remaining there a few years we then moved down to Frio County in the fall of 1858 and located on the Leona River, where we found a fine country, with wild game and fish galore. We brought with us about 400 head of cattle, which were allowed to roam at will over the excellent range, there being no fences to keep them confined to the immediate vicinity of our ranch.

But they did not get far away from us for some time, or until other ranchers began to locate around us, when the cattle began to mix with other cattle and then began to stray off, some drifting as far as the Rio Grande or the coast.

Soon the settlers began to organize cow hunts and work the cattle. I have been on cow hunts when there were as many as one hundred men working together from different counties.

Stockmen of today do not know anything about the hard work and the strenuous times we encountered in those days. Sometimes we would be out for weeks at a time, starting every morning at daylight, and probably not getting in before dark, tired and hungry, and having to do without dinner all day. Our fare consisted of cornbread, black coffee and plenty of good beef.

We were not bothered by the Indians very much until the Civil War, when the troops were largely withdrawn from the frontier posts, and the country was left unprotected. The Indians came in great numbers then, killing many settlers and driving off a great many of their stock.

Also, Mexican cattle thieves became troublesome, and stole thousands of cattle off the range, which they would drive across the Rio Grande into Mexico.

Many of the ranchmen were compelled to take their families back to the settlements for protection. After the Civil War cattle soon became plentiful on the range, and Sam Allen of Powder Horn soon had a monopoly on the shipping by chartering every boat from there to New Orleans.

He sent men out all over the country to buy fat cattle, which made times pretty good for a while, but as no one could ship by water except Allen, the demand was soon filled, and in order to reach the market for their stock the cattlemen began driving their cattle to Kansas.

In 1872 I took my first herd, starting from Uvalde and going up that long and lonesome trail to Wichita, Kansas. We had a pretty good time going up, with only a few storms and stampedes, and lost no cattle. We crossed the Red River at Red River Station, then took the old Chisholm Trail and went out of the Indian Territory at Caldwell, Kansas.

After holding my herd at that point about three months I sold to A.H. Pierce, and came home by way of Kansas City, St. Louis, New Orleans, Galveston, and then to Austin on the new railroad, and from Austin by stage to San Antonio and Uvalde.

In 1873 I took another herd of steers up the trail. Had a pretty hard time that trip and lost many head of cattle and about all I received for them. Nearly all of the Texas cattlemen went broke that year, as it was the year of the severe panic, when silver was demonetized.

During the years 1874 and 1875 occurred what is still remembered by the old-timers as the "Big Steal." Cattle were driven off and the country was left bare. They drove them off in all directions, some to Kansas, Wyoming, Colorado, New Mexico, Arizona and California.

Then came the sheep men with large flocks, and prosperity again smiled upon us. With the advent of the man with the plow, the sheep men moved further west, and the scream of the panther and the howl of the wolf began to give place to the whistle of the locomotive and the hum of the cotton gin. It would require volumes to record all of the hardships and dangers we went through during the sixty years I have lived in the West, and I merely contribute this brief sketch to add my testimony to that of the other pioneers that helped to blaze the trail through the wilderness.

During the Civil War, and for many years after the war, the people of this station hauled their supplies out from San Antonio in ox wagons, and in looking back to those times and comparing them with the present we cannot but discern the great change that has been wrought.

Our manner of travel was necessarily slow in those days. Sometimes we were on the trail for four and five months. It usually required three months to take a herd to the Red River.

Only a few days ago the papers gave an account of an aviator flying from San Antonio to Oklahoma City, a distance of over 600 miles, in the short space of three hours! Such a feat was undreamed of in those old days, and if even a prediction of such things happening had been made no one would have believed it would ever come to pass.

May we not venture to predict that in another sixty years somebody will have established a trail to Mars or other planets, and our descendants may be signaling the latest market quotations to the cowmen of those parts?

# Courage and Hardihood on the Old Texas Cattle Trail

SOL WEST, ONE OF THE BEST-KNOWN CATTLEMEN IN TEXAS, who is a part owner of a ranch of 30,000 acres in Jackson County, worked a whole year for seventy-five cents and board, when a young man.

Mr. West belongs to the old school of cattlemen. He received his business training in the early days in Texas when the chief occupation of its citizenship was raising cattle, but the more difficult proposition was to find a market for them. Texas had no ways then except in the eastern portion of the state, and these were not available, for the reason that they did not go to Kansas and the Northwest. Men were forced to do some farming, for they had to raise corn in order to have bread.

In the early days an occasional buyer who resided in Southwest Texas would purchase a herd of 8,000 or 10,000 steers on time. There was no payment made at the time of the purchase, for the reason that the buyer needed all the money at his disposal to defray the expense of the drive.

The seller did not even take his note for the purchase price, because he knew he was dealing with an honest man. The only evidence of debt was the tally of the cattle, giving the numbers in each class, including the mark and brand they bore.

The purchaser would head north with them. Sometimes he would go to Ellsworth, Abilene or Dodge City, Kansas, or some other point at the southern terminus of railroad transportation where the chief occupation of the cowboy at times was to see that his shooting irons were in good working order.

Sometimes the herd would be headed for Montana, Dakota or Nebraska. The seller did not exact any promise from the purchaser to pay for the cattle at a certain time, for neither of them knew whether it would take one, two or three years for the buyer to dispose of his holdings, and get back to Texas again. There was always a satisfactory settlement, however, when he returned. If he had the money to pay for them it was all right, but if he had lost half of them in a blizzard, the seller did not take his note for the balance due and insist on its being secured by a mortgage. The slate was wiped clean and work began again shipping up another herd on the same terms.

The trite old saying that "man's inhumanity to man makes countless thousands mourn" had no place in the lexicon of the Texas cattlemen in those days. He was then, as he is now, ready to lend a helping hand to a deserving fellow man, and he could shed tears as easily as a woman when his friends were bowed in grief.

It was amid such surroundings that the firm of McCutcheon & West of Lavaca County, composed of the late Willis McCutcheon of Victoria and George W. West, was preparing another herd of cattle to go North. Sol West, now a resident of San Antonio, was a younger brother of George W. West.

While still a mere stripling he had made three previous trips up the trail, and the firm made a deal with him in 1874 to take a herd to Ellsworth, Kansas, for half the profits. He was the youngest man who ever "bossed" a herd up the trail.

"It was a trip fraught with some adventure, considerable responsibility, and very little cash," said Mr. West a few days ago, while he was in the reminiscent mood. "I was the first man to reach Ellsworth that spring, notwithstanding the trials and tribulations, which beset us, and as a mark of their appreciation, the business men of the town presented me with a suit of clothes, hat, boots and, in fact, a new outfit entirely.

"I stayed around up there all year, selling a few steers here, a few there. There never had been such a spree of weather as greeted us in the Indian Territory on our way up. Myself and the men got back to Lavaca County about December 1.

"My brother George was the bookkeeper for the firm of McCutcheon & West, and when I turned over to him the list of my receipts and expenditures, and what cash I brought back with me, he proceeded to figure up results.

"I had to check it up very carefully to be sure that he made no mistake. We had agreed on a price for the cattle when I started with them, and I was to have one-half of all they brought over that price, after deducting the expenses incident to the trip.

"The net profit on the year's work was $1.50, and when my brother handed me the seventy-five cents, he made some jocular inquiry as to whether I expected to buy a herd of my own, or start a bank with it.

"I left Lavaca County on Feb. 27, 1874, with the herd, and on the night of the 28th reached Gonzales Prairie, in Gonzales County. On the 1st day of March we crossed the Red River into the Indian Territory without any mishap, having had a splendid drive, with clear, open weather all the way. But this was not to last long. We pushed on north, and late in the afternoon of April 6th we reached Rush Creek, where the two prongs came together just above the trail. The range had been burned off by the Indians and was black, but, being protected by two streams, the grass between these prongs was fine.

"We stayed there for two days, and on the morning of the 8th took an early start for a camp on Hell Roaring Creek, about fifteen miles further north, which I had selected because grass and water were plentiful there. The cook, with the wagon, had preceded us, but we got sight of camp about three o'clock in the afternoon. The day had been a bad one, misting rain and snowing lightly all day, with a brisk wind from the north.

"Just as the head cattle came within about one hundred yards of camp at the foot of some high hills the blizzard broke forth with increased fury. The cattle at once turned their heads to the south and began to drift with the wind. I knew we were in for a bad night of it, and there was not a man in the outfit over 20 years old.

"We held them back as best we could until after dark. In the meantime the horses ridden by the boys had actually frozen to death, and their riders on them during our progress of about five miles. My horse was the last to go down.

"I had instructed the boys that when the horses went down they should go back to camp. When I was forced to leave my horse there were two men with me, both on foot, of course.

"One of them was Charles Boyce of Goliad County, who is now a prosperous stock farmer, and who will easily recall that fearful night. The other was Jake Middlebrack of Lavaca County, who returned to that county with us, but of whom I have lost sight for many years.

"We finally got the cattle checked, after the wind had subsided a little, and as we had not touched a bite to eat since early morning, we began to cast about for something to break our fast. We had each a box of matches, but our hands were so numb that we could not strike one, even if we could have gotten the box out of our pockets.

"Presently I saw a light in the hills about two miles away. We started for it and reached the dugout, for such it proved to be, after a weary trudge of an hour or more. The dugout had two rooms and the men took us in after we told them our hard luck story. They gave us a fine supper and put us to bed in the spare room, with plenty of good warm bedding.

"The next morning at the peep of day I roused out the boys. I found a dun pony under a shed on the outside with a bridle and saddle convenient and I appropriated it and told the boys to follow me down in the direction of the herd, provided it was where we had left it.

"They followed me down and I found the herd intact, just where we had left it the night before, after one of the coldest nights I ever experienced.

"Soon after I reached the herd the other boys hove in sight and we started the cattle back toward the camp, the snow, sleet and ice being a foot and a half deep. Hell Roaring Creek and all the other streams in that section were frozen hard.

"We had traveled a couple of miles down the creek when I discovered a man on foot coming toward us. He proved to be Al Fields of Victoria. He was what was known as my neighbor on the trail, having a herd just behind me. He was overjoyed to see me, as he feared we had all frozen to death that night before.

"All of his horses and work oxen had frozen to death and his herd was scattered to the four winds. When we finally reached the camp Jim Taylor, the man who had entertained us in the dugout the night before, and about fifteen of his men, were there.

"Charles Boyce had told me previously that he was not in a very good humor about the plan I had adopted to borrow his horse. I proved to be a good talker, however, and when I got through Jim said he guessed one dollar and fifty cents would be enough for the use of the horse. I told him that the price was cheap enough, but I didn't tell him there was only ten cents in cash in the whole outfit.

"I traded him some steers for three horses and a mule, and included the one dollar and fifty cents in the trade. Our troubles were not to end here, however.

"Two men were behind with the remuda of sixty five horses used by the men on alternate days in coming up the trail. I sent two of the boys back to meet them, and led them into camp.

"Going back about eight miles, they met the men coming toward camp on foot, as the whole sixty-five head had frozen to death the night before in a space not larger than an ordinary dwelling house, and the boys had only saved themselves from a like fate by building a fire in the blackjack timber and keeping it going all night.

"We held the herd there for a couple of days with the three horses and the mule, and I traded some steers to the Indians for three more horses. We then started on north and reached Ellsworth on May 20. This heavy loss of horse-flesh was a prominent factor in the hindrance, which cut the net profits of the drive down to one dollar and fifty cents. Not a single one out of seventy-eight head of horses survived the terrible blizzard of four- or five- hours' duration."

Mr. West made twelve successive trips over the trail from the coast of Texas to Colorado, Kansas, Nebraska and other Northern markets with large herds of Texas cattle. His first trip was in 1871 – a good many trips for a boy to make without break, and he didn't ride in any automobiles on these trips.

# Lived on the Frontier during Indian Times

*by Joe F. Spettel, Rio Medina, Texas*

I WAS BORN IN THE HABY SETTLEMENT IN 1856, and have lived in Medina County all my life. My parents were Castro colonists and came to this country in 1844, locating in the Haby Settlement.

My father, John Spettel, was a "forty-niner," and went to seek his fortune in the California gold fields. He, with two companions, made quite a lucky strike, but in returning homeward they were overtaken by a band of robbers, his companions were killed and father received a bullet wound which eventually caused his death, although he lived for several years afterward.

He came home and remained a while, and again went to California, but did not find mining so successful as on his former trip. However, he brought back some gold nuggets that are still in the possession of our family.

In 1852 he married Miss Mary Haby, and of this union were born three children, respectively, John B., Mary and Joseph F. Spettel. My father died in 1857, his early demise being due to the wound he received while prospecting. My sister became the wife of my partner, Louis Schorp, and she died in 1905. My brother died in 1909, so I am the sole survivor of one of the most courageous men that ever resided in this vicinity, who overcame all obstacles to penetrate the unknown Western land to accumulate a fortune.

After my father's death my mother had to depend on hired help, as we were not large enough to take care of the farm and stock. At this time we had but one horse, and the Indians stole him.

As time went on we began to prosper, our cattle increased and we had a fine bunch of saddle horses, but fate was against us, it seemed, for in 1866 the Indians made another raid in our settlement and drove off every cow pony we owned. We did not let this misfortune discourage us, but purchased more horses and soon were able to take the proper care of our cattle.

During the Civil War we were troubled a great deal by the soldiers, who would come into the community and gather up all the able-bodied men and boys. But the settlers would keep out of their way as much as possible and hide out their work oxen and horses to keep the soldiers from taking them.

In 1870 the Indians made another raid in our neighborhood, but failed to take any of our horses, as we had heard of their approach and penned our stock. My uncle had two horses in a small pasture, which he trained to come home when he whistled to them.

That night he called them up and staked them near the house, armed himself with a shotgun, concealed himself behind a tree and waited the results. About one o'clock the horses began to snort and caper around, and he knew Indians were near.

Looking around he saw three Indians coming along the rail fence in a trot. Just as the Indians were opposite him the foremost put his head inside the fence between the upper and second rails, and my uncle cut down on him with that old shotgun, which was loaded with buckshot. The Indian dropped in his tracks and his companions instantly vanished.

The following full moon another raid was made, probably by the same band, but they did not steal any horses this time. They went into a field about 300 yards from home and cut up many melons. One of our dogs came home with an arrow sticking in his neck.

During the seventies two companions and myself drove a hundred fat steers from Medina County to Luling, the nearest railway station, from where they were loaded and shipped to New Orleans.

In the spring of 1873 I assisted in driving 500 aged steers from Haby Settlement to a place above San Antonio, where we delivered them to John F. Lytle and Bill Perryman, and were met by another herd owned by the same men, who drove them up the Kansas trail to Northern markets.

In 1875 Julius Wurzbach, my brother and I put up a herd of 1,100 steers for the firm of Lytle & McDaniel. It was in charge of Gus Black, who now resides in Kinney County. We continued to gather herds for Lytle & McDaniel for several years.

In 1878, while on a roundup near the Medina and Uvalde County line, one night the Indians made a raid and tried to steal our horses, but succeeded in getting only four.

From 1878 to 1887 my brother and I looked after our stock and sold steers near our home. In 1883 Louis Schorp married my sister, and we formed a partnership, and our ranches are still known as the Schorp & Spettel Property. In 1887 we purchased a ranch in Frio County and drove our aged steers there every fall and shipped them to market each following June.

# Played Pranks on the Tenderfoot

*by Henry D. Steele, San Antonio, Texas*

EARLY IN THE SPRING OF 1882 I WAS EMPLOYED by Mark Withers of Lockhart, to go up the trail with a herd to Kansas. Before starting on the trip I went to San Antonio and purchased a complete cowboy equipment, broad-brimmed hat, leggins, Colt pistol, scabbard, cartridges and the usual trimmings.

We went down into McMullen County to get the cattle, and I was selected as horse-wrangler for the outfit. The cattle were bought from a man by the name of Martin. While we were at Tilden, George Hill came up with some of the boys and helped to gather the herd.

I was pretty much of a "tender-foot," just a slip of a boy, and the hands told me this man Hill was a pretty tough character and would steal anything he could get his hands on, besides he might kill me if I didn't watch him.

They loaded me up pretty well on this kind of information, and I really believed it. They would steal my matches, cartridges, cigarette papers and handkerchiefs, and tell me that Hill got them. I reached the time when I was deprived of almost everything I had and even had to skin prickly pears to get wrapping for my cigarettes, believing all the while that the fellow Hill had cleaned me up.

Things were getting serious and I was desperate, and if Hill had made any kind of a break the consequences would probably have been disaster. At last Hill, who was fully aware of the game that was being played on me, called me aside and told me that it was all a put-up job, and said it had been carried far enough. We all had a good laugh and John Story was our cook until we reached Coleman County, but there he left us and returned to Lockhart, to engage in the blacksmith business.

After Story left us I had to do the cooking some time, and, getting tired of that work, I quit the herd and returned home, George Hill accompanying me as far as Austin.

In the spring of 1883 I was employed by Dick Head of Lockhart to go with a herd. Monroe Hardeman was boss. We gathered the cattle in Mason and Coleman Counties. The cattle were pretty thin, as the range was dry and had little grass. We passed through McCulloch County, through North Texas, and into the Indian Territory. Crossed the Washita River when it was on a big rise. That night we had a severe thunderstorm and I lost my hat during the rain.

When we reached Dodge City, Kansas, we remained there several days to allow the herd to rest, and from here we proceeded to Ogallala, Nebraska, where Mr. Head sold the cattle, and most of the crew came home, but Joe Lovelady, Pat Garrison, myself and Charlie Hedgepeth, a Negro, went on with the herd to Cheyenne, Wyoming, where we arrived in August. When we started back we bought our tickets for Austin, and the price was $33.35 each.

It has been just thirty-seven years since I went over the trail. I do not know what has become of the men who went with me on that trip. One of the hands, Charlie Hedgepeth, the Negro, was hanged at Seguin by a mob some years ago. I saw Mark Withers at the Old Trail Drivers' reunion in San Antonio in 1917.

# When a Man's Word was as Good as a Gilt-Edged Note

*by George N. Steen, Bryan, Texas*

TAKING THE ADVICE OF JAKE ELLISON, in 1867 I decided to go into the cattle business. I had no money, but the people let me take their cattle on credit, and I gathered enough to start a herd from San Marcos, Texas, to Abilene, Kansas, in the spring of 1868. I had six cowboys and only one hundred dollars to start on the trip with, but I knew I would get through somehow.

When we reached Gainesville my money was all gone, and our stock of grub was low. I went into the town to see if I could buy enough groceries to last until we could get through the Indian Territory. I was a perfect stranger there, and did not know a man in the town.

I went into George Howell's store, told Mr. Howell my circumstances, and asked if he could credit me for what I needed. He looked me straight in the eye for a few seconds and said he would do so. And he didn't ask for a mortgage or a note or anything to hold me bound except my word to pay.

Our bread gave out before we got through the Indian Territory, and I started foraging. One of the boys in my outfit had a ten-dollar gold piece and loaned it to me to use in buying flour. I struck a small trail and followed it until it led me to a little old log cabin. I got off my horse and went inside and found an old Indian who could not speak very much English, and did not seem to understand what I wanted. Looking around the room I saw a sack of flour and said to him, "How much take?" He said "Ten dollars," so I gave him the gold piece and went back to camp rejoicing.

Capt. Bill George of Seguin joined me while going through the Indian Territory. We had some trouble with Indians on the trip. One night our herd was stampeded and we discovered that it was a ruse played by the

Indians to get possession of our horses. I heard them rustling about and put after them, with the result that I captured a horse and bridle.

Next morning when we started the herd we tied the horse at the edge of a mot of timber, and I concealed myself in the thicket to watch for developments. Pretty soon an Indian came to the horse and I covered him with my gun. He thought his time to depart to the happy hunting grounds had arrived. After giving him a good scare I made him promise to quit thieving and to never again attempt to steal horses from trail drivers. Then I let him go.

I was in Abilene when Tom Bowles and Wild Bill, the city marshal, had a shooting scrape and a policeman was killed by a stray bullet. While we were there one night a man was drinking at a bar in a saloon, and somebody fired in from outside, the bullet striking him in the mouth and instantly killing him. Later one of the boys with a Texas herd was shot and killed by one of the Mexican hands. The Mexican skipped out. A reward was offered for his capture dead or alive, and Wesley Hardin got the reward.

# My Experience on the Cow Trail

*by F.M. Polk, Luling, Texas*

MY FIRST EXPERIENCE ON THE COW TRAIL was in 1872. I went with Joe Tennison and Warnell Polk, my father. We traveled the trail known as "the Old Chisholm Trail." We left for Lockhart, Texas, on the first of April and went by way of Fort Worth. Fort Worth was a new town then and, of course, we had to stop over and see the sights. After leaving Fort Worth we made good time until we reached Red River, which we crossed at Red River Station. The river was swollen by the heavy spring rains and we were forced to swim our cattle through very deep and swift water. We lost a few, but felt lucky in getting off light.

We were a carefree bunch, had lots of fun and also lots of hard work. It was the spring of the year and the woods were very beautiful. We would pitch our tents at night, get our work all done, and after supper would light our pipes and sit or lounge around the campfire and listen to the other men spin their hair-raising yarns, of their earlier trips.

We would then make our beds, using our saddles for pillows, stretch our tired limbs and soon be sound asleep and know nothing else until morning, unless something happened to disturb the cattle, when we would bound up and be ready for action.

I recall one stampede especially on this trip. We had camped on the south side of the North Canadian River one stormy night and after retiring we heard a big noise and we were up and out to the cattle in a very few minutes. We soon realized that we had our hands full, for the cattle had scattered everywhere and it required two days to get them back together again.

As we went through the country, it kept us busy looking out for Indians and buffalo. One man was always sent ahead to keep the buffaloes out of the herd and scout for Indians, for they were very savage at this time and we never knew when they would attack us. We landed in

Wichita, Kansas, some time near the middle of July without serious mishaps or the loss of very many cattle.

I decided I would take it easier coming back, so bought a wagon and left Wichita the middle of August. I came down through Arkansas and the edge of Missouri and landed at home the 20th of September with five head of horses.

As I was only eighteen-years-old, my father thought I was too young for such a strenuous life and persuaded me to farm a few years before returning to the trail, but I did not like farming and after two years' trial of it, I was more than ready to go back to the wild, carefree life of a cowboy.

In 1875 I went to work for J.W. Montgomery, better known among the cowmen as "Black Bill." He moved his cattle to Lampasas County and I worked for him three years, 1875, 1876 and 1877. I returned home then and worked on a ranch until the spring of 1881, when I went to work for W.H. Jennings and John R. Blocker. I bought cattle over Caldwell County until the first of April.

We left the ranch near the San Marcos River on the first day of April for Kansas. We landed at the Blocker Ranch in five days and received twenty-eight head of outlaw horses. Blocker and Jennings always took several herds up the trail at the same time.

On this trip they bought 200 head of Spanish horses from someone on the Rio Grande. Bob Jennings, the boss of our herd, and I, were sent after this bunch of horses. They were the worst horses we ever handled. We had lots of fun and lots of falls trying to ride them. It was Ab and Jenks Blocker's job to rope, down and put shoes on them, and let me tell you it was a worse job than some ladies have in trying to put a No. 3 shoe on a No. 5 foot.

We made our way to Taylor, Texas, and received 300 head of steers. It was then the 18th day of April and it required several days to put the road brand on this bunch before we were ready for the long, long trail.

The boys had a rough time, but we certainly had lots of fun. Nothing ever happened that we didn't get a good laugh out of it. We had one "greener" with us on this trip and we never missed a chance to play a prank on him.

His name was Joe Hullum. Cal Tuttle, Charlie Roberts and I all knew him well and, of course, delighted in teasing him. When we reached Lampasas County we told him we were getting into a country where the Indians were very bad and that they didn't mind wearing a few scalps on their belts.

He pretended not to care, but before we had gone very much further he bid us farewell, saying that he didn't care anything about being buried on the lone prairie for the wild coyotes to howl over his grave and, besides he was getting too far away from "dear old Caldwell County." He bade us good luck and the last we saw of him he was taking the newly traveled end of the trail, and he wasn't slow about it, either.

For the next few days everything went on fine, the weather was fair, the cattle were quiet, and we began to say to each other : "Cattle driving is just about the easiest job I know of," but, alas, peace never lasted long on the cattle trail. I don't remember just where we struck the Western Chisholm Trail, but as we neared Little River we had a terrible storm and rain.

The cattle became frightened and pulled off a big show. It took us three days to get them all together again, and when we reached the river we had to swim the cattle. They were restless and unruly and it took us two days to get them all across.

We had a fellow by the name of Rufe Fuller taking care of the horses, and in crossing the river he drowned the horse he was riding and one of the bunch he was driving. We made pontoons and fastened them to our wagons to float them across.

We made good time after that until we reached Pease River, but here we had a big stampede and had to lay over two days to gather up our cattle. The country was lined with antelope and prairie dogs and we found great sport killing them.

We crossed the Red River into the Indian Territory at Doan's Store, and here we struck the Indians by the thousands. We kept our eyes open and managed to keep peace by giving them a beef every day. They would come to us fifty and one hundred at a time. Some would ride with us all day and they always asked for a cow, which they called "Wahaw, Wahaw," and, of course, we acted like we were glad to give it to them, but we were not very badly frightened. We all had our guns and knew how to use them if we got in a tight.

As we went through this part of the country we had great sport roping buffalo and elk. You could look across the prairie and see hundreds of them in droves.

J.R. Blocker and W.H. Jennings overtook us at Bitter Creek. They were to deliver the cattle at Mobeetie, a little town in the Panhandle. I quit the herd at Bitter Creek. Mr. Blocker sent Will Sears and I on to overtake Givings Lane, one of Blocker & Jennings' bosses. We overtook Mr. Lane in three days at Bluff Creek, and while camped there we had a big rainstorm, which put the creek up and caused a big stampede among our cattle.

We stayed with Mr. Lane until he got the cattle rounded up and across the creek, when we decided to go to La Junta, Colorado. I had a cousin there running a ranch for J.J. Jones.

We left Dodge City the first of August and traveled up the Arkansas River on horseback. We reached the Jones Ranch on the fifth of August. I rested one day and went to work.

J.J. Jones was at that time the biggest cattleman in Colorado, so you may guess that we had lots of work to do. I worked here until the first of December, and as it was getting very cold up there by that time, and we were having some heavy snowfalls, I decided I would strike for a warmer climate, and back to Texas I came.

I hired to M.A. Withers on April the first, 1882, and struck the trail again. He sent several herds this time and I went with a bunch under Gus Withers.

We had lots of hard work and plenty of bad horses to ride. They were the worst bunch I ever saw with the exception of the Blocker bunch. The stampedes were so numerous that I could not keep track of them, but we had a well-trained bunch of men and lost no cattle, but had to work hard and sleep with one eye open.

There was so much rain and the cattle were so restless, we never knew what to expect. Lots of times I never pulled off my boots for three days and nights. After one of these strenuous times, we would lay over some place and rest for a few days. We would have lots of fun trying to prove who was the best rider, but oftentimes the horse would prove that he was on to his job better than any of us.

At Pease River we had a big stampede and would have lost a great many cattle if we had not been near Millett's Ranch. Millet worked only desperadoes on this ranch, but they were all good cattlemen and came nobly to our rescue.

We ran across one boy in that crowd from Caldwell County. He had decided quite a while ago that Caldwell County was getting too warm for him and his cattle rustling and had struck for a cooler climate. It seemed awfully good to us to see anyone from home, even a cattle rustler. He enjoyed our stay very much, as he learned of lots that had happened at home since he left. We rested here a few days and struck out again.

We crossed the Red River at Doan's Store and there we found a large number of Indians camped, but they were peaceable, for they were fast finding out that it didn't pay to molest cattle drivers. M.A. Withers overtook us here and sent Gus Withers on with his herd, which was going to Dodge, while he went ahead to get Mr. Johnson, who had bought these cattle for an English syndicate, to come to Mobeetie to receive our herd. He put Tom Hawker over us and also changed my brother, Cal Polk, to our bunch, which pleased me very much. We had been separated for quite a while and had lots to tell each other.

After leaving Doan's Store we traveled up Bitter Creek for forty or fifty miles and then turned west to Mobeetie, when we turned our herd over to John Hargroves to hold on the L.X. Ranch until fall, as we could not take them on to Tuscosa until after frost on account of a quarantine they had on at that time.

After Mr. Johnson received our bunch he and M.A. Withers returned to Dodge to receive the herd he had sent there. After reaching Dodge and counting the cattle, Mr. Johnson was struck and killed by lightning while returning to camp. Mr. Withers was knocked from his horse, but wasn't hurt further than receiving a bad fall and shock.

About the first of October, the boss and I had a row and I decided I was ready for the back trail. I took the buckboard for Dodge, which was about 300 miles from Mobeetie. On reaching Dodge, I bought a ticket for San Antonio.

On my way home I reviewed my past life as a cowboy from every angle and came to the conclusion that about all I had gained was experience, and I could not turn that into cash, so I decided I had enough of it, and made up my mind to go home, get married and settle down to farming.

# Punching Cattle on the Trail to Kansas

*by W.B. Hardeman, Devine, Texas*

I WAS JUST A FARMER BOY, started to church at Prairie Lea one Sunday, met Tom Baylor (he having written me a note several days before, asking if I wanted to go up the trail) and the first thing he said was, "Well, are you going?" I said, "Yes," so he said, "Well, you have no time to go to church." So we went back to my house, got dinner and started to the "chuck wagon and remuda," which was camped some six miles ahead. There I was, with a white shirt, collar and cravat, starting on the trail. You can imagine just how green I was.

We put the herd up below Bryan. We were gone seven months, so I had plenty of time to learn a few things in regard to driving cattle. We were a month putting up the herd.

I was always left to hold the cattle, and when we finally drove out of the timber and reached the prairie, the grass was ten inches in height, green as a wheat field and the cattle were poor and hungry, so went to chopping that grass as though they were paid. There was a nice little shade tree right near, so I got off my horse to sit in the shade for a few minutes and watch the cattle.

The first thing I knew Tom Baylor was waking me. I thought, "Well, I have gone to sleep on guard. I had just as well put my hand in Col. Ellison's pocket and take his money."

I never got off my horse any more when on duty, though I have seen the time when I would have given five dollars for one-half hour's sleep. I would even put tobacco in my eyes to keep awake. Our regular work was near eighteen hours a day, and twenty-four if a bad night, then the next day, just as though we had slept all night, and most of us getting only thirty dollars per month and grub, bad weather making from twenty-four to forty-eight hours, never thinking of "time and overtime," or calling for shorter hours and more pay.

In Kansas one day for dinner we bought some pies, eggs and milk from a granger. He informed Baylor that a certain section of land that had a furrow plowed around it, did not belong to his neighbor, but was railroad land and the number was 115. When I came to dinner Baylor told me about the section. He also told me we would not strike any more water that evening.

This creek on Section 115 had fine water, and he asked me if I thought best to water there. I said, "Yes," knowing I had to herd that afternoon. Ham Bee protested, and said we should not treat that old man that way, but Ham did not have to hold the herd that evening, so I insisted, and Baylor said, "Get your dinner and fresh horses, I will start to the water."

The old man lived in a dug-out on the side of a hill where he could see everything, so when he saw the cattle cross that furrow he came out with a shotgun, rolling up his sleeves, waving his arms and shouting, "Take those cattle off my land or I will have every damn one of you arrested."

Baylor, being in the lead, came in contact with him first. He said, "'Old man, there must be a mistake; we have some fat cattle and the agent of the railroad (some four miles to the depot) said he had no stock cars and for us to throw the cattle on Section 115."

Well, sir, you should have heard that old man curse that (innocent) agent, as well as the country in general, stating he had moved his family out there, the drought came and it looked like starvation, so he was trying to save that little grass for winter.

Baylor compromised by telling him he had a family and knew how it was, and would be willing to water on one-half of the section and would give him a doggie calf that had got into the herd several days before and we did not want it. The old man got in a fine humor, had us to send the wagon by the house to get a barrel of spring water – that was the kind of a neighbor the old man had.

While in the Indian Territory one day at noon, about a dozen head of range cattle got in the herd. We did not discover them until we threw the herd back on the trail, so we had to cut them out and run them back some three miles. Sometime during the night they trailed us up and came into the herd, and we did not discover it until we were out of that range.

After we got up into Kansas I saw two men riding around the herd with Baylor and when he left them he came to me and said, "Bud, those men are butchers, and said they would give us $300 for those range cattle and do not want a bill of sale." I said, "Tell them the cattle are not ours, so we can't do that; we will turn them over to Col. Ellison and he can find the owner," and we took them on.

We delivered that herd at Ogallala, Nebraska, took another from there to the Bell Fourche in Wyoming – a sixty-mile drive without water for the cattle. We were just twelve miles from the buffalo. By the time we branded out the herd we were short of grub, so did not go buffalo hunting, and right there I lost my only chance to kill buffalo. We were 500 miles from a railroad, but I wish I had gone anyway.

Tom P. Baylor was a son of Gen. John R. Baylor. He died some twenty-one years ago. He was as fine a man as I ever knew. Ham P. Bee is now in San Antonio, express messenger on a railroad.

In 1883 I went on the trail with W.T. Jackman of San Marcos. We started the herd from Colorado County at "Ranches Grande," owned by Stafford Brothers.

While in the Indian Territory one evening two Indians ate supper with us. I was holding the herd while first relief was at supper. Dan, a fifteen-year-old boy, was holding the "remuda" (saddle horses). We really had two herds with one wagon, had 3,000 cattle, 400 horses and one hundred saddle horses, fifteen men in all, and only three six-shooters in the outfit.

Just as I went to eat my supper and the horse herders were going to relieve Dan, we heard him give a distress yell and shoot several times. Jackman and Lee Wolfington mounted their horses, drew their guns and started in a run for Dan.

That was one time I wished for a gun. Twelve men and nothing to defend ourselves with. Those two Indians that had eaten supper with us had mounted their horses and ostensibly started for their camp, but slipped around and drove off two saddle ponies. Dan discovered them by skylight, hence the alarm. Jackman and Wolfington followed them and recovered the horses, but did not see the two Indians. W.T. Jackman is postmaster at San Marcos. He was sheriff there for twenty years, and as good as Texas ever had.

In 1886 I went with J.C. Robertson. We drove for Blocker, Davis & Driscoll. They drove 40,000 head of cattle, and had 1,400 horses. We started for Uvalde, went up the East Fork of the Nueces River, the roughest trail I ever went. We could not see all of the cattle, only at bedding time.

When nearing the Territory one evening, a young man and young lady came galloping by us. The girl was well mounted, and had on a handsome riding habit. We had not seen a woman for months, so we were all charmed and thought she was the most beautiful object we had ever beheld. All wanted to see more of her. Joe Robertson being the boss, found out we would pass near where the family lived the next evening and there was a fine spring of water where they lived, so that noon he had me to trim his hair and whiskers, his intention being to take the chuck wagon by to get a barrel of spring water. Of course we all knew it was just an excuse to get to see that pretty girl once more.

Sandy Buckalew called out to me to "fix the boss right," and I did my best. Sandy was pointing the herd and had a chance to pass right near the house before Robertson could get up there, so he galloped over to the house to get a drink of water. The old mother, who was a very kind and nice lady, brought him some water. He thanked her and began to brag on the beautiful country, to all of which she agreed, but deplored the fact that there was no school.

Sandy saw his chance and said, "Well, that can be arranged, I think, as our boss is married and his wife is a splendid school teacher, and he is well pleased with the country, so I feel confident that you will have no trouble in having him to locate here. He will be by to get a barrel of water and you can mention it to him."

You can imagine how the boss felt when the good mother did all the entertaining all the time, urging him to bring his fine little wife and teach their school. I don't think he even got a glimpse of the girl. We had lots of fun out of it, anyway, though none of us ever laid eyes on that most beautiful woman again.

Joe has never married, but has more children to look after than any of us, as he has charge of the San Pedro Springs Park in San Antonio and looks after the children there, and a better man can't be found.

In the final roundup, may we all meet again.

# Exciting Experiences on the Frontier and on the Trail

*by C.W. Ackermann, San Antonio, Texas*

I WAS BORN IN THE YEAR 1855 on the Salado Creek four miles east of San Antonio, Bexar County, Texas.

My first adventure I can remember was when I was six years old. One day my brother, ten years old, asked me to go with him to hunt some cows. We both rode on one horse. After we had ridden for several miles we found a cow with a young calf. My brother told me to stay with that cow while he hunted others, then he would return for me.

While he was gone the cow and calf rambled off and I got lost from them in the high grass. I kept on hunting the cow and in the meantime my brother returned for me, but could not find me. After hunting for me a while he concluded I had followed the cow home, so he went on home.

My parents immediately began to search for me.

In the meantime I kept on walking in the direction the cow went, believing I was going home, till night came. The wolves began to howl and scared me so I climbed up a little tree, where I remained till they stopped howling. Then I crawled down and slept soundly under the tree till the sun woke me up.

I got up and started off again. I walked all day with nothing to eat but chaparral berries and I was fortunate enough to find a small pool of water that afternoon. By night I had not reached home, so I made my bed under a tree as I had done the night before.

That night there was a big thunderstorm and rain. I was completely drenched. But my courage never failed, so in the morning bright and early I started out. I heard some roosters crowing, so I went in that direction, thinking I had at last found home. But, to my disappointment, it was only a Mexican house. The dogs began to chase me, but the old man called them back, then took me in his house where they were just ready to eat breakfast.

I was scared almost lifeless, for I could neither speak nor understand Spanish. I could picture them roasting me for dinner and all kinds of horrible things they might do with me. Nevertheless, I greedily drank the cup of coffee and ate the piece of bread they gave me and asked for more, because I was almost starved, but they would not give me any more.

Immediately after breakfast the old "hombre" saddled his horse, tied a rope around me and put me behind him on his horse. Then he rode to an American family and got a written note from the white man that he (the Mexican) had not kidnapped me, but was taking me home.

The old Mexican took me on home and received a generous reward from my father. Afterward I learned that I had roamed to Chipadares, a distance of about twenty miles from my home. At that time that was the nearest settlement southeast of home. During the Civil War I was just a mere boy of nine years. Nevertheless, I recall some thrilling adventures.

My father was exempted from the army on account of owning a flour mill. This mill was located on the San Antonio River about sixteen miles from our farm. Father had to run the mill himself, so he and mother moved there and left my older brother, thirteen years old, and I at the farm to take care of the stock and everything.

One day while I was alone the Confederate soldiers came around gathering up horses. They threatened to take mine and had me scared to death. I begged hard for my horse and I told them that I needed him to get supplies with. After frightening me real good they told me I could keep my horse. I was the only one they left with a horse around that neighborhood.

The schools in those days were very much different to the schools of today. We only had private schools and these lasted the entire year. Our only vacation was two weeks in August.

The only subjects they taught were reading, writing, arithmetic, spelling, history, geography and grammar. On Monday, Tuesday and Wednesday we studied reading, writing, spelling and arithmetic. On Thursday and Friday we had history, grammar and geography.

I started to school when I was eleven years old and attended three years. After that I was sent to San Antonio, where I studied surveying.

When I was a boy, rounding up cattle was a very exciting event. In those days people did not have their pastures fenced, so the cattle often wandered many miles from home.

About the beginning of spring we would start on the roundup. Three or four neighborhoods would send out ten to fifteen men together. Out of these one man was selected as captain. I was just fourteen years old when I went out on my first roundup. My father put me in the care of our captain and from him I learned how to rope and brand cattle and many other important things one should know about roundups.

I often roped and branded as many as eight or ten calves by myself in a day. Branding was not a very easy task, either, for we had to run the brand. We had no ready-made brands as now. Many times we had to gather the wilder cattle at night. When they went out on the prairie we would sneak a tame bunch of cattle in with them and thus drive them in a corral. Sometimes we would build a stockade around water holes, leaving only one opening for the cattle to get in. Even with such a trap we were often unable to hold the wildest ones in.

Licenses permitting one to carry arms was unheard of in my earlier days. Every man always carried his "six-shooter" buckled to his side. This was necessary on account of there being so many robbers. There were about forty or more highway robbers scattered over the country in squads of five or six men.

I remember one time as three of the other boys and myself were coming from the market in San Antonio we were waylaid by some robbers. Fortunately we spied them in time and each of us galloped off in different directions. They fired at us, but we all escaped unharmed.

When I was sixteen years old I had a little experience with horse thieves. My father noticed a suspicious looking man riding around our place one day, so he told us boys we had better watch the horses.

My brother and I went out to guard the horses that night and just about midnight the thieves came in two or three different squads. How many there were we never knew. We watched them give signals to each other with the fire of their cigarettes. Then we fired at them and scared them away. We hit one of them, but never knew if we killed him or not. After that we were never bothered with horse thieves.

The robbers were certainly skillful. I recall one day when my brother and I were out on a hunt, we laid down to rest. We used our saddles for pillows and put our belts and "six-shooters" under them. And while we were resting someone sneaked up and stole my belt and "six-shooter" right from under my head. I suppose whoever it was thought I had money in the little money pouch on my belt, but they sure got fooled.

In 1872 we were not allowed so much liberty. A law was passed, which prohibited men from carrying concealed arms. In 1874 horse thieves and highway robbers were so bad something had to be done. The ranchmen formed an organization known as the "Stock Association" to rid the country of these marauders. I was one of the fifty deputies elected. After a year's time we had Bexar County clear of robbers.

My first trip up the old cow trail to Kansas was in the year 1873, when I was just a boy of eighteen. My father decided to take some of his cattle to the Kansas market, as they sold so cheap here. At that time 1,000-pound beeves sold in San Antonio for eight dollars per head and in Wichita, Kansas, for $23.80 per head.

Father asked a bunch of young cowboys if they thought they could take his cattle to Kansas. As we were all young fellows, between the ages of eighteen and twenty-two, eager for adventure, we willingly consented. So on the first day of February we began gathering our cattle and finished rounding up a herd on March 14th. Early next morning we started on our journey. We traveled all day and that night made our first camping place where Converse, Bexar County, now stands, but at that time it was only an open country.

That first night was one never to be forgotten. It rained all night long and our cattle stampeded eighteen times. During one stampede they ran into one of our men. His horse was run over by the cattle and crippled, while the man was carried off about a fourth of a mile on top of the cattle. He escaped with only a few bruises. We were lucky not to lose any cattle that night, but fifteen head were crippled.

The next morning we bought a two-wheeled cart to carry our bedding and provisions in. Then, with a yoke of oxen hitched to it, we began our journey again and made our next stop on the Santa Clara, where now stands the little town, Marion. That night there was an electric storm, which was followed by cold weather and frost. After a few days' rest we resumed our trail. When we reached the Guadalupe River it was up about six feet. Our cattle had to swim across and our cart was taken on a ferryboat.

At our next camping place we had another stampede and lost thirty-five head of cattle, which we never found.

When we reached the Colorado River it also was up about four feet. After swimming that we kept on the trail to Round Rock, where our yoke of oxen was stolen, so we had to rope and hitch two wild steers to the cart. When we reached Fort Worth, at that time a small town of one hundred inhabitants, we sold our cart and bought a wagon and team of horses.

It was a very rainy year and every river we came to was up; however, we crossed them all without loss. When we reached Washita River, in Indian Territory, we had to stay there eight days on account of heavy rains. There I had my hardest time of the trip. For six nights I slept only about one and a half hours and never pulled off my slicker and boots.

Upon reaching the Canadian River we found that so high we could not cross for two days. Our next stop was on Bluff Creek, on the line of Kansas. There one of our men, Joe Menges, roped a buffalo calf, which we carried with us to Wichita and sold it to "Buffalo Joe," who was running a beer garden for the amusement of the trail men.

We camped on the river called Ninnesquaw for three months in order to fatten our cattle for the market. Then my father came to Kansas by train and sold them. On the seventh of September we began our return trip, bringing with us forty-five head of saddle ponies. It took us twenty-seven days to make the return trip to San Antonio. Only five of us made the return trip, Hartmann, Eisenhauer, Markwardt, Smith, and myself.

On my journey I saw many buffalo, but killed only one great big one. I also killed seven antelopes. One morning while I was eating breakfast one of the boys came running up and said, "Chris, come on quick, buffalo ran in the herd and they have stampeded." I jumped on my horse and went with him. The first thing I saw was one of the boys, Philip Prinz, galloping after some buffaloes trying to rope one. When he spied me he came and asked me for my horse. I would not give it to him and told him to let the buffalo alone if he didn't want to get killed. He got a little sore at me, but we rode on back to camp together.

I think we were the youngest bunch of trailmen on the "Trail" that year. The oldest man, Ad Markwardt, our cook, was only twenty-five years old, and the rest were between eighteen and twenty-two years. Those that rode the "Trail" with me were Alf Hartmann, Steve Wooler, Joe Menges, Phil Prinz, Louis Eisenhauer, Ad Markwardt, Henry Smith, a Negro, and my brother, Fred.

Besides making trips over the "Trail" to Kansas, I often made trips to the coast. Years ago there were no trains we could ship our cattle on as nowadays. Whenever we wanted to take cattle to the seaport we had to drive them. We usually drove them in herds of about 200 head.

In the spring of the year we usually began rounding up our cattle, as the beef buyers usually came in the early fall. Our captain would give us orders for the trip, then we would start out, each man with his pack-horse and two saddle horses. There were large stock pens scattered over the country. We would each go in different directions and all meet at one of the pens. At night when we went into camp we would hobble our tamest horses with buckskin hobbles and staked the wilder ones. We hung our "grub" up in a tree so nothing could bother it.

After we had all the cattle together we would start for home. As we came near to each man's house he would cut his cattle out of the herd. Then came the beef buyer. After he bought as many as he wanted he would get ready for the drive to the seaport. I helped him out many times just to take the trip.

We would often lose cattle on these trips, for they would stampede and, of course, we seldom found those that got lost. At one of our camping places an Irishman had built a pen on rollers. When the cattle stampeded in that pen there was no danger of losing any. When they would run the pen went right with them. It was often carried as far as fifty yards.

In the year 1874 I had another very thrilling experience. On account of such a dry year my father decided to move to a different location. He did not know where to go, so he gave me the job of hunting a suitable place. In August of that year I started out with two saddle horses and one pack horse. I went in a northwestern direction, then turned toward the Concho country. I went as far as the New Mexico boundary line, then started back home.

The country I traveled through was very wild. There were just a few small settlements scattered here and there and the people even seemed uncivilized. I saw antelope and buffalo by the thousands. It was that year the government was trying to kill out the buffalo. I passed many mule teams loaded with buffalo hides. Even though the country was wild I found some excellent locations for a ranch, especially in the Concho country.

When I returned home and told father about the wild country and people he decided not to move so far away. So he bought a ranch close to where now stands Wetmore. Later he gave me this ranch. I moved up there in 1877 and lived a bachelor's life till I married Emma Bueche in 1882.

We lived on that same ranch until 1905. Then I bought a small farm of 500 acres at Fratt, about nine miles from San Antonio, and left one of my sons in charge of the ranch.

I am now living a quiet, peaceful life on my farm. Every time I go up to my ranch memories of those old wild, happy days come back to me. Now I am 65 years old and have a clear record of never being arrested and never was involved in any kind of lawsuit.

# Observations and Experiences of Bygone Days

*by Louis Schorp, Rio Medina, Texas*

IN THE SPRING OF 1873 JOHN VANCE, a merchant of Castroville, decided to drive a herd of cattle up the Kansas Trail. In company with my neighbors I helped to round up and deliver steers to Mr. Vance, this being my first work along this line. Bladen Mitchell, a pioneer of Bandera County, was engaged by Mr. Vance as trail boss.

All of the cattle were received by Mr. Mitchell and driven to Bandera County, to a point about two miles north of the Mormon Camp, where Mr. Mitchell had his herding pens, and what was known as the Mitchell Crossing. This property was purchased during the early eighties by the firm of Schorp & Spettel, but at the present time it is entirely covered by the Medina Lake, a vast body of water impounded by a great concrete dam. After delivering my bunch of steers I went over to Elm Creek, a tributary to the Medina River, where I found a crowd rounding up cattle for Perryman & Lytle, among whom were the Spettel, Habys and Wurzbachs.

The following day five men out of this crowd, including myself, were going to Bandera to see the Vance cattle inspected and road branded, As we were getting ready to start the steers became frightened and stampeded. I was the only one horseback, and one of the men yelled to me to "turn the leaders toward the bluff and mill them." I did not understand the meaning of this, for I had never seen a stampede before. I knew how to turn the crank of a coffee-mill, but when it was necessary to "mill" a bunch of outlaw steers I did not know where to look for the crank.

I turned the lead cattle from running into camp and crowded them against the bluff, but they did not mill, and when I looked back I saw that most of the cattle had turned behind me. By this time all of the men in camp were on their horses and it took about an hour to get all of the cattle together again. Every steer had his tongue out, and an ox tongue never looked so cheap to me before or after.

The next day I went with the boys to take the herd out to graze, and when several miles southwest of Bandera one of the men pointed to a large live oak tree and said six men were hung to its branches during the Civil War by Confederate soldiers.

The next day the cattle were inspected by a man named Pue. During the inspection a dispute arose about a certain steer belonging to a Frenchman named Cordier at Castroville. I had delivered this steer to Mr. Mitchell, and knew it by the flesh marks, and it was branded R I, but the party calling the brand called it B I.

The inspector asked for water with which to dampen the brand and, finding the bucket empty, he took out a bottle of whiskey, wet the brand with the liquor, smoothed the hairs, and the brand showed R I very plainly. Thus twelve dollars were saved for the old Frenchman.

I rounded up steers every spring thereafter and delivered most of them to Lytle & McDaniel of Medina County.

During the year 1874, while riding over the range one day looking after stock, I noticed a cow running about and bellowing and rode over to see what was the matter with her. I found she had a very young calf by her side and three wolves were trying to get the calf. I chased the wolves away and drove the cow toward shelter. The calf had been wounded, and had I not happened along when I did the wolves would have killed it I am sure. I have been on the range more or less since 1870 and this is the only time that I ever saw wolves attack a calf.

During the winter of 1878 and 1879 grass in the Medina Valley was very short and many of the stockmen lost heavily. My father at this time owned about 500 cattle, and I remember that I skinned seventy head of father's cattle that winter.

In the fall of 1879 I moved the remainder of our cattle to San Miguel in Frio County, to where the Keystone pasture is now located. In the spring of 1880 I purchased all of the stock belonged to my father. I sold the steers to John Lytle and delivered them to him in the Forks Pasture at the mouth of the Hondo. This was the last bunch of steers I sold and delivered to go up the trail.

In the fall of 1882, the land in this particular part of Frio County where I ranched was purchased by a company from Muscatine, Iowa, known as the Hawkeye Land & Cattle Company. I sold all my land and stock to this company and moved back to Medina County, where I have resided ever since.

In the spring of 1884 I formed a partnership with Ed Kaufman, who now resides in San Antonio, and we drove a herd of horses to Pueblo, Colorado. In the outfit were George Gerdes, now with the Schweers-Kern Commission Company, John Saathoff of Hondo, Eames Saathoff of New Fountain, and a cook whose name I have forgotten.

# Met Quanah Parker on the Trail

### by John Wells, Bartlett, Texas

I WAS BORN IN GORDON COUNTY, GEORGIA, July 19, 1859. My father died when I was three years old. I left home in July when only ten years of age, and from that time on earned my way. The family moved to Texas in 1866 and in the winter of 1867 to Bell County.

First started on the trail when I was twenty-three years of age with thirteen men, including boss, cook and horse rustler. Worked for Hudson, Watson & Co. in spring of 1883. Gathered about 8,000 cattle from Lampasas, Burnet, Llano, Williamson, Gillespie and San Saba Counties. The company sold 3,000 cattle to Bob Johns and 2,000 cattle to Bill Shadley, also eighty-five horses, chuck wagon and trail outfit, drove them to Taylor and shipped to Wichita Falls.

Alex Webb and I were sent to San Antonio to receive and bring 2,000 cattle and twenty-four horses to Wichita Falls. This bunch was then unloaded and thrown with the Burnet County herd, making a total of about 4,000 cattle and 115 horses. The cattle ranged from one-year-olds to seven. We held them fifteen miles from the town between Wichita and Red River for a rest period of ten days to fit them for the trail.

While crossing at the mouth of Pease River we had ten steers to bog in the quicksand, and after digging them out we threw the herd on the prairie and camped for the night. The boys were all thirsty, having nothing to drink but gyp and alkali water.

I saw a settlement down the draw, a mile away, and went down and asked the people for a drink of water. They told me to ride to the spring, where I would find a cup and help myself. I went and found a bubbling spring as clear as crystal, which on tasting was gyp water too.

So I went to the house and asked if they had some buttermilk they would sell. They sold me about two gallons for fifty cents. I took it back to the herd and I and four other boys drank it. We were very glad to get our thirst quenched.

The next evening we camped near Doan's Store and there we saw our first Comanche braves.

The next day the range men cut the herd. We crossed the South Fork of Red River that evening where thirteen steers bogged and had to be dug out. One steer was bogged and I and Henry Miller, the boss, went to dig him out. The boss hobbled his horse.

I told him he had better hitch to the horn of my saddle, as the steer might catch him before he could unhobble his horse. I hitched my horse to his saddle, but, being boss, I guess he thought he needed no advice. He had the spade in his hand and we walked down and dug out some sand from the animal. The steer began to lunge and I thought he was going to get out, and so I got my horse in between the steer and my boss in time to keep him from being run over by the steer.

We continued up Red River for four- or five-days' drive. Had plenty of grass and a good supply of fresh lakes of water until we came to Wichita Mountains, where we crossed the North Fork of Red River.

There we found Quanah Parker and his friend waiting for us. He wanted a yearling donated, and said, "Me squaw heap hungry." After the boss. and five of the boys had gone to dinner I and four of the others were left on herd.

I rode around the herd to where I came up to Quanah Parker and his friend. Quanah was dressed like a white man. His friend wore breech clout and hunting skirt with a Winchester to his saddle. Quanah had on a hat and pants with a six-shooter in cowboy style. I made friends with Quanah, but I didn't like the looks of his friend. When the boss returned to the herd after dinner he gave Quanah a yearling and by that time four or five other warriors had appeared. They drove the yearling to their camp.

We passed through a gap of the Wichita Mountains and camped on the east side of the trail. After we had bedded our cattle and eaten our supper we saw a prairie fire in the foothills on the west side of the trail.

The first relief was on herd. The boss was afraid the fire might cross the trail and burn out over camp or cause a stampede, so he called the boys up and told them to get their horses and named two to go to the herd, the remainder to go with him.

Alex Webb was to go to the herd, but the cook asked Webb if he was going to leave his six-shooter with him. Webb told him no, he needed it.

But Cook says, "By Jacks, when it begins to thunder and lightning you fill this wagon full of six-shooters, but when the Indians are around the guns are all gone, and who is going to protect me?" The men rode far enough to find out that there was no danger of fire crossing the trail, then they returned to camp and all spent a peaceful night.

We saw no more of the Comanches and the next tribe was Kiowas, who were frequent visitors to the camp. There were seventeen for dinner one day. Three squaws sat down together, and two or three papooses went to looking for lice on each mother's head and eating them.

While passing through the Kiowa Indian country one of our men at Alverson had a close brush with one of the warriors, which might have resulted seriously had it not been that the boss was close at hand with his six-shooter. The Indian, after being forced to put up his Winchester, ran into the herd and killed two steers before he stopped.

I was riding with the herd in the Cheyenne country when a brave asked for a cartridge from my belt. I told him my cartridges were forty-fives and his gun was a forty-four.

He made signs to show me how he would reload it, and I had to give him one. Then he wanted to run a race. Our horses were not at all matched, mine being far superior, but I managed to hold him in for a short distance alongside the herd, so the brave could join.

The Indian parted with me saying, "Me heap hungry." I told him to come to Po Campo at night. He came, bringing three friends, one of them a youngster from college, out in full war paint, breechclout and hunting shirt. He traded quirts with Jim Odell, giving him a dollar to boot. The Indian wanted the quirt to ride races with.

About that time Frank Haddocks rode up and was mistaken by a 200-pound warrior for one of their tribe. He began talking to Frank in Cheyenne, at the same time advancing for a friendly bout. The college Indian, acting as interpreter, called him aside and told him that a family in their tribe had lost a baby years before and they believed Frank was this child.

They concluded then that Frank had been stolen from the Kiowas and that white people had stolen him before he learned to talk. Nothing seemed to shake their belief that he was an Indian. They urged him to go to their camp. Frank asked me to go with him and I believe he would have gone had I consented.

While we were at supper the Indians were sitting on piles of bedding, which the cook had thrown from the chuck wagon. One of the boys said, "Those damned Indians will put lice on our beds." The cook heard this and, angry at having extra company, said, "I'll get the fire shovel and get them off."

The young Indian of course understood, and at a word from him they moved and sat on the grass nearby. Early next morning the Indian who supposed himself to be Frank's brother, came and for an hour or more tried to persuade him to come and live with them. Frank asked me again to go along, and finally refused, when he saw I couldn't be persuaded. Looking back I can see we might both have been benefited by staying.

We reached Dodge City, Kansas, about six weeks after leaving Wichita Falls. There the boss bought provisions and after crossing the Arkansas River threw the cattle out on the tableland and camped for the night.

One incident broke into the regular trail life between this place and Buffalo, which it might be well to relate. A Kansas jayhawker had been in the habit of exacting toll from the herds crossing his land at Shawnee Creek. The boss, riding ahead, found out that he asked a cent apiece for the cattle, and decided to put one over on the gentleman.

At noon the boss came back to us with instructions to get the cattle across as quickly as possible and not tell the Kansas man how many head we carried. To say about 2,500 if he pressed us.

The next morning the boss wrote a check for twenty-five dollars and proceeded at once to Buffalo, where he wired Bob Shadley, the owner, not to honor the check.

The trail led through Buffalo and on beside the grave of two of Sam Bass' men, Joel Collins and his partner, who were killed by officers at that place some years before.

Through Kansas and Nebraska we had good water, plenty of grass, and the cattle thrived. Reaching Ogallala our cook quit and his cloak fell on my shoulders as the only one of the bunch qualified to fill it. We crossed the South Platte River and hiked out up the North River about sixty miles, where we stopped to brand for nearly ten days.

We proceeded to Sydney Bridge and crossed below the Block House. From this place we took the right-hand trail and went to Fort Robertson on the White River, past the famous Crow Burke Mountain, through the Bad Lands of Dakota, and crossed the Cheyenne River three miles below Hot Springs at the foot of the Black Hills.

We proceeded seventy-five or a hundred miles further to the Company Ranch on Driftwood Creek. Webb and Odell stayed at the ranch. The remainder went to Julesburg, Nebraska, with the provision wagon, where we bought tickets and came back to Texas.

Should any of my companions read this sketch I would be glad to have them write John Wells at Bartlett, Texas, or better known on the range as John Arlington.

QUANAH PARKER, dressed in European-American business attire, was the last chief of the Comanche Indian tribe, c1890.

# Texas Cowboys at a Circus in Minneapolis

### by S.H. Woods, Alice, Texas

I WAS BORN IN SHERMAN, Grayson County, Texas, Jan. 29, 1865, and left home in Sherman in the spring of 1881, when a lad sixteen years of age, and worked for Suggs Brothers on the IS Ranch, near the mouth of Beaver Creek, in the Chicksaw Nation, about twenty-five miles north of Montague, in Montague County, Texas.

In the month of July, 1881, we left the IS Ranch for Wyoming with about 3,000 head of Southern steer yearlings. I was second boss – the horse rustler. We started from the Monument Hills, about fifteen miles north of Red River Station on the old Chisholm Trail, which was known at that time as the Eastern Trail.

About the third night out the Indians stampeded our herd at the head of Wild Horse Creek, which delayed us for a few days. Leaving this point, we had fine weather and moved along rapidly until we left the Eastern Trail at Red Fork Ranch, on the Cimarron River, to intersect the Western Trail. Here we had some trouble, but nothing serious.

When we arrived within eight or ten miles of Dodge City, Kansas, a beautiful city, situated on the north bank of the Arkansas River and about one month's drive from Red River, we could see about fifty different trail herds grazing up and down the valley of the Arkansas River.

That night we had a terrible storm. Talk about thunder and lightning! There is where you could see phosphorescence (fox fire) on our horse's ears and smell sulphur.

We saw the storm approaching and every man, including the rustler, was out on duty. About ten o'clock at night we were greeted with a terribly loud clap of thunder and a flash of lightning, which killed one of our lead steers just behind me. That started the ball rolling.

Between the rumbling, roaring and rattling of hoofs, horns, thunder and lightning, it made an old cowpuncher long for headquarters or to be in his line camp in some dug-out on the banks of some little stream. After the first break we were unable to control the cattle longer, for just as soon as we could get them quiet, some other herd would run into us and give us a fresh start.

Finally so many herds had run together that it was impossible to tell our cattle from others. When lightning flashed we could see thousands of cattle and hundreds of men all over the prairie, so we turned everything loose and waited patiently for daybreak.

The next morning all the different outfits got together and we had a general roundup. It took about a week to get everything all straightened out and trim up the herds. We then crossed the Arkansas River just above Dodge City and traveled northwest across the State of Kansas and struck North Platte River at Ogallala, Nebraska.

Following the North Platte River, we passed Chimney Rock, old Fort Fetterman and Fort Laramie and camped on the north bank of the North Platte River, where we rested one day grazing cattle, bathing and washing our saddle blankets. We then started on a four-days' drive without water (about sixty miles) across the mountains from the North Platte River in Nebraska to Powder River in Wyoming.

When we arrived on the divide or the backbone, between the two rivers, we passed along where a train of emigrants had been murdered by the Cheyenne Indians about two years before.

For about the distance of half a mile the trail on both sides was strewn with oxen bones, irons and pieces of wagons where they had been burned, but did not see any human bones because I didn't take time to make a close examination.

From the appearance of the surroundings there must have been twenty-five or thirty wagons and ox teams. We were told by old Indian fighters that there were 150 persons in the train, including the women and children, all murdered – none left to tell the tale.

By this time the cattle were getting dry. They had been two days without water, and these little Southern steers began to look like race horses. All the men were in front of the cattle except myself, the drag driver and the cook. Of course, we had to take good care of the grub wagon and cook. This was in the evening about four o'clock, and we did not see the men nor the lead cattle until the next day about five o'clock in the evening.

The boys reported that the lead cattle reached Powder River about ten o'clock, while we did not arrive until about five o'clock. After resting two or three days we proceeded down Powder River to the mouth of Crazy Woman, a small stream that empties into Powder River, and then up Crazy Woman River to near the foot of the Big Horn Mountain to our Wyoming headquarters.

It took us just exactly three months and twenty days to drive a herd of Southern "dogies" from Red River and deliver them at the Wyoming Ranch. We rested a few days while the Wyoming outfit gathered a beef herd for market and delivered it to us, and then we continued our northward drive with the beef herd to a station on the Northern Pacific Railroad called Glendive, on or near the Yellowstone River in Montana.

When we loaded our cattle on the railroad for Chicago all the Texas outfit, numbering about twelve, took the cow trail for Texas by the way of Chicago.

Our first stop was at St. Paul, in Minnesota, to feed and water the cattle, and while the cattle were resting we all took the interurban street car for Minneapolis, about five miles from St. Paul, to see the Barnum & Bailey Circus. We arrived at the circus, still wearing our trail garb, just a short time after the performance had begun.

Of course we were feeling good by this time, and just as we entered the clown had his trick mule in the ring and was offering anyone five dollars that could ride him.

Twelve Texas cowboys fresh from the range, thought that was easy money, and all wanted to win the five dollars, so, we selected one of our party to earn the money. (He is now one of the wealthiest and most prominent stockmen of Texas, but I won't tell his name.)

The clown let out his mule and we let out our Texas cowboy. One of the boys had a pair of Texas spurs in his pocket and we fastened them on the boots of the party that was to pull off the Wild West stunt.

The mule was blindfolded and our man got on, and when the word was given one of our boys pulled off the blindfold, halter and all, and left the two in the ring ready for business. The rider fastened his spurs in the mule's shoulders and struck him in the flank with his Texas hat and that started the performance.

There were thousands of people in the audience to witness the stunt. The mule made two or three jumps and roared like a mountain lion and our rider yelled like a Comanche Indian; the mule would pitch and roar, but our rider stuck to him like a postage stamp.

As the rider could not be dismounted, the mule laid down on the ground and rolled over like a ball. Our rider stood by, and when the mule would get on his feet he would find our rider again on his back until, finally, the mule sulked and just stood in the middle of the ring with our rider still on him spurring and whipping him with his hat.

The audience went wild and uncontrollable and the police had to interfere and pull our rider off the mule. The five dollars was given the rider, and after the performance we returned to St. Paul, reloaded our cattle and continued our journey for Chicago, where we delivered them and left for Texas.

I stopped at Sherman and went to school that fall and winter and the next spring I returned to the IS Ranch in the Indian Territory.

For six years I worked for Suggs Brothers during each spring and summer, returning in the late fall to Sherman, where I attended school during the winter months.

After those six years spent on the trail and the range I returned to Sherman and attended one full term of school, after which I took up the study of law in the office of Woods & Brown, of Sherman, was admitted to the bar in the year 1888, then left for the West to grow up with the country.

I first located in Haskell, Haskell County, Texas, but in the spring of 1890 one of those blizzards struck me and I drifted south, and as there were no wire fences to stop me, I landed in Laredo, Webb County, Texas, on the Rio Grande River, where I remained a short time, then moved to San Diego, in Duval County, Texas, where I hung out my "shingle" and commenced the practice of law.

In the spring of 1893 I was appointed county judge of Duval County, but in the spring of 1894 I resigned as county judge to accept the appointment of district attorney for the old 49th Judicial District of Texas (a warm district about that time), composed of the counties of Webb, Duval and Zapata. I received this appointment from the Hon. C.A. Culberson, then governor of Texas.

I served as district attorney for one term and in 1896 I was again elected county judge of Duval County, which office I held continuously until August, 1915, when I resigned and moved to Alice in Jim Wells County, Texas, where I am now practicing law.

# The Remarkable Career of Col. Ike T. Pryor

A HISTORY OF THE TRAIL DRIVERS OF TEXAS would not be complete without a sketch of the career of Col. Isaac Thomas Pryor, whose achievements during the past sixty years have been remarkable, to say the least. His life story reads like a romance, for it is made up of thrills and pathos, struggles and hardships, failures and triumphs that befell but few men who successfully overcame such obstacles that Col. Pryor met and conquered.

A pioneer of the early days of the unfenced range, he has become the most widely known cattleman of America, and his reminiscences, if ever written, would afford a complete panorama of the cattle industry of the United States.

From the early days of the grass trails, when the great herds of the Texas longhorns were driven thousands of miles to market, down to the present, with its bred cattle, its modern marketing system and rail transportation, he has been an active participant.

At all the various stages that mark this period of Texas' development, his has been an important part. His has been the directing mind in determining many of those steps where the decision meant either the advancement or downfall of the livestock industry.

At these times of peril he became the trusted leader, just as in the earlier days of his young manhood he was looked upon to lead and direct when brawn and courage were needed to assure right by might.

Born at Tampa, Florida, in 1852, the third child of three boys, the subject of this sketch was left fatherless in 1855 at the age of three years, through his father's death.

Shortly after his father's death, Mrs. Pryor took her three boys to Alabama, where two years later she passed away. She gave one each of the boys, ranging in age from five to nine years, to her three sisters. Ike, the last one, being with an uncle at Spring Hill, Tenn.

At the age of nine years he ran away from the home of his relative and boldly struck out into the world for himself. He plunged at once into some of its most awesome and thrilling scenes.

It was in the year 1861 with the Civil War just beginning its devastating reign. Into the midst of it he entered. Attaching himself as a newsboy to the Army of the Cumberland, he lived among the hardships of the campaign.

He witnessed the scenes enacted at Murfreesboro, Chickamauga, Lookout Mountain and other desperately fought actions of the war between the States in which the loyal sons of the North and of the South fought to the end, each for what they held was right.

It was in such environment that tried the very souls of men, that an impressionable boy not yet in his teens, had the early molding of his character.

In it was seasoned the courage that had sent him, inexperienced and frail, to challenge for life and fortune. In these scenes, in which were born the reunited nation with its brilliant future, he imbibed the spirit of empire, the broadness of vision and the inspiration of immensity that determined the wide bounds his later activities in life were to reach.

In addition to helping mold his character, the great maelstrom into which he had thrust himself had a decisive effect upon determining his immediate life and actions.

The little newsboy, unafraid where many a man knew fear, won numerous friends among both enlisted men and officers. So personal was the interest they took in him that after his pony had been shot from under him in one of the sharpest engagements, an army surgeon decided it was no place for a boy of his years and had him sent to his home in Ottawa, Ohio, where he arrived in 1863.

As a background to this remarkable part of Col. Pryor's boyhood there is a story of a kind woman's influence over a motherless boy and her persevering search for him that ended in a manner that cannot but be considered providential.

In one of the former homes to which the boy was sent he found an elder cousin, a beautiful young girl just entering into womanhood, who felt the warmest sympathy for the orphaned boy brought into the home of her sisters and brothers. She was his defender in the reckoning over childish scrapes and his comforter in times of childish grief.

Following his transfer to the home of his uncle at Spring Hill, this girl had married Mr. John O. Ewing and removed to Nashville, Tenn. The orphan boy frequently thought of her in his new home and longed for her comforting. It accordingly happened that when he was severely, and, as he felt, unjustly punished for a prank in which he had played an unwilling part, he determined to leave his uncle's home and go to Mrs. Ewing, who, he felt, would gladly give him a home with her.

He was resolutely making his way toward Nashville when a sudden advance of Federal forces passed beyond him and left him within the Union lines, thus determining his further wanderings. Incidentally, the sudden shifting of battles around interrupted the pursuit of the runaway and prevented his being returned to Spring Hill, Tenn.

More remarkable still was the manner in which eventually he was found by Mrs. Ewing. Never losing faith that ultimately he would be located, she religiously asked every person who came from the Union lines for information of him.

One day a Federal forage party reached the country home where she was living outside Nashville. The commanding officer, after taking the supplies wanted, courteously offered to issue a receipt for the property taken so that later claim might be made for the amount.

He approached Mrs. Ewing to give her the document and, pursuing her usual course, she asked him if by chance he knew aught of a boy she described who was thought to be among the Federal troops.

To her unbounded surprise and joy the officer not only knew the boy; he had frequently shared his couch with him, bought papers from him and assisted him. More important still, he knew of his being sent to Ottawa, Ohio, by the Federal surgeon. Means were at once adopted to get in communication with the boy in his new home.

It was just in time, for the adventurous lad, thus placed on the very shores of Lake Erie, had determined upon a maritime career. He had even selected the vessel upon which he was to embark and had made overtures to her captain. Only the strong love he felt for the good woman who had protected him in his earlier childhood deterred him from becoming a seaman.

President Johnson, himself, became interested in the story of the boy, which reached him, and in 1864 had him returned to his relatives in Tennessee. He remained with them until 1870, when he took the step that was the real determination of his future career. At that time he turned his steps to the wide expanse of Texas. His first employment was as a farm hand. For this he received fifteen dollars a month.

The next year he entered the cattle industry. His first connection with it was as a trail hand, driving his cattle to Coffeyville, Kansas. This was but the first of a number of trips he made over the now almost forgotten trails upon which are found today some of the greatest cities of the country as successors of the hamlets of those times. In 1872 he helped to drive a herd of cattle from Texas to Colorado.

From then on his activities for many years were uninterrupted in the raising and marketing of livestock as practiced in those years. In 1873 he was employed on the Charles Lehmberg Ranch in Mason County and there he really began his upward climb in the cattle business.

Within a short time he had become ranch manager and in 1874 he had the responsibility of driving the cattle to Fort Sill, then Indian Territory, in fulfillment of contracts for their delivery to the Indians. The following year he was engaged largely in driving cattle to Austin for sale to the butchers there.

In 1876 he became a ranch owner, buying land and cattle in Mason County. The next year he again had charge of a herd of cattle driven overland, this drove including 250 head of his own cattle, which, together with those of John W. Gamel, were taken to Ogallala, Nebraska.

Each season he reinvested and as the years passed in succession he drove ever-increasing herds of his own to the Northern markets. In 1878 he drove 3,000 head on his own account, in 1879 he drove 6,000 and in 1880 he drove 12,000. About that time he formed a partnership with his brother in Colorado and by 1881 he had so increased his drive that the total that year was fifteen herds of 3,000, making a total of 45,000 head in a single year.

These were taken to the North and Northwest over the much-discussed Chisholm Trail, being marketed in Kansas, Nebraska, Wyoming and the Dakotas. Profits of from three dollars to five dollars a head were reckoned for the enterprise, but a period of reverses came with the winters of 1884 and 1885, and despite the large operations that had been carried on, Pryor Brothers showed a loss of half a million dollars and their liquidation resulted.

Nothing daunted, Mr. Pryor again resumed his operations, centering his activities again in the Texas field, where he had achieved his first successes. By this time the innovation of the railways and barbwire fencing had greatly changed the conditions that existed in the earlier days of the open range and the trails. Adapting himself to the new conditions, Col. Pryor again achieved success, and this time a lasting one.

The Texas Cattle Raisers' Association had been organized by leading cattlemen of the State in order to afford themselves mutual protection for their cattle. Col. Pryor early became identified with the organization and in 1887 he was elected a member of its executive committee.

This was the beginning of a long and distinguished service in the interest of organized cattle industry.

In 1902 Mr. Pryor was elected first vice president of the Texas Cattle Raisers' Association, and in 1906 he became its president under conditions, which made the honor one especially great. This was due to the fact that Col. Pryor was one of the heads of one of the largest livestock commission firms in the country (the Evans-Snider-Buel Company).

Some opposition developed in the convention to electing as president a man who was so prominently engaged in the commission business, where it was felt that there might arise conditions in which the interests of the cattle raisers and the commission merchants would be at variance. Those who knew him personally and therefore trusted him to the limit, were sufficiently strong to bring about his election.

During his administration for the year the others became so thoroughly convinced of his unfaltering devotion to their interests that the 1907 convention witnessed the dramatic and touching incident of his reelection without opposition by unanimous consent, attested by a rising vote.

It was thus he was recognized by an organization that had grown to a membership of 2,000 cattlemen, owners of an aggregate of five million head of cattle.

Even this tribute was not the full measure of their reliance upon him. The succeeding year the members of this organization, which had grown to be one of the most important in the commercial life of the nation, broke the time-honored rule of limiting the presidency to two terms.

They passed an amendment to the constitution permitting a longer term and enthusiastically named him for his third term. In 1909 he was again importuned to stand for re-election, but resolutely declined.

In the meantime, Col. Pryor had also been elected president of the Texas Live Stock Association, which included all classes of interest in the livestock industry of the State. He was importuned to accept another term as its head, but declined reelection. Later he was chosen to head the National Live Stock Shippers' Protective League, which was organized at Chicago for the purpose of protecting the interests of livestock shippers all over the United States.

On Jan. 8, 1917, at the convention held at Cheyenne, Wyoming, there was added to the other honors conferred upon him by the live stock interests of the country, the presidency of the American National Live Stock Association. Again at the convention held in January, 1918, at Salt Lake City, Utah, he was elected to succeed himself. A speech made by Col. Pryor before that convention made definite recommendations to Congress for national legislation affecting the cattle and meat-packing industry and attracted nationwide interest and endorsement.

This was perhaps the beginning of the active campaign in behalf of the Kendrick or Kenyon bill, as it is generally known.

In 1919 Col. Pryor retired from the presidency of the American National Live Stock Association, being succeeded in that office by Senator J.B. Kendrick. Last September Col. Pryor went to Washington and testified before the Senate Agricultural Committee favoring the Kendrick or Kenyon bill. This testimony was given wide publicity through the American press at that time and is believed to have exerted a wide influence.

While centering his greatest efforts in the livestock business, Col. Pryor has not attained prominence in it alone. He was first chairman of the Texas Industrial Congress. In 1908 he was elected president of the Trans-Mississippi Commercial Congress at Denver, Colorado, and it was in a large measure through his instrumentality that San Antonio was selected for the 1909 session of that great body.

In 1909 he organized and accepted the presidency of the City National Bank of San Antonio. He was at the same time vice president of the R.E. Stafford & Co., bankers, of Columbus, Texas, and vice president and one of the managers of the Evans-Snider-Buel Company.

Keeping constantly in touch with all conditions affecting the cattle market, he has been able successfully to manage affairs that many would deem impossible. At the outbreak of the Spanish-American War he sent a special agent to Cuba to keep him advised as to the cattle conditions on that island.

This foresight and enterprise resulted in his sending the first shipload of beeves that arrived in Cuba after the blockade had been lifted. Other shipments followed in quick order until 7,000 head in all had been landed at Havana, bringing the unusually high prices that they could command. Interested with Col. Pryor in this bit of enterprise was J.H.P. Davis of Richmond, Texas.

Such is his character that it is his great fortune not to be envied in his success and honors. This is because in his rise to prominence and wealth he has never been other than the same true-hearted man of the plains. To this day his office in San Antonio is the gathering place of the greatest of that great clan of Texas empire builders, the early cattlemen.

# Habits and Customs of Early Texans

### by L.B. Anderson, Seguin, Texas

I WAS BORN IN AMITE COUNTY, Mississippi, March 24, 1849. Came overland with my parents to Texas in the spring of 1853. Our outfit consisted of two wagons and a buggy, and we also brought several of our Negro slaves. My mother and the youngest children rode in the buggy, which was drawn by an old mule.

We crossed the Mississippi River on a ferryboat. I do not know how long it took us to make the trip, but we must have made very slow progress, for the older children walked almost all of the way and drove an old favorite milch cow that we called "Old Cherry."

I remember one amusing incident about that old cow. She had a growing hatred for a dog, and never failed to lunge at one that came near her. One evening about dusk as we were driving her along the way we came to a large black stump by the roadside, and "Old Cherry," evidently thinking it was a dog, made a lunge at it and knocked herself senseless.

The one thing that stands out most vividly in my recollection of that trip is the fact that I was made to wear a sunbonnet all the way. I hated a bonnet as much as "Old Cherry" hated a dog, and kept throwing my bonnet away and going bare headed, so finally my mother cut two holes in the top of the bonnet, pulled my hair through them and tied it hard and fast.

That was before the days of clipped hair, and as mine was long enough to tie easily, that settled the bonnet question, and I had to make my entrance into grand old Texas looking like a girl, but feeling every inch like a man.

We stopped in Williamson County, near Georgetown, then in the fall of the same year we came to Seguin, Guadalupe County, where I have lived ever since, except when I was following the trail.

My father bought a tract of land west of Seguin for $1,000 cash. As it had not been surveyed by either the buyer or the seller neither of them knew how much land the tract contained. Twenty years later father sold it for just what he had paid for it, and when it was surveyed it was found to be several hundred acres, and is now worth one-hundred dollars per acre.

There was but little farming carried on in those days, the settlers depending on grass for feed for their work teams and other stock. The crops of corn and cane were made with oxen. Many times I have seen the heel flies attack a yoke of oxen and they would run off, jump the rail fence and get away with the plow to which they were attached, and sometimes it would be several days before they were found.

Of course we did not make much farming after that fashion, but we did not need much in those days. We lived carefree and happy until the outbreak of the Civil War, when father and my older brother went into the service to fight for the South, leaving me, a lad of only 11 years, the only protection for my mother and younger brothers and sisters, but mother was a fearless woman and the best marksman with a rifle I ever saw, so we felt able to take care of ourselves.

My duties during the war were many and varied. I was mail carrier and general errand boy for all of the women in the neighborhood. Among other things it was my duty to look after the cattle.

During this trying time the cattle accumulated on the range and after the war when the men returned cow hunting became general. From ten to twenty men would gather at some point, usually at old man Konda's, in the center of the cow range, and round up the cattle.

Each man would take an extra pony along, a lengthy stake rope made of rawhide or hair, a wallet of cornbread, some fat bacon and coffee, and plenty of salt to do him on the roundup. Whenever we got hungry for fresh meat we would kill a fat yearling, eat all we wanted and leave the remainder.

On these trips I acquired my first experience at cow punching. Our route usually would be down the Cibolo by Pana Maria and old Helena to the San Antonio River, and up Clate Creek, gathering all the cattle that belonged to our crowd and some mavericks besides.

The drives would generally wind up at old man Konda's, from where he had started, and here division was made, each man taking his cattle home, where they would be branded and turned out on the range again. Some of the men who went on these trips were Gus Konda, considered the best cowman in Guadalupe County, John Oliver, Frank Delaney, Dud Tom, Whit Vick, W.C. Irvin, John and Dud Jefferson, Pinkney Low and sons, and Gen. William Saffold.

There was no local market for the cattle, and the Kansas drives started about that time. Eugene Millett and his two brothers, Alonzo and Hie, engaged in buying beeves and work oxen to send up the trail in 1869. My father sold them several yoke of oxen, which he had freighted to Mexico with, and I helped deliver them to Mr. Millett at the Three Mile Water Hole north of Seguin. I was already a cowboy in my own estimation, those hunts on the range having given me a taste of the life.

Hearing Millett's men tell of their trips up the trail, I decided at once that that was the life for me, so I told my father I wanted to go with the herd. He very reluctantly gave his consent, but made me promise that if I was going to be a cowman that I would be "an honest one." He then proceeded to give me a lot of advice, and presented me with a ten-dollar gold piece for use on the trip.

My mother sewed that money in the band of my trousers (breeches, we called them in those days) and I carried it to Kansas and back that way, and when I returned home I gave it back to my father.

The next fall and winter I worked for Pinkney Low, gathering cattle on the range to be taken up the trail in the spring. I went on the trail every year thereafter until 1887, when the trail was virtually closed.

I went twice as a hand and sixteen times as boss of the herd. I drove over every trail from the Gulf of Mexico to the Dakotas and Montana, but the Chisholm Trail was the one I traveled the most.

The men I drove for were E.B. Millett, Alonzo Millett, Hie Millett, Col. Seth Maberry, W.C. Irvin, Tom and John Dewees and Jim Sherrill. The places I most often delivered cattle to were Baxter Springs, Great Bend, Newton, Abilene, Ellsworth and Dodge City, Kansas, Ogallala and Red Cloud Agency, Nebraska, Fort Fetterman, Wyoming, and Dan Holden's ranch in Colorado on Chug River. Some of the most prominent cattlemen I knew in those days were Pressnall and Mitchell, John Blocker, Jim Ellison, D.R. Fant, John Lytle and Dick Head.

My experiences on the trail were many and varied, some perilous and some humorous.

I remember one exciting time in particular, when I was taking a herd for Millett & Irvin from the Panhandle Ranch to Old Fort Fetterman in the Rocky Mountains. The Sioux Indians made a raid on us, got off with most of our horses and all of our provisions. We had nothing to eat except buffalo and antelope meat until we reached North Platte City, a distance of 200 miles.

In 1871 I went up the trail with T.B. Miller and Bill Mayes. We crossed at Red River Station and arrived at Newton, Kansas, about the time the railroad reached there.

Newton was one of the worst towns I ever saw, every element of meanness on earth seemed to be there. While in that burg I saw several men killed, one of them, I think, was Jim Martin from Helena, Karnes County.

One fall after I returned from Wyoming, Millett sent me to the Indian Territory to issue beef to the Indians on a government contract. I was stationed at Anadarko on the Washita River, and issued but once a week at Fort Sill and Cheyenne Agency on the Canadian River.

There I saw my first telephone. It was a crude affair, and connected the agent's store and residence, a distance of several hundred yards.

The apparatus consisted of one wire run through the walls of the store and house with a tube at each end through which you had to blow to attract attention of the party called, and then you could talk over it as well as any phone of the present time.

I was in Abilene when Wild Bill Hickok had full sway in that town and it was dangerous for a man to walk the streets. I was there when he killed Phil Coe. Some of the old cowboys who followed the trail from this country were the twin brothers, Cap and Doc Smith, Dud Tom, Joe Ellis, Haynes Morgan, Mit Nickols, John and Fenner Jefferson, Whit Vick, Bill Coorpender, Frank Rhodes, Leroy Sowell, Billie McLean, Billie Thompson, Pat Burns, Tom Terrell, John and Tom Lay and many others.

The journeys up the trail were beset by many dangers and difficulties. Savage Indians often attacked the herd in attempts to cause a stampede. Few outfits were strong enough to repel the Indians by force and were compelled to pay them tribute in the form of beef. To do the work required on those drives took men of strong nerves, iron bodies and alert brains.

The last trip I made was in 1887, when I drove horses. I bought them from Redman and his partner through Mr. George W. Saunders. They were a bunch of Spanish mares just from Mexico, and I remember a squabble I had with two other buyers over a big white paint stud that happened to be in the bunch. I got the stud, all right, and made big money on him as well as all of the other horses.

In 1888 I married and settled down on my farm, but never could quite give up the cattle business, and on a small scale have handled some kind of cattle ever since, but the Jersey or any other kind of milch cow has never appealed to me as the Texas longhorn did. After thirty years of settled life the call of the trail is with me still, and there is not a day that I do not long to mount my horse and be out among the cattle.

# Hit the Trail in High Places

*by Jeff Connolly, Lockhart, Texas*

I WAS BORN AT PRAIRIE LEA in 1863 and moved to Lockhart in 1876. My experience in the good old days gone by was as follows:

Drove on the trail for old Capt. King of Nueces County in 1880 with a man by the name of Coleman as boss, and when I got as far as Taylor, King sent me back and I helped another brother of this man Coleman drive another herd of the King cattle to Red River.

The only white men with the herd were Coleman and myself, the balance of the bunch being Mexicans. All the old-timers know how King handled the Mexicans – he had them do the work and let the white men do the bossing.

I was on the trail that year about three months and drew a salary of one dollar and fifty cents per day, and board was furnished me.

During the winter of 1881 and spring of 1882 I drove cattle for George W. Littlefield of Austin, who I am sure all the old-timers remember and regard very highly. I went with A.A. Woodland, who all the old-timers in Lockhart knew very well and who lived here during his latter days.

When we got to old Fort Griffin we cut the stock cattle all out, which amounted to about 1,000 cows at that time. Myself and two other men held these at Foil Creek, this side of Fort Griffin, until another herd reached us, which was about thirty days. Then we turned them in with another herd of Littlefield's cattle that was being handled by a man by the name of McCarty, another Irishman who looks about like I do.

From there we went on to the Pecos River, where the LFD Ranch of Littlefield was established, known to be one of the foremost ranches in that part of the country.

We had plenty of good horses on this drive, and McCarty and Littlefield bought fifty more when we reached Fort Griffin from a Mexican at that place. These last horses they bought had a colt every once in a while as we were mounting them in the mornings.

This herd of cattle McCarty was looking after was bought from Jim Ellison, a noted cowman in Caldwell County in the seventies, who owned what was then known as the Ellison Ranch, where these cattle were delivered to Littlefield.

Last time I was in Austin, about six years ago, I went into the American National Bank with a friend of mine and I asked the teller of the bank where the Major was. He told me he was back in his private office. This friend of mine wanted to know why I was asking about Major Littlefield and asked me if I knew he was a millionaire?

I told him that I knew that, but that I used to drive on the old trail for him and was anxious to see him. I went back and told the Major who I was and he treated me as fine as any man was ever treated. If I had been a millionaire myself he could not have treated me any better, and that's what makes us common fellows like him. He is just as plain as if he didn't have any more than we have.

We talked about old times when the other fellows like Bud Wilkerson, Phelps White, Tom White, some of his men, used to work with me for him. He told me these three fellows were still with him on the ranch and making good.

In 1884, I drove a herd of horses from Banquette in Nueces County, for a man by the name of Frank Byler. Right at the edge of Lockhart, where we camped that night, and from where we started to town next morning, we were arrested by Sheriff Allie Field for trespassing.

We had no money and Frank did not know what in the world to do, and I told him to go to Dr. Blanks of Lockhart, a great friend of the old trailers, and he would loan us the money to pay the fine.

We borrowed fifty dollars in money and bought fifty dollars worth of grub on credit, and when we got to Onion Creek we sold two horses for one-hundred dollars and in a few days sent the money to Lockhart, and from that time on we had plenty of money to do us.

When we got to Hillsboro it was very cold and raining, and we broke our wagon down and had to stop. Our horses stampeded all over that country and twenty-seven froze to death that night.

We remained there about four days waiting for it to thaw out, and when it did we sold about forty-five saddle horses to an old cowman of the Red River country. We headed from there to Red River, and when we got there the river was up and we got a little of that stuff that livens up.

The herd attempted to stampede, but we held them and put them across all right.

Everything went well until we got to the Washita, where the herd stampeded again and we were two days crossing the river. One night I stayed over there with the Indians.

This side of Okmulgee we went out hunting a place to camp one evening and came across a little clump of trees where we saw a man hanging there by the neck with a sign on him, "Death to the one who cuts him down." We saw he was dead and we did not cut the rope. We went on further to camp that night.

We reached the Arkansas River in a few days, where we had to lay four days on account of the river being up.

Just before we crossed we found that the Indians had stolen a lot of blankets from our Mexicans. I made our bunch of Mexicans go up to their camp and steal some of the Indians' blankets and slickers, and the next day when we crossed the river the Indians were pointing at the Mexicans, noticing that they had stolen their blankets and slickers.

They were talking Indian and our Mexicans did not know what they were talking about.

We had no further trouble until we got to Baxter Springs, Kansas. The first night we were camped on the state line we had a big stampede. The Indians were there to count us up for grass fee, and we run them through so fast they could not count them and lost count.

They accepted our count and, of course, we guessed them low enough to take care of ourselves.

We did very well, selling these out to people all over the United States, as there were traders there from everywhere.

In 1885 I drove cattle with Bill Jackman of San Marcos, the herd belonging to Hez Williams and Bill Goode of Kyle. This herd was put up at Rancho Grande, in Wharton County, by Bob Stafford of Columbus.

When we got to old Texarkana we had a big stampede that night and whipped them in and ran them over one another trying to hold them until they looked like they had been in a wreck. They had "run" on the brain all the way until we got to Kyle.

When we reached there every fellow was about on foot, as our horses had played out, so we put the herd in Desha Bunton's pasture and stayed there several days to get a new outfit of horses, and had them all shod up to go through the mountains and get a new outfit of men also, as the boys all quit except Fisher, Jackman and myself.

We pulled out from there with a new set of men and horses headed for Deer Trail, Colorado, south of Cheyenne.

A few nights after we left Kyle we had a big rain and the cattle drifted pretty well all night, and Tom Fisher and myself came upon a man camped in a wagon and told him to get up, for it was daylight. When he got up we both crawled in with our wet clothes on and went to sleep and left him on the outside. When morning came we got up and began rounding up the herd and none of the bunch had missed us.

We traveled along all right then until we reached Bell Plains one evening. There a Dutchman came out and told us to move on, and we told him to hunt a warmer climate, that we were going to camp there that night.

About twelve o'clock that night he and the sheriff came to our camp hunting the boss and couldn't find him. They went away and next morning before breakfast they came back and wanted to know where the boss was, and we told him we didn't have any.

He wanted to stop our herd of cattle, but we told him if they did they would have to give a $30,000 bond, as these cattle were mortgaged and could not be stopped without somebody giving bond. The sheriff called us off and talked with us a while and told us he would see us about it, and this was the last we ever heard of the matter.

Everything went all right from here until we got up to Doan's Store, when one night the wagons caught fire and burned the wagon sheet. We got busy just at this time trying to save our coffee and a little meat we had picked up from the 3 D cattle.

From there we had to rustle a wagon sheet to keep everything dry when the rains came up. We got along all right from here until we got to Wolf Creek at old Camp Supply, where they quarantined us, and we had to go down to No Man's Land, a strip between the Panhandle and Kansas, now a part of Oklahoma.

Crossing the plains it drizzled very nearly every night, just enough to make the cattle walk till about eleven o'clock at night.

When we got to Beaver, this side of the Arkansas River, in Colorado, we sold the cattle.

After we turned them over Bill Jackman and myself came back over the trail and met Alex Magee and his cattle and stopped him for a few days to let his cattle rest up, as we knew the people that had contracted his cattle were waiting for him, and we wanted his bunch to look good when he got there. Wanted them to show up all right so there would be no kick.

When we brought the cattle up to turn them over to the buyers they received them with the understanding that we had to brand them. We carried them up Beaver Creek for about 40 miles, where we branded them, and after we had done this they asked us to carry a bunch of about 300 white-face Herefords, the first I ever saw, up in the Rocky Mountains and put them in winter quarters. When we got them there he fitted us up with fresh horses and everything and started us for West Los Angeles to ship us back home.

In 1886 I started to go up with Bill Jackman again, but when I got to the Hutcheson Ranch near San Marcos, Jackman was there and told me he had sold the cattle to John Blocker, who would be there directly with his outfit to receive them.

When they came he recommended me to the man who was in charge of the cattle – a man by the name of Murchison, who was also in charge of the horses and outfit.

Next day we rounded up the pasture, but they didn't take the cattle, and we went from there on to Kyle to the Vaughn pasture. Arch Odem in a few days bought about 1,500 head of cattle down on the Guadalupe River and brought them up to where we were and turned them over to us. We went on up in a few days to the Hez Williams Ranch and got about 800 more steers.

In a few days we got about 700 head more from places near there, then pulled out for the trail, being the first herd of the Blocker cattle for that year. When we got between Runnels and Abilene we laid in wait there until ten more herds of the Blocker cattle caught up with us.

Then we shaped up ten herds to go on to Colorado, and I and my bunch cut cattle all the way until we got to Red River.

At Red River we took the lead cattle out of two herds and put them together in one herd and left the drags together in another herd.

When we reached the Wichita Mountains, in Indian Territory, the Indians met us there and wanted beef. I had a big black range steer I had picked up in Texas, and when I got up in the roughest part of the mountains I cut this steer out and told them to go after him.

The steer outran them and got away and directly I saw them coming back, one after another, like they travel, but without any beef.

The next day the trail cutters looked us up and did not find anything. Then we went on until we got to Camp Supply, where we had to go across the plains again, and it was very dry.

The first evening we struck the plains we drove right square until night and I held up the lead cattle and the wagon was not in sight at this time. We camped there that night and there came the hardest rain I ever saw fall, and it was so cold we nearly shook ourselves to death.

It rained all the time from there on to Hugo, Colorado, where Blocker turned these cattle loose and where they were rebranded and turned loose again.

From Hugo I helped take about 1,000 head of saddle horses and put them in winter quarters, and when that was done I came back home.

# The Men Who Made the Trail

*by Luther A. Lawhon, San Antonio*

BY A DEGREE OF GOOD FORTUNE it fell to me to be reared from infancy to manhood in Southwest Texas in the midst of that favored section when it was one vast breeding ground for cattle and horses, and from which was afterward to be driven those herds that, moving across the prairies of Texas and through the Indian Territory, from 1869 to 1886, poured into the wild and unsettled area from Kansas to the British Dominions.

In the days and in the section of which I treat the railroad, the telegraph and the telephone were unknown. A greater part of the land still belonged to the state and was prized in the main for the grasses, which grew upon it. Fencing wire had not been invented, and in consequence the entire country, except where dotted with ranches, was unfenced and uncontrolled – a common pasture in which thousands of horses and cattle roamed at will.

In imagination reverting again to those bygone scenes, I shall endeavor to describe briefly some of the conditions, which surrounded the old-time Texas ranchman, his peculiarities and his customs.

The country at large was sparsely settled. In a majority of the counties there was barely sufficient population for county organization. The largest and, in most instances, the only town in the county, was the county seat village, with its rock or lumber court house, which was rarely of two stories, and nearby, as an adjunct, a one-cell rock or lumber jail.

Around the public square were built the few unpretentious storehouses, that flaunted the proverbial signs, "Dry Goods and Grocers," or "Dry Goods, Boots and Shoes," as the case might be.

That the weaknesses as well as the social predilections of the sturdy citizenship might be readily and conveniently catered to, a saloon or perhaps several, could always be found on or near the public square.

Clustered about the commercial center, and growing further apart as the distance increased, were private residences, which went to make up the hamlet.

After the courthouse and jail, the hotel – generally a two-story building – was considered the most important, as it was frequently the most imposing structure in the village. In addition to the official and business edifices, there was always a well-constructed schoolhouse (there were no free schools in those days) and a commodious, comfortable church house at convenient distances.

I purposely use church house in the singular, for in the days under consideration the tabernacle of the Most High was a union structure, erected by the joint contributions of the various and divergent church members, as well as of philanthropic citizens who made no "professions," and in which those pioneer men and women with their families, irrespective of denomination, met together with good and honest hearts and worshiped God in spirit and in truth.

Such, in brief, was the frontier village. Beyond it confines the country, as stated, was unfenced and uncontrolled. Luxuriant grasses and fragrant wild flowers covered prairie, hill and valley for two-thirds of the year. Herds of cattle and horses grazed in every direction, and each ranchman, by his mark and brand, was enabled to identify his stock and secure its increase.

Trained to the range and keen of eye as they were, the old-time ranchmen and their cowboys would necessarily fail to find some of the year's increase when they worked this vast territory.

As a result there was a small percentage, yearly, of unmarked and unbranded calves. These animals, after being weaned from the mother cows, would thenceforth be abroad on the prairies, the property of whomsoever found and branded them, and in cowboy parlance were called "mavericks."

This name had its origin in the fact that Mr. Sam Maverick, now deceased, an honored and wealthy citizen of San Antonio, was the owner of a large brand of cattle that ranged throughout Southwest Texas.

During the Civil War he was unable to "brand up" the increase in his stock, and in consequence there was a marked augmentation of unbranded and unmarked cattle on the range from San Antonio to the coast. This fact, and the cause of it, was a matter of general knowledge throughout this section.

Therefore, when the old-time ranchman and his cowboys in this territory found an unmarked and unbranded yearling or two-year-old on the range, it was assumed that the animal had at one time been the property of the San Antonio citizen. Hence the term "maverick" soon became universal as a designation for an animal whose owner could not be definitely determined, and has now become a permanent fixture in our English nomenclature.

The "roundup," with its chuck wagon, its high-priced chef and bill of fare a la carte, had not as yet been introduced. Those old-time ranchmen were content to simply cow hunt twice a year and brand their calves. As a rule those whose ranches were the nearest hunted together and thereby made up an "outfit."

Their provisions, flour, coffee and dried beef, with the beddin', was loaded on a pack horse, which was driven with the saddle ponies. They worked the country and branded through the day and camped at night where water was in abundance and where grass was good.

There was an unwritten law, recognized by the good women of the towns as well as of the country, that whenever a party of cow hunters rode up and asked to have bread baked, it mattered not the time of day, the request was to be cheerfully complied with.

Not from fear of insult in case of refusal – for each and every cowboy was the champion defender of womanhood, and would have scorned to have uttered a disrespectful word in her presence – but from an accommodating spirit and a kindness of heart, which was universally characteristic in those frontier days.

My father was a lawyer and therefore my boyhood home was in the village, but I remember the many times that cow hunters rode up to my father's house, and telling my mother they were out of bread, asked that she would kindly bake their flour for them.

Everything was at once made ready. The sack was lifted from the pack horse and brought in, and in due time the bread wallets were once more filled with freshly cooked biscuits, and the cowboys rode away with grateful appreciation.

These acts of consideration on the part of my mother were entirely gratuitous, but the generous hearted cowboys would always leave either a half sack of flour or a money donation as a free-will offering.

One of the cardinal virtues of the old-time ranchman was hospitality. This commendable trait was not alone possessed by him, but was an attribute of his entire family. The cordial welcome was not restricted to nearby neighbors, friends and acquaintances, but was as freely extended to "the stranger within the gates."

The way-worn traveler was never turned aside, and while a guest at the ranch, did illness overtake him, the watchful vigils and tender hands of the ranchman's wife and daughters ministered to his sufferings as though he was one of the family, until health was restored, and he was sent on his way rejoicing.

The wife of the old-time ranchman! How kind, how considerate she was! It mattered not that at the approach of every full moon the saddle horses were rounded up and more closely guarded, and the guns and pistols on the ranch were overhauled and minutely inspected in anticipation of an Indian raid there was no excitement or complaint on her part!

Amidst the dangers and the deprivations of frontier environment, she gathered her little ones closer about her, and with faith in God and reliance on the strong arm of husband, neighbors and friends, went forward uncomplainingly with the stern duties of life. All honor to those noble mothers in Israel!

The methods of business were in keeping with the primitive conditions of society. There were no banks in the country. Owing to this fact every ranch home was the depository of more or less money. The coin, if of considerable amount, was put in saddle bags, morrals, etc., and secreted in remote corners of the house or up under the roof, or buried on or near the premises, and was brought forth from its hiding places as occasion demanded.

A somewhat ludicrous incident arose from this peculiar custom. One of the "old-timers," whose ranch was near the line of Karnes and Goliad Counties, finding himself with considerable money on hand, and having no immediate use for it, decided to bury it.

Choosing an especially dark night, he went down to his cow pen and, removing one of the posts of the fence, dropped his bag of gold in the posthole. He then replaced the post and returned, satisfied that he had put his treasure where moth and rust could not corrupt nor thieves break through and steal.

After considerable time had elapsed he found himself in a position to use his secreted fund. But, unfortunately, he had failed to note the particular post under which he had buried his money, and all signs of his former visit having been obliterated, he was compelled to dig up one-half of his cow pen before he secured the coveted deposit.

When the ranchmen bought stock of any kind they brought the money in gold and silver to where the animals were to be received and paid it out, dollar for dollar. They generally carried the money in leather belts buckled around their waist, but the silver, being more bulky, was placed in duckin' sacks, and was loaded on a pack horse or mule.

It was necessary in those days to know the weight as well as the value of money, and therefore it was a matter of current knowledge that $1,000 in silver weighed sixty-two and one-half pounds. Robbery was a crime unknown among those rugged and honest old pioneers.

Brave, hospitable and generous, the old-time ranchman believed in justice, simple justice, stripped of all technicalities of law. According to his ethics, the man "who'd forsake a friend or go back on his word," was a scoundrel, and the thief, it mattered not who he was, had forfeited his right to live.

But those nice distinctions of judicial import, murder in the first or second degree, manslaughter, etc., did not appeal to him. In the enforcement of the code he did not subscribe to the theory that an accused could be morally innocent and at the same time legally guilty of a crime.

When a killin' occurred he asked, "Was there a grudge between 'em, and wuz it a fair fight?" If so, he could not understand why, when the best shot or the coolest nerve had slain his adversary, the great state of Texas should want to prosecute and punish the survivor. And as a juror he would not be a party to such prosecution and punishment.

In illustration of his personal application and influence in the enforcement of law, I am reminded of the following occurrence: One of the old-time ranchmen and forceful characters in Southwest Texas was a certain Capt. Blank.

He had been at the head of a vigilance committee, which had hung a number of men under his personal supervision. He was well known throughout his section as a firm, fearless and implacable leader.

During the progress of a murder trial in his home county he was summoned to attend as a special venireman. In due time he was called to the stand, and on voir dire the district attorney propounded the statutory question, "Have you any conscientious scruples in regard to the infliction of the punishment of death for crime?"

To the surprise of the district attorney, as well as of all those present, Capt. Blank replied, "I have." Then noting the incredulous smile on the faces of the audience, he turned to the court and said, "Judge, it's this a-way. I don't want to hang a man unless I've got somethin' agin' 'im."

The old-time ranchman never turned a deaf ear to a worthy appeal. His generosity and his warm-heartedness knew no bounds. On the other hand, he would not tamely submit to what he considered an unjust imposition. With a Hampden spirit, it was not the amount, but the principle for which he was ever ready to fight, if need be to the death.

The following will perhaps serve to illustrate this phase of his character: One of the cowboys on a Southwest Texas ranch in the olden time, when gas was the principal municipal illuminant, decided to go up to San Antonio for a few days and see the sights and, incidentally, "pike" a little at the Bull's Head or the White Elephant gambling tables.

In due time he returned to the ranch. The boys gathered around him to learn what had been his experiences in the big town.

After recounting at some length the incident of his sojourn, he casually remarked, "Fellers, I come damn near havin' to kill a hotelkeeper." "Why, how was that, Bill?" queried his auditors. "Well, it wuz this a-way," explained Bill. "The fust night I wuz thar, when I got ready to go to bed a nigger showed me up to my room an' lit the light. On lookin' around, I saw a great big sign tacked to the wall, sayin', 'Don't Blow Out the Gas.'

"Of course then I didn't blow it out, bein's as they said not to. I jest let the light burn, an' by pulling my hat over my face managed to sleep tolerable well.

"The next mornin' when I went to settle my bill, that low down hotelkeeper tried to charge me two dollars extra, because I didn't blow out the gas. He shore did. An' I jest looked that hotelkeeper in the eye, an' I told him that I'd fight him till hell froze over, an' then skate with him on the ice, before I'd pay one cent of that two dollars. And I meant jest what I said."

The boys all unanimously agreed that if Bill had killed that hotelkeeper, under the circumstances, it would have been a clear case of justifiable homicide. Such were some of the conditions, characteristics and peculiarities of a society now long since passed away.

To conclude: In 1880 a combination of circumstances gave me the long-coveted opportunity to go up the trail.

I was one of Mr. Cal Mayfield's "outfit" with a herd of 1,000 head of ML horses. Our party, with but one exception, was composed of Karnes County boys.

We left the Hill pasture in Live Oak County for the long and arduous drive to Dodge City, Kansas. After a halt of three days in the vicinity of Fort Worth, where the chuck wagon was replenished with food sufficient to sustain us to our destination, we virtually bade adieu to civilization, and moved into the wild section of Northeast Texas, and on, on, through the Indian Territory (crossing Red River at Doan's Crossing), until at last, after many hardships and exciting experiences, we again enjoyed the comfort of "God's land," in the frontier town of Caldwell, Kansas.

The year above mentioned was one of the worst ever known on the trail. Storms, rain and lightning. We had our first stampede in the Blue Mounds country, north of Fort Worth, and from there on it was a run night after night, with but short intermissions.

When we had crossed the Cimarron River, out of the Indian Territory, and came to where the Dodge and the Caldwell trails forked, Mr. Mayfield decided to follow the latter trail, as Caldwell was somewhat nearer. After resting at Caldwell for a few days, the herd was "split up" and I was assigned to go with a bunch, which was loaded on the cars and shipped to Kansas City. From there, back to Texas and home.

In closing this article, I crave the reader's pardon for what may be an unwarranted intrusion of personal feeling. But the old-time ranchman, his bravery, his rugged honesty and his nobility of character, is a theme, which is near and dear to me.

The purest, sweetest draughts of happiness that I have quaffed in this life, were drawn in those good old days, when as a boy and as a young man, I dwelt in the little village of Helena, the then county seat of Karnes County, in Southwest Texas, in the midst of a noble pioneer people, among whom were many of the men who made the trail.

Time's cruel hand has wrought many changes. The silken ties of early association have been severed for years, but the treasured memories of that golden time have kept green in my heart throughout every change and vicissitude of fortune. These hallowed recollections have walked with me thus far and will continue so to do to the end of the chapter. Then:

> "Let Fate do her worst, there are relics of joy,
> Bright dreams of the past, which she cannot destroy;
> Which come in the nighttime of sorrow and care,
> And bring back the features that joy used to wear.
> Long, long be my heart with such memories filled,
> Like the vase in which roses have once been distilled –
> You may break, you may shatter the vase if you will,
> But the scent of the roses will cling 'round it still."

# A Few Thrilling Incidents in My Experience on the Trail

### by L.B. Anderson, Seguin, Texas

ONE TRIP I DROVE FOR DEWEES, ERVIN & JIM ELLISON. I got the herd at Rockport, in Coleman & Fulton's pasture, and drove to the Millett & Irvin Ranch in the Panhandle, camping right where the town of Seymour is now located, and remained there several months helping to round up several thousand head of cattle.

Among those who were with me there on the range were Tom Peeler, Billie Bland, Sam and John Wilson, Billie Gray, Charlie Reed and Whit Vick. We started from that point with 3,000 yearlings for Major Wolcott's ranch in the Rocky Mountains.

Had good luck all the way until we reached Fort McPherson on the North Platte River, where our horses stampeded and ran right through our herd, causing the yearlings to stampede, also going in every direction, several hundred running into the river. We finally rounded all of them up and delivered the herd in fine shape.

I took one herd of cattle up into Colorado for John and Tom Dewees to a man named Cheatem.

We killed many buffalo on this trip, but in Kansas in 1874, on the Ninnesquaw River, I saw more buffalo than I ever saw anywhere else. As far as the eye could see over the plains was a solid mass of moving buffalo, all drifting northward.

I remember my first experience in trying to kill one of these animals. I did not know the huge hump on their backs was a row of ribs, and that I could not kill one unless I shot below that hump, but I learned that much while trying to shoot my first buffalo. I had an old cap and ball pistol and, taking careful aim at a bull's hump, I began to shoot, but the only effect my shots had was to make him run faster. I kept up with him, firing as we ran. Sometimes all six loads would go off at the same time and I would reload, going at full speed. I ran him several miles before I finally killed him.

Besides buffalo, deer and antelope, we used to kill ducks, geese, prairie chickens and other wild fowl, which were plentiful in the uncivilized part of the state. I always enjoyed hunting, and I guess I killed as many deer as the average man.

Speaking of deer, reminds me of a peculiar thing that happened in Atascosa County one day. The outfits of Dudley Tom and myself were gathering cattle on Dewees' ranch, when one morning a Negro and myself were rounding up a bunch of cattle, when several deer jumped out of a thicket directly in front of us. Of course we gave chase and ran them so close one of the bucks ran against a tree and broke his neck.

At another time, when we were camped near John Tom's ranch in Atascosa County, we were driving a herd of old Mexican beeves down a long lane, and they stampeded, turned around and started back up the lane.

A man and woman had just passed us, riding horseback. When they heard the noise of the stampede and saw the herd coming they began to ride for dear life to get out of the way of the frightened cattle. The woman was riding sideways, as was the custom in those days, and it seemed to us that the cattle were surely going to overtake her.

Looking back and seeing the cattle gaining that woman suddenly swung herself astride of the horse she was riding and pulled off a race that beat anything I ever saw. She outdistanced everything in that herd and rode safely away.

Stampedes were very common occurrences. Sometimes they were just tame affairs, but at other times they afforded all the excitement anyone could want. It was hard to tell sometimes the cause of a stampede.

Often during a clear, still night, when the cattle were contentedly bedded and the nightriders were dozing in their saddles, a sudden run would take place and the remainder of the night would be spent in trying to keep the herd together.

One of the worst stampedes I ever witnessed was at Kilgore's ranch near Hondo. Tom Lay was having some fun with a Negro boy and the cattle became frightened at the noise the boys made and the stampede that followed cost us several days' hard work and some money to get them together again.

Another bad stampede in which I had to do some tall riding occurred while I was taking a big herd of the Millett beeves to Paul's Valley. When we reached the Devil's Backbone, between Cash Creek and Washita River, we found the country had been burned off except a small scope of ground between the creeks where fire could not get to the grass, and on that ground I camped at the edge of a strip of timber.

I think every prairie chicken in that whole country came there to roost. They were there by the thousands. The next morning, when these chickens began to leave the noise they made frightened the cattle and caused them to stampede.

The 3,000 beeves ran over that rough country in every direction, and they went several miles before we were able to check them. Several were killed and about a hundred got away.

During the eighteen years that I followed the trail life I was never arrested for any infraction of the law, but on two occasions I came very near being arrested – the first time just before we crossed a herd at Red River Station. I had started a herd of the Millett cattle to the Indian Territory to turn them into the cornfields to fatten.

Mr. Millett said he thought I could make it for a day or two without inspection papers, saying he would overtake me in a few days and bring the papers with him. I got as far as Red River Station without interference, and while we were stopped there for dinner a cattle inspector rode up and demanded my papers. When I told him Mr. Millett would come with them in a few days he said nothing, but turned and rode away toward the county seat.

I knew he was going to get the officers and arrest me, so we hastily rounded up our cattle and rushed them across the river. Just as I succeeded in getting the last hoof across the inspector came with the officers, but he was too late, for I was out of their reach. Mr. Millett arrived in a few days and everything was all right.

The next encounter I had with an officer of the law was near Fort Worth. My outfit had encamped near a settlement. The boys, in a spirit of fun, caught two or three hogs that were foraging about the camp and the squeals of the swine led the settlers to believe that we were stealing the hogs.

Early the next morning just after we had strung the herd out on the trail and the cook was getting the chuck wagon in shape to start, the officer rode up, threw a villainous looking gun down on me and told me I was under arrest, accused of stealing hogs.

He said he would have to search the wagon, and I told him to proceed, and gave orders for the cook to unload the chuck wagon. When the officer was satisfied we had no hog in the wagon he told us we were free to continue on our trip.

Then I sent him off on a "wild goose chase" by telling him that there was another herd several miles ahead of us, and the cowboys of that outfit were the fellows who had stolen the hogs.

My experience with the Indians were like my other experiences – some laughable and others serious. The friendly Indians would sometimes follow us for days and torment us with their begging.

Old Yellow Bear, a chief, came to our camp one day at noon and wanted bread. I told the cook not to give him anything, and this made the old chief so mad he stamped his foot right down in the dough the cook was working up to make bread for our dinner.

The Indians at the Red Cloud agency in Dakota did not bury their dead under the ground, but would erect a scaffold some eight or ten feet high, place the body thereon and cover it with a red blanket, besides placing a bow and quiver of arrows, with a pot of food on the scaffold for the deceased Indian to use on his journey to the "happy hunting grounds." Every animal the dead Indian owned was brought to the scaffold and killed. I have seen as many as twelve dead horses at one scaffold and several dead dogs.

One of the most perilous things encountered on the trail in those days was the electrical storm. Herds would always drift before a storm and we would have to follow them for miles, while vivid lightning and crashing peals of thunder made our work awesome and dangerous. Only one who has been in a Kansas storm can realize what it means. Sometimes several head of cattle or horses were killed by one stroke of the lightning, and many of the cowboys met their death in the same manner.

# Memories of the Old Cow Trail

*by C.H. Rust, San Angelo, Texas*

AS ONE OF THE OLD COWPUNCHERS that enjoyed the life on the Chisholm cow trail that led from Texas to Kansas between 1867 and 1885, the object, as you will readily see, is to keep alive the memories of those early pioneer days.

My own interest in these matters is no more than that of any other old-time cowboy who enjoyed the life of those days, but I would like to see in my own day and time some record left to perpetuate the memories of the life of the old cowboy on the trails and the men that followed them.

What happened on these old trails between 1867 and 1885 is history, but at this present time there is no milepost or stone to mark their location. I wish to call your attention to the information I can give of those days, the conditions that led up to them, the effect they had on the men who experienced them and on the development of the great Southwest.

In fact, it is not too much to say the reclamation of the Southwest created a class of men that have made and will make a deep and permanent impression on our government. The conditions under which they lived prevented their being bound by conventionalities of an established community. They were creators of a new society.

For nearly a hundred years, some in Texas, men have been solving problems that required courage, self-reliance, willingness to assume responsibility and the peculiar quality called long-headedness, which is the ability to foresee the effect of untried experiment.

The proof is shown in the influence, out of all proportion to their number, that Texas representatives or delegates exercise in legislative or deliberative bodies outside their own state. The causes that produced this power should be preserved for the study and instruction of those who come after us and who will have to carry on our work. The preservation is surely worthwhile, and for that reason I am willing to give my own experience, much as I dislike recalling part of it.

I was born in the old red hills of Georgia in 1850. My father and mother emigrated to Texas in 1854. In 1863 my father pushed far out, almost to the danger line, to where the Caddo Peaks and Santa Anna Mountains stand as silent sentinels overlooking the valley of the Colorado River and the great Concho country to the west, far out where countless thousands of buffalo roamed at will, where deer, antelope and wild turkey seemed to have taken possession of the whole country.

This wonderful panorama loomed up to me, as a boy, as the idle and happy hunting ground that I had long dreamed of, with the silvery watered streams, like narrow ribbons, winding their way toward the Gulf of Mexico.

I am so tempted that I cannot refrain from quoting from Chapter 1, *The Quirt and The Spur*, by Edgar Rye, it fits so well in the time and condition:

"Far out beyond the confines of civilization; far out where daring men took possession of the hunting ground of the Indians and killed herds of buffalo to make a small profit in pelts, leaving the carcass to putrefy and the bones to bleach on the prairies.

"Far out where cattlemen disputed over the possession of mavericks and the branding iron was the only evidence of ownership.

"Far out where a cool head backed the deadly six-shooter and the man behind the gun, with a steady aim and a quick trigger, won out in the game where life was staked upon the issue.

"Far out where the distant landscape melted into the blue horizon and a beautiful mirage was painted on the skyline.

"Far out where the weary, thirsty traveler camped overnight near a deep water hole, while nearby in the green valley a herd of wild horses grazed unrestrained by man's authority.

"Far out where the coyote wolves yelped in unison as they chased a jackrabbit in a circle of death, then fought over his remains in a bloody feast.

"Far out where the gray lobo wolf and the mountain lion stalked their prey, killed and gorged their fill until the light in the east warned them to seek cover in their mountain lairs.

"Far out where bands of red warriors raided the lonely ranch house, killing, burning and pillaging, leaving a trail of blood and ashes behind them as a sad warning to the white man to beware of the Indian's revenge.

"Far out into this wonderful country of great possibilities, where the sun looked down upon a scene of rare beauty."

The sad thought to this writer is the passing out of those scenes so well portrayed in the above by its author; the old free grass, saddle farmer and line rider and range, through mystic regions, it is strange.

I turn my face west. I see the red lines of the setting sun, but I do not hear the echo come back, "Go west, young man, go west." I turn my face east and I hear the dull thud of the commercialized world marching west, with its steamroller procession, to roll over me and flatten me out.

I ring my Ford car's neck, and go off down the street.

I drifted down into San Antonio, Texas, in the winter of 1869. I was about nineteen years old, long lank and lean; my height was full six feet. My weight was about 140. I had no business in San Antonio. I just went there. I found board and room with a Mrs. Hall on Alamo Street.

This being the largest town I ever was in, I was somewhat "buffaloed," but Mrs. Hall and her husband were old Texas folks. Mrs. Hall was good to me, tried to advise me, but I knew it all.

About all I did during my stay in San Antonio was loaf around such places as the Old Bullhead Saloon that faced south on Main Plaza, piked at monte some, saw big old grizzly gamblers get rich, and poor, in a few hours.

When the spring of 1870 opened up I found work with Myers and Roberts. They had just recently bought out the old NOX Ranch, seventy miles west of San Antonio, on the Frio River, thirty-five miles north of Uvalde.

I believe it was about the first of April when Meyers and Roberts sold 1,500 head of mixed cattle to Ewing and Ingrams of California. We began to put the cattle up at once. About the middle of May we delivered the 1,500 head near San Antonio, five miles west of the Alamo.

Ewing and Ingrams made me an offer to lead the herd up the trail to Kansas. This offer I accepted. We held the cattle up a few days to organize, as the outfit was all new hands – green.

Some of them had never seen a horse or a cow, much less ridden one. Will say here, I had never been over the trail as far north as Fort Worth. My duty was to look out for good places to camp, bed grounds and crossing of streams.

We made only one drive a day, eight to ten miles. We followed the old cow trail from San Antonio to San Marcos, Austin, Round Rock,

Georgetown, Salado, Belton, Cleburne, Fort Worth, Boliver, crossing the Red River near Gainesville, through Nation to Oil Springs, Fort Arbuckle to Wild Horse and Washita.

Here we met forty Comanche Indians. Every one of the redskins had a parasol. I asked them where they had been. One spoke up, in fairly good English, and said they had been in on the Arkansas River making a treaty with another tribe.

We went through the Osage Nation, striking the line of Kansas at Caldwell Bluff Creek. At Ninnisquaw we turned to the left up the Ninnisquaw to the Sand Hill, crossing the Arkansas River at Rayman, Kansas, to Great Bend.

Out ten miles north, on Walnut Creek, we held the cattle up, cut out all the steers to fatten, leaving about 800 cows one-, two- and three-year-olds. They were taken on to Nebraska and put on a ranch.

Here I left the outfit. Traveled down the Arkansas River about ninety miles to Wichita, Kansas, all alone. Wichita was then about a mile long, one hundred yards wide and an inch thick. Here is where the Long and Shorthorns met and fought it out right. I remained here about ten days, struck an outfit bound for Texas with a bunch of old trail horses and chuck wagon. We traveled slowly back down the trail, easy gait, telling each other our experiences on the trail going up.

My last trail and range work was in 1877, around old Fort Griffin.

I have been a citizen of San Angelo, Texas, for over thirty years. It is not what I might have been, it is what I stand for today. I believe I have made good. I was all wrong at one time in my life. I am all for the right now.

My business is dealing in fuel. I have been right here in one place for twenty years, handling coal and wood, and belong to the old M.E. Church South, and I am proud of her record as a church.

I am thankful for my own record that I have lived to get right and do something. I know there are hundreds of the early-day trail hitters doing well and living good, clean lives.

It might be that the old trail driver has something buttoned up in his vest that he won't tell. Well, he is not supposed to tell all he knows, but will tell all he can.

I was a grown-up man before I ever saw a Sunday School, but I owe much to my mother for the lesson she taught me at her knee. I departed from her advice in early manhood, but I came back. She and my father are buried side by side here in Fairmont Cemetery, in the great Concho

Valley, having lived to a good, ripe old age, over eighty years.

The boys that have passed over the Divide, I do not know where they are, but I hope they got right.

# Trail Driving to Kansas and Elsewhere

### By W.F. Cude, San Antonio, Texas

IT IS THE DUTY OF THE CATTLE DRIVERS to do their bit in giving to the people of the great state of Texas some important facts that happened more than two score and ten years ago.

In the year 1861 war broke out between the States and it lasted four years, and during all this time there was no market, so the country was beginning to be overrun with cattle so much that thousands died.

Some people went out with a wagon and an ax and killed and skinned them for their hides, which sold for one dollar apiece, though there was not much killing of animals for the hides except where the animal was down on the lift or in a bog hole. This was in 1869 and 1870.

Up until 1872 there was not over 150 miles of railroad in the state; that was from Galveston to Houston, and a short line from Houston to Brazoria, twenty-five miles in length, and one road from Harrisburg to Alleyton, three miles east of Columbus.

So the cattle driving to Kansas was the only hope at that time, and it proved to be a great help before the railroads got around. Trail driving to Kansas lasted from 1866 to 1886, and it was estimated that fully eight million head of cattle and horses were driven and sold during the twenty years above mentioned to Kansas, the drivers paying for the cattle on an average of ten dollars per head, although most of the horses came back to Texas and were used the next year.

There were all sizes of herds, from 500 to 2,500 cattle in a drove, usually seven or eight men to the small herds and twelve to fifteen men with the large herds.

My first trip to Kansas was in the year 1868. I went with men by the name of Forehand and C. Cockrell. The cattle were steers, 600 in number, and were gathered near Cistern Post Office, in Bastrop County. There were eight hands besides the owners and the cook.

After we passed Dallas lightning struck the boys in camp, killing one, and three others were so badly burned that one of them quit, so we only had six all the way to Kansas.

We were told by the citizens of Dallas that we would reach the Chisholm Trail a few miles north of Dallas, and we followed it through Fort Worth, a small town, then through the Chickasaw Nation on to Wichita, Kansas, and thence to Solomon City on the Kansas Pacific Railroad, nine miles west of Abilene.

There were but few settlements on the way after we passed Dallas, and when we reached the settlements in Kansas we were all joyful again. We passed through many prairie dog towns and over rattlesnake dens, and lost only one horse from rattlesnake bite.

Many kinds of wild animals were to be seen along the way, such as antelope, elk and buffalo, and we killed one buffalo calf and brought it into camp, though I did not like the meat as well as that of our cattle.

The country was one vast stretch of rich land, no timber except on creeks or rivers, and when we came in sight of timber we knew there would be water. In some instances we had to haul our wood to cook with, but generally we would have to gather buffalo chips (dry dung) for that purpose.

In the fall of 1869 I drove a herd of cattle to Shreveport, Louisiana. We made some money, but the buffalo flies were so bad we never went any more to Shreveport.

Sometimes we would get farms to put the cattle in at night and the farms were stocked with cockleburrs and the cattle's tails would get full of burrs, and when the buffalo flies would get after them they would lose their tails fighting flies.

Their tails would become entangled in small pine trees and there they would stand and pull and bellow until they got loose. You could hear them bawl a mile. Some of the cattle would run off and lay down, crazed with misery, and it was hard to drive them back to the herd.

We sold the cattle in Shreveport and down Red River some 15 miles distant. This herd was gathered in Gonzales County near where Waelder is now.

In the fall of 1870 I gathered another herd near the town of Waelder, Gonzales County, and went to New Orleans.

On this trip we had many rivers and bayous to swim. Ferrymen wanted five to ten dollars for their services. The largest stream was Burwick's Bay at Brazier City, 900 yards wide straight across. Here a man led an ox to the edge of the stream and drove him into swimming water, when two men in canoes, one on each side, pointed the herd across.

I shipped a carload from Brazier City to New Orleans and drove the rest, selling to plantations until I reached the Mississippi River. There I sold the balance, getting a much better price than I received for those I shipped to New Orleans, many of the farmers giving me checks on banks and merchants in New Orleans, very few paying the money down.

Another herd of cattle went along at the same time, owned by Col. Fred Malone of Beeville, Texas, and Capt. Gibney of New Orleans, and as the latter knew the city well, I got him to assist me in locating the banks and merchants.

One of the merchants had moved, however, so we went to the city register to find his location. When I reached this place I found it to be a house made of beeswax and tallow, and I began to think that fellow could not pay a check for $500, but it was all paid.

I also drove another herd that same year to Natchez, Mississippi, and sold to two men by the name of John McKen and James Gainer, who lived on Black River, thirty miles from Natchez. We made some money on this herd of cattle.

Some of the hands came back with the horses and wagons, myself, Charles Edwards and Henry Crozier taking a steamboat on Black River, thence down to Red River and on down to the Mississippi River to New Orleans. This boat took on board sugar and molasses all along the way.

It was a very pleasant trip and somewhat amusing to see the hands load on the barrels of sugar and molasses. They loaded that boat until the deck was right down to the water's edge. At New Orleans we took a train to Brazier City, there we took a ship to Galveston and from there came by train to our home in Gonzales County.

In the year of 1871 I saddled up "Old Ball," my favorite horse, and rode away to Kansas, this time for N.W. Cude, whose herd was gathered in Gonzales, Caldwell and Bastrop Counties. When we reached North Texas I found the Old Chisholm Trail had been abandoned and went far to the west to cross Red River.

One morning about eleven o'clock I rode on ahead of the herd to some timber, where "Old Ball" stopped very suddenly, and then I saw an Indian standing near the road. The Indian had a gun, and I suppose he was out on a hunt, but I gave my horse more slack on the bridle and passed on, and neither of us spoke.

A few days later two Indians came up to the herd and wanted beef, but I told them that I had bought these cattle and had none to give away. They talked some English and asked to see my gun. I gave it to one of them and they looked it all over and soon rode away as fast as their horses could carry them.

The cattle market was very low that year, so I failed to sell out all, wintering the balance in Nebraska, but they turned out bad. In crossing the Missouri River, it being frozen over, the cattle milled out on the ice and broke through, and we lost sixteen. The expense of wintering was so heavy we came out behind that year.

The first cattle I ever drove to a market was in 1867, to Houston, Texas, for a man by the name of Tumelson, from Gonzales County, and the last herd was in 1872, for a man by the name of O.J. Baker. R.D. Cude and myself bought the cattle from a Mr. Wimberly, in Hays County. We drove to Kansas and stopped our herd about fifteen miles west of Ellsworth, near the Kansas Pacific Railroad.

Everything went well except when we got into Kansas, Bluff Creek being the line. We lay over a day to rest and clean up. Next morning just about sunup, I heard a gunshot down the creek and in a few minutes we saw two Indians running two mules as fast as they could go.

They had shot a white man with a gun and arrows. He came dragging up to our camp with one arrow still sticking in him, and one of the boys pulled it out and we carried him to a tent not far away.

The trail drivers had many narrow escapes and were exposed to many storms, cyclones, hail and all kinds of weather, stampedes of cattle, running over ditches and bluffs at night. Some few never came back, but were buried along the lonely trail among the wild roses, wrapped only in their bed blankets; no human being living near, just the coyote roaming there.

# When Lightning Set the Grass on Fire

*By George W. Brock, Lockhart, Texas*

I WAS BORN IN CALDWELL COUNTY, TEXAS, three miles west of Lockhart, Jan. 25, 1860. Beginning at the age of nine years, I commenced to handle stock, but at that time I was too small to get on a horse unaided and my father told me not to get off, but every time I saw a rabbit I would get off and throw rocks at it and then I would have to be helped back on my horse.

About 1871 or 1872 I started on my first trip on the trail, going with my father. When near Fort Worth father concluded I was too young to go on account of the danger of Indians, and he sent me back home.

I continued to work with cattle until 1876, and at this date I went to work for M.A. Withers, herding 300 cows, penning them at night, sleeping at the pens and doing my own cooking.

In 1878 M.A. Withers took a bunch of boys to Fayette County, Texas, and bought about 800 head of cattle.

At the crossing on the Colorado, at Judge L. Moore's ranch, we had a great experience in two or three ways. We tried first to swim the cattle across the river, but we only succeeded in getting about ten head across that way and had to rope and drag them.

We then crossed the others on the ferryboat. Here I saw my first Jersey. She was a heifer and belonged to Judge Moore, and it was a hard matter to keep her out of our herd.

Judge Moore thought very much of this heifer and would watch everybody passing there with cattle. When he came out and found the thing in our herd he threatened to prosecute us for attempting to steal her.

In January, 1879, Blanks and Withers began buying cattle and pasturing them, preparing for a drive in the spring. On the first day of April we rounded up the pasture to start the herd north. On the second we left the pasture and went about three or four miles and camped for the night. We had so few men with us that night we lost about 3,200 out of 3,500 head. They just simply walked off and everyone seemed to take a different direction, and, being short of men, they went their way, with the result as stated.

The next morning G.W. Mills (Pap) and myself held the 300 until the others ate breakfast. When we went to camp there were two horses tied up for us. Not one of us knew anything about these horses, but the general opinion of the camp was that one of them was bad. The cook said, "Withers left instructions for Brock to ride the one supposed to be bad and for Mills to ride the other one."

So "Pap" had lots of fun while eating breakfast at the thought of seeing Brock thrown and losing his saddle. Breakfast over, Brock saddled the bad horse and mounted him and he walked off perfectly quiet, but it was entirely a different case with "Pap's" horse. "Pap" was the one that went heavenward and had to call for poultices, which was so often the case on the trail, for the fun did not always show up just where you were expecting it.

Going back to the herd, we got them all together by the next day, moved back into the pasture and for four or five nights these cattle would walk off; so the first night we held them we put them on the trail proper the next morning and drove them as far as possible. We had no other happenings except an occasional storm or high water stampede, which belonged to the business.

In the edge of the state of Kansas the cook accidentally set the grass on fire and we had to move into rough country.

One night Mark Withers cautioned me to tie my horse good so that if anything happened I would be ready. About twelve o'clock the cattle stampeded, and when I got to where my horse had been he was gone. I told Mark my horse was gone and he said, "Durn it! I told you to tie that horse good."

And when we went to where his horse was tied he was gone also, and I said, "Durn it! Why didn't you tie him good?" We could do nothing but listen to the running of the cattle, and every once in a while Mark would exclaim, "If I only had a horse!"

After I returned from this trip I worked on the ranch until 1883 and then went to La Salle County for Blanks and Withers and worked on the ranch for four or five months. In 1884 we left home for the Blanks and Withers Ranch in La Salle County.

The first herd prepared was turned over to G.B. (Gus) Withers, numbering 4,000 three's and four's. I started to help Gus with this herd to Uvalde County, but we had a stampede just above Cotulla and lost 400 or 500 head. Willis Hargis and myself were left to gather them up. We got all but 200 head of the cattle and most of the horses. Some of the horses went back to the ranch before stopping.

In this stampede my horse ran into a ditch that night. The cause of him doing this was because I was trying to point the cattle away from the ditch and a Negro (Russ Jones) was on the opposite side of the herd trying to do the same thing, and the result was that instead of pointing them away from the ditch, we drove them straight into it.

The banks of this ditch were five or six feet high, and I was fortunate in escaping unhurt.

The stampede occurred in a very brushy place and the men next morning all looked like they had been to an Irish wake, all bloody and bruised.

In this drive we rounded up one of those notorious outlaw steers, which were to be found in the country at that time. Withers said if there were any two or three men in the outfit that had the nerve to rope that steer and lead him to a good place he would kill him for beef.

Well, I caught him, but if I had not have had others close at hand who came to my rescue and also roped him and spread him out, so to speak, I might not have been writing this story.

But between us we killed him and enjoyed his carcass. The outlaw steer above referred to was rounded up while we were on the ranch after Hargis and I turned over the cattle we gathered after the stampede.

I went back to the ranch and we gathered another herd and shipped them to Wichita Falls, Texas. Drove from there to Julesburg, Colorado., Sam Childress being the boss. We crossed the Red River at Doan's Store, where we laid in supplies to last us until we reached Dodge City, Kansas.

They told us at the store that someone was stampeding horses across the river and driving them off. So when we camped at night after crossing the river, Childress and myself tied our horses to the wagon and examined our six-shooters to see that they were in working order.

After we had gone to sleep the cook jumped up and said, "The horses are running." Childress and I jumped on our horses with our pistols in our hands, but just then the cook discovered that it was only a pot of beans boiling, which he had built a big fire around before going to bed.

After crossing North Red River in the Wichita Mountains, we met a Comanche chief, who said he had 300 bucks besides the women and children. I gave him five crippled yearlings to keep his bunch away from our outfit, and he kept his promise.

After we got to the top of the ridge I looked down in the valley of Washita River and the whole face of the country was alive with herds. I went back and stopped the herd until I could survey the route, and found that by going above the trail and crossing about five miles up and swimming the river we could get ahead of everything, so we proceeded to swim the river and get ahead in the lead of all other herds.

Monroe Hardeman was just behind us with another herd for Blanks and Withers, and he helped us swim our herd and we in turn helped him. After we got both herds across I found that the sun had taken all the skin off my back. Swimming the river and an occasional stampede was about the only excitement until we reached Kansas.

Childress at one time had been shot all to pieces by a bunch of soldiers who mistook him and others for horse thieves, causing him to have a natural hatred toward all soldiers, and at Bear Creek he spied about 300 Negro soldiers coming toward us.

He squared himself with gun in hand and was ready to open fire. I tried to stop him, but saw there was no use to talk to him, so I roped his horse and pulled him around and led him off. I think that was all that saved our whole outfit, as we were so badly outnumbered it would have meant suicide to have started anything like that. However, we had just left Longhorn Roundup and Childress had been celebrating considerably, and that might have had something to do with his display of nerve that he exhibited there.

From there to Dodge City everything went well. At Dodge City every man, including the boss, except myself, celebrated in great style, while I was left to handle and hold the outfit.

After disposing of our lame cattle we shaped up and moved on to Ogallala. About four or five days' drive out of Dodge City, Tobe Swearingen came to our herd to count the cattle, and he and I did the counting.

According to my count the cattle were all there, but he made a mistake of 100, making us out that number, and, it being too late to recount, I spent an awful restless night. I couldn't understand how we could lose that many cattle in a prairie country like that. The next morning we recounted and found that my count was correct. Then my nervousness left me.

Several days later we had to make a long drive for water. We watered at the North Republican. The lead cattle struck the Frenchman about sundown, and from then until next morning about ten o'clock they kept coming in, and every once in a while a man would show up.

The morning we started this particular drive I ate breakfast at daylight and the next meal I ate was at ten o'clock the next day.

For the next day or two we grazed along the stream, so appropriately named Stinking Water. When crossing the Frenchman the cook broke down the wagon tongue, and we fixed it by wrapping it with ropes so that it held out for the balance of the trip.

After leaving Stinking Water for Ogallala everything went nicely. Leaving Ogallala we went up the south side of the Platte River to Julesburg Junction, where we delivered our cattle to Governor Rout and ex-Governor Brush of Colorado.

Going up the river our only trouble was to keep our stock off the farmers. They had no fences and it took very careful watching to keep them out of those patches. To let your stuff get on those patches meant the highest price grazing that a Texas horse or steer ever got.

One night I woke up and heard the horse bell and I knew it was in the wrong direction, so I got up and found them grazing on one of those high-priced corn patches. I quietly drove them to camp, woke up everybody and moved everything away that night. I believe that corn actually did the horses good; at least they seemed that night to travel stronger than usual.

After reaching Julesburg Junction we crossed the Platte and began delivering. I was then sent to meet Gus Withers, who had not yet come up with us.

I had three horses, riding one and leading the others. When crossing the Platte my horses were so weak from the trip from Texas, and the quicksand so very bad, they could not carry me, so I led them, wading water up to my chin.

After crossing the river and about the middle of the evening, I met with something entirely different from anything I had ever before been up against. I had thought up to this time that I knew what a Kansas storm was, but that evening I was shown that I had never been in one before.

The lightning would strike the ground and set the grass on fire, then the rain would put it out. I got off my horse and tied the three together, took off my spurs, six-shooter and pocket knife, laid them down and moved away.

After the storm was over the sun came out and it looked as though nothing had ever happened, so I moved on. At night, not knowing where I was, I stopped at a good hole of water, but I had nothing to eat. After lying down I heard the lowing of cattle. I saddled up, putting my bedding in front of me, and started in the direction of the cattle I had heard and, to my good luck, it was Gus' herd.

The boys were all very glad to see me, as I had heard from home and they had not. They had been in the same storm that I had just passed through and the lightning killed one steer for them. Very shortly after I reached them their herd stampeded, but they did not lose anything, and Gus said, "The cattle did that to show they were glad to see Brock." I then piloted them back to Julesburg the same route I had traveled in going to them.

After all our cattle had been delivered we naturally felt that we could sleep as long as we cared to. So Childress and myself slept until ten o'clock the next morning. The sun was unusually bright and, we both being without whiskers on the top of our heads, the boys said our heads made very good mirrors.

The dinner that Mark Withers gave us at the station when we were ready to come home paid me fully for all the meals I had lost on the trip.

The balance of my work with cattle has been on ranches at home.

*Old age and parting of ways in life*
*Will not erase the cowboy's strife.*
*In after years let come what will,*
*He proves to be a cowboy still.*

# Experiences 'Tenderfeet' Could Not Survive

*by G.W. Mills, Lockhart, Texas*

MY FATHER AND MOTHER were both born in Somerset, state of Kentucky. I first saw the light of day on June 2, 1857, and in the fall of 1872 my father, with his family, including myself, emigrated to Texas. Our mode of transportation was by way of wagons, there being no railroads convenient at that early date.

My father came to look after some land somewhere in the broad domain of Texas (he knew not exactly where) that had been left him by an older brother, Henry P. Mills, who died while serving as a soldier in the Texas War for Independence.

We settled near Lockhart in 1874, and at the age of about seventeen I went to work on the M.A. Withers Ranch, one of the biggest ranches of this section at that time, which was due west of Lockhart about four miles, as the crow flies.

I think it would be of interest to the reader to have some idea of the appearance of that ranch as it appeared to me, then a mere lad. It was located on a little flowing stream known as Clear Fork and abundantly fed by many springs. This creek was fringed with timber, pecan, walnut, elm, hackberry and wild plum on either bank, and dipping into its crystal waters were the weeping willows.

The creek abounded with an abundance of fish, such as bass, channel cat and the silver perch. The old ranch house stood back about 300 yards east of the creek, on the summit of a gradual sloping hillside, which commanded a view of the beautiful stretch of valley country roundabout and where it was swept by the gentle southern breeze.

About 150 yards from the house were the corrals, covering about four acres of ground, and these corrals were divided into various pens, in which we "rounded up" from time to time the great herds for marking and branding. As a matter of course these pens were built to endure and were very strong, as cattle in those days were wild, and in this exciting work none but well-built pens would hold them.

The uninitiated will probably be interested in knowing just how these corrals, as we termed them, were built, when material was not so plentiful as now.

The material was largely post oak rails, which we had cut and hauled by ox teams about five miles from the timbered country of Caldwell County. The posts were of fine cedar timber obtained from old Mountain City in Hays County.

These corrals had to be much higher than the ordinary fence, as the infuriated longhorns would, in their desperation to be free, try to go over the top or break them down.

Once the material was on the ground, we dug deep, wide holes, about seven feet apart, and in these we placed two of the cedar posts in such juxtaposition as to hold the long rails, which we piled one on top of the other until they reached the top of the high posts.

That being done, some of the old-timers bound the ends of the posts together with wire or stout strips of rawhide, but at about the time of which I write we began to bind them with smooth wire.

The subdivisions spoken of above were divided into branding pens and horse corrals. We would not be true to the picture we are now attempting to paint in words if we fail to mention the singularly attractive feature of the setting of these particular corrals.

They were shaded by large spreading live oaks, hoary with age, where we hung up our saddles and leggins and various and sundry camp equipage, under which we slept on our blankets and saddle pillows, and partook of our frugal fare. Some of these grand old monarchs of the forest still stand – the pride of the Texas cowboy.

It must be realized that we had no fences arbitrarily deciding the bounds of our little empire, and our cattle and horses roamed at will over the hills and valleys, covered with the rich, luxuriant curly mesquite grass, upon which they grew sleek and fat.

After three years' work on this busy ranch none but the life of a cowboy appealed to me. Around the old campfires at night I heard the tales of the older men of their exciting life on the trail, and naturally I felt like going the route that those I knew, admired and trusted had gone.

Right here I want to put in that, fortunately for me, I was associated with a few of the grand old stockmen of early days, to whose fine, though rugged characters, I am indebted for that training, which carried me safely through many trying times.

In March, 1877, as our boss was not to drive that year, I secured employment with Ellison and Dewees, who were going to drive about six herds up the trail from this section to Ogallala, Nebraska, on the South Platte River.

In the six herds there were about 15,000 head of mixed cattle, being about 2,500 head to the herd, each herd having its boss and trail outfit, which we will now attempt to briefly describe.

The boss is the man in charge of the herd; then there were eight cowboys, one "horse wrangler" and cook, who drove the wagon, drawn by two yoke of oxen – the wagon containing our provisions and bedding, the provisions being replenished from time to time from the "outposts," sometimes hundreds of miles apart.

We received our herd in the western part of Gonzales County, the herd being in charge of N.P. Ellison, a cousin of Col. J.F. Ellison, a grand old cowman, who owned the cattle.

On this trip we had with us the following boys, not a one over twenty-three years of age: W.M. Ellison, son of the boss; E.F. Hilliard, W.F. Felder, E.M. Storey, Albert McQueen, Ace Jackson, myself, two Negro cow hands and a Negro cook.

We left the Lockhart pasture about the first of April, took the Chisholm Trail and "lit out." My first stampede was on Onion Creek; as usual, this occurred at night, about twelve o'clock.

The herd was bedded about one hundred yards from the wagon, two men on guard. In their fright the cattle broke for the wagon, and we asleep at the camp, being aroused by the roar of tramping hoofs, scrambled up on the wagon.

One of the older men jumped up and shook a blanket before them and turned them off the other way. The first thing I remember was the boss calling out, "Boys, get down and get your horses."

It was then that I discovered that I had quit my pallet and was astride one of the hind wheels. Of course, we hurriedly got our horses, went around the cattle, after about a mile's run, held them, and they quieted down.

Old hands at the business will know that we slept no more that night. This trip was marked by excessive rainfall, big rains falling at night, and one hailstorm, adding greatly to the hardship of the cowboy's lot; but we didn't mind it much and, with songs and jokes, kept up our spirits.

When we arrived at old Red River Station, where the old Chisholm Trail crossed, we found the river up and several herds waiting to cross. We stopped on the east side of Panther Creek and pitched camp.

I want to say here that that stream was rightly named. We killed a fat yearling – I won't say whose it was – tied a rope to one end of the front bow of the wagon, the other to a small tree; the cook hung the beef on the rope. When the boys came in at twelve o'clock to wake up the third guard he discovered a panther standing on his hind feet eating the meat off of the rope, just on the opposite side of the wagon from where we were sleeping. He opened fire with his forty-five on the panther.

We thought "horse rustlers," now commonly called horse thieves, had attacked the camp. The noise of the firing stampeded the cattle. As the boys sprang out of their blankets some had their forty-fives ready and some made for the horses, where it took but a moment to saddle and then off for the cattle.

In the rush E.M. Storey sang out, "What is that? If you don't speak out I'll cut loose at you," and then we recognized the voice of E.F. Hilliard, calling out in the inky darkness from the direction of the firing in excited tones, "It's a damned panther; he's eating our meat off the rope."

This was about twenty feet from where we were sound asleep, sleeping as only Texas cowboys can. By that time the herd had gotten a good distance away.

We made a run to overtake the herd; finally rounded up a part of them that night, and the man on guard checked another part further away. The balance we found next morning in the valley of Red River; rounded all up and started back to camp about five miles away. We counted them – always a part of the program – to see if we had lost any.

To show that our work was not all "rough work," and that we had our "bookkeeping" department, though ever so simple, I shall tell how this counting was done.

The herd was allowed to string out; two men went on ahead, some distance in width between them, the others pointed the herd in their direction and so that they would slowly go between them; then they counted, and with a knot on the saddle string or some other convenient method, tallied them by hundreds, each calling out to see if they had agreed; then knowing the number that we started with, we knew if our roundup had been complete.

We bedded the cattle on the same bed ground that night; I and my pal stood guard from two o'clock in the morning until day. On guard, one rides one way and the other the opposite direction around.

As I got on the round on the side next to the creek I heard the most horrifying yell, or more of a scream, that I had ever heard in all my life. This blood-curdling scream came from a bending tree about sixty yards from the herd. My thick hair went straight up and has never thoroughly settled down since that memorable night.

The cattle jumped up, and about that time I met my pal coming toward me. Instantly I said, "What's that?" His reply betrayed his fright also, although he had been up the trail before. In language picturesque and accurate he replied, "The scream of a panther," with some adjectives before that name, which assured me that my hair was not standing on end for nothing.

From then on until daylight we just rode around together. Next morning we told the boss that we had rather swim Red River (then 300 yards wide in swimming water) than to stand guard assisted by panthers ready to spring on man or beast. A conference was held among the bosses and it was decided to cross some of the herd that very day.

We hit the water about ten o'clock and crossed our herd first, four other herds following.

Of course, the outfits assisted one another in this hard and dangerous work. In this crossing one of the boys had a horse, which refused to swim, and the man had to jump off onto a wild steer's back, but with pluck made a safe landing on the other side.

This put us into the Indian Territory and new precautions had to be taken to save us from attack by the Indians, the several herds keeping close together to be of mutual help in case of a surprise attack. The next river was Washita, and we had to swim that also; narrow but deep and very swift.

About a hundred miles further on we came to the North Canadian River, swimming also, narrow, deep and swift. When I swam across and came out on the opposite side on the second bank I got down to pull off my boots to let the water out, and wring my socks.

A few scattering elm trees were ahead and about the time I got my boots off I looked up toward the trees and saw my first Indian, who looked about six and one-half feet tall to me, standing backed up against one of those elm trees, with the eagle feathers in his head, a long rifle standing up in front of him. He had on buckskin clothes with a dandy fringe on them.

My hair rose again very suddenly, so I lit straddle of my horse and ran out to the front cattle. The other two boys thought I was just seeing things because I was badly scared.

They did not believe there was an Indian down there, but when they finished crossing the herd and came on up with the wagon there were about fifteen Indians showed up with the one I had first seen acting as chief, who claimed that he was the noted chief, "Spotted Tail."

He told the boss he wanted "Wa-ha," meaning beef. Then I had it on the boys and it was their time to get scared. The boss knew it was best to use a little diplomacy, and so he told us to cut out four or five of the "drag yearlings" and turn them over to them. The Indians had just as soon have these lame or given-out cattle as any. Of course, Indian-like, they wanted more, but we outtalked them, telling them there were more herds behind and they would gladly give them some of theirs.

Then the chief put up his spiel for "chuck," meaning flour, bacon, etc. And they talked like they meant to have it. We explained that our supply was short, but just to wait on the big supply coming on behind.

They left us and went on to meet the other herds, so we moved on out of their zone that evening. We saw no more Indians on that trip, and we did not look for any.

On Salt Fork there came up a rain and lightning storm, and I saw unbelievable doings of the lightning; it beat anything I ever saw.

The lightning would hit the side of those hills and gouge out great holes in the earth like a bomb had struck them, and it killed seven or eight head of cattle in the herd back of us and two horses out of the "remuda," which, being interpreted, means the saddle horses.

Nothing more eventful occurred and in about a week we arrived at the famous and renowned Dodge City, Kansas, a familiar name to all cowmen in that day.

Then we provisioned and started on the tail-end of the journey to Ogallala, about 300 miles. We arrived there about Aug. 1, our cattle all in good shape in better condition a long ways than when we left. They were there delivered to the various purchasers, who removed them to their respective ranches in that great cow country. Our faithful saddle horses, wagons and all were disposed of with the cattle.

On the night of Aug. 20, this being 1877, I went to call on Col. J.F. Ellison, he being indisposed and stopping at the Gass House, and also to get my "time," which really means wages, about $180, then a small fortune for a young cowboy. Upon this visit to Col. Ellison I was introduced to two guests who had called to pay their respects. They were two brothers, Joel and Joe Collins, handsome young men, products of the West.

About a week afterward, in that very neighborhood, the Union Pacific was held up eighteen miles west of Ogallala and the robbers rifled the express car, taking $100,000 in gold, but scorning to take a huge amount of silver, which perhaps was too heavy to take with them in their hasty flight.

Joel Collins was in this very holdup, being with the notorious Sam Bass gang, who successfully did the trick. About a week afterward Joel and George Hereford were killed by a detachment of United States soldiers and their part of the loot recovered, about three miles south of what was known then as Buffalo Park, on the K.P. Railroad.

Upon getting my time I lit out for home over the U.P. Railroad. On the way back I fell in with some wild and woolly green cowboys making their first trip on a train, just like myself. At Grand Island the train stopped for breakfast; we got off and on the way to the eating place a Negro suddenly came around the corner of the house, beating one of those huge gongs, making a most terrific din of noise.

We were scared senseless, and it was all I could do to keep one of those boys from shooting that darkey. He contended that he would let no damn nigger stampede him by beating on a tin can.

It is hard for you who have always traveled and become accustomed to the ways of the city to understand just how puzzling civilization is to a boy raised up on the Texas frontier, whose life is very simple, and who knows cow trails far better than he does paved streets, and the campfires the only hotels he ever saw until forced out into the world.

We arrived at Austin on time and there I took one of those old-fashioned stages to Lockhart, feeling like I had seen the world, and with much pride telling the boys all that I had seen and been through.

The younger boys looked upon us fellows who had been up the trail as heroes, and of course this very thing incited others to want to go. It was the life ambition of many a one to make such a trip. You were not a graduate in the cowboy's school until you had been.

In 1878 I was back on the comfortable old Withers Ranch. In 1879 my old friend and boss, M.A. Withers, took through a herd and I went with him. We crossed the Colorado at Webberville and arrived at Taylor about the 22nd of April. A rain, a terrible rain, came up about four o'clock in the evening, raining all evening and all night. It was very cold and we came very near freezing to death.

At that springtime period several horses and cattle died of the cold. Every horse that we rode that bitter night was unfit for service the balance of the trip, so dreadful was the exposure.

You understand cattle drift before wind-driven rain, and by morning we were at Hutto, eight miles away; we had had no supper and no breakfast, and not until noon did we have anything to eat. When these "drifts" take place every man and the boss is in front of the herd, holding them as much as possible; there are no shifts then, but every man to his post all night long; and the nights are long, too.

On this memorable night I well recall my associates: M.A. Withers, in charge; G.B. Withers, G.W. Brock, A.N. Eustace, C.W. Pope, W.M. Ellison, Joe Lewis, the scout; Barney Roland, better known as "Pard;" and Edmundo Martinez, the Mexican horse wrangler.

Next day it was still bitterly cold, but the rain had let up, leaving that country covered with water.

About noon we got back to camp and our appetites, always good, were now ravenous, and we looked forward to boiling coffee and hot grub of some kind. Instead, imagine our disappointment at finding the trifling cook housed up in the wagon covered in his blankets, and hadn't prepared a thing – hadn't even started a fire.

Mr. Withers, always mindful of his men, was outraged and hauled him out of there with a demand to know why he didn't have the boys something to eat. He evasively replied that he couldn't build a fire in that water. Mr. Withers gave him his time and told him to "light a shuck." I can see that cook now making it over those hog-wallows, filled with water, to the nearest town.

Under a camp wagon is usually suspended an old cowhide called the "caboose," and in that we throw stray pieces of wood, etc., as long as we are in a country where it can be had, just for use in such emergencies.

It came in handy that time, sure, and some of the boys got it out, and with a lavish use of the oil can, we soon had things going, some of the boys doing the cooking. We were not particular and after a hearty meal our spirits were up again ready for any turn of fate in the cowboy's lot.

The next day we picked up a boy from old Gonzales County, filled with the spirit of adventure, by the name of Joe Knowles, and he cooked the balance of the way up. He was a good lad and some of the boys have seen him since, just lately, and he is doing well, we are glad to know.

We went the old Chisholm Trail and crossed the river at Red River Station. Nothing exciting occurred until we got to Turkey Creek, Indian

Territory. There the trail had been changed to turn northwest and hit the western trail at the Longhorn Roundup on the Cimarron.

The new trail had been marked out by a buffalo head set up about every half of a mile. It was a hundred miles from Turkey Creek to Longhorn Roundup.

We arrived at Dodge City early in July, sold our steer yearlings there to the well-known cattle firm of Day Brothers, moved on up to the Smoky River, sold the cows to J.R. Blocker, then lit out for Ogallala, Nebraska. At about thirty miles from the last named place we pitched camp about a mile from the spring, which, curiously enough, opens up right in the bald prairie and forms the head of the stream known as Stinking Water.

Here I had an experience with lightning that I know rivals the experience of any man who ever went up the trail. How we escaped death I have never understood.

The storm hit us about twelve o'clock at night. There was some rain, and to the northwest I noticed just a few little bats of lightning. Then it hit us in full fury and we were in the midst of a wonderful electrical storm.

We had the following varieties of lightning, all playing close at hand, I tell you. It first commenced like flash lightning, then came forked lightning, then chain lightning, followed by the peculiar blue lightning.

After that show it rapidly developed into ball lightning, which rolled along the ground. After that spark lightning; then, most wonderful of all, it settled down on us like a fog. The air smelled of burning sulfur; you could see it on the horns of the cattle, the ears of our horses and the brim of our hats.

It grew so warm we thought we might burn up with it, and M.A. Withers and Joe Lewis, old-timers, told me afterward that they never had seen the like in all of their experiences. Needless to say, we were all on guard that night. The cattle did not give us so much trouble as the constant flashes keeping them moving so much. We delivered at Ogallala and lit out for Texas.

Under the same leadership we drove two herds in 1880 to Fort Griffin, going what was known as the Western Trail. We threw them together at Fort Griffin, M.A. Withers taking full charge. There were about 4,500 mixed cattle in that herd. It looked like a "roundup" when turning them off the bedding ground.

When we arrived at Beaver Creek, near Pease River, we had a terrible rain, a veritable cloudburst, raining all day, all night and all next day. The ground got so soft it was belly deep to a horse, and they would give out in a short distance, as tough as they were. For two days and nights we were without sleep. We were in the saddle all of the time except when we snatched a bite to eat, and to change saddle horses. The prairie was simply covered with prairie dogs, which had been run out of their homes in the ground by the water.

On this trip when we left Washita, we were expecting to find plenty of water at the South Canadian, and found it as dry as a powder house. That was nearly thirty miles through the hot sun dunes to Wolf Creek – sixty-five miles without any water. The cattle milled all night, suffering for water, and "lowed" piteously. Next morning we hit the trail early. Late that evening we arrived at the brow of the old slope, down to Wolf Creek, with six men ahead to hold the lead cattle back. They made a run for the water, which they had smelled for some distance, ran through an Indian camp, stampeding the Indians and their horses. Cattle and men all went off in the river together.

Here we sold the cows – about 500 – cutting them out of the great herd. Then we moseyed along up to Dodge on the Arkansas, camped just opposite old Fort Dodge, five miles down the river. Held there for ten days.

On the Fourth of July, 1880, about two o'clock, the awfulest hailstorm came up a man ever saw. The hailstones nearly beat us to death; it knocked over jackrabbits like taking them off with a rifle.

It even killed a few yearlings and many fleet antelopes, but the cow hands had to stick to their posts, although we nearly froze to death – on the Fourth of July.

We had knots and scars all over our hands and backs. The ice lay about four inches deep on the ground next morning.

Ten miles back, at Mulberry, next morning we found ourselves when day broke. It was so dark during that storm, in the daytime, that you could not see a man ten feet away. We had no supper nor breakfast; getting back to camp next morning at ten we found the cook fixing to leave, thinking surely that all the men had been killed. We were a hardy lot or we should have been, no doubt. No wonder "tenderfeet" did not survive those experiences.

I guess this about concludes my story. I met many brave and fearless men during those times. I want to say in conclusion that many of these men were tenderhearted and as gentle as a woman; they were rough outside but refined in heart and soul. Of all of them I shall always remember Mark Withers, who was always thoughtful of and a few thrilling incidents in my experience.

# His Father Made Fine 'Bowie' Knives

### by John James Haynes, San Antonio, Texas

I WAS BORN IN THE REPUBLIC OF TEXAS, Aug. 6, 1843, where Gonzales is now located. My father, Charles Haynes, who arrived in Texas some ten years previous, risked his life in helping Texas to gain her independence from Mexico. I was raised in Llano County, then on the frontier.

When I was quite small I was taught to ride, shoot, hunt and run wild cattle, and all the other things necessary to withstand the requirements of those strenuous times.

At a very early age my father presented each of his three sons with a gun, and as he was a mechanic and smith by trade, he made for each of us a long "Bowie" knife, and gave instructions how to use it. The rule in those days was to use the "Bowie" knife and save powder and shot.

I have been in many close quarters when that knife came in mighty handy, for in my time I have killed every kind of wild animal that roamed in this wild country.

Besides the wild animals we had worse foes to contend with – the savage Indians, who often made raids upon the white settlements. But as this writing is for our experiences with cattle on and off the trail, I will confine myself to those experiences.

When I was eighteen years old I joined the Confederate Army and was sent out of the state. I served the entire four years of that desperate struggle, and came home with a crippled arm. When we were discharged we were given transportation home, as far as the train went, and it didn't go far into Texas in those days.

We came by water to Galveston, and while our "high-up" officers were having a "peace treaty" somewhere in town, we "high up privates of the rear ranks" decided we had been away from home long enough, and as we did not see anything of special interest or excitement to us there, we concluded to leave the "peace subject" with the officers, so we captured a waiting train and ordered the engineer to "charge," which order was promptly obeyed.

When any of the boys reached a point anywhere near a beeline to his home, he would pull the bell-cord and drop off. I fell off at Brenham, which was the end of the road at that time.

From Brenham I went by stage to Austin and from Austin I took the "ankle express" for my home in Llano County, seventy-five miles away. After a tramp, tramp, tramp with the boys in gray for four long years, I was alone now, but the thoughts of getting home spurred me on, and I did not mind the fatigue as I covered the distance.

One night I stopped at what was known as "Dead Man's Water Hole," so called from the fact that the body of an unidentified man was once found there. I used a soft log that night for my pillow, and slept to the tunes of the hoot owls and the coyote wolves.

When I reached home I found my neighborhood was still being raided by hostile Indians. I was soon rigged out with a new saddle, horse and gun, and ready to defend my home against the red men. But I realized that I must seek a livelihood, so, in company with my younger brother, Charlie Haynes, and Harve Putman, we decided to go out and round up mavericks and drive them up the trail.

Each of us having secured two ponies and a pack horse and other equipment for a long camping trip, we started out, establishing our camp in the forks of the North and South Llano Rivers where Junction City now stands.

At that time there were no fences and very few ranches in that region. The cattle from the open country of the north and northwest had drifted into that wild and unsettled wilderness without being sought after and naturally had become very wild.

But we came with the intention of securing our herd, despite the wildness of the brutes. At a point near our camp we found a natural trap that was of material assistance to us. It consisted of a long strip of land about twenty-five feet wide, with a deep hole of water on one side and a very high bluff on the other.

This was the watering place for the cattle of that particular range. We built a pen and fenced in one end of this natural chute, leaving the other end open so that when a bunch of cattle came down for water we crowded in on them and ran them into our pen through the trap. We often started after them out on the range, and in order to get away from us, they would make for the water hole, and right into our trap they would go. We usually kept them in this pen without water or grass until they became tame enough to drive to our other pens some distance away, when, of course, they were then driven regularly for water and grazing. We kept this up until we had about 1,000 head of maverick yearlings.

Harve Putman and my brother, Charlie, decided to sell their undivided interest in these yearlings, and John Putnam and myself bought them for $2.50 per head, on credit, to be paid for on our return from the Kansas market.

We drove the herd by way of Fort Worth and crossed the Texas line at Red River Station. We put a bell on an old cow for a leader, and when a yearling got lost from the herd, and came within hearing of that bell it generally came back to the herd.

We reached Abilene, Kansas, with our yearlings in good shape, and we sold them for eight dollars per head. We found ourselves in possession of $8,000, and had started out without a dollar. But any old trail driver who found himself rich in Abilene, Kansas, in 1871, knows the rest.

In 1872 my brother, Charlie, and I took a mixed herd of about 1,000 head up the trail. This time we made a general roundup. It was the custom in those days for the party or parties getting up a roundup to take along cattle belonging to people they knew.

Owners were glad to have them driven to market and sold. The distance between ranches was so great that a consultation was not possible every time, and it was usually left to the driver's own judgment.

Be it said to the credit of those early cowmen, everyone was honest with his neighbor and trusted each other absolutely. The only requirement of the law was that the cattle be inspected by the county inspector, the marks and brands being recorded, and it was agreed among the stockmen that certain value be placed on certain grades, ages, etc., as assessed by the assessor.

After driving the cattle up the trail to market, we then, on our return home, paid for cattle as the claimants appeared, according to the assessment, our profit being the selling price, together with those not claimed or unknown.

Our second trip was somewhat different from the first one on account of having so many mixed cattle in the herd. They were easily stampeded by the smell of buffalo, and other things encountered on the trail.

We had several storms on this trip. The lightning during these storms seemed to be playing all over the heads and horns of the cattle, and the loud claps of thunder greatly disturbed them, and often caused a stampede.

When cattle stampede they all move in one direction, with the exactness and swiftness of one body. During a storm we would ride among them, doing our best to get them settled, but in the darkness of the night, the blinding rain, loud peals of thunder, with vivid flashes of lightning to keep them excited, our efforts were often of no avail.

When we saw that they were going, in spite of all we could do, we left two of our Mexican cow hands to "tough it out" with them. No matter how many miles away we found the herd the next day, the faithful Mexicans were still with it.

In a mixed herd many calves were born on the trip, and it was the custom to kill them before starting the herd each morning. Some outfits tried taking along a wagon for the purpose of saving the calves, but it did not pay.

We drove this second herd to Council Grove, Kansas, on the Indian reservation, and as we did not find ready sale, the businessmen of that place secured permission for us to hold them there until the market opened.

While we were in camp here an incident occurred that was a bit interesting to us. We had two Indian blankets, which my brother had captured during a fight with Indians in Blanco County, Texas, some years before. In this fight the chief of the tribe had been killed. We used the blankets for saddle blankets, and one day we hung them out to dry, when an Indian on the reservation came along and saw them. He called others, and they had a general pow wow over them, and the result was that they exchanged us two new government blankets for the Indian blankets.

That night the Indians all got together and had a big war dance around those blankets. We found out later that the two blankets in question had belonged to their chief. Although we anticipated trouble with the redskins on this account, we were not molested, and we remained here for some time.

As the market was crowded, we had to take our time and sell as the demand came for our cattle. In one deal we got a new wagon and a span of good mules. These mules were afterward stolen by Indians from my brother's home in Blanco County, during a raid when the Indians killed a man named Hadden.

# Scouting and Routing in the Good Old Days

### by J.M. Custer, Alias Bill Wilson

I WAS BORN IN 1865 and got my first experience on the cow range in 1876. Capt. Hall was moving cattle to West Texas from the Colorado River coast country, and as they passed through Live Oak County I joined them and worked with them through the fall of 1876.

In 1877 I went to work for Dillard Fant, and John Dumant was my boss. When Fant sold out to George West I worked in the Mustang Camp on Spring Creek catching wild horses and breaking them. In 1879 I went up the trail with horses for Mr. Neall, and we delivered at Dodge City, Kansas.

On our way up we had several stampedes, but had no trouble with the Indians. In 1880 I again went up the trail, this time to Ogallala, Nebraska, and we had skirmishes with the redskins.

One night I was on herd north of Doan's Store on Red River, near the mouth of Cold Water Creek, and had for a night mare a small Spanish mule. That mule smelled the Indians, his tail went right up against his belly, and it was impossible to hold him. In fact, I did not try to hold him, just let him take the lead through the darkness, and we traveled all night.

Next morning I found myself about twenty miles from camp. When I got back to the bunch we were short thirty-three head, so we started out to look for the lost horses.

The boss sent me up the creek to the divide where there was no timber to hide in, in case a fellow should get after a bunch of Indians. After riding about twenty-five miles up the creek, and reaching a point not far from the Indian Territory line, I discovered several Indians at a distance of about 200 yards coming toward me, but we did not meet, for their guns looked as long as the Chisholm Trail, and I did not care for them to get in closer range.

At that time I weighed only ninety-five pounds, but I picked up my pony on my spurs and when I let him down I went down his hind leg with my quirt. I pointed him back down the creek, with the yelling red devils in full chase, and I working in the lead.

My boss had often told me that in a stampede I should stay in the lead, and I was bent on carrying out his instructions. Finally, after I had raced them for several miles, I came to a crossing in the creek, which was about forty feet wide and in deep sand.

Here my horse gave up and refused to go further. I shook him up, but he had done his best, and that was all he could do. It was then up to me and the Indians to do the rest.

So I went into a small ravine, took the cartridges out of my belt and put them in my hat, and waited for a fight, but the red rascals went out of my sight, leaving me as mad as a hornet and wanting to scrap, for I had not had time to fight them during the chase.

I went back to South Texas in the fall of 1881, and worked on the mustang range again in 1882, when I got into trouble and had to leave that region, and was "on the dodge" for twelve years during which time I fought cattle for nine years almost night and day.

My little case of trouble caused a "moving" disposition to take a hold on me, and for two years it seemed that everywhere I went the officers were after me.

During those two years I went under my own name, from place to place, and state to state, but they chased me out, so I returned to the plains, changed my name to Bill Wilson, and went up the trail several times, until 1892.

During one of these drives I was in an Indian fight on the Canadian River. We had a stampede one night and lost a few head of cattle, and next day I was sent out to hunt for them. While riding down the river a bunch of Indians jumped me. We had a short race for a thicket of cottonwood trees. As usual, I worked in the lead, and when we got to the thicket I went into it like a rabbit.

There were seven Indians in the party, and they immediately surrounded the thicket. I had dismounted, and had my Winchester ready, so when I saw one of the redskins standing up on his horse, I raised old "Betsy" and cracked down, and there was a dead Indian. For about thirty minutes we had a pretty lively time. The battle ended with five dead Indians and one scalp scratch on my head.

In 1885 I took a herd for Chadman Brothers to Butte, Montana. I delivered the herd, shot up the town, and rode out to camp. The next morning I went back and asked the amount of damage I owed for shooting a saloon glass to pieces. The bartender said $1,500. We asked him to take a drink. We took one more, and then took off down the trail.

The next year, 1886, I had charge of a herd of stock cattle and started from Las Vegas, New Mexico, to Nebraska. On this trip I killed a smart Mexican in a shooting scrape. I went out of there under fire, but I held my ground, as all of the Mexicans in that region were on my drag.

But a boy raised on the frontiers of Texas always had a way to beat that kind of a game. As George Saunders said about Jack West: "If it did not go right, we always had a machine to make it go right."

The kind of a machine the cow-puncher had was sometimes called a "cutter," and sometimes it was called a "hog-leg," but it was better known as a six-shooter gun, and we frequently had a use for it, for it was a "friend in need" in those days. The Western boys always stood pat no draw pat or showdown.

I ran a maverick brand on the head of Double Mountain Fork, on the 00 Range. O.J. Warren was the owner. It got so big I lost my job and had to change my brand. That was my headquarters in winter after I got off the trail.

A great many so-called cowboys nowadays think it is fun to work cattle. It is really play, for they have nothing to do. In the early days we had no pens or railroads or wire fences. When we gathered cattle it was to hold them. Sometimes they would run all night.

The boss would yell out to us, "Sing to 'em, boys," and we would sing a song as only a cowboy can sing, but something would go wrong and they would be off on a rampage once more. The worse the weather the closer we would have to stay, for then was the time they gave the most trouble. Once I was on guard six days and nights without going to bed.

This was written in September 1919, just after I had passed through a great Gulf storm, in which we lost everything, house washed away, and everything lost. There are nine in my family, but I did not lose any of them.

We were in the storm for twenty hours and during that fearful period I thought of the old times on the trail, when the rain, hail and thunderstorms used to play such havoc with us.

Those were strenuous times, and we endured many hardships that will never be recorded for the perusal of oncoming generations, but, just the same, we had our day, and the world is better for it.

# An Indian Battle near the Leona River

*by L.A. Franks, Pleasanton, Texas*

IN 1865 OCCURRED ONE OF THOSE sad frontier tragedies where the settlers were unable to sustain themselves in an Indian battle, and wives and mothers were made to mourn for loved ones who never returned except as mangled or inanimate bodies. This noted fight occurred on the 4th day of July in the above named year near the mouth of the Leona River in Frio County.

The settlers in the vicinity at that time were the Martins, Odens, Franks, Bennetts, Hays, Parks, Levi English and Ed Burleson. These were all in what was known as the Martin Settlement.

On the morning in question Ed Burleson went out a short distance from his ranch to drive up some horses. He was unarmed and riding a slow horse. Suddenly and unexpectedly to him he was attacked by two Indians, who ran him very close, one on foot and the other mounted.

The one on foot outran the horseman and came near catching Burleson, but he ran through a thicket and, coming out on the side next his ranch, arrived there safely.

Quite a lot of people had collected at his house, men, women and children, to celebrate the Fourth and wind up with a dance. Ere the sun went down on that day, however, the festivities were changed into mourning. Instead of the gay tramp and joyous laughter of the dancers, wailing and the slow tread of a funeral procession was heard.

Excitement ran high when Burleson dashed in and gave the alarm. Most of the men mounted in haste to go in pursuit and others were notified. When all the men had congregated who could be gotten together on short notice, they numbered eleven and were as follows : Levi English, L.A. Franks, G.W. Daugherty, Ed Burleson, W.C. Bell, Frank Williams, Dean Oden, Bud English, Dan Williams, John Berry and Mr. Aikens. Levi English, being the oldest man in the party and experienced to some extent in fighting Indians, was chosen captain.

When the main trail was struck the Indians were found to be in large force, and going down the Leona River. They crossed this stream near Bennett's ranch, four miles from Burleson's. They then went out into the open prairie in front of Martin's ranch, ten miles further on.

The settlers first came in sight of them two miles off, but they went down into a valley and were lost to sight for some time. Suddenly, however, they came into view again not more than 200 yards away. They were thirty-six Indians, mounted two and two on a horse. The Indians now discovered the white men for the first time and at once commenced a retreat.

The white men were all brave frontiersmen and made a reckless and impetuous charge and began firing too soon. The Indians ran nearly a mile and, thinking likely they had well-nigh drawn the fire of the settlers, checked their flight at a lone tree at a signal from their chief, and each Indian who was mounted behind another jumped to the ground and came back at a charge, and for the first time commenced shooting.

The mounted ones circled to right and left and sent a shower of arrows and bullets. Some of the Indians went entirely around the white men and a desperate battle at close quarters ensued.

The red men had the advantage of the whites in point of numbers and shots. The latter, having nearly exhausted their shots at long range, had no time to reload a cap and ball pistol or gun in such a fight as was now being inaugurated.

Capt. English in vain gave orders during the mad charge, trying to hold the boys back and keep them out of the deadly circle in which they finally went. Dan Williams was the first man killed, and when he fell from his horse was at once surrounded by the Indians.

English now rallied the men together and charged to the body of Williams, and after a hot fight drove them back, but in so doing fired their last loads. The Indians were quick to see this, and came back at them again, and a retreat was ordered. Frank Williams, brother to Dan, now dismounted by the side of his dying brother and asked if there was anything he could do for him, and expressed a willingness to stay with him. "No," said the stricken man, handing Frank his pistol, "take this and do the best you can – I am killed – cannot live ten minutes. Save yourself."

The men were even now wheeling their horses and leaving the ground, and Frank only mounted and left when the Indians were close upon him. The Comanches came after them yelling furiously, and a panic ensued.

Dean Oden was the next man to fall a victim. His horse was wounded and began to pitch and the Indians were soon upon him. He dismounted and was wounded in the leg, and attempted to remount again, but was wounded six times more in the breast and back, as the Indians were on all sides of him.

Aus Franks was near him trying to force his way out, and the last he saw of Oden he was down on to his knees and his horse gone. The next and last man killed was Bud English, son of the late captain. His father stayed by his body until all hope was gone and all the men scattering away.

The Indians pursued with a fierce vengeance, mixing in with the whites, and many personal combats took place, the settlers striking at the Indians with their unloaded guns and pistols. In this fight all the balance of the men were wounded except Franks, Berry and Frank Williams. Capt. English was badly wounded in the side with an arrow; G.W. Daughtery was hit in the leg with an arrow; Ed Burleson also in the leg; Aikens in the breast; and W.C. Bell in the side.

In this wounded and scattered condition the men went back to the ranch and told the news of their sad defeat. Other men were collected and returned to the battleground to bring away the dead, led by those who participated but escaped unhurt. The three bodies lay within a hundred yards of each other and were badly mutilated.

The Indians carried away their dead; how many was not known, but supposed to be but few, on account of the reckless firing of the men at the beginning of the fight.

Bud English was killed by a bullet in the breast, and there was also one arrow or lance wound in the breast. The head of Dan Williams was nearly severed from the body, necessitating a close wrapping in a blanket to keep the members together while being carried back.

Oden and Williams were brothers-in-laws, and were both buried in the same box. Eight out of eleven were killed or wounded.

This is a very good description of the early day life in Texas.

# A Woman Trail Driver

*by Mrs. A. Burks, Cotulla, Texas*

MY HUSBAND, MR. W.F. BURKS, and I lived on a ranch at Banquette, Nueces County, during the days that Texas cattle could be marketed only by driving them over the old Kansas Trail. At this time in this section of the country good steers could be bought for fifteen dollars, and were often killed for the hides and tallow. The meat was fed to the hogs.

In the early spring of 1871 Mr. Burks rounded up his cattle and topped out 1,000 head of the best to take to market. Jasper Clark (better known as "Jap") was getting ready to take the Clark herd also, so they planned to keep the two herds not far apart.

They started in April with about ten cowboys each, mostly Mexicans, and the cooks. The cattle were road-branded at Pinitas and started on the familiar trail.

They were only a day out when Marcus Banks, my brother-in-law, came back with a note to me from Mr. Burks asking me to get ready as soon as possible and catch up with the bunch. He also said to bring either Eliza or Nick (black girl and boy who worked for us) to look out for my comfort, and suggested that Nick would be of more help than the girl.

So Nick and I started in my little buggy drawn by two good brown ponies and overtook the herd in a day's time. Nick, being more skilled than the camp cook, prepared my meals. He also put up my tent evenings, and took it down when we broke up camp.

It was intended that he should drive my horses when I was tired, but that was not necessary, for the horses often had no need of anyone driving them. They would follow the slow-moving herd unguided, and I would find a comfortable position, fasten the lines and take a little nap.

The cattle were driven only about ten miles a day, or less, so that they would have plenty of time to graze and fatten along the way. They were in good condition when they reached Kansas.

Except when I was lost, I left the bunch only once after starting. On this occasion I went to Concrete, where my sister lived, to have a tent made for the trip.

The night before our herd reached Beeville the Clark herd stampeded and never caught sight of us until we were way upstate.

All went pretty well with us till we neared Lockhart, and here we lost thirty cows in the timber. They were never recovered.

Whenever we came to timber we had to rush the cattle through, sometimes driving all day without stopping, for if they were scattered it was almost impossible to gather them again in the thick undergrowth.

Being springtime, the weather was delightful until we reached Central Texas. Some of the worst electrical and hailstorms I have ever witnessed were in this part and also in North Texas. The lightning seemed to settle on the ground and creep along like something alive.

Over in Bosque County late one evening a storm overtook us, and Mr. Burks drove me off into a more sheltered part of the timber. He unfastened the traces from the buggy and gave me the lines, but told me if the horses tried to run to let them go.

Hail had begun to fall by this time and he had to hurry back to help the men hold the frightened cattle. Harder and heavier fell the hail, and rain was pouring down in torrents.

The horses worked their way around to one side of the buggy, seeking protection, and it seemed that it would be only a few seconds until they pulled away from me entirely.

Determined not to let the horses go, I left the shelter of my buggy top and tied the horses with a rope I always carried with me. I got back in the buggy and sat there cold and wet and hungry and all alone in the dark. Homesick! This is the only time of all the months of my trip that I wished I was back on the old ranch at Banquette.

After what seemed ages to me I could hear the rumble of wagon wheels on the trail, and later still the sound of the beat of a horse's hoofs going the same way; but no one seemed to pay me any mind.

Later I learned that it was the cook driving the wagon, not knowing which way to go after being lost in the dark woods; and that Mr. Burks rode after him to bring him back to cook supper for the hungry men who had had nothing to eat since morning.

After I heard the return of the wagon the woods rang with the sound of Mr. Burks' voice calling me, and I lost no time in answering. It was one o'clock in the morning when I reached camp.

Mr. Burks and several of the others had big blood blisters on their hands caused by the hail. One of the boys said, "The beat of the hail on my head made me crazy. I would have run, but didn't know which way to go."

There were few people living along the trail, but when going through Ellis County we saw an old woman sitting in the doorway of a small house stringing beans.

We remarked to her that we saw very few women in that part of the country. She answered, "Yes, sir, I'm the first woman that made a track in Dallas County, and I would be back in Tennessee now, only I would have to go through Arkansas to get there. I guess I'll stay right here."

Once when we were camping in Johnson County I heard the bark of dogs followed by several rapid pistol shots. I ran to my tent to see what the trouble was. The Mexican who had charge of the cattle on this relay said that two dogs ran right in among the grazing herd and were about to stampede them when he shot them.

The owner of the dogs appeared soon after the shooting and seemed very downcast over his loss. He said he had "sure been having hard luck." He had first lost his two sons in the Civil War and had now lost his two dogs, which he had trained to keep cattle out of his tiny nearby field. We were sorry for the poor old man, but knew the Mexican did the right thing in preventing a stampede.

We camped a long time at Fort Worth, waiting for the Trinity River to fall low enough to cross our cattle. I counted fifteen herds here waiting to cross.

After we had crossed the Red River we seemed to have left all civilization behind. There were no more fresh fields, green meadows, and timber lands. The sun was so blistering that we hung a cloth inside the top of my buggy to break the heat that came through. Evenings and mornings were so cool that we were uncomfortable.

We had heard of the treacherous Indians and cattle rustlers of the Territory and were always on the lookout for them. The cattle and horses were kept well guarded.

One day one of the Mexican cowboys who was on guard duty fell asleep. Mr. Burks could not permit such negligence and told the man that he had to go. All the Mexicans notified Mr. Burks that if this man was "fired" that all would go with him. Of course there was no one else to be employed in this uninhabited territory, so we kept the man who had to have his afternoon nap.

We had no unpleasant experiences with the Indians, although they came to camp and tried to trade with the men. We narrowly escaped having trouble with a couple of what we supposed to be rustlers. While alone in camp one afternoon two men came up and were throwing rocks in among the grazing cattle. I called to them to stop and said, "Don't you know you'll stampede those cattle," and they answered, "That's what we're trying to do." Just then some of the men rode up and the rustlers left hurriedly.

Mr. Burks always kept his horse saddled at night so that he would be ready to go at a word from the boys. As he often helped the men watch the cattle when they were restless, I was sometimes alone in my tent till late at night. On these occasions I sat up fully dressed for any emergency.

On one of these nights it was thought that Indians were near, so a guard was left at my tent, but he was soon called to help with the cattle. A man from the other camp begged me to go over to his camp and stay until the trouble was over, but I told him I preferred my own tent. The men thought me very brave to stay alone at such a time.

Both the Clark and our herds were stampeded one day, supposedly by Indians. It was a horrible yet fascinating sight. Frantic cowboys did all in their power to stop the wild flight, but nothing but exhaustion could check it.

By working almost constantly the men gathered the cattle in about a week's time. They were all thrown into one big herd, and the roar of hoof-beats of 2,000 milling cattle was almost deafening. The herd was divided into two, then worked back and forth until every cow was in her rightful bunch.

After an experience of this kind the men would be almost exhausted. I felt so sorry for one of them, Branch Isbell, a young tenderfoot, that I persuaded Mr. Burks to let him rest. The boy lay down and was soon sleeping so soundly that he did not hear us breaking camp, and we forgot him when we left. I wanted someone to go back and wake him, but Mr. Burks said that it would be only a little while till he appeared again.

The boy overtook us late in the evening, and said that he would not have awakened then if an approaching herd had not almost ran over him.

We seemed to be pursued by fire during our entire trip. The first night we were in the territory Mr. Burks and I went to sleep, leaving a candle burning, and before we were awakened a box full of trinkets and small articles, including my comb, were in a blaze.

On one occasion a prairie fire ran us out of camp before breakfast. We escaped by fleeing to a part of the plain, which had been burned before, called "a burn" by people of that section.

Two days later my ignorance was the cause of an immense prairie fire. I thought I would build a fire in a gulley while the cook had gone for water. Not later than I had struck the match than the grass all around was in a blaze, which spread so quickly that the men could not stop it. They succeeded in beating out the flanks of the fire so that it did not spread out at the sides at the beginning.

The fire blazed higher than a house and went straight ahead for fifty miles or more. Investigators came next day to find out who the culprit was, and when they learned that it was a woman, nothing was said, except for a remark one of the men made that he was glad that he didn't strike that match.

Once when we were encamped on Emmet Creek a fire crept upon us so quickly that the men barely had time to break up camp and get the cattle to safety. There was not time enough to harness the horses to my buggy, so the men tied ropes to it, told me to jump in, and we again fled to a burn. Birds and animals fled with us before the flames.

Many of the prairie fires were started by squatters on land who wanted to keep strangers away. They would plough a safety boundary around their stake and then set fire to the grass outside.

Fuel was very scarce because of these fires and the cook often had to go miles to get enough to cook a meal.

We crossed many nice cool streams whose banks were covered with wild plums. I noticed the ripe ones first when crossing the Washita, and wanted to stop to gather some. Mr. Burks wasn't ready to stop, so told me that the Indians were very troublesome at this place, and I needed no coaxing to start the horses on.

Later, when we came to the Canadian River, the red, blue, and yellow plums were so tempting I had one of the Mexicans stop with me to gather some. We wandered farther away from the buggy than I realized, and when we had gone back a short way I thought the horses had run away and left us. I was panic stricken, but the Mexican insisted that we go farther upstream, and we soon found the horses standing just as they were left. I forgot my scare when the cook served me with delicious plum pie made from the fruit I had gathered.

Being the only woman in camp, the men rivaled each other in attentiveness to me. They were always on the lookout for something to please me, a surprise of some delicacy of the wild fruit, or prairie chicken, or antelope tongue.

In the northern part of the territory we left the trail a while to graze the cattle, and I drove on ahead of the bunch to a stream. "Jap" Clark motioned to me to stop, but I misunderstood him and thought he meant "go on," and plunged my horses in the swollen creek. One of the horses stumbled and fell, but was on his feet in a moment, and somehow I was jolted across to the other side. I was the subject of much chaffing because of this alleged attempt to break my neck. The crossing was so bad that the banks had to be chopped down to make it safe for crossing the cattle.

On the banks of the Arkansas River we saw two Yankees who called themselves farmers. When we asked to see their farms they showed us two plots about the size of a small garden. They said they had never farmed before, and we easily believed them. Vegetables were a great treat to us, so we bought some from the "farmers" and enjoyed them immensely.

The camp cook on this trip was a very surly Negro. He was a constant source of trouble, and everybody was glad when he was "fired" and a white man took his place. I heard a commotion in the camp kitchen one day and when I looked out of the tent door I saw the cook with a raised axe and a Mexican facing him with a cocked pistol. Mr. Burks rode up in time to prevent a killing.

We were three months on the trail when we arrived at Emmet Creek, twenty-two miles from Newton, Kansas. We summered here, as did several other Texas ranchmen. Market had broken, and everybody that could do so held his cattle hoping for a rise.

While going to town we would often stop at the different camps for a few minutes' chat.

On stormy and rainy nights a candle always burned in my tent to guide the men. One very stormy night Mr. Burks had to help the men hold the cattle, and he saw the light in the tent flare, then all was black. He rushed through the rain to the place where the tent was and found it flat on the ground, me buried under it, unhurt.

The rain had softened the ground and the wind easily blew the tent down. That night all the matches got wet and it was late next morning before we got others with which to start a fire.

When cold weather came the market was still low and Mr. Burks decided to winter his cattle, with others he had bought, on Smoky River.

Mr. Burks wanted me to stay in town at Ellsmore, but after being there a few days, and witnessing another fire in which a hotel and several residences were burned, I preferred camp.

A man who lived some distance from camp was paid to feed the horses through the winter, but soon after we heard that he was starving them. A boy was sent to get them and as he was returning, the first severe snowstorm of the season overtook him at nightfall and he had to take refuge for himself and horses in a wayside stable.

Next morning he was awakened by a commotion among the horses, and found the owner of the stable trying to punch out the horses' eyes with a pitchfork. Such was the hatred felt for strangers in this region.

Nine horses were lost in this snowstorm. Many of the young cattle lost their horns from the cold. Blocks of ice had to be chopped out of the streams in order that the cattle could drink.

The first taste of early winter in Kansas decided Mr. Burks to sell his cattle and leave for sunny Texas as soon as possible, and he met with no discouragement of his plans from me, for never had I endured such cold.

So in December we left Kansas, dressed as if we were Esquimaux, and carrying a bucket of frozen buffalo tongues as a souvenir for my friends in Texas.

Our homeward journey was made by rail to New Orleans via St. Louis, and by water from New Orleans to Corpus Christi via Galveston and Indianola. I arrived home in much better health than when I left it nine months before.

Please don't think, now that I've finished telling the few stories of my trip over the Old Kansas Trail, that the journey was one of trials and hardships. These incidents served to break the monotony of sameness of such a trip.

One day Mr. Von said as we were resting along the way, "In the heat of the day, when I am riding behind my cattle, I think of you and am sorry for you," and added, as I hope you will, "but when I see your smile of happiness and contentment I know all my sympathy is wasted."

What Mr. Von said is true. For what woman, youthful and full of spirit and the love of living, needs sympathy because of availing herself of the opportunity of being with her husband while at his chosen work in the great out-of-door world?

# The Experience of an Old Trail Driver

*by Richard (Dick) Withers of Boyes, Montana*

I WAS RAISED ON MY FATHER'S RANCH eight miles north of Lockhart, Caldwell County, Texas, and made my first trip up the trail in 1869. Col. J.J. Myers, who had a ranch near my father's, had a large stock of cattle, and after the war he commenced to drive them north, and that year I gathered 110 steers and put them in one of the herds, Billie Campbell being boss.

I traded a beef steer for a pair of goat-skin leggings, bought a slicker and a pair of blankets and started up the trail. I was then eighteen years old. We crossed the Colorado River below Austin, went by Georgetown, Belton and Waco, where we had to swim the Brazos, crossed Red River and struck the Chisholm Trail.

Right there is where I ran my first antelope, and thought it was crippled. I was riding a bay horse I called "Buck," so I took down my rope and Buck and I lit out after the antelope, but we did not go far until we quit the chase and went back to the herd.

We had a stampede in the territory while Noah Ellis and myself were on herd together. In the run that followed my horse fell with me, and I thought the steers would run over me.

But I soon learned that steers will not run over a man when he is down under foot. They will run all around a fellow, but I have yet to hear of a man being run over by them. Ellis and I held those cattle all night.

After we got rounded up the next day we moved on to the Arkansas River, where we found three herds belonging to Billie Campbell, Dan Phillips and John Bunton, who were traveling together. The river was up and no ferry to help us across, so we had to swim the stream.

We made a raft to carry our wagons and supplies over, which took some time. This was at a point fifty or a hundred miles below Wichita, then consisting of a supply store, post office and saloon, all in dugouts.

We went from there to Abilene, Kansas, our destination, where we sold our cattle and started for home.

M.A. Withers and J.W. Montgomery had a large number of cattle at home and I had a good bunch, so in 1870 we gathered a herd together. George Hill was also with us, and Bill Montgomery, George Hill and myself started with them to Abilene, Kansas. In those days 1,000 head was considered a large herd, but we had 3,500 head in that herd, and it was called "the big herd" all the way.

A few days after we crossed this stream we had a big stampede, in which we lost some cattle and had to lay over a day while George Hill and myself went to look for the missing cattle. Returning to camp that night, my horse gave out and I was compelled to roost in a thicket the remainder of the night while George went on to camp, a distance of about five miles.

We had two wagons and two cooks with us, Uncle Gov. Montgomery and Jerry Head.

A few days after the stampede mentioned above, the wagons went ahead of the herds to get dinner, and when they made camp a bunch of Indians came up, and when I arrived at camp I found Uncle Gov. and Jerry were about to give them all the tobacco and coffee we had. I gave them only a portion of our coffee and tobacco and they left.

All went well until we got to the North Canadian, which was also on a rise, and we had to swim our cattle across. There being three herds of us together, we all made a raft to carry our wagons over.

Our herd was in the lead, and when the cattle reached the opposite bank and started out the embankment gave away and 116 head of the cattle were drowned before we could turn them back. We found another going-out place and all three herds made it across all right. When we commenced the getting of wagons over with the three outfits there was a general mix-up.

Somebody in the other outfit had a big lot of Confederate money, and Doom, a silly Negro that was with us, found this money, $10,000 in large bills, and he hid it, and if we had not been on the north side of the river he would have left us and tried to make away with it. He showed the money to me and I told him it was worthless. I do not know what he did with it, but we would have lost Doom if the river had not been up.

We moved on and crossed the Arkansas River at Wichita, then on to Abilene, our destination. There Montgomery sold his cattle, to be delivered in Idaho, beyond the Snake River. George Hill, W.F. Montgomery, Bill Henderson and George Mohle left for Texas, while Bill Montgomery and myself started with the herd to Idaho.

We went from Abilene to the Big Blue River, from there to the South Platte, below South Platte City, going up that stream to Julesburg, and crossed the river, from there to the South Platte, below South Platte City. We had to have the oxen shod at Cheyenne, as the gravel had worn their hoofs to the quick. After leaving Cheyenne we struck the North Platte River below Fort Fetterman.

A few days before we got to Fetterman we made a long drive to water, and when we reached the water, there being no other herds there, we turned our herd loose that night. During the night a herd of 500 big, fat steers came in, which were being driven to Fetterman, and the drivers, not knowing we were there, turned their herd loose also and mixed with our herd.

The next morning we told them that as we were going to Fetterman, they could cut them out when we reached that place. When we arrived at Fetterman we rounded up our herd for them and they went to cutting out, but as they were tenderfeet, they did not succeed very well, and now and then one would come back on them.

You old Texas cowboys know what it means for a wild Texas steer to come back on you.

When they were through cutting there were sixteen of those big fat steers in our herd, which they could not cut out, and we told them our horses were "all in," and we could not cut them, so I made a trade with them, giving sixteen head of lean cattle for their fat ones, and they sure came in mighty handy, as will be shown later on.

We went up the North Platte and struck across to Sweetwater, following the old California immigrant trail, going by the Enchanted Rock and Devil's Gate. There the cook broke one of the ox yokes and we could not get one, so we had to camp and cut down a small cottonwood tree to make a yoke with a dull axe and the king bolt of the wagon to burn the holes with. Bill assigned that job to me.

It took me all evening and all night to burn the six holes in the yoke. We pulled out the next day, and all went well until we reached the Rocky Mountains. It was forty miles across these mountains and 200 miles around, so we decided to go across them. This was in October and the weather had been good, but we were getting short of grub.

The first night in the mountains there came a snowstorm, and twenty-five of our horses died and our cattle scattered considerably. All we could do was to push them in the old trail from each side and let them drift along. At this time our sixteen fat steers came in might handy, for when our supply of provisions gave out we began killing them. The meat would freeze in just a little while, so we lived on nothing but beef for over a month.

We had no flour, salt or coffee, and nowhere to purchase these things. Only a few trappers and miners were in the country, and they did not have enough to supply us. Our horses all gave out and we had to walk and drive our diminishing herd. We had plenty of money, but could not buy any horses because there were none to buy.

However, one day a miner came along with eight big U.S. mules, and Bill purchased them. We thought those big mules would relieve our troubles, but when I saddled one of them and went after the cattle he did not last an hour, for he could not climb the mountains.

We managed to secure a few more horses from miners, and after pushing on for another ten days we reached Salt Valley, where we laid over for several days while three of the men went back into the mountains to gather up cattle we had left, numbering about 300 head.

Bill Montgomery pulled on with the herd and I took a man and a pack mule and also went back into the mountains to try to gather more of the missing cattle. I found about fifty of them and hired a trapper to take them to Ogden, while I and my man returned to overtake the main herd, which was about ten days ahead of us. We camped one night near a big lake on the trail and next morning we found the tracks of a big grizzly bear in the snow within ten yards of where we slept. We had our heads covered up, and I suppose he could not smell us as he passed our camp.

We did not overtake the herd until they reached Snake River. There Noah Ellis, who had taken one herd on to the man we had sold to, returned to us. From there on we had no trouble, but soon reached our destination and delivered the cattle to Mr. Shelly. Bill Montgomery then bought 150 mules from Shelly, paying $75 to $100 each for them, and started them to Branyon to ship them to Missouri, where he expected to sell them for good prices.

I took stage for Ogden to get the cattle I had sent there by the trapper, and when I arrived there I sold the cattle and went on to Branyon to meet Bill. I had to wait several days for him to arrive, and when he got there, Noah Ellis and I pulled out for Texas, arriving at Lockhart on Christmas Eve.

In the spring of 1871 my brother, M.A. Withers, and I gathered a herd and started it to Kansas, but when we reached Belton we sold the herd and I returned home.

In 1873 M.A. Withers, Bill Montgomery and myself drove two herds to market. I was boss of one herd, and a man named Page bossed the other. That was the wettest year I ever saw on the trail. It rained all the time and we had to swim every stream from Red River on.

At Fort Worth the cook broke a wagon wheel and after we got it fixed and went on some distance further he broke another wheel. Red River was on a big rise, and the stream was lined with herds, for no herd had been able to cross for a week or more.

I asked some of the bosses of the herds there if they were going to tackle the river, and they said they were not, so I told them to give me room and I would tackle it, for I would rather undertake the crossing than to take chances on a mix up of the herds. They all gave room and helped me to start the cattle into the water.

I strung my herd out, had them take the water several hundred yards above where I wanted them to come out. I never saw cattle swim nicer than those steers; they kept their heads and tails out of the water. I ferried my horses across.

We proceeded on our way and when we reached the Washita and Canadian Rivers they were high also, but as they were small streams we had no difficulty in crossing them. Before we reached the Arkansas River I killed a buffalo cow and roped her calf. Intending to take the calf with me, I necked it to a yearling, but it was so wild and stubborn it fought until it died.

After crossing the Arkansas at Great Bend I pulled on to Ellsworth, where I found brother Mark with the front herd, and we delivered our cattle, sent our horses back to Texas and returned home by rail.

In 1874 I sold all of my cattle to Driscoll & Day of Austin, Texas.

My next drive was in 1879, when I bossed a herd for Jim Ellison, which was delivered to Millett Brothers at their ranch on the Brazos River, north of Fort Griffin.

The herd was the first to cross the Colorado at Webberville. For about ten miles after crossing the river the country was brushy, but other herds followed us and soon made a good trail through there.

We went by way of Georgetown, up the Gabriel and on toward Brownwood. Near Brownwood we turned north, struck the Western Trail near Albany, and on to Fort Griffin to the Millett Ranch and delivered the herd. When we started back with the horses I received a telegram from Mr. Ellison instructing me to take stage for Fort Worth and hasten home, as he had another herd for me to take to Ogallala, Nebraska. When I arrived at the ranch Mr. Ellison had two herds, which he had purchased from Bob Stafford at Columbus.

Bill Jackman was to take one of those herds to the Millett Ranch on the Brazos, so we traveled together, and when we reached Millett's ranch he would not take the cattle, so we threw the two herds together and drove them to Ogallala. We had 5,500 head in this herd, and it was the largest herd ever seen on the trail.

It was getting late in the season and water was scarce. We had nine men besides myself, the cook and the horse rustler. All went well until we reached Red River at Doan's Store. There one of my men was taken sick and two of the hands quit, leaving me with only six men to handle the herd. But we made it all right until we reached the Washita River, which was the last water until we got to the Canadian River, a distance of about thirty miles.

I made a long drive after leaving the Washita, made a dry camp, expecting to reach the Canadian the next day. But we made slow progress as the weather was hot and we were short three men.

About three o'clock the next day after leaving the Washita we were within five miles of the Canadian and the big herd was strung out about four miles. They were as dry as fishes.

You old-timers know what that means. We were going up a long divide, the wind was from the west, and about a half mile west of us were some alkali springs. The herd smelled the water from these springs, and back about the middle of the herd they began to break away and go for that water. Right then I thought Mr. Ellison's open Y's would be scattered clear to the Red River.

The old-timers know that you had just as well try to handle a bunch of mixed turkeys as to try to keep a thirsty herd away from water. We found good grass at these springs and stopped there for the night and the Indians ran off thirty head of them for us. Next morning I took the trail and went back about five miles to look for the cattle, and when I came up with them I found that the red rascals had killed one old stag. I took the others back to the herd. We reached the Canadian about noon.

When I arrived at Dodge City, Kansas, I hired three men to help us take the herd on to Ogallala, about eighteen days' drive. Mr. Ellison met me at Ogallala and sold the cattle, to be delivered at Sidney Bridge on the North Platte.

After replenishing our grub supply, we pulled on and struck the North

Platte, which we followed up to the Narrows. The "Narrows" is a name given to a ledge of hills, which run from the divide to the North Platte River. A herd cannot be driven over these hills, but is forced to travel up the bed of the river for about a mile.

The North Platte is a treacherous stream, and full of quicksand. We had to send our chuck wagon around over the hills, and it required all day for the wagon to make the trip.

Just above the Narrows, in the valley, we found about one hundred graves, which I was told mark the resting place of men killed in a fight with Indians. From here we traveled up a beautiful valley all the way to Sidney Bridge, where we delivered the cattle, returned to Ogallala, paid off the men, and all hit the train for Texas.

During the fall and winter of 1880 I bought cattle in Bastrop and Lee counties for Mr. Ellison. In the spring of that year I drove another herd of the Y cattle for him, making the start in April.

This was a very dry year on the trail. While crossing the Washita we broke a wagon wheel and had to use a pole drag for 150 miles to Wolf Creek. As there was no grass in Kansas and it began raining, I laid over on Wolf Creek and sent the wheel fifty miles down the creek to have it fixed. We rested here two weeks.

After leaving the Canadian I went ahead of the herd about five miles looking for grass and water and was overtaken by about 500 Indians. I felt a bit scared as they came up, and they wanted tobacco, and I willingly gave them all I had and moved back to my herd.

As we proceeded on our journey Mr. Ellison came to meet us in a buggy. He remained all night with us, and we slept on a pallet together. Mr. Ellison undressed, but I did not, as I always slept with my entire outfit on, pants, boots and spurs, so as to be prepared for any emergency.

During the night the cattle made a run, and when I started to get up one of my spurs caught in Mr. Ellison's drawers and he was rather painfully spurred. The next morning we cut out the weakest cattle in our herd and Mr. Ellison sent them back to his Panhandle Ranch.

I have been around cattle during many bad nights, but the night Otis Ivey was killed by lightning was the worst one I ever experienced. Ivey and his horse and about twenty head of cattle were killed during the storm. Mr. Lytle sent out from Dodge after his body and had it sent to his mother in West Fork, Caldwell County, Texas.

We often used lanterns around the herds at night, but on that night a lantern was not needed, for the lightning flashed so continuously and so bright we could see everything plainly and smell burning brimstone all the time.

When we reached Dodge we had our last grass, for there was not enough on the range to feed a goose. From Fort Dodge to Stinking Water was usually fifteen days' drive, but I made it that year in twelve days. I would leave the bed ground in the morning, drive until noon, round up in the trail for two or three hours, drive on until night and round up again.

For twelve days the cattle had no grazing, but had plenty of water. Cattle, if given plenty of water, can go a long while with but little to eat. But unless you give them water at least every twenty-four hours you will have trouble. After reaching Stinking Water we had plenty of grass and we grazed them on to Ogallala.

I had to wait at Ogallala for Sam Moore, for Mr. Ellison had told us to take some steers to a man near the Red Cloud Agency. Bill Jackman came up and Mr. Ellison told us the contract called for 1,000 cows, 1,000 yearling steers and not less than 700 two-year-old steers.

He found us cutting some long yearlings for twos, and said, "Dick, a Texan is going to receive those cattle, and he knows ones from twos." Anyway, we cut and got our supply, then pulled out over to the North Platte up to Sidney Bridge, then followed the Deadwood road.

When near the Red Cloud Agency I saw my first Indian buried on a scaffold. I was ahead of the herd at the time, and saw something I took for a well and, being pretty dry, I decided to go to it and get a drink. But instead of being a well it was a dead Indian on a scaffold. It was the custom of the Indians to bury in that fashion, and everything the dead Indian had owned in life was left there. After that we saw a great many Indian graves like that.

Reaching the ranch where we were to deliver these cattle I found the Texan that Mr. Ellison said knew one-year-old steers from twos, and we went to work classing the cattle. We never disagreed on a single steer, and when we were through I found that out of 1,000 yearlings and 700 twos, I had delivered 800 ones and 900 twos.

When we got back to Ogallala I gave Mr. Ellison the receipt, and after looking at it he said, "Dick, bring all the boys to the hotel for dinner," and he paid my fare home.

Early in January, 1881, I commenced buying cattle for Mr. Ellison. That year, when starting up the trail, I went through the mountains by way of Llano and Brady City. I had bought 500 head on the Colorado near Buffalo Gap and had to take that route to receive them. They had been gathered when I reached there, so I road-branded them and pulled out for Fort Griffin, Doan's Store on Red River, Dodge City, and Ogallala. When we reached Ogallala Mr. Ellison told me he had 6,500 cattle he wanted me to take to Belle Fourche, Wyoming, deliver them and bring the horses back to Ogallala, sell them, pay the men off, and return home.

So I got my supplies, pointed the herd over to the North Platte, followed that stream up to Sidney Bridge, where we took the Deadwood road to Running Water, then turned west to Crazy Woman, thence to the Cheyenne, up that river to Lodge Pole, leaving the Black Hills and Devil's Tower to our right. Then there was nothing there but a ranch, but now there is a railroad and the town of North Craft.

I am living at Boyes, Montana, now about one hundred miles from where I delivered those cattle on the Belle Fourche River below the old ranch. I went from Lodge Pole down the canyon to the Belle Fourche River, and within a week had the cattle branded and delivered.

That was in September, and as some of the boys wanted to wash up before starting back to Ogallala, several of our outfit went buffalo hunting and we killed all the buffalo we wanted. Those were the last buffalo I have seen.

In 1882 Mr. Ellison sent me to East Texas and Louisiana to buy cattle, as they were getting scarce in our country. I bought two trainloads and shipped them from Longview, Texas, to Kyle. In March we began rounding up for the spring drive. Mr. Ellison said he wanted me to drive a herd of beef cattle, and told me to pick out my remuda. Out of 500 horses I selected ninety head of the best that ever wore the Y brand. I started on this trip with 3,520 fours and over, and delivered 3,505.

Mr. Ellison asked me just before we started when I would get to Dodge City. I figured a while, and then told him June 10th. He said he didn't think I could make it by that date, "But," he added, "if you do, you can make it to Deadwood, South Dakota." He informed me that it was an Indian contract and had to be made on time. "You make it on time and I will pay your way home and give you a good suit of clothes," said Mr. Ellison. I got my clothes and my fare paid back home.

That was the most enjoyable trip I ever made. I could drive as far in a day as I wanted to. Those steers walked like horses, and we made good time all the way. Mr. Ellison went broke that year.

# Days Gone By

*by Hiram G. Craig, Brenham, Texas*

IT WAS IN THE YEAR OF 1850 that my father and mother, John and Caroline Craig, decided to make their home in that great state of the future – Texas.

Suiting the words with action, they hitched up their two bay (baldfaced) mares to the wagon, taking such belongings as were absolutely necessary, and started on the long and perilous journey from Tennessee to Texas. Their destination was Washington County, and they landed in the western part, in the neighborhood called Sandtown – so named by my uncle.

My parents must have suffered many hardships in those days of privations, raising as they did, a large family of seven boys and two girls. My father was a teamster. He hauled freight with an ox team from Houston to Austin, hauled cotton from Washington County to Brownsville, on the Rio Grande, and hauled salt, loose in the wagon bed, on his way back from the King Ranch, home. He made several trips to Brownsville, and also, one to Eagle Pass, Texas.

I remember one trip I made with him from our home to Alleyton, Colorado County. This was our nearest railroad station, and at that time the terminus of the Southern Pacific Railway. We were hauling cotton. In those days wagons had wooden axles with an iron skean, and linchpins to hold the wheels on the axle.

On these trips father would take one horse along to round up the oxen. At night, or when camping, he would have a bell for each yoke of oxen, would neck them and put a hobble on one of the oxen of each yoke. I made a number of short trips with my father, as I could be of some help in rounding up the oxen and hold them while he put the yoke on them.

Often he would also be breaking in a yoke or two of wild oxen. On this particular trip when we got as far as Frelsburg, where we broke an axle, and as there were few people living in the country at that time, we were in a bad way. No houses, no tools to work with, not a blacksmith within twenty miles.

Here my father accomplished something that nine men out of ten of these days and times would fail in. The only tool at hand was an axe. With this axe father cut down a hickory tree, cut it the proper length, and with the axe hewed out an axle. He got on his horse and rode to the next neighbor, where he got an auger.

At that time such a thing as a "brace and bit" were unheard of. With the auger he bored the holes for the hound and skean and put the wagon together. He unloaded and loaded the cotton by himself, as I was too small to do any lifting. We wound up our trip by delivering the cotton to the railway company and returned home to Washington County.

I used to plow many, many a day with a single ox and a plow, made entirely of wood, with the exception of the point, which was of iron. Even the moldboard (the part that turns the dirt) was of timber.

Father would cut a short piece of some twisted oak tree, split it open – which would almost have the shape, then hew it down to fit the point of iron and attach the handles with wooden pins – and the plow would work fine.

A word about my dear mother: During the Civil War such things as clothing, shoes, flour, salt, sugar and coffee were scarce and high – very often not to be had at any price. Flour was selling at twenty dollars per barrel.

Mother, my oldest sister and my second oldest brother, carded the roll and mother spun the thread that made our clothes during the war. The work allotted to me was to hand the threads through the sleigh – at which I became quite an expert. If these threads, in any way became crossed, they would not weave.

Often mother would send me to the neighbor ladies to help them with this line of work. I also peeled the blackjack bark and gathered the wild indigo to dye the cloth that made our clothes. My second oldest brother was a cripple and could not work in the field, so mother kept him in to help her with the weaving. In my mind I can still see my mother at the old spinning wheel.

The young people of today do not realize what "hard times" are. Imagine that most of the flour you were to see would be a feast of biscuits on a Sunday morning for breakfast, and then some more the next Sunday morning.

Imagine for your coffee a substitute of corn, roasted potato peeling and cornmeal bran. These were some of our luxuries. Of meats we were more bountifully blessed. Cattle were more plentiful and cheap; pork was more abundant. Hogs were running loose in the woods, and the mast was so good that hogs were generally fat in winter.

Father died at Bellville, Texas, at the age of fifty-four, and mother died in Washington County at the age of forty-four. This left the family in the hands of my oldest brother, who faithfully and conscientiously administered to our wants until we were able to take care of ourselves.

I was born at Sandtown in 1855 and lived here with my parents to the end of the Civil War, when we moved to Bellville, Austin County, Texas.

Father was the proud possessor of a small bunch of cattle, and created a desire in me to be a cowboy to have a good horse, saddle, leggings, spurs and to handle cattle. At fourteen years of age I ran away from home and went to work for Foster Dyer of Richmond, known as one of the biggest ranch owners of that time.

I was proud of my job, which, however, was of short duration. My brother learned of my whereabouts and came and took me home. I remained at home with my parents for three years, when the call to the "wild" again overcame me.

This time it was T.J. Carter, who was studying to be a doctor, and I, that went on a wild goose chase in 1872. We landed at Sweet Home and hired out to George West, to help gather a herd of steers for the trail for Kansas.

We gathered between 1,500 and 2,000 head of steers. There were no pens or corrals to hold such a large herd. We held and herded these steers on the prairie by day and by night. The boys would herd them in shifts, or reliefs; one shift of men would herd them from four to six hours (according to the number of shifts), when the next shift would relieve them, so that the cattle would be continually guarded.

This work is hard and trying, and at our age seemed severe; however, we stayed with the herd until they were actually started on the trail, and then went home to Washington County. Carter went back to his profession, and is today a practicing physician in Fayette County, having made good.

In the fall of 1873 J.D. McClellan and I went to Oakville, Live Oak County, and worked for Andrew Nations and his son, Bob Nations, helping them gather 1,500 stocker cattle to be moved to the Wichitas. Our headquarters were at Sulphur Creek, about ten miles north of Oakville. We gathered up and down the Nueces River, as far down as Lagarto. We were short of cowhands – who were hard to get.

Bob Nations decided to make a trip to San Antonio and get the necessary complement of men. The best he could do was to get a bunch of "brakemen," as he called them. These men were no good at riding or at handling cattle, being unaccustomed to the work.

We were holding the herd on a prairie near the Nueces River bottom. The cattle were wild and some of them would make a break every now and then and, as sure as an animal would make a run, the trained cow pony, with his "brakeman," would take after it – and we would be minus a "brakeman."

Tom Johnson was our trail boss. He was one of the best men I ever knew, when it came to handling stock cattle on the trail. He taught me every detail in "grazing" a herd. Johnson was very fractious and hard to get along with, and Bob Nations said he doubted very much in our going through on the trip with Johnson.

The herd was started early in the spring with Johnson as foreman, everything progressing nicely. We were obliged to swim all the rivers on account of heavy spring rains, but suffered no loss of cattle. We reached Lockhart and then Onion Creek, near Austin. Here at Onion Creek we had a little stampede, for which I was blamed. It brought on words between the foreman and I. Naturally, I was discharged and McClellan quit.

Bob took McClellan and me on to Austin, and asked us to accompany him and his family west, and assured us work as long as we cared to stay. As he started out of Austin we told him we would overtake him on the way later. But, alas, there was a drawing card back home, in Washington County, that was stronger than even a promise. McClellan had a girl there and so did I, so we went home.

That summer J.W. Nunn bought out a meat market in Brenham, and McClellan went to work for him, while I did the buying and supplying of livestock for the market. McClellan lived only three months after that, leaving me without a pal. I continued working for Nunn.

In June, 1876, we gathered about 1,400 head of Nunn's cattle and started for the Plains. We left Dime Box, Lee County, June 10, 1876. We herded the cattle on the first night at Lexington, Lee County, in a wide lane. The second night we camped near Beaukiss in the woods. There were two of the Nunn boys, both much older than I, but neither they nor any of the other hands had ever "bedded" a herd.

It was up to me to take charge of my first large herd. We rounded the cattle into a circle in the woods, dragging logs around the bed grounds and built fires. There were clouds rising and about eleven o'clock that night it began thundering, lightning and raining. The cattle got restless and stampeded, running all night. The third day we crossed the Brushy Creek, camping near the Olive pens on the Taylor prairie. From here on we had plenty of open country and could handle the herd more easily.

We had many ups and downs, being short of horses. Our horses got very poor and were worn out from overwork; also the cattle got thin in flesh by the time we got to Buffalo Gap in July, and we were also out of provisions, no beef, no coffee, no money. Nunn borrowed a small sum from one Ben Anderson, one of our hands, and started me off with one yoke of oxen for Coleman City, sixty miles distant, to lay in a supply of "grub."

I bought mostly breadstuffs and coffee, returning to camp a week later. This left us still shy of meat, our cattle being too poor for slaughter. We were told that fifty or sixty miles west there were lots of buffalo, so Nunn got us to rig up a wagon and to go on to the Sweetwater Creek to kill some fat buffalo.

We engaged a man by the name of Jim Green at Buffalo Gap, who was a buffalo hunter, and he was to pilot us to the Sweetwater country, and incidentally give us a few pointers on buffalo hunting.

Dr. John Obar, J.T. McClellan (a brother of my former pal), Jim Green and I formed the outfit. We went to Sweetwater, camping near Dan Trent's ranch, and hunted here for two days and saw only two buffalo bulls in this time. The first bull I chased until my horse gave out, shot away all my ammunition, and only drew a little blood.

It will not be amiss to state what our artillery consisted of at that time. We used a long and trusty cap and ball rifle, familiarly known as "Long Tom." Then the old cap and ball six-shooter, sometimes called "outlaws." At times they would behave and fire one shot, and again they would fire two, three or possibly all six chambers at one time. But to revert to our buffalo hunt:

On the second day we found another old, poor buffalo bull. I handed my long rifle to one of the boys and took his six-shooter, and told them I was going to get meat, in which I eventually succeeded. I was riding my own horse, one that I had bought from one of my German friends in Washington County. I had named him "Dutch," had taken good care of this horse, using him only for night herding on the trail, and so he was in good time. He was a keen runner. I took after the buffalo bull, ran him about three miles, emptying my pistol as I chased him. He was a monster and looked like an elephant to me.

Some of the buffalo hunters claimed that our "outlaw" pistols would not kill a big buffalo bull, but I demonstrated that they were wrong, for I put one ball in the right place and stopped the bull. After a bit the boys came up and finished the animal with their "Long Tom" rifle. It took two horses by the horn of the saddle to turn the carcass of the bull on his back so we could skin him. This will give you an idea that he was some bull. We built a fire and kiln-dried the meat. It was not fat, nor what we wanted.

We broke camp and drifted ten miles further north, where we came on to a herd, which we estimated at about 1,000 head. This herd of buffalo was on the move, and going pretty rapidly.

When I first got sight of them they were traveling west; they would go downhill on the run, while up the incline of the next hill they would be grazing. I rode around the foot of the hill to head them off and when I reached the ridge of the hill they were coming toward me, and about the same time I heard some shooting, which later proved to be our pilot, Jim Green, who had already got into the herd and put them on a full run.

I had some trouble holding down old "Dutch," my horse, when the herd of buffalo came toward us on the run.

There was one big red one leading the herd. I killed him first. He proved to be a big red steer, instead of buffalo, and belonged to John Chissum. I then killed one fat buffalo.

As I came over the hill I came on to our pilot, who had shot down five, of which one got up on his feet and was making for Jim Green who, by the way, was afoot. I tried to get Green to get on the horse behind me. He declined, saying he "would get him in the sticking place directly," deliberately shooting at the buffalo as he came on. He was holding his six-shooter with both hands to steady his aim and downed him. This gave us six buffalo and one fat steer, with which we struck out for Buffalo Gap.

Another little stunt with a buffalo we pulled off while at Buffalo Gap. Don Drewry and I were riding out among the cattle, where we came on to a two-year-old buffalo bull. Don boasted that he could and would rope him.

I pleaded with him not to risk such a thing, but he declared "old Browny," his horse, could handle him, and had the loop on him in no time. He threw the bull several times, but finally wore out his horse and called to me to shoot the bull. I did so to save his horse. Don admitted that he had taken in "too much territory" that time, and said he would never rope another buffalo larger than a calf.

Old man Drewry, Don's father, and his son-in-law, Tobe Odem, had come to Buffalo Gap from Oakville with cattle and horses. Don was then quite a boy, about 17 or 18 years of age.

Along in September we gathered up the cattle and moved on out to Sandrock Springs, where Nunn located his ranch on Rough Creek, and is now living and accumulating cattle. That winter I went back home and engaged in buying and selling cattle, at which trade I worked for several years, buying quite a lot of work steers to be shipped to Havana, Cuba.

On Dec. 15, 1881, I was married to Johanna Awalt at Burton, Texas, and lived there about one year. I went west again, locating at Snyder, Scurry County. My brother, J.M. Craig, and I carried a nice bunch of about 300 head of stock cattle with us, but one hard winter put us out of the cattle business and took us back to Washington County, where I now reside.

While working our cattle at Snyder, I took a trip west to the head of the Colorado River and here witnessed the largest "roundup" that I ever saw or heard speak of. It was the C.C. Slaughter "roundup," was estimated at 10,000 head of cattle in one herd, covering a prairie one-half mile each way.

For the benefit of those readers who have never seen a large "roundup" like those on the plains in the early days, I shall endeavor to describe this "roundup," the wonderful system and efficient way in which such an immense number of cattle were handled, cut and assorted, and how each rancher got his cattle.

You will understand that these cattle in this roundup were not owned by one individual, but belonged to ranches from a radius of many, many miles, comprising possibly a number of counties. With the exception of perhaps a small corral for the horses at the ranch houses in those early days, fences or pastures were unknown. The country was an open range, and the cattle were grazing in the open prairies, drifting to the four winds. Cattle were known to drift as far as 150 miles north.

Each stockman, or ranch, had a line rider, who rode the line or limits of his particular ranch in order to get his cattle "located," or used to their grazing grounds. However vigilant, this would not hold all of his stock. The line rider had to sleep at night, or sometimes, or had so much territory to cover and to guard, that cattle would drift away from their stamping grounds at night, or when the rider may have been engaged at other points of the line.

This made it necessary to have the "roundup," and to get the different brands of cattle to their respective owners and ranches.

The custom was to have a roundup in the spring of the year, and one in the fall. Word was sent to stockmen for many miles around when the roundup was to take place at a certain ranch. Then eight or ten neighboring stockmen would rig up a "chuck wagon" and place a cook in charge. One of the men would furnish the wagon one time, and the next time someone else – turn about. These stockmen going with the "chuck wagon" would meet at the appointed time with their saddle horses. Each man having his bedding lashed to a horse when they met the chuck wagon, would pat all their bedding in the wagon. This "chuck wagon" was drawn by two and sometimes four horses.

Next they would turn all their saddle horses in a bunch, detail one of their number as "horse wrangler" and start off for the roundup. At the roundup there would be a number of these chuck wagons or outfits – possibly six or eight or ten such wagons, according to the notices sent out, or the size of the roundup.

In the Slaughter roundup there were ten chuck wagons, and each wagon would receive a number from the roundup boss, making ten numbers – in this case representing some ninety men, or stock owners.

On the evening before the roundup Billy Stanefor, the roundup boss, went to all the wagons and called for two or three men from each wagon to go out from ten to fifteen miles and make what is called a "dry camp."

Each man was to stake his horse so that when daylight came every man was ready to follow out instructions to bring all the cattle toward the grounds. The men so sent out, all going in different directions, formed a veritable spider's web, with the roundup grounds in the center. As soon as the boys would "whoop 'em up," the cattle were on the run, and would make for the grounds.

There was little danger or chance for any cattle escaping, as when they would leave the path of one man they would drift into the path of the next man, and the nearer they came to the grounds, the more men would come in sight – finally forming one big herd, and then the fun would start.

We found on bringing in these cattle in this manner that five buffalo and twenty or more antelope had drifted in with the cattle. Several of the boys, I, for one, were sure we were going to rope an antelope. We got our loops ready and started for them. Our horses were too short, and also a little too slow. We did not rope any antelope. Some of the other boys fired into the buffalo, but did not bring in any meat either.

The herd was now ready for cutting. The roundup being on Slaughter's ranch, the foreman, Gus O. Keith, and his men, including old man Slaughter, cut their beef cattle, cows and calves first, and drove them back on the range to avoid "housing" them. As soon as Slaughter was through with his part the herd was ready for general work.

Now Billy Stanefor calls out, "No. 1 cut and No. 2 hold," meaning that the men from wagon No. 1 were to go into the herd and cut all of their cattle, while the men of wagon No. 2 would hold the herd. No. 1 finished, the roundup boss would call, "No. 2 cut and No. 3 hold" – when No. 2 would go into the herd and cut, while the men from wagon No. 3 were holding the herd, and so on in this manner until the cutting was finished.

Then, to the branding of the cattle. This was also all done on the open prairie.

We made our fires to heat the branding irons, would rope the calves or cattle, as the case may be, on horseback, drag them to the fire and put the brand on them.

It was also the duty of the roundup boss to see that no large calf was cut out of the roundup herd unless it was accompanied by its mother. The roundup boss had to act somewhat in the capacity of a judge. He had to see that all disputes were satisfactorily settled.

If trouble arose regarding ownership of an animal the roundup boss would find out what brand each one of the disputing parties were claiming the animal under, and if they could come to no agreement, the animal was roped, the brand moistened with water to make it plainer, or he would shear the hair off where the brand was located, and in that way determine the ownership.

All this was done immediately, and then the work would proceed. In those early days the earmark would not always be proof of ownership and an animal without brand was called a "sleeper."

A sleeper was nominally everybody's property, and was so called because someone had overlooked branding this animal in a previous roundup – had slept on his rights.

Naturally, all hands had a leaning toward these sleepers; and I have seen a sleeper cut out of the roundup by one man and during the day changed several times to other bunches. The man that was lucky to get away with a sleeper would put his brand on him. However, if such an animal had an earmark and any of the parties claimed the mark he would then hold the best title.

The roundup boss would let no one ride through the herd and "chouse," or unnecessarily disturb them; these fellows found guilty of such misconduct were called "loco'ed." Oft times it was known for the roundup boss to put him out of the herd and cut his cattle for him. The whole roundup was conducted in a strictly business way, and such a thing as "red tape" was unknown.

This work being finished, each wagon with its little herd would start for the next roundup. Possibly night would overtake them and pens, being unknown, it would be up to the boys to herd them and "sing" to them, as it was usually called. Each man would rope his night horse and they would herd in shifts.

This night herding is nice and novel in fair weather, and on a nice moonlit night; but when it comes to one of those dark nights of thunder, lightning and the rain pouring down on you, your life is in the hands of God and your faithful night horse.

There is to my mind no nobler animal in God's creation than a faithful horse. We would always pick out the clearest-footed, best-sighted horses for this work. All horses can see in the night, and better than a man, but there are some horses that can see better than others.

Boys, in this connection, I wish to relate a little incident of what a horse can do and did at the Slaughter roundup. We were told that the Slaughter Ranch possessed two horses that would cut without a bridle, and we asked Gus Keith, the foreman, to let us see the horses perform this feat.

He called for two horses, "Old Pompy," a black pacing horse, and "S.B.," a slim bay horse. They rode into the herd and worked an animal toward the edge of the bunch and slipped the bridle. Each horse brought out the right cow and without a miss. This was great work for a dumb animal.

At this roundup I also saw the last wild buffalo.

It was in the year 1880 that I sold Hugh Lewis and Jim Holt, of Brenham, 700 steers on a contract to Mr. Runge. The steers were to be delivered at the Runge Ranch near Yorktown, De Witt County. They were short of both horses and men and hired my brother and me to go through with the herd to Yorktown.

On our way we came to the Colorado River at LaGrange and found the stream on a rampage. We were told of a man that had been drowned at this crossing three days before in trying to cross a herd of cattle. The man had all his clothes on besides a six-shooter. In swimming across he had taken the left point (or lead) to point the cattle across.

The cattle began milling in the stream and tried to turn back. He had made the point on his horse, but got into the bunch of milling cattle and both he and his horse went under. He was found two days later some 400 yards below the crossing.

This brought up the question to us: Who would venture to point our herd across; and, what would it cost to have them pointed? Crowds of people had come from LaGrange to witness the spectacle of a large herd of cattle swimming across the river; there were men, women and children, all eager to see. I was about the poorest swimmer in the outfit, but had lots of experience in my time, no doubt more than the rest all together.

Holt sauntered up to me and asked if I was afraid to point the herd, and what would I charge extra to pull off the stunt. I confessed to him that I was not a good swimmer and was afraid of water, but that I was a hired hand and would not shirk my duty. I had a first-class pony for the work, and told him that I would point the herd if allowed to strip my clothes. He told me the work had to be done, women or no women.

When everything was arranged I stripped, mounted my pony bareback and took the left (or lower) point. I struck the water with the cattle and stayed near the lead until they saw the opposite bank, then I led out for the bank and crossed the cattle without a mishap. From there on we moved along smoothly until we got to the Guadalupe River.

Here, at night, my brother, I, and two other boys were herding on first relief. Some old-timers had told us that it "never rained at night in June," but we had all doubts dispelled here. As we were short of horses, we herded in only two reliefs.

After midnight, as I rode into camp to wake up the second relief, I noticed an approaching storm cloud in the northwest, and before the boys could saddle their horses and get around the herd it was thunder, lightning and a downpour of rain, all in one.

The herd started drifting south and there was no way to hold them. They did not stampede, but kept moving, and as it was very dark, we could only see them by the flashes of lightning and drift with them. We must have traveled some three or four miles when I called to my brother to ask what had become of the other two boys. He said they had found a tree and had climbed up in it. We had not heard a sound from them since leaving camp.

I knew the man near me was my brother by his voice, as he was always in the habit of singing and talking to the cattle to quiet them. In a stampede there are no "road laws," everything in its path must clear out or get run over. After a few minutes' silence my brother called out: "Everybody look out, trouble ahead; my horse won't go any further!"

A flash of lightning revealed the banks of the Guadalupe River, the cause of his horse refusing to go further. We worked our way back through the cattle, as the river would hold the cattle at this end, and waited for daylight. We found that we had drifted seven miles during the latter part of the night, and just the two of us in charge of the whole herd.

Our horses were "all in," for we had ridden them since noon the day before. We figured that we would be off at midnight, when our relief was up, and had not changed for the night relief. This was our last obstacle to speak of from there to the Runge Ranch.

Steers those days were bought and sold "by age." When the classing and turning them over to Runge's foreman began, some trouble arose between Jim Holt and the foreman of Runge's ranch as to the age of the steers. Runge's foreman asked Holt if he did not have a man in his outfit that he would entrust with classing for him. Jim Holt had never handled many cattle, and asked me to his classing with Runge's man. We got along fine and more than pleased Holt, for when we were through Holt found himself to the "good" several hundred dollars above contract price he paid, and the amount of my classing.

On our way home Holt stopped at a hotel in Yorktown. In this hotel I saw a sign that I shall never forget. It read:

PASSENGERS WITHOUT BAGGAGE
PAY IN ADVANCE
AND DON'T YOU FORGET IT.

Holt had no baggage and had to dig up the cash. He was considered a good-hearted man, but when drinking would not stand for any foolishness. He was known as a good fighter and soldier from his Civil War record.

I recall one time at Burton, Texas, when Holt and Dr. Watt met, disagreed, and both pulled their "smoke wagons" and got busy. When the smoke cleared away both men were found wounded, Dr. Watt going to

Knittel's store and Holt into Hons & Bauer's establishment.

Holt was wounded in the hip, the bullet lodging in the backbone. Dr. Hons, his brother-in-law, who now lives in San Marcos, probed for the bullet while I was holding Holt's leg. I could feel the forceps slipping off the leaden missile as the doctor was trying to extract it. Dr. Hons failed to remove the ball and advised Holt that it would take an operation and which would be a dangerous one.

Holt sent to San Antonio for Dr. Cupples, who had been a surgeon in the army with Holt. Dr. Cupples and Dr. Hons performed the operation and Holt got well. He lived about two years when he and Joe Hoffman, also of Burton, were waylaid and shot in a saloon in Brenham.

Dr. Hons treated me during my illness with meningitis about 33 years ago. At the same time he was also attending Charles Hohmeyer's three children, who were suffering from the same malady. We all got well but I, minus one eye. There were at the time fifty-six cases of meningitis in Burton and Brenham, of which forty-four did not recover.

I considered myself very fortunate in securing the services of my friend, Dr. Hons, and know he is one of the finest physicians in the State of Texas.

In 1884 Sam Hale and I put up for Curtis & Cochran of California 800 head of cattle. We bought these up in Washington, Lee, Burleson and Austin Counties.

Curtis & Cochran bought some 600 head more from their kins-people and others near Bellville, and gathered them at Buckhorn, Austin County. My oldest brother, J.M. Craig, was employed by Curtis & Cochran to boss the herd through to New Mexico. He moved their 600 head from Buckhorn to Burton, where Hale and I joined him with the 800 head, making a herd of 1,400 cattle. This was entirely too large a herd to handle in the woods and among the farms.

The first day we only moved the herd some seven miles and camped at Charlie Tarno's, in Sandtown, within 300 yards of where I was born. Old Man Tarno had a field of about ten acres fenced with post oak rails. Into this field we turned our herd. Cochran had made the arrangement and knew nothing about cattle. He said: "Put them in there and give the boys a good night's rest."

We had some sixty miles of the worst kind of brush ahead of us before we would get to the Taylor Prairie. I warned my brother and Cochran that the herd would break the fence and scatter in all the directions of the globe; and I, for one, would sleep with my bridle in hand. Hale and my brother followed my suggestion.

Curtis & Cochran had hired every man that came to the herd, having some fourteen hands, besides a cook. The firm had all their money in this herd and were down here in Texas where they did not have confidence in Texas people. They were so "darned" crooked themselves that they thought everybody was trying to beat them, so they hired all these men to be sure of their cattle, and to hold the herd.

Hale, my brother and I had our horses saddled and ready. We took up our stations around the herd, one in a place. About ten o'clock that night the expected happened – the cattle stampeded. My brother was ahead of me, but could not make the lead; so he called to me: "Go to the lead of the herd and hold them up."

I made the lead and on my way I passed Arthur Jones, who was in the middle of the herd, whipping for dear life to get out of the way, and caused the cattle in front to run so much faster. I did not see Jones any more that night. Later I located Sam Hale by his voice. The herd split up on us; my brother being with one part, and Sam Hale and I held the other part. At daybreak we drove our cattle toward the balance of the herd. We had the cattle counted before a single man from camp showed up – three of us holding 1,400 head of cattle in a herd through a dark night.

The cook told us that Curtis & Cochran had talked and wailed all night about their fortune being scattered in those woods, and that they would never get them back. Old man Cochran came to us in the morning, accosting my brother: "Well, John, how many of the 'band' (meaning the herd) are gone?" My brother said: "Here is the count."

He handed him the envelope on which we had jotted down the numbers as we cut the cattle by in small bunches and had counted them. The figures proved we were none short.

Cochran was a happy "old Yank," and declared: "You boys must have eyes like an owl, to run through these woods at night and not get killed."

With the delivery of these cattle to Curtis & Cochran my contract expired. The next day at noon I left for home. My brother carried the herd on through to New Mexico, somewhere near Las Vegas, and told me later that he had undergone many hardships. In crossing the Plains he had been without water for the cattle, at one time, for two days and nights.

After all the hard and faithful work, these two old Yanks tried to beat my brother out of half of his wages. They hired him at $100 per month and paid him fifty dollars. Curtis & Cochran had lost a few cattle at Bellville while herding them and authorized me to gather and dispose of them and send them the money. I gathered these cattle, sold them, paid my brother his balance, and have never heard from them since.

One night while we were putting up cattle for the Curtis & Cochran herd we had some 150 head in my pen at Burton. After turning in for the night my brother took his money and some money that Joe, my wife, had given him for safekeeping, together with his six-shooter, stuck them under his pillow and turned in. He was sleeping on the front gallery.

All of a sudden I heard a noise and found something had frightened the cattle, and they had broken fence and stampeded. They ran south, through the town of Burton. We were after them in no time and overtook them on Whitener's Prairie, rounded them together and finally succeeded in quieting them.

Now, it happened that my brother began to get restless and confided to me that he came away and had left all his and my wife's money under his pillow on the front gallery. He figured that possibly my wife might have thought of it after our departure and had taken care of it, but "seeing is believing," and he was ill at ease. He rode back to assure himself while I held the herd.

Luckily he found the money and six-shooter in possession of my wife, and, to say the least, he felt much relieved. There were but few banks in the country, and we were in the habit of carrying the cash with us. The German people, as a rule, would not take anybody's check, and quite often demanded payment in silver, as they did not like paper money.

Whenever I had too much money I would turn it over to my wife. This was not a "force of habit," but quite convenient. My wife would put it in what she termed the "First National Bank" – her stocking. You know that is a woman's money purse.

In 1893 Dr. Hons of San Marcos and I were buying up 1,000 head of one and two-year-old steers on contract. We sold them to H.C. Beal for Louis Runge of Menardville. We had leased the McCoy pasture, near Wetmore, on the Cibolo Creek, to hold these steers until we had the required number. We were to deliver these cattle to them at the Las Moras Ranch, on Elm Creek, near Menard.

This was really the hardest trip that I ever made with cattle. The cattle ran the first four nights that we were out and gave us no end of trouble.

The first night we herded in a wide lane or pocket, some three miles this side of the Guadalupe River on the Blanco city road. The cattle stampeded. Sam Craig, Billy and Ed Eckert were holding the north end of the pocket, toward the river, while Stock Wesson, I and the other hands held to the south end. The cattle headed for the river and went onto the boys with such force that they were unable to hold them.

Sam Craig was riding a little black pony named "Nigger Babe," a sure-footed and fast animal. Sam went into the lane with the cattle, taking all kinds of chances.

He worked his way toward the lead, but before they got to the river he crowded them into the fence, which broke and got into a pasture. Sam was with them. He turned their lead and brought them all back to the herd. I considered Sam the best hand I ever had, day or night work, with cattle. Next morning's count showed that we had not lost any of the herd. On this trip I also had my boy, Walter A. Craig, then eight years old, with me. He had his own horse, leggings and spurs, and made a splendid little hand in daytime. I caught him asleep but once. He was on his horse under a tree and two other grown men were down on the ground sound asleep. He was too young to do any night herding.

The second night we held the cattle in another pocket or wide lane, near Krueger's store. The fences were good on either side, just two lanes to hold, but that night we had a rainstorm. I took Walter, my boy, on my horse behind me and brought him to Krueger's store.

Sam Craig and Stock Wesson held the south end of the lane. They had orders to force the cattle through the fence in case of a stampede, rather than let them go back the way they had come. The other boys, Billy and Ed Eckert, held the north end of the lane.

The storm came from the north and the cattle ran south, throwing them on Craig and Wesson. They fought them with their slickers for dear life until they succeeded in turning their lead. Into the six or eight-wire fence they went. They broke through, cutting up a number of them badly, and we were obliged to kill several of them. They made another run, going north; broke through the line, and scattered all over the mountains near Blanco City.

We worked for three days gathering these cattle, and Cavaness Brothers and others rendered us great assistance.

The third night we moved in above Blanco and had pretty "bed grounds." The cattle made one little run, but we did not lose any in the stampede. However, some of the boys were careless and let quite a number drift out of the herd during the night and we gathered all next day to get them back.

The fourth day we moved into an ideal "bed ground," an open prairie with mountains all around. The boys had good grounds to run on. I gave

Sam Craig and Stock Wesson each two horses and told them to run the cattle down if they could do no better; also, to take their slickers and run the herd in a circle all night or hold them.

I put Walter, my boy, and my little nigger boy, Bill, on the chuck box in back of the wagon, and told them to stay there till the cattle quieted down. These boys said that the cattle ran twenty-two times that night.

The next morning we tried to stampede the herd with our slickers, but they refused to be stampeded. They never made another run on us. We had no more trouble of this nature, but we were quite a few short on account of so many stampedes. H.C. Beal having passed on these cattle, stayed by his classing and did, not cut us any cattle on account of wire cuts.

This was an exceptional trip and I was very foolish in taking my child along at his age. The trip kept him away from his mother for two months. We returned in the chuck wagon and on the way gathered what cattle we had lost and could find.

In 1914 one day I was en route from Brenham to Ledbetter with my two favorite ponies, Johnny and Charlie. I was riding Johnny and leading Charlie. Some two and a half miles north of Carmine, on the Houston and Texas Central Railroad, I met Crawford Gillespie. He was section foreman, Section 7, and was trying to push one of those motor cars down the track to where his men were at work.

In some unaccountable way the motor started and the car got away from Gillespie. It went through his bunch of men, who tried to board it, but failed. He called to me to ditch it by throwing a tie across the track. The track was fenced, and I had no chance. In fact, I did not hardly have any time to "hesitate."

It was all my horse could do to outrun the car, and I saw my only chance was to beat the car to Carmine and rope it. There was no way of getting close to the track on account of it being fenced.

I got to Carmine in time enough to jump off my horse and throw a near-lying plank across the track, and ditched it directly in front of the depot. It was a test of horse flesh against gasoline, in which the horse won out. This little pony is now playing polo in New York.

In the early days there were in Washington County as well as in many other counties of Texas, some pretty tough people. Horse and cattle thieves were quite plentiful.

The officers, knowing that my oldest brother and I were handy on horseback and ready at day or in the night to uphold law and order, would call on us to assist in running down this element. We kept this duty up more or less all of our lives, and neither of us ever held an office higher than a deputy sheriff or constable.

The fact is, the courthouse ring were playing "safety first," and knew that some of their crooked bunch would get locked up if occasion warranted.

In those days we could not prohibit horse stealing, but nowadays you seldom hear of it in this country.

The horse thieves were very bad and bold, and something had to be done. You might, for instance, go to bed at night leaving your work team in the barn or lot and awake next morning to find your team had disappeared. Every possible means were resorted to stamp out this evil, but of no avail.

Finally they experimented with "hemp" for several years. A strong dose of hemp would always tend to kind of "deaden" the desire to steal and today there is very little of it going on.

With reference to the old-time cowmen with whom I have spent all of my life, I candidly believe them to be the best people on earth today. They do not all profess to be Christians, but they are a noble and big-hearted set of men that you can rely upon when you, or your country, gets into trouble. They will divide their last dollar with you, and fight their weight in wildcats for you, their friends and their country. They are always ready to help the poor and needy.

Only the other day at one of the local commission offices, a boy who had come from Arkansas with cattle told us of lending his last ten dollars to a gambler and losing it. He had a "pass" back home, but nothing to pay for meals or lodging. The boys chipped in and made up enough money for him on his way home.

As he was walking out of the office, John Draper asked me to call him back, and handed him a ten-dollar bill. This is the kind of material the stockmen in general are made of, and may the good Lord favor every one of them.

May we all meet at the final roll call and accompany the chuck wagon to the last and great roundup. Beware, if you are a "sleeper!"

# When George Saunders Made a Bluff 'Stick'

### by T.T. Hawkins, Charlotte, Texas

I WAS BORN IN GUADALUPE COUNTY, near Seguin, April 7, 1859, and spent practically all of my life on ranches. I first went up the trail with a herd of horses, in 1879, from Corpus Christi to Cherryvale, Kansas.

This was one of the hardest trips I ever made. Our chuck wagon consisted of a Mexican mule about fourteen hands high. The next trip I made was in 1879, this time with a herd of two-year-old steers owned by G.W. Littlefield, driven from the O'Connor Ranch near Victoria to Yellow House Canyon.

This was a very pleasant drive, and we had good grass and plenty of water on the way.

The next year I went with a herd of 1,800 cattle bossed by Nat Jackson, going from Kyle, Texas, to Ogallala, Nebraska, where we delivered them to Col. Seth Maberry, after which we drove from there to the Red Cloud Agency to supply a government contract.

The fourth trip was made in 1881, when I went from Taylor, Texas, to Caldwell, Kansas, with a horse herd owned by Kuykendall, Sauls & Burns, with John Burns as boss.

During 1882 and 1883 I worked in the Panhandle of Texas, but in 1884 I went on the trail again with a horse herd owned by H.G. Williams and bossed by Bill Williams. On this trip, somewhere in the vicinity of Abilene, Texas, we came up with George W. Saunders' outfit as they were going up to Kansas. Here we had a stampede, our horses mixed together, so we just let them stay together and drove them from there to Dodge City.

On this trip several things took place that should be mentioned for the benefit of the readers of this book, for they give a clear idea of some of the dangers that beset the men who traveled the trail in those old days.

When we reached the Comanche reservation, the Indians demanded horses and provisions from us.

As George Saunders could talk Spanish fluently, and was good at making a bluff stick, our outfit and Carroll Mayfield's outfit, which had overtaken us, decided to appoint George to settle with the Indians as best he could.

Accordingly he accompanied the chiefs and some of the bucks to a tepee and held a council with them. The old chief could speak Spanish, and when he learned that George was familiar with his old raiding range, he became quite friendly and told him that he knew every trail on the Rio Grande from Laredo to El Paso, knew all of the streams by name, the Nueces, Llano River, Devil's River, Guadalupe River, Pecos River, the Concho and Colorado Rivers, besides many creeks.

He became very talkative and, going to a rude willow basket he had in his wigwam, he brought forth several burrs, which he said he had taken from cypress trees of the head of the Guadalupe River. He told Mr. Saunders that he had killed "heap white man" on his raids, but that he was now "heap good Indian, no kill no man."

Saunders offered to make settlement by giving them one horse and some provisions, and the Indians seemed well pleased with this offer.

When we started our herd about twenty young bucks riding on beautiful horses came and helped us swim the cattle across the Canadian River. A number of our horses bogged in the quicksand and had to be dug out, which sport the Indians enjoyed immensely. They fell right in with our boys and helped in every way they could to pull the horses out, and when this work was finished they gave us an exhibition of their riding. Some of the bucks would run by our crowd and invite us to lasso them.

Saunders finally decided to rope one of them, a tall young fellow who was mounted on a well-trained horse, so getting his lariat ready, he waited the coming of the Indian, and as he passed, laying flat on his horse, George threw the rope and it encircled both horse and rider.

The Indian's horse shied around a tree and the Indian and his horse and George and his horse were all thrown heavily to the ground when the rope tightened. The Indian was painfully injured, but when we ran to their assistance we found no serious damage had resulted, although it was a narrow escape for both of the performers. The rope had been drawn so tight around the Indian that it required some time for him to get his lungs in proper action. We thought the Indians would be offended by the accident, but they laughed and guffawed over it in great fashion, and we left them in fine spirits.

As we proceeded on our way we heard the Kiowas were in an ugly mood, and the next day the old chief, Bacon Rind, and about 200 Kiowa bucks and squaws came to us and they, too, demanded horses and provisions.

We sent them to Saunders, of course, for he had so successfully managed the Comanches the day before we trusted him to handle these Indians the same way. We told them Saunders was "heap big boss," and to talk to him. Saunders parleyed with them for some time, finally telling them to come back the next day. They left grudgingly and came back that evening, renewing their demands, so Saunders had all of the wagons drawn up together, and offered the Indians a small amount of flour, some sugar, coffee, bacon, prunes, beans and some canned goods out of each wagon.

All of this stuff was placed where they could see just what he was offering to give them to depart in peace, and he also told them two horses would be given in addition to the provisions. Some of the Indians seemed satisfied and were willing to accept the offer, but others wanted more. In the band of Indians was a pockmarked half-breed who had been the most insistent that more be given them, and he finally got all of the bunch demanding more.

Saunders finally lost patience with them and told the cooks to put all of the stuff back in the wagons, and the men to straddle their horses and start the herds. As George mounted his horse and started off the pockmarked half-breed and a dozen bucks made a dash at him, and before he realized what was happening they had grabbed him by the arms and caught his horse by the bridle.

He had drawn his pistol, but was unable to use it because of the vise-like grip that held him. At the same time forty or fifty buffalo guns in the hands of the Indians were leveled at his head, and for an instant things looked bad. The half-breed, who spoke English fluently, was cursing and abusing Saunders, and telling him they were going to kill him right there. The squaws had all vanished, nobody knew where.

Harry Hotchkiss and several of the other boys, including three of Saunders' Mexican hands, ran to his assistance, and their bravery no doubt saved his life. They leveled their pistols on the Indians, the Mexicans in a rage screaming, "Dammy you, you killee Meester George, me killee you."

This was a critical moment for George Saunders, but he kept his nerve, for he realized that if there was one shot fired he would be a "goner." He talked to the Indians in every language except Chinese, telling them they were making a serious mistake, and that he would send to Fort Sill and get the soldiers to come and protect him.

This talk had the desired effect, and they lowered their guns and departed without provisions, although Saunders gave them a stray horse in our herd, which I think belonged to the Comanches. The Indians were in an ugly mood when they left, the pockmarked Indian swearing vengeance and saying, as he rode away, "We will come back and take all we want from you when the sun comes up."

While parleying with the Indians, Saunders offered to give them orders for provisions on men behind, who, he told them, were rich men and would gladly give them cattle, horses and money, naming Bell, Butler, Jim Blocker, Jim Dobie, Forest, Clark, King, Kennedy, Coleman, O'Connor and many other prominent trail men of that time. But the Indians said, "All no good. Pryor man give order last year; no good."

Saunders was worried and told us we had given him a hell of a job, but he was going to play it strong.

That night Saunders put on only two reliefs, some of them to hold the herd and the others to reconnoiter and give the alarm at the first sign of Indians. He told all of the boys to get their shooting irons in good shape, for there was likely to be trouble.

The Indians did not molest us during the night, and early next morning Mr. Saunders told us they would probably show up in a little while, and he gave us instructions as to what to do. He told us to congregate behind this herd when the Indians appeared, keep in line and not mix with the Indians, for in case of a fight we should not run the risk of shooting some of our own men. We were to keep cool while he was parleying with the Indians, and if he saw that a fight could not be avoided he would give a keen cowboy yell as a signal, and every man was to act.

Just after sunrise we saw the Indians coming across the plain in single file and in full war garb, headed by two chiefs, Bacon Rind and Sundown, and the pockmarked half-breed. The Indians came right up to us, and as they were approaching Saunders said, "Remember, boys, we must win the fight. If I give the signal each of you must kill an Indian, so don't make a miss."

They looked hideous in the war garb, and as they rushed up one of the chiefs said, "How, big chief bad man, no give poor Indian horse or grub. Indian take um." Saunders told them they would get nothing. They began to point out horses in the herd, which they said they were going to take, and George informed them that he would shoot the first Indian that rode into the herd.

The pockmarked Indian held a short whispered conversation with the two chiefs and started toward Saunders, seeing which the boys, who were already on their mettle and tired of waiting for the signal, began pulling their guns, and the Indians weakened. They instantly saw that we were determined to give them a fight, and withdrew.

Saunders had to do some lively talking then to hold our crowd back. There were about thirty-five men in our bunch, including the cooks and wranglers, and the Indians numbered about 200 warriors. As they left, the pockmarked half-breed showed the white feather, and Saunders called him all the coward names in the Indian, Spanish and English language that he knew, but the rascal knew he had lost and his bluff was called.

In resentment the Indians went to Neal Manewell's herd, which was nearby, and shot down ten beeves. Saunders and several of our boys went over to the herd and offered assistance to the boss, Mr. Cato, but he said they were too late to save the beeves, and it was best to let the Indians alone, as we could all drive out of their reservation that day.

We pointed our herd up the trail and had no further trouble with them.

The pockmarked Indian was known to most of the old trail drivers. He was an outlaw and thief, and was regarded as a desperate character all around. I learned that he was killed by a cowboy in 1886.

George Saunders had lots of experience in dealing with Indians during those days, and he often told me that when he made a bold bluff, if it did not stick he was always ready to back it up with firearms or fast talking.

In 1885 and 1886 I carried herds for H.G. Williams from Kyle, Texas, to Arkansas City, and made my last drive in 1886, when I delivered a herd to Miles Williams at Abilene, Texas. I have been in the cow business ever since, the greater part of the time associated with H.G. Williams.

*How dear to my heart are the scenes of my trailhood,*
*When fond recollections present them to view—*
*The water barrel, the old chuck wagon,*
*And the cook who called me to chew.*

# Reminiscences of the Trail

*by Jasper (Bob) Lauderdale, Texas*

I WAS BORN NEAR BELTON, BELL COUNTY, TEXAS, Aug. 17, 1854. My parents moved to Belton in 1849 from Neosho County, Missouri, coming in by ox wagon, then moved to Gonzales, where, after remaining a short time, they returned to Belton and maintained the stage stand until 1854, when all earthly possessions were wiped out by a flood.

My parents both died when I was young, and I was raised by Uncle Alex Hodge until I came to Atascosa County in 1873. During my early boyhood in Bell County I rode the range and helped with herding and branding cattle, enjoying the experiences of the then early conditions existing in Texas, one of which caused so much amusement that I am going to recite it here.

One day a Mr. Isabell came traveling through the country trading eight-day clocks for cattle, giving one clock for four cows and calves, and as no one had a clock, it did not take Isabell long to gather a herd.

One of the settlers with whom he traded, took his clock home and, after winding it, set it on the mantle, and when the family gathered round after supper, the clock struck eight. It scared the family so that they scattered, thinking it was something supernatural, and it took the old man until nearly midnight to get them together and in the house.

I helped Isabell drive his cattle as far as Comanche Springs on his way to Fort Worth and returned to the range, remaining until 1872, when, with Isaiah Mock, Hoffman and Moore, we drove a herd of cattle to Alexandria, Louisiana, with W.C. Wright, who loaded them on boats for New Orleans; then we returned home.

During the fall we branded "mavericks" and put up trail herds and in the spring of 1873 Olley Treadwell came through with a herd for Kansas belonging to Sim Holstein of Gonzales. Bob Allen and I hired to Treadwell and went to Wichita, Kansas, this being my first trip over the

Chisholm Trail, with nothing unusual or exciting except we saw some buffalo.

At Wichita during the summer, Bud Chapman, Bud Hilderbrandt, Bill Bennett and I helped "Shanghai" Pierce cut and load a train of steers for the market at St. Louis. This was the first bunch of cattle I ever saw loaded on cars.

In the fall of 1873 I went to work on the range for Bill Fountain and we gathered and drove 200 head to W.B.G. Grimes' slaughter house on the coast, near Powder Horn, where they were slaughtered for their hides and tallow. On our return we gathered a herd of 250 cattle and drove them to Harrisburg, then five miles from Houston, and on this trip I led the pack horse and cooked for the outfit.

I then went with Bud Chapman to Fort Ewell, where we gathered cattle and brought them back to his ranch, and in the spring of 1874 started 3,000 head up the trail, going as far as the Salado with them. Upon returning I worked for "Billy" Childress, John Slaughter and Mrs. O'Brien.

In the spring of 1875 three Mexicans and I were herding 400 head of cattle near Carrizo Springs, Texas, when Lem English and Len Hay, two boys, who were playing close by, discovered a bunch of Indians.

The children ran to the house and gave the alarm and Ed English came out and helped us put the cattle in his pen, and we stood guard all night, although the Indians did not attack us, as they had previously had a taste of old English's rifle. On their way out the Indians killed one of Ed's sheepherders.

In the spring of 1876 Dick Horn, Jack McCurley and I, with some Mexican hands, gathered and delivered by Billy Childress and John Slaughter, to Bill Dougherty two herds of about 5,000 head at Indian Bend Ranch.

In the fall of 1876 I went to Runnels County and took charge of a herd for J.W. Murphy and George Hindes and wintered on Elm Creek, above where the city of Ballinger now stands, and the following spring drove them to Dodge City, Kansas.

On the trip I saw old Sitting Bull and about 1,200 of his bucks and squaws in charge of government troops; these were the Cheyenne and Sioux Indians, who had massacred Gen. Custer and his men and were being taken to Fort Reno.

There were about 2,000 horses with the Indians. The troops had one-hundred pack mules so well-trained that you could not make them break line. They moved in single file and were taught this to enable them to travel through the mountains.

The Indians were traveling in their usual way, poles tied to the necks of ponies like shafts in a buggy, but much longer, and in willow baskets lashed to these poles the old bucks and squaws rode who were too old to ride horseback their tepees and supplies were also carried in this manner. Squaws with their papooses strapped to their backs rode bareback, and in passing through their camp I saw one old buck dressed in moccasins, breechclout, a frocktail coat and an old-fashioned preacher's hat.

Upon my return from Kansas, in 1877, I went to a point near Oakville and received a herd of cattle for Lewis & Blunzer and drove them to Saddle Creek, near the mouth of the Concho, where it empties into the Colorado, at a point near where Paint Rock now stands. Shortly after I left the horse wrangler, Lebora Chappa, who had remained with Joe Reame, was killed near Salt Gap by the Indians.

In November 1877, George Hindes, Volley Oden and I took an outfit to Laredo and bought and received a herd of cattle on the Gonzales and Ambrosia Rodriguez ranches and returned to the La Parita Ranch, in Atascosa County, on Christmas day, 1877, then road-branded, and in the spring of 1878 started up the trail.

On the trail with me was Joe Collins with his herd and a herd of Bill Dewees in charge of Joe Eggle, and when crossing the North Fork of Red River, at the foot of the Wichita Mountains, Joe Collins' cook was killed by a Mexican, who we were unable to capture. We rolled the cook in his blanket and dug his grave with an axe and a broken-handled spade, the only implements at hand.

On the Mobeetie Road crossing at the North Fork of the Red River, near Fort Sill, the Indians – Cheyennes and Sioux – were holding a medicine dance and afterward went on the warpath. They killed Tuttle & Chapman's cook, took thirty-five head of horses on Crooked Creek, near where I had camped, shot Foreman Rainey's horse and headed for the Bad Lands of the Dakotas.

We reached the H&D. Ranch on Sept. 7, 1878, and remained there until the cattle were ranch-branded, and returned to Cheyenne and then to Denver by train.

In the spring of 1879 I started for Dodge City with a herd for John Camp, and a little above San Antonio our oxen gave out, requiring us to use Mexican "stags" with Mexican yokes to Dodge City. In the fall and winter of 1879, C.F. Carroll and I made several trips down the Rio Grande below Laredo and bought cattle from the Tortilla Ranch in Mexico and from Pedro Flores, Juan Benavides, Jesus Pena and others for Camp, Rosser & Carroll.

In the spring of 1880 Carroll and I started to Kansas, and at Bandera we threw our herds together because several of Carroll's hands quit him, and I drove the combined herds to Ogallala and delivered them to Charles and Joe Shiner, who then sold 1,000 head of two-year-olds, steers and heifers, to Billy Campbell, and I drove this lot to Pine Bluff, Wyoming, turning them over to Campbell's men.

In the spring of 1881 I took a herd of three- and four-year-olds for Mitchell & Pressnall to Ogallala and turned the big steers over to Seth Maberry and then shaped up another herd of 2,500 one- and two-year-old steers and 1,000 one- and two-year-old heifers out of the Mitchell, Pressnall and Ellison herds and went to Crazy Woman Fork of Powder River at the foot of Big Horn Mountains, and delivered them to Stoddard, Latman & Howard.

Returning in 1881, I worked my own cattle until 1884, and that year shipped to Dryden, on the Southern Pacific. In 1885 I traded with John Camp and the Pecos Land & Cattle Company, and "hit" the trail again.

John Doak, Dan Franks and I gathered a herd and sold out to Zook & Odem and I went to Independence Ranch, in Pecos County, and turned them over to Billy Alley. Returning home in 1886 with Jess Pressnall, I went to Fort Stockton and gathered a herd, drove up the Pecos to Fort Sumner, and remained six weeks cutting out steers; then drove to Las Vegas and loaded them for Cheyenne, Wyoming, and upon my return to Fort Sumner I took the balance of the herd, 1,000 one- and two-year-old heifers, to Grant, New Mexico, and delivered to a Kansas City outfit.

# An Old Frontiersman Tells His Experience

*by Joe Chapman, Benton, Texas*

I WAS BORN IN TENNESSEE, FEB. 18, 1854, and came to Texas with my parents when I was about five years old. My father stopped in Parker County for a short time, then bought a tract of land in Jack County, nine miles north of Jacksboro, on Hall's Creek, and opened up a fine farm there.

At that time we were on the extreme frontier, and the country was infested with hostile Indians, who made raids almost every full moon, and we had to keep our horses locked with trace chains to trees in the yard to keep the redskins from stealing them.

In July, 1860, my father was waylaid and killed by the Indians while he was out deer hunting in a little ravine near home. This tragedy happened just at sundown, and was so near home I heard his gunfire, and we all thought he was shooting a deer. But when he failed to return we became uneasy and gave the alarm, and next morning the neighbors found his body.

He had been shot eighteen times with arrows, scalped and his clothing taken. His gun had been broken off at the breech, evidently in the hand-to-hand struggle that took place when the Indians closed in upon him.

Some time previous to the killing of my father, the Indians had murdered a man named Cooley, our nearest neighbor, three miles away. Also in the same year one of the Browning boys over on the West Fork was killed and his brother shot through the breast with an arrow. Before that the Loss Valley murder took place, in which several women and children were killed, one of the women, Mrs. Cameron, being scalped and left for dead, but recovered.

After father's death we went back down in Parker County and remained there until the winter of 1861-2, then moved to Cooke County, and often had to leave there on account of the Indians, sometimes going as far east as Collin County.

In 1863, on Christmas day, the Indians made a raid on the head of Elm, where the large town of Saint Jo now stands, and all of the people went to the old Spanish fort on Red River for protection. They killed many people and stole lots of stock in this raid.

I knew a little boy and girl named Anderson who escaped and came to old Fort Wallace the next day. Their parents and other members of the family were murdered, and the little boy's throat was cut and gashed with lances. Another family was killed and their home burned. The Indians also killed a little boy named Guinn, cut his arms off and stuck his body on a pole.

Near the same place later on the Box family were captured, the father being killed before their eyes and the mother, two grown daughters and an infant being carried away into a captivity worse than death. Up near Fort Sill one of the daughters, a beautiful girl in her teens, was treated in a most shocking manner by the savages. These tragedies occurred when I was but a child, but I remember many of them vividly.

During the four years of the Civil War the people of the Red River country, Montague, Cooke, Wise and Denton counties, had a severe struggle to get along. Everything was of primitive style, and we had to get along the best we could.

Most of our houses were built of logs, some of them roughly hewn and with the bark on, and the cracks "chinked" with sticks and mud, with dirt floors and a big, wide chimney. Sometimes a family would get "tony" and hew logs on one side and make a puncheon floor for their home and thus get into the "upper class."

In the summer we would move out and live in these log houses, but in the fall and winter the Indians kept us in the forts. We had plenty to eat, although we had to take our grain fifty miles to a mill to have it ground. We had no money, but did not need much, for we could not buy such things as coffee, sugar, soap, matches, pins or anything to wear, and we were compelled to spin and weave all of the cloth that made our clothing. Rye, corn, wheat, okra seed and roasted acorns were used as a substitute for coffee.

In 1868 my brother, about eighteen years old, was waylaid and killed by Indians between Gainesville and Fort Wallace while on a trip to the fort. Thus the savages had killed two of our family, in each instance our chief support and protector.

That same year we moved to Atascosa County, where we had relatives, and as I was about fifteen years old, I was considered large enough to be of help in working with cattle, on the roundups and roping and branding on the range. In those days every waddy had two crooked irons attached to his saddle and a pocketful of matches, and the maverick that got away was sure enough a speeder.

In the fall of 1870 I worked on the Redus Ranch on the Hondo, working cattle with George, John and Bill Redus and Tally Burnett. Later I worked for V.A. Johnson, but mostly for Lytle & McDaniel. I learned all I know about handling cattle from V.A. Johnson and Tom McDaniel. If a boy working under them did not make a good hand in the brush or on the trail there was simply nothing to him. There is Uncle Bob Ragsdale, Will Lytle and Capt. John Lytle, with whom I worked, who were all good men and true. All have reached the end of the trail and gone over the great divide, except Uncle Bob Ragsdale.

I made my first trip up the trail in 1872 with a herd for Lytle & McDaniel with 1,800 head of cattle from yearlings up to grown beeves and cows. We routed them across Mustang Prairie to the Medina, then up the Louse and over to the Lucas to the old John Adams Ranch, on to San Antonio, skirting the northwestern part of the town, and passed on to the Salado. After we passed San Antonio we had quite a rainstorm and our cattle split up in small bunches and scattered everywhere.

We lost about thirty head in this stampede, which we did not get back. Tom McDaniel was selected as boss of the outfit, which consisted of sixteen men. Four men had interest in this herd, viz.: Tom McDaniel, Jim Speed, Uncle Ben Duncan and Newt Woofter. Gus Black, Tom Smith and myself were the only white hands with the outfit, the other hands being Mexicans, except old Jack Burckley, the cook.

Jim and Dock Watts, who lived at the Man Crossing on the Medina, came to us further up the trail. Woofter went with us, but did not come back.

In 1874 I made a trip up the old Chisholm Trail with 1,000 beeves, which had been selected and put in the Shiner pasture below Pearsall. We went to work gathering them about the 20th of February and it took us until the 5th of March to get them out of the thickets, inspected and road-branded. These cattle were in good shape and as fine beeves as you ever saw, no she stuff, and mostly threes and up. There were a few twos, but they were all fours when we got through and ready for the market.

On the morning of March 5 we pointed those old moss-headed

beeves up the trail and made it to the Davis Ranch that night. Uncle Bob said we could pen them there and perhaps get a little sleep, but a norther and a dry thunderstorm blew up and everybody had to get around that old pen and sing to them while they were milling around like a grindstone.

We pulled out from there at sunrise the next morning and drove to the old John Adams Ranch on the Castroville road, where we penned the beeves again and had another bad night. Nobody got any sleep, but we kept them in the pen. When the herd reached New Braunfels Uncle Bob, who was acting boss, turned the herd over to Bill Perryman and turned back. Our regular boss was V.A. Johnson, who had been detained in San Antonio on account of sickness in his family.

We crossed the Guadalupe River in a rain, and just after nightfall we had a severe storm with lots of thunder, lightning and cold. It was so dark most of the hands left us and went to the chuck wagon except W.T. Henson, myself, and old Chief, a Negro. We had to let them drift, and it took us two or three days to get them back together.

We were about thirty head short when we counted and pulled out from there. When we reached the vicinity where Kyle is now located we had another big storm and a general mix up with some other herds that were near us. We had quite a time cutting our cattle out and getting them all back, especially some strays that were in the herd.

We had storms and stampedes all the way up to Red River, which we reached about the 16th of April. We never did succeed in holding all of them at any time. We had a few old trouble-makers in the herd, which, if they had been shot when we first started, would have saved us a lot of worry. They ran so much they became regular old scalawags. But, strange to say, we never had a single stampede while passing through the Indian Territory. The Indians did not give us as much trouble on this trip as they did in 1872.

Ed Chambers was killed at Pond Creek, while in charge of a herd for Tucker & Duncan.

We had some exciting times getting our herd across Red River, which was on a big rise, and nearly a mile wide, with all kinds of large trees floating down on big foam-capped waves that looked larger than a wagon sheet, but we had to put our herd over to the other side. Henson and I were selected to go across and hold the cattle when they reached the opposite side.

We were mounted on small paint ponies, and the one I was riding got into some quicksand just under the water and stuck there. I dismounted in water about knee deep, rolled him over and took off my saddle, bridle and leggins, then undressed myself and called some of the boys to come in and get my things, while I headed my horse for the north bank with just a rope around his neck.

I figured that if my little pony could not make it across I would use one of those moss-headed steers for a ferry boat, but the little fellow took me safely over. He swam all of the way with his nose just out of the water.

Three herds crossed the river that day and one man was drowned, besides several cattle. Hub Hunt of Gonzales got away from his pony in some way and we had to fish him out, and a fellow named Barkley was knocked off and pawed in the face by his horse, and we got him out too.

We had one horse, which I had intended to ride, that would not attempt to swim at all, and we had to take him across on the ferryboat. We tried to get him to swim the river, but he would only turn up on his side, curl his tail, and float back to the bank. He was a fine looking red roan, was raised on the Noonan Ranch near Castroville and branded circle dot on left shoulder. He fell on me one night during a stampede at Wichita, and seemed to be a Jonah all around.

It took about four weeks to move our herd across the Territory, during which time we had some fun killing and roping buffalo. Some of our outfit returned by way of the old Coffeyville Trail, as the Indians were on the warpath on the Chisholm Trail because some buffalo hunters had killed some of their bucks and they wanted revenge.

# Reflections of the Trail

### by George W. Saunders, San Antonio, Texas

I WAS BORN AT RANCHO, GONZALES COUNTY, TEXAS, Feb. 12, 1854. My father and mother settled in that county in 1850, coming with several other immigrants in ox wagons from Mississippi. In 1850 they moved to Goliad County and settled twelve miles west of Goliad, on Lost Creek, where father previously selected a place to start a cattle ranch.

At that time I was only five years old, but I can remember riding a side saddle belonging to one of my sisters and helping keep up the tail end of the herd part of the time on this trip. At Helena I saw my first white house, and when we crossed the San Antonio River at Wofford, I remember how excited we all were when our herd was in the swift water.

Part of them floated down below the ford, and it required a great deal of time to get them out at different points for half a mile down the river. Never having seen anything like this before, my mother thought all of the cattle were lost when she saw them going down the stream.

In a few days we reached our new home and camped on the site, which father had selected, and father and my two oldest brothers, Mat and Bill, assisted by some hired help, began cutting and hauling timber to build houses and stock pens, while myself and brother, Jack, a third brother older than I, range-herded the cattle to locate them.

Fish and game were plentiful, deer were constantly in sight of our camp; in fact, that country was in a perfectly wild state. Only a few cattle were on the range, which was as fine as could be found anywhere. In a few months we were comfortably quartered and happy in our new location. Father had taken a herd of cattle on shares from William Rupe, getting every third calf for attending to them, and we all kept busy looking after the stock.

We soon became acquainted with the settlers, with whom we worked the ranges, and neighbored with them in every sense of the term.

This being before the days of the chuck wagon, the men would set a date and place to meet for what we called a "cow hunt." Each man would bring bedding, coffee pot, tin cup, a wallet of biscuit, salt, sometimes sugar, four or five horses each, and we would work the surrounding range until all cattle belonging to the outfit were gathered and held under herd, then we would select a pack horse for our equipment and move to some other part of the range, gathering cattle as we went.

When grub got scarce we would send after more supplies to some nearby ranch. Usually it required from ten to fifteen days to make these trips, then each man would take his cattle home, put all the calves in a pen in order to locate the mother cows, and range herd the dry cattle for a few days and locate them.

We were prosperous and happy until the Civil War started, and father and my oldest brother entered the service the first year, and another brother enlisted the second year, which left brother Jack and myself to take care of our stock with the assistance of a few old men and some Negroes.

We worked the range constantly during the war. The range was full of wild mustang horses, and they caused us a lot of trouble, for we had to keep our horse stock from getting with them, for once they got mixed with the mustangs they soon became as wild or wilder than these wild horses. In order to capture or kill these mustangs the stockmen built pens around water holes and prepared traps to ensnare them.

To these pens wings would be constructed in the shape of a V, forming a chute through which the mustangs would be compelled to go to water.

Once a bunch of mustangs passed through the chute to the water hole the gate would be shut by a watchman, who had lain in wait in concealment for the horses, and the animals were securely snared. They would then be forced into a small, well-built enclosure constructed of rails to a height of eight or ten feet, where they were roped and made gentle.

These animals were of Spanish origin and were noted for their endurance on the range and trail. The settlers used various unique methods of capturing them, one way being to walk them down.

Some men would take three or four days' supply of provisions, start a bunch of mustangs, follow them as closely as possible, and when they got out of sight of the pursuer would pick up their trail, keep right after them, never giving them time to eat or rest day or night.

Usually on the second day of the chase he could get closer to them;

the third or fourth day he could drive them in home with a bunch of gentle horses and easily pen them. They were caught in many different ways and oftentimes shot in order to rid the range of their presence. Before long they disappeared entirely.

Our cattle increased to such proportions with new herds coming into our country from East Texas and Louisiana that by the time the war ended our range was overstocked. We sold a few cattle to the government and a few to Mexican freighters for work oxen.

I shall never forget the first stampede I experienced. George Bell, who was exempt from military service on account of one eye being blind, agreed to take a herd of beeves to Mexico and exchange for supplies for the war widows. The neighbors got together about 200 of these beeves, my mother putting in twenty head. We delivered the herd to Mr. Bell at the Pettus Ranch where Pettus Station now stands.

This was in 1864, when I was ten years old. We put our cattle in the herd and brother Jack and I agreed to help hold them.

That night shortly after dark something scared the beeves and they made a run. I had never heard anything like the rumbling noise they made, but I put spurs to my horse and followed the noise. We ran those cattle all night and at daybreak we found we had not lost a beef, but we had five or six bunches four or five miles apart, and two or three men or boys with each bunch.

We soon had them all together and Mr. Bell started them on the trip. When he returned from Mexico he brought us one sack of coffee, two sets of knives and forks, two pairs of spurs, two bridle bits, and two fancy "hackamores," or bridle headstalls, for which he had traded our twenty beeves, and we were well pleased with our deal, for in those days such things were considered luxuries, and we were glad to get them, particularly the knives and forks, for we had been drinking bran coffee and were using wooden knives and forks we had made ourselves.

Those were hard times in Goliad County during the Civil War, and when the internecine strife ended, the soldiers came home broke and all anxious to make up the time that had been lost during the four years that had passed.

Reconstruction set in. Some outlaws and crooks drifted into our country; considerable friction and hatred existed between the boys of the Blue and the Gray; Negro soldiers were stationed at different points to keep order, but it soon resulted in serious clashes that called for more Texas Rangers and U.S. marshals.

As is usually the case, right and justice finally prevailed. During this time our stockmen were hunting markets for the cattle on our overstocked ranges. We sold a few steers to Foster & Allen, Shanghai Pierce and Joel Collins, which were shipped from Powder Horn. Slaughter houses at Rockport killed considerable beeves at the time, but we needed a greater outlet for the ever-increasing herds on the ranges.

In 1868 or 1869 a few stockmen drove small herds to Baxter Springs, Kansas, or other northern points, and met with such success that everybody had caught the trail fever. My two brothers, Mat and Jack, took a herd to Baxter Springs in 1870, and their reports of thrilling encounters with the Indians, stampedes, buffalo chases, and the like, filled me with a wild desire to go on the trail, too.

I was barely seventeen years old, and felt that I was able to take care of myself on a long trip as well as any man. My parents finally consented for me to go, and I hired to Monroe Choate, of the firm of Choate & Bennett, to go with a herd. The firm was receiving herds in different parts of the country to send up the trail. They sent fourteen herds that year.

Mr. Choate told me the name of the boss of each herd and asked me which boss I would rather go with. I told him I wanted to go with the first herd that started, and he informed me that Jim Byler would boss the first herd and would start at once.

That suited me fine, so I said, "Put me with Byler." Mr. Byler was asked what he thought about taking a seventeen-year-old kid on the trip and remarked, "His age is all right, if he has staying qualities, but most kids are short on sleep, and generally sleep on watch." I told him I would not sleep during stampedes or Indian fights, and he promised to give me a trial, and that made me exceedingly happy.

We left Helena with a full chuck wagon, the necessary number of horses and men, and went to the Mays pasture on the Cibolo near Stockdale, Wilson County, and received 1,000 steers.

Dunk Choate counted the cattle and Mr. Byler pointed the herd north and Dunk said, "Adios, boys, I will see you in Abilene, Kansas, I must go now and start other herds."

We went by Gonzales, Lockhart, Austin and Georgetown, without any unusual happenings, but on the Gabriel we had a bad stampede during a thunderstorm, and the herd was split up into several bunches.

They were all found the next day. Some of the bunches had men with them and some did not. They were all trailed and found except me and seventy-five steers. By ten o'clock the boss finally located the trail of my bunch and found it ten miles down the Gabriel.

When he rode up he asked, "Are you awake? Why didn't you bring these cattle back to the herd" I said I could not find the trail the steers made, and I did not know what direction to go to find the herd.

We got back to the main herd about four o'clock in the evening, and I was so tired and sleepy I told the boss I was just bound to eat and sleep a little. He said, "Go, go eat and sleep all night; I will herd your relief. You deserve a rest." This sounded good to me, for up to this time I thought the boss was mad.

After a good night's rest I was on the job early the next morning, ready to do my share in keeping the herd on the move. The cattle were easily scared and for several days were very nervous and made many runs, but the boys kept strict watch on them, and they finally became reconciled.

We went by Waco, Cleburne and Fort Worth. Between the last named places the country was somewhat level and untimbered, and was full of prairie chickens and deer. When we reached Fort Worth we crossed the Trinity River under the bluff, where the present streetcar line to the stockyards crosses the river. Fort Worth was then but a very small place, consisting of only a few stores, and there was only one house in that part of the town, where the stockyards are now located.

We held our herd here two days, finally proceeding on our journey, and crossed Red River at Red River Station and took the Chisholm Trail through the Indian Territory.

Here we saw lots of Indians, who came to our herd with the usual greeting, "How, John," to beg tobacco and provisions. Byler got by these Indians without any trouble, but we found all the streams in that region up and had to swim them or lose time, for Byler wanted to keep the lead, and we therefore crossed many rivers at a time when other men would have hesitated.

At Pond Creek we encountered our first buffalo. The plains were literally covered with these animals, and when we came in sight of them all of the boys quit the herd and gave chase. It was a wonderful sight to see these cowboys dashing after those big husky monsters, shooting at them from all angles.

We soon learned that it did no good to shoot them in the forehead, as we were accustomed to shooting beeves with our pistols, for the bullets would not penetrate their skull. We would dash by them and shoot them between the eyes without apparent effect, so we began shooting them behind the shoulder and that brought them down.

I killed two or three of the grown buffaloes and roped a yearling, which I was glad to turn loose and let him get away with a good rope. I soon became satisfied with the excitement incident to killing buffalo, swimming streams, being in stampedes, and passing through thunderstorms, but I still longed to be mixed up in an Indian fight, for I had not yet had that sort of experience.

We crossed Bluff Creek into Kansas and passed Newton during the latter part of May.

A blacksmith shop, a store, and about a dozen dwellings made up this town at the time, but when we came back through the place on our return home thirty days later, it had grown to be quite a large town, due to the building of a railroad. It did not seem possible that a town could make such quick growth in such short time, but Newton, Kansas, sprang up almost overnight.

We stopped our herd on Holland Creek, twenty miles from Abilene, Kansas, where we were met by Pink Bennett and a buyer. Pink sold 300 fat beeves out of our herd to this man, and I went to Abilene with them to help load them on the cars. They were the first cattle I had ever seen loaded on a train, and I was anxious to see how it was done.

We held our herd there until several more herds belonging to Choate & Bennett arrived. They sold some out of each herd, and we soon had a surplus of men and horses. W.G. Butler had done likewise and he also had too many men and horses to continue on with the cattle, so it was arranged that some of us could start home, and accordingly about fifty men, with five chuck wagons, five cooks and about 150 horses, hit the back trail for Texas.

We had a lively time en route home, for we had nothing to do but drive the horses, make camp, eat and sometimes sleep. When we reached the Washita River we found it out of its banks. We cut timber and made a raft by tying the logs with ropes, but could not ferry the rude craft until a rope had been stretched across the river, which was some 300 yards wide and very swift and deep.

Several of the boys attempted to make it across with the end of a rope, but each one failed. Some of them got half way across, turned the rope loose and swam back. One of them got near the opposite bank, but lost the end of the rope and landed without it. I was the fifth one to try this difficult feat, and determined to succeed, so taking one end of the rope in my mouth, passing it over my shoulder, I entered the water, the boys on the bank releasing the rope gradually as I swam out, and I made it across, but grasped an overhanging willow limb and pulled myself ashore with the rope still in my mouth.

The man who had preceded me across came to my assistance and helped me up the slippery bank, then there was a cowboy yell of approval from the other side as the boys realized that I had succeeded in accomplishing a dangerous feat.

I felt very proud of myself, and think I added several inches to my stature right there, for I was only seventeen years old, and had succeeded in an undertaking in which four stalwart men had failed, but I am willing to confess I could not have gone ten feet further in my exhausted condition.

We soon put our outfits across with the raft, but lost the hind wheels of one of Butler's wagons. We carried the wagon beds over on the raft, but pulled the wagons across with ropes, for we had to draw the wagons and effects up a steep, slippery embankment, and this required a great deal of time, patience and profanity. When we got everything across, we rigged up our outfit and resumed our journey.

We crossed Red River opposite Denison, rode into town and visited all of the stores and saloons. The people there were glad to see us come and glad to see us leave. Our next town was Denton, where the officers demanded our pistols.

The law prohibiting the carrying of pistols had been enacted only a short time before and was then in effect, but we could not think of parting with our lifelong friends, so when a demand was made for us to surrender them we pulled our pistols and rode out of town shooting into the air. The officers did not follow us.

We stopped at Fort Worth and all the other towns on our route, as we leisurely traveled homeward, finally reaching our destination safely. I was mighty proud of this, my first trip, and reached home with a pair of shop-made boots and two good suits of clothes, one of which was a black changeable velvet affair that I had paid fifty dollars for in Kansas.

I carried these clothes in a pair of saddlebags all the way home, and found after I reached there that I could have purchased them cheaper from a local merchant. But little did I care, for I was determined to "cut a shine" with the girls when I got back off that notable trip.

Referring back to some of the incidents that occurred on the trip, I can recall several amusing things that happened.

The prairies near Abilene, Kansas, where we held our herds, were partly taken up by grangers, who lived in dugouts, a square hole in the ground, or on the side of a bluff, with timbers placed across and covered with dirt. Each granger had taken up about 160 acres of land, part of which was cultivated. They had no fences, so to mark the boundaries of their homesteads, they would plow a furrow around it. As there was no timber in the country, except a few cottonwoods, which grew along the streams, the grangers were compelled to use buffalo chips for fuel.

While we were there with our herds many other herds came in and the whole prairie was covered with cattle for many miles around. I visited lots of camps and met many old friends from Texas. Buyers were plentiful, cattle sold fast, and the grangers were active among the herds asking the cattlemen to bed cattle on their lands so they could get the chips for fuel.

One evening I noticed several men and women in buggies and buckboards going to different herds and begging each boss to bed his herd on their respective lands.

They soon got into a "squabble" with each other, claiming they had asked a certain boss first, and this caused the cowboys to congregate around to see the fun and encourage the row. Levi Anderson was the boss in question, and they all claimed he had promised to bed cattle on their land.

Levi was puzzled, for he was not used to the customs of the country, and said the reason he had promised was because he thought they were all joking. He said those dugout people were somewhat different from the folks where he lived, remarking that "Down in Texas, if you gave a man dry dung he would fight you, but here in Kansas they will fight you for dry dung."

The grangers figured that 1,000 cattle would leave enough chips on the ground in one night to give them 500 pounds of fuel in a few days.

Ben Borroum and I were herding together one day, and as all of the cattle were in sight, we did not notice that they had gotten on a small patch of corn just coming up, until they had pawed and trampled the corn, crushing twenty little chickens to death, and ran all of the family into the dugout. This negligence on our part cost Choate & Bennett about $100.

Jack Potter once told me that while he was up in this part of Kansas he got lost from his outfit one night and rode up to one of these dugouts and asked if he could stop with them until morning. The granger told him he was welcome to do so, although their accommodations were very limited.

They fed his horse for him and then invited him down into the dugout, which contained one room about sixteen feet square, but as neat as could be. In this room there was a nice clean bed, one table, four chairs, a stove, cooking utensils, the man, his wife and two small boys. The wife soon prepared a good supper for Jack, and after he had eaten they sat up and talked to him for quite a while, during which time the little boys fell asleep on the bed, while the parents, who seemed to be a very intelligent couple, told Jack about themselves and their plans.

They were enthusiastic over the prospects to make a fortune in that new country, and talked about everything in general, but all this time Jack was puzzling his brain over how all of them were going to sleep on the one bed in that dugout. Finally the mother picked up the two boys and sat them over in a corner, leaning them against the wall still asleep, and then she informed Jack that he could occupy the bed and she and her husband went up the steps.

Potter turned in and was soon asleep, and slept soundly all night long, but when he awoke the next morning he found himself sitting in the corner with the two little boys and the man and woman were occupying the bed. Jack told me he knew that couple was just bound to prosper anywhere, even in Kansas.

After breakfast he gave them five dollars, but they protested, saying that fifty cents was enough to pay for the poor accommodations he had received, but Jack informed them that what he had seen and learned right there was worth five dollars to him.

Remember this was Jack Potter, not Jim Wilson.

I passed through this same old herding ground some twenty-five years later, and I was astonished to see the changes that had taken place. Pretty farms and new dwellings covered the whole region, and there were fine herds of good cattle, horses, sheep, mules and hogs everywhere, and the whole country looked prosperous.

After I reached home from my first trip I went to work on the range driving cattle to Rockport packeries in summer and winter and putting up trail herds each spring, following this occupation for several years, selling our family's cattle to the well-known trail drivers, J.D. Reed, Dillard Fant and others.

Cattle accumulated fast on the ranges. Many ranches were established, each ranch owner running his own outfit and exchanging brands with stockmen in different parts of the state.

The ranchmen would brand calves and sell beeves for each other, then meet and make settlement once a year. Such arrangements were made between stockmen from San Antonio to Brownsville and from Victoria to Laredo. It was nothing strange for one man to own cattle throughout the above-mentioned territory.

The cattle business gradually moved westward, forcing the redskins back; many of our stockmen began buying purebred bulls and improving their stock. Among those who first began to grade up their cattle were King & Kenedy, Reynolds, Coleman, Matthis & Fulton, W.A. Pettus, N.G. Collins and others. The chuck wallet and pack horse disappeared and their places were taken by the chuck wagon.

Fences came and the open range passed away forever.

During those days I belonged to Uncle Henry Scott's Minute Company for two years. This company was organized at Mission Refugio in 1873 to protect the citizens of the border against Mexican bandits.

During these two years a number of massacres were committed by these bandits, many of whom paid the penalty for their lawlessness. Among the families that were murdered by the Mexicans were the Swift family near Refugio; John Maden, near St. Mary's; the Nux family and others at Nux Store twelve miles west of Corpus Christi; Lee Rabb; the Penescal family and others whose names I cannot recall.

When our company was called out for duty we went at a moment's notice, regardless of what we were doing or where we were, and we rode with such vengeance that our company soon became a terror to the invading murderous Mexicans.

For one year I was a deputy under Sheriff James Burk of Goliad, during which time I had some narrow escapes and made some dangerous arrests of desperate characters.

For a few years after the war there was a woman in that region by the name of Sally Skull, who was quite a character. She traded horses through our country, and operated alone, with a band of Mexican helpers, from Texas into Mexico, and had a record of being the most fearless woman ever known. Nearly all of the old citizens of that section remember Sally Skull.

In those early days cattle buyers usually met the sellers at some appointed place to close a deal for stock, and they would bring the purchase money in gold and silver in sacks on the backs of pack horses. When they reached the meeting places the sacks of money would be carelessly dumped on the ground where sometimes it would remain for two or three days without molestation, then when the settlement was made for cattle bought the sacks were opened, the money dumped out on a blanket in camp and counted out to each man who had participated in the trades.

I fear that kind of an arrangement would not work today, but in those days those rugged pioneers dealt strictly on the square.

Pasture fencing commenced on the coast in 1872 – 3, and in a few years each cattleman had a pasture of from 1,000 to 50,000 acres, which stopped the exchanging of brands, for before a great while every man had his cattle in his own pasture and ran his own cow outfit.

Space will not permit mention of the cattle stealing, fence-cutting, trouble between cattlemen and others, which called for the assistance of Texas Rangers and U.S. marshals, with whose aid the cattlemen established law and order.

With the organization of the Cattle Raisers' Association a few years later the doom of the cattle and horse thief was sealed, for the organization soon grew to such proportions, with its expert inspectors at all markets and shipping points, that it made it almost impossible for a thief to exist.

In 1874 I was married to Miss Rachel Reeves, who was the daughter of W.M. Reeves, a well-known stockman of Refugio County. We began housekeeping on my ranch, eight miles from Goliad, where the present railroad station, Clip, is now located.

I later sold this ranch to W.A. Pettus (better known as Buck Pettus), one of the most prosperous stockmen of Goliad County, and years later, when the railroad was built from Beeville to Goliad, it went across my old ranch and the station was named Clip, in honor of Mrs. Pettus, whose maiden name was Miss Clip Lott.

In 1880 my wife's health failed and I took her to San Antonio for treatment, and as I had to be near her, I could not follow my work as a stockman, so decided to get into some line of business in San Antonio to make a living in the big city.

I finally bought several hacks and teams and ran them day and night, carrying passengers over the city. The I. & G.N. and the S.P. Railroads were just building into San Antonio, the city was flourishing and full of prospectors and stockmen. As I was acquainted with many of the visitors, mostly stockmen, I did a thriving business.

My wife died in January 1883, and the following March I sold out my business, carried my two little girls to the home of my parents in Goliad, then returned to San Antonio and bought 300 Spanish mares, which I shipped to Vinita, Indian Territory, and drove them through Eastern Kansas, selling a few and paying fines for damage they did to unfenced fields along the way.

I shipped from Springfield to Hannibal, Missouri, where I decided to try to dispose of all of these mares. At this place I advertised "Wild Texas Ponies for Sale at William L. Fry's Stables, with an Exhibition of Roping and Riding Wild Horses."

I put my stock in a large lot adjoining the stable on the morning of the sale, and everybody in the town was there to see them, all anxious to witness the bronco busting. I mounted a dry goods box and announced that these horses were for sale and invited buyers to come forward and select the mares they wanted, and in order to hold the crowd, I told them the bronco riding would be the last act of the show, but that they would not be disappointed.

Quite a number bought horses, and as each animal was sold two of my expert cowboys would lasso it and hold it by the jaws and ears until a hackamore was securely placed on its head, then it was led through a gate and delivered to the buyer, who in turn employed Negroes to take it home for him.

We kept this up all morning, when word was passed around that all of the horses that had been sold were running loose in the town and surrounding country with ropes dragging. It seems that the Negroes who had undertaken to lead the horses away, in each instance did not understand how to handle these broncos, and they would get away.

One Negro said it would take a long time to learn the nature of such horses, for they would lay down and kick and paw all of the rope around their bodies and legs and leave him nothing to hold to, and he just had to let go the rope.

The buyers were good-natured and did not blame me in the least. I sold fifty head of the mares here at good prices, and when the buying slacked up, I roped an outlaw horse, saddled him Wild West fashion, and Anderson Moreland, one of my cowboys, mounted him. This horse was a professional and on that occasion he did full credit to his past reputation, to the great delight and enthusiasm of the crowd of spectators.

When we drove our herd out of town several of the citizens went with us for several miles. From here we drove them to Pittsfield, Illinois, selling and trading as we went, finally disposing of all of our Texas horses, but we still had about twenty large native horses that we had taken in exchange. We shipped these by boat down the Mississippi River to St. Louis. This was our first boat ride, and was greatly enjoyed by myself and my companions. We sold out at St. Louis and came home by train.

After returning to Texas I bought 150 saddle horses, or cow ponies, and shipped them to Wichita Falls, then the terminus of the Fort Worth & Denver Railroad. From this point we drove them to Atascosa, on the Canadian River above the LIT Ranch, where I sold them to Will Hughes at a big profit. After the sale was made we went to the ranch house together, and there I discovered that Hughes and I were boys together at Goliad, but his Goliad name was not Hughes.

When I returned to San Antonio, Harry Fawcett and myself bought the Narcisso Leal livestock commission business, with offices and stables opposite the Southern Hotel on Dolorosa Street. We put up our sign in September 1883, and our business thrived from the very start. We sold horses by thousands on commission for parties who drove to the San Antonio market from South Texas and Mexico.

During the fall and winter we bought considerable horse stock ourselves, which we sent to the Bluntzer pasture near San Patricio and also to the Tobey pasture in Atascosa County, expecting to sell them the next spring to trail drivers.

Not being able to get as much for them as we thought they were worth, we decided to drive these horses up the trail ourselves, so we sold our commission business back to Leal, gathered our horses, brought them to San Antonio and for several days held them on Prospect Hill, which is now in the city limits.

On April 5, 1884, we loaded our chuck wagon and hit the trail for Dodge City, Kansas. We went by Kerrville and Junction City, following what was then known as the Upper or Western Trail. At Seymour we crossed the Brazos, and at Doan's Store we crossed Red River.

I will not attempt to describe the trouble we had on this trip with Indians, stampedes and swollen streams, as other sketches in this book have treated those subjects with full justice. There were many herds on the trail that year, and we wanted to keep in the lead, but to do so required systematic work, so I kept my herd moving forward all the time.

I would go on ahead and select herding ground for nights and grazing grounds for nooning, grazed the horses up to these grounds and grazed or drove them off, never allowing them to graze back at all, for in this way I gained a great deal of valuable time, for I had learned that good time and lots of it was lost by the old way of stopping a herd and allowing it to graze in every direction, sometimes a mile or more on the back trail.

In such cases the stock would travel over the same ground twice, which, in the long run, would amount to considerable mileage when you consider that the distance from Texas to the markets was from 1,000 to 1,500 miles. Good trail bosses who made quick time with stock in good shape were always in demand.

We reached Dodge City minus a few horses, which were lost on the trail, but they were brought up by other herds and delivered to me at this point. One night while we were there a storm came up and caused several herds to stampede, and there were about 15,000 horses mixed up. Two men were killed by lightning that night. It took several days to gather and separate the horses.

Several outfits from different parts of Texas gave the same road brand and this caused no end of trouble. Mr. Fawcett, my partner, had come up to Dodge City by train, and was present during the big stampede, which he thought was great sport. He said he would buy the leaders if we could pick them out, as he wanted to ship them to England to show the chaps over there what a running horse was like, and if he could ever get the blooming rascals gentle he would run foxes on them.

Just before we started this herd up the trail Harry Hotchkiss, who is now manager for the Houston Packing Company, arrived in San Antonio from England and helped us to get our herd together. Harry was an old friend to Mr. Fawcett and was so delighted with the prospect of getting into the horse business that he bought 100 head and put them into our herd.

He made a good hand from the very start and was of great assistance to me on the trail. We had told him we expected to make $15 to $20 per head profit on our horses when we sold them up the trail, and he was looking forward to making a neat sum on his investment.

One night while we were camped in a rough region between the Saline and the San Saba River, west of Maberry's pasture, our herd stampeded, during a storm. I had told the boys on first relief not to attempt to hold the herd if they stampeded, as the country was too broken and that I would rather trail the horses the next day than to take any chances of some of my men getting killed.

The boys all came to camp and at daybreak the next morning we were all ready to start cutting sign. In a few hours we rounded up most of them, while Hotchkiss was holding the herd and counting his horses as they came in each bunch.

I brought in several bunches, and each time Hotchkiss would come to me and want to know if I thought he would ever get all of his horses back. I would tell him I did not have time to talk to him, for I was in a hurry to go after other bunches. The herd was pretty badly scattered, and had left plain trails in every direction. Some were followed for ten or fifteen miles before they were overtaken and brought back.

This required fast work by all of us, for we had to gather them before they could mix with other range horses and be lost entirely. I brought a bunch into the herd about two o'clock and found we were still about 200 head short.

Hotchkiss rushed up and commanded me to stop and explain to him how I could figure $15 or $20 per head profit for him on his horses when half of them were gone on the first ten days out, adding that it was a "blawsted rotten misrepresentation," and that Fawcett and I must make it good.

I told him not to worry, that we would get them all back, and as I left him he was cussing and cavorting around in great fashion; in truth he was about the maddest man I ever saw.

In a little while I met some of the boys with about twenty of Hotchkiss' horses in the bunch they were bringing in, and I told them to assure him that he would get all of them back before night, for he was in great suspense and needed consolation. By five o'clock that evening we had recovered all of our horses and Hotchkiss was a happy boy. Ten men riding at full speed all day, changing horses each time they brought in a bunch, accomplished a wonderful work that day.

We had another Englishman in our outfit on that trip who was also a tenderfoot and fresh from England. His name was Lambert and he had begged to be permitted to go with us, agreeing to furnish four horses and help us free of charge, as he wanted to learn to be a bronco-buster. He was game and would undertake anything he was told to do.

He insisted that he be allowed to do night herding, and when given the work, went to sleep, his horse drifted into the herd and he fell off, causing a stampede. After that I set him free to go and come as he pleased. He would visit other herds in front and behind us, getting all the news, so we called him our reporter.

My Mexican hands were riding wild horses when in open country and during good weather. Lambert begged me constantly to let him ride a bucking horse, so one day at noon, while we were camped in a beautiful prairie country, I had the boys to rope the worst bucking horse in the herd, saddle him, tie the stirrups, and fix a roll in front of the saddle. Then I mounted a well-trained horse, took firm hold on the rope attached to the bronco's hackamore, while Lambert was assisted to get on.

As soon as all was ready I gave the bucker slack enough to get his head down. Lambert was eager to show what he thought he could do, and said to the horse, "Gaddup, Gaddup, old Chap, I've rode worse 'orses than you."

But "old Chap" did not move, just stood there all humped up. I told Lambert to hit him over the head with his hat, as the other boys did bucking horses. He took his big hat in his hand, reached forward and brought it down between the horse's ears. At that same instant the horse and the Englishman went straight up in the air with their heads toward the north, turned in the air and came down with their heads toward the south.

Lambert quit the horse and hit the ground running, yelling, "'Old the blooming rascal. 'E made such peculiar movements I lost my balance." The boys who had bet on Lambert riding the horse, raised their bets, Bill Williams betting two to one on the Englishman; so he tried it again. That horse threw Lambert five times before he gave it up, and said if the horse had a straight back he could ride him, but his back was too crooked for him to stay on.

Lambert pulled off a lot of stunts for our amusement on the trip, but decided that bronco-busting was too hard to learn. One day he accidentally roped a wild mare with a rope that was tied around the neck of a little mule he was riding. The mare dashed through the herd and caused a stampede. Some of the horses ran across the rope and threw mare, mule and Englishman all to the ground. When the dust cleared Lambert was found holding the mule by the tail while the mule held the mare, until the boys roped her and removed Lambert's rope.

Lambert was the possessor of a red saddle blanket, and when we were in the Comanche country the Indians got friendly with our outfit and made signs that they wanted that red blanket. Tel Hawkins and some of the other boys told the Indians to take it, and when they began to pull it from under Lambert's saddle he pulled his pistol and I rushed up just in the nick of time to prevent bloodshed, for Lambert meant business.

While the boys were trading and hurrahing with the Indians I went to the old Comanche chief's tepee and had quite an enjoyable conversation with him. He told me he knew all of the region in South and Southwest Texas, and named many of the streams, and told of raids he had made down there. He also said he knew Creed Taylor, Capt. John Sansom, John R. Baylor, Bigfoot Wallace, and other citizens of that section, who, he said, were "Heap bad mans. Killie heap Indians," and indicated that his warriors always dreaded to meet these well-known characters, for they always "shot to kill."

In July, 1884, I bought two cars of saddle horses and a chuck wagon and shipped them from San Antonio to Alpine, where I received a herd of cattle for Keeney, Wiley & Hurst, which they had bought from Millett & Lane. John Kokernot delivered this herd to me and I took them to Seven Rivers, New Mexico, via Saragosa, Pecos City and up the Pecos to Seven Rivers, where I turned them over to Mr. Keeney. It was a long, dry drive, and I was glad when through with it.

After delivering this herd I went to Tat Huling's ranch in Rattlesnake Canyon, thirty-five miles west of Van Horn, in El Paso County, and remained there two months helping Huling do ranch work and prospecting for gold in the Delaware and Guadalupe Mountains with an old miner named Dyer, who claimed that Indians had told him where he could find a rich mine near an old Indian camp.

While prospecting we camped at a spring where the Urcery boys of Oakville, Texas, later established a cattle ranch. We searched through the Delaware Mountains, going up into the Guadalupes, and came back by the salt lakes. These lakes cover a territory fifteen-miles long and two- or three-miles wide with salt three to seven feet deep.

By appointment I met N.H. Hall at Toyah in October. He was in quarantine there with several thousand head of cattle, and was anxious to get 1,000 two-year-old heifers to his ranch in Luna Valley, Arizona, for spring breeding. Mr. Hall offered me extra big wages to take them through, and as I had previously promised to make the trip for him, I consented to start as soon as the herd could be made ready.

The weather was getting cold, and the route was through a dangerous region occupied by old Geronimo's band of Apaches, and I knew that I would have a hard trip, but I picked 1,000 of the best heifers in the best condition, selected the best horses and secured the best men I could find, all well armed, and pulled out with the herd, going by Cottonwood Ranch, the Gran Tinnon Ranch, passed the head of Delaware River, Guadalupe Peak, and stopped several days at Crow Springs, just over the line in New Mexico, to prepare for a 107-mile dry drive to the waters of the Sacramento River.

When I started the herd from Crow Springs I left my horses there until the next morning, so as to have fresh mounts when they overtook us the second day, then we sent the horses on to water thirty miles up the Sacramento. From the mouth of the Sacramento the channel of the river was a dry bed of gravel for thirty miles with great bluffs on either side hundreds of feet high.

The herd strung out up this canyon for several miles and we pushed forward as rapidly as possible. When we reached the water I turned the cattle up the steep mountainside as fast as they arrived and got their fill. It was ten hours from the time the lead cattle reached the water until the tail end got there. They were in very poor condition and a pitiful sight to see, with their sunken eyes, and some of them barely able to creep along.

There was no grass in the canyon, but we found good grass and water on the mountains and range herded them several days, then put them back in the canyon several miles above and followed it up to the divide, where we crossed over to Dog Canyon.

On this divide I saw my first wild elk, and some of the tallest pine trees I had ever seen. Dog Canyon was very steep and we had to lock all the wagon wheels to pass many places. At the mouth of Dog Canyon our route was around White Mountain, and in this region was where old Geronimo was depredating.

We often saw the signal fires of the Indians at night, and in order to play safe we would bed our herd in the evening, eat supper before dark, then take our horses and wagon and camp a mile or more away from the herd so the Indians would not find us if they attacked the herd. No fire was built at those camps to guide the redskins.

Next day we would round up the herd and move on. We were not attacked and I suppose it was because our cattle and horses were in such poor condition the Indians did not care for them; and, further, they were not seeking a fight with a bunch of Texas cowboys.

We went by Tularosa and La Luz, across the Melphia at the government crossing, and crossed the Rio Grande at San Marcial, proceeding on to Magdalena, where I was taken seriously ill. Mr. Hall met us here and took the herd on to Luna Valley, Arizona. Remarkable as it may seem, I lost only five head of these cattle on the entire trip, which were bogged in a marsh at La Luz. At this marsh we had considerable difficulty in pulling out about fifty herd that were bogged, but we could not save the five head mentioned above.

The trip was made in cold weather, part of the time freezing temperatures prevailed, and we suffered a great deal from the cold and exposure.

This made the third herd, or trip, I had taken that year, which was a record-breaker, and I decided to recuperate, so I went to Socorro, New Mexico, reaching there the 20th of December, 1884, and after spending a while there I went to El Paso, and found employment with the Newman & Davis outfit, which was working in Chihuahua, Mexico, just across from the mouth of Van Horn Canyon.

I was over there during the Cutting trouble, and helped to get many cattle across into Texas before the threatened confiscation occurred.

In the spring of 1886 I returned to San Antonio, and again went into the livestock commission business under the firm name of Smith, Oliver & Saunders, being associated with Frank Oliver, now of Victoria, and Capt. Bill Smith, one of San Antonio's most respected citizens, who is now deceased.

I am the oldest livestock commission man in the state today who is still actively engaged in the business. I incorporated my business fifteen years ago, sold shares to leading stockmen all over the country, and today I am the president and general manager of the firm, which is known as the George W. Saunders Live Stock Commission Company, with offices at San Antonio and Fort Worth.

The Fort Worth branch is managed by my son-in-law, W.E. Jary. We enjoy a liberal patronage from all parts of Texas, New Mexico, Oklahoma, Louisiana and Old Mexico, and do a gross business of between $5 million and $6 million annually.

Besides actively giving my attention to my commission business, I supervise the management of four small ranches and a 700-acre farm.

I have always tried to follow the policies of my father and deal justly and fairly with all men, but considering the bad influences that many times engulfed me, the many temptations to deal unfairly, and the glowing prospects to greatly profit by yielding to them, it required an iron will and determination to resist, hence I feel proud that my record is not worse.

I have made money in almost every undertaking, but my sympathy for suffering humanity, and my liberality in dealing has kept me from accumulating a fortune. I believe that ninety-five per cent of the people who know me are my friends, and I value them more than the millions of gold, which perhaps I could have accumulated by sacrificing their friendship by unfair dealing.

I have always been willing to give to charity or any laudable purpose that had for its object the uplift of my fellow man, and have always lent aid and encouragement to every undertaking that was for the up-building of our state and my home city, San Antonio.

I served two terms as alderman of Ward 2 in San Antonio during the

Clinton Brown administration, during which time we voted $3.5 million city bonds, had them approved and sold and spent the money in municipal improvements, building sewers, widening streets and paving thoroughfares, making a modern city of the old Mexican town.

During the World War, I served as chairman of the Exemption Board, Division No. 1, free of charge, and did all I could to help win the war.

I have seen and participated in many unpleasant things during my sixty years of active life, but I think they are best forgotten. I do not think it would be amiss, however, to mention some of the hardships and examples of self-denial endured by the people of the early days.

During the Civil War our family and all of our neighbors were compelled to make almost everything they used or wore; all ropes were made from hides or horsehair, all of our clothing was spun and woven at home, and I have carded and spun many nights until late bedtime.

Leather was tanned by the settlers with bark from oak trees and used to rig saddles and for other purposes. Our shoes were made by country shoemakers; our saddle trees were made at home; we used water from creeks and rivers. Before the country was stocked all the streams contained pure, clear water.

We carried corn in sacks on horseback fifteen to twenty-five miles to mills to be ground into meal, or ground the corn at home with small hand grist mills; wagons, ox yokes, looms and spinning wheels were made at home; hats were plaited and made from palmetto. The rich and the poor in our days were on equal footing, because these necessities could not be bought.

As I look back to those times I am impressed with the marvelous changes time has wrought. The people of those good old days were brave and fearless, but if a high-powered automobile had gone speeding through the country at night with its bright headlights glaring and its horn screeching, I am sure the inhabitants would all have taken to the brush, thinking it was some supernatural monster.

The descendants of the early settlers of Texas are today identified with every industry in the country.

Their intelligence and traits of character are not surpassed by any people on earth, because they are quick to learn, quick to act, brave, honest and true to God and country.

A quarter of a century of my life, from 1861 to 1886, was a continual chain of thrills, not by choice, but by the customs of those times.

The dangers through which I passed during those days make me shudder when I recall them, but I attribute my preservation to the earnest prayers of my devoutly religious father and mother, who continually entreated Almighty God to protect their reckless boy.

They taught me to trust in the Divine Father from infancy, and their admonitions have continued with me to this day, never dimmed but brightening as the years pass. I do not claim to have followed their teachings to the letter, but the training I received at their knees has been a guide and great support to me through life. Had I not received this early training to fortify me against the many temptations I cannot think what would have been the outcome.

I want to say a word about some of the men with whom I have been associated during my business career, for I feel that such affiliation has contributed to my success in the business world.

As good fortune would have it, I fell in with the best men of our country, men of honesty and integrity, and leaders in the affairs of county and state. They helped me to attain that, which I think I now possess, a good name that is "rather to be chosen than great riches." They were loyal at all times, and ever ready to advise and assist me.

And right here I want to pay a tribute to the noble women of our land, for they are more deserving of praise than all of the men combined.

Consider the pioneer mothers and wives of our glorious state, and think of the hardships and privations they endured for the sake of being near and helping husband or father to make a home in the new country.

Their social pleasures were few, their work heavy. Dangers lurked on every hand, but bravely and uncomplainingly these women endured their hard lot, cheering and encouraging the men who were their protectors.

God bless them! I often heard it said in the days of my youth that the women were the hope of our nation. They have fulfilled that hope in every sense of the term, and I believe they will ever continue to do so.

I was the first man to introduce roping contests in this state some thirty years ago, but the practice was so badly abused and so many cattle crippled and killed, that I regretted the introduction, so accordingly in after years I was the first to petition the legislature to pass a law prohibiting the sport.

From 1868 to 1895 it is estimated that fully 35,000 men went up the trail with herds, if the number of men computed by the number of cattle driven is correct. Of this number of men about one-third were Negroes and Mexicans, another third made more than one trip.

Let us conclude that one-half of the white trail drivers who made one trip have died, and we still have some 6,000 survivors of the trail scattered all over the world, all of whom ought to be members of our association.

This would give us the strength to forever perpetuate our organization, for as it is now our sons are eligible to membership and they in turn can make their sons and grandsons eligible as they grow to manhood.

I have urged the organization of the old trail drivers for thirty-five years. Many of my old comrades promised to participate in the organization, but it was put off from time to time, until 1915, when I called a few together and started the movement, which has steadily grown until today. I feel that my efforts in this matter have been in a large measure successful. If we had organized earlier, however, I am sure we would have preserved the record of many of our old comrades who have crossed over the Great Divide, and retained much of the trail slang and customs that have passed away.

I have carefully read most of the sketches that appear in this book. They tend to show that the early settlers and old trail drivers did more toward the development of this state than all other things combined, and it would be the father of all mistakes to allow the record of these men to go down in unwritten history.

Therefore, this book was prepared to preserve that record. My greatest wish is that the proceeds from the sale of the book will be used for the purpose of erecting a monument, one-hundred-feet high, to the drivers of the famous old trail, somewhere on the trail near San Antonio or Fort Worth.

# Some Things I Saw Long Ago

*by George Gerdes*

HERE ARE MY CREDENTIALS: I solemnly swear and affirm that I went the length of the trail up to Dodge City, Kansas, and from there to Pueblo, Colorado.

I further solemnly swear and affirm that I will tell "not" all I saw and heard. Who would? It's a long time back to remember; and if you remember, would you care to tell? If you cared to tell, would you dare to tell? And if you dared to tell you'd be afraid; and if you weren't afraid, you'd be "skeered" as Helmar Jenkins Booth.

My credentials further state that I was born when quite young, in 1863, at a little "jumping-off-in-the-road" place called Quihi, Medina County, Texas, on what was then known as the old John Heven place. We moved later to Sturm (meaning "storm") Hill, where I spent most of my childhood days.

Father was a stock raiser, and also took cattle on shares attending to the handling and care of them on the open range. My sister and I were sent to school in an old school house nearby, on the Klappenbach Ranch, to be "edjicated."

As children we were warned and taught to be on the lookout for Indians. We were told wild and weird stories of massacres and how Indians would steal children and torture them; and which was not a "fairy story," but a fact.

We were on our way home one evening after school when we saw in the distance a band of Indians coming in our direction. It took us but a moment to hide in a cluster of white brush. The Indians passed uncomfortably close to us on their way to some other place, as the settlement was not molested that night.

They confined their raids mostly to stealing of stock, such as horses and mules. However, they did not hesitate in "lifting a scalp" if chance offered. Some time later Indians appeared at night and made a raid on our settlement, taking with them a number of horses, and happened to lose one of their own – a little dun pony.

We took up this pony and fed him so that he was soon nice and fat. One evening we took him out to graze near the house, and had gone back some 300 yards when we saw a bunch of redskins leading away our fat little pony, and we lost no time in hiding.

We found the cut hobble next morning about ten feet from where we had left the horse, and I guess the Indians had watched us and waited long enough for us to leave and then took the animal. That very night the Indians stole horses all over the settlement.

They also visited a place belonging to Nic Haby.

He had his horses and mules in a pen and was guarding them, hiding behind a large live oak tree. Early in the night he noticed his horses becoming restless, and directly an Indian appeared above the fence and jumped into the corral among the horses. Nic Haby was a good shot and the Indian found it out.

The following morning a neighbor of Haby's came over to tell Haby his trouble with Indians and the loss of horses he had sustained, when he spied the dead Indian. He drew his dirk and plunged it into the redskin's body, exclaiming, "That is the son-of-a-gun; he stole my horses."

They put a rope around the Indian's head and dragged him up on the mountain, turning him over to the mercies of the buzzards and hogs. They accorded him the same burial that the redskins gave their white victims. For a long time thereafter nobody would eat pork.

After I was large, or old enough to work out, I started freighting, my first trip being with a two-horse wagon from San Antonio to Fort Clark. There were generally from six to ten wagons making the trip at the same time, partly for protection and also for assistance, which in the rainy season was quite imperative.

After a trip or two I bought a three-and-a-half-inch Studebaker wagon and hitched up six animals. We freighted to Del Rio, to Eagle Pass and to Fort Clark from San Antonio, Texas. We would take out merchandise and bring back raw material – wool and hides, and sometimes a load of empty beer bottles, or "dead soldiers" as we called them.

We had some experiences with our work teams stampeding at night, and sometimes we would catch up with them next day ten or twelve miles away, homeward bound. In those days there were no graded roads; a wagon track, or a number of them, would be called a road if it had the name of its destination tacked to it.

Sometimes a road would be 100-feet wide or wider, according to where the ground was most solid and suitable for travel. When the rainy spell set in the roads were almost impassable.

Sometimes we hitched as many as sixteen animals to a wagon to pull it out of the mud, and would move it 100 feet or so, then hook on to the next one, until we had them all out of the mud. I have seen the time that we were camped for weeks on this side of the Frio River on account of high water and impassable roads.

We had an old mule team that we used in swimming the river when going to Uvalde for bacon and meal. We had plenty of meat, such as rabbits, venison and also fish. In 1881, with the coming of the Southern Pacific Railroad, our trade went "blooe." I became foreman of the Judge Noonan Ranch southwest of Castroville, Texas, and worked there until I went up the trail in 1884.

Ed Kaufman and Louis Schorp, both of them alive to this day, gathered a herd of some 450 head of horses in Medina County, Texas. With them were J.M. Saathoff, Ehme Saathoff, a cook by the name of Ganahl Brown, and myself. We started from Castroville and drove by way of Bandera, Kerrville and over the "old trail," crossing the Red River at the old Doan Store.

We herded the horses the first few nights and later let them graze or rest during the night to themselves. We had a very wet trip, it raining almost every day while we were on the way. Feed for the horses was plentiful and our crew fared on wild game, cornbread and black coffee. We came across our first Indians when we arrived in the Indian Territory. They were very friendly and would eat tobacco and sugar "out of your hand."

These articles were always on their mind and after their preliminary "How" they would never fail to ask for them. When the meals we were cooking were ready there would always be some "self-invited" Indian guest or guests to fall in and help themselves and eat to their heart's content.

One day an old buck rode up to me in the usual way and asked for "terback." I handed him a plug and after he gave two or three of his "compadres" each a chew he took one himself and stuck the balance in his pocket. I argued and asked him to give me back my plug, but he said: "Pony boss, he be good," and rode off.

It was customary to pay a duty on horses crossing the reservation, and our boss paid the Indians in horses, but they also stole some twenty-five head from us before we got away from them.

We did not have very much trouble with the horses, and our trip took up something like four months from Castroville, Texas, to Dodge City, Kansas. We camped with our herd about six miles south of Dodge City, on Mulberry Creek.

The first thing we did when we arrived there was to go to town, get a shave and haircut, and tighten our belts by a few good strong drinks. Here I also met George W. Saunders, the same George who is now the worthy president of the "Old Trail Drivers' Association."

While here, our boss, Ed Kaufman, got summons that some important business demanded his immediate return to Medina County. He left the herd in our charge until such a time when he should return, in about thirty days. After he got back to the herd he sold it to Mr. Wilson, of Pueblo, Colorado, where he had to deliver the horses for him.

After delivery of the horses at Pueblo, Colorado, I hired to Wilson, and worked for a couple of months, when I was sent back to Dodge City to receive and take charge of a herd of 3,500 head of two-year-old stocker steers for Wilson.

I started the herd and the cattle would stampede every blooming night. Often in the morning we had to help from thirty to forty of the poorer steers on their feet by a tail-hold and lift. This was repeated for some eight or ten days, and we could only make from five- to six-miles per day. We tired of herding the cattle at night, so would scatter the herd over a large area of ground to give them more elbow room. This worked like a charm, for as long as the cattle were not in close formation they would not get excited so easily – and we had no more runs.

We took the herd about sixty miles below Pueblo to the Wilson Ranch, branded the 3,500 head, and six more herds, which had been delivered there, amounting to another 3,500 – 7,000 head in all; besides branding, we dewlapped every animal. We built our own pens and chutes to do this, and hard work it was.

Still, we had lots of old-time pleasure to relieve the monotony. Every Saturday afternoon at two o'clock we would quit work and go to a dance, start dancing at 4 p.m. and dance till after sunrise Sunday morning. We had lots of refreshments, booze, beer and kindred "exhilarators."

Sometimes a little shooting scrape would change the scenery, but was of passing interest. From the Wilson Ranch I returned home by way of Kansas City.

I remained at home a short time and took up some state land in 1885, fenced it – and then went west to Brewster and Presidio Counties, where I worked for Sam Harmon of Alpine, Texas.

Harmon was a roundup boss and attended to the branding and gathering of stock. The first work we did was out of the ordinary – we tried to dig a well. We blasted through sixty-five feet of solid rock and left a "dry hole." Later I worked for F. Collins a long time.

In 1892 I left Alpine and went home to Medina County, got married to Johanna Schweers and settled down five miles north of Quihi – on Sturm Hill.

# Spent a Hard Winter Near Red Cloud

*by D.S. Combs, San Antonio, Texas*

MY EXPERIENCE COVERS A GREAT DEAL OF TIME, as I am now just past my eighty-first birthday.

You, perhaps, have lived long enough to know that a man frequently forgets many things he would like to remember and remembers many things he would like to forget, but to me the memories of the Old Trail days are very pleasant, principally on the account of my good fortune to be associated with many of the pioneer cowmen of Texas, who made the country famous by their display of nerve and grey matter.

We did not know anything about the so-called hard times; we were trained to meet conditions, overcome obstacles and accomplish what we started out to do.

My first experience on the trail was in 1866, when I drove a herd of cattle from San Marcos, in Hays County, to New Iberia, La. William Earnest owned these cattle, he put the value on them at six dollars per head, I did the work, and we divided profits. I had with me young men with the grit necessary to accomplish this undertaking.

In those days we did not discuss hardships; it seemed to be a pleasure to accomplish our undertaking. We cooked our own food, slept on the ground, worked in the rain in daytime and at night, but all this was D.S. Combs pleasure. Having made a real success of my first venture, I was determined to tackle it again.

My next drive was in 1867. I took a herd of horses to Kansas and on to Waterloo, Iowa. This time I had as a financial partner L.W. Mitchell. The horses cost us $10 per head. We made a profit and were pleased with our results.

In the year of 1871 I drove with Dock Day a herd of steers from San Marcos to Red Cloud, Nebraska, where we concluded to winter. This was my first bad setback, for the winter was the worst I ever saw or heard of;

the country froze over early in November and never thawed until spring.

Our cattle literally starved to death, snow covered the grass and the water froze so they could not drink. I left in the spring, a busted and disgusted cowman. I have never been back to that particular country and have tried all these years to forget it, but the memories of that dreadful experience will forever remain with me.

In 1876 I drove a herd for Ellison & Dewees. That year about 40,000 head of cattle were put on the trail, known as the Western Trail.

This was real experience. We started from San Antonio over an unknown route and where no road or trail was to be followed. We were the pioneers who made the first tracks that marked the Western Trail. We reached Ogallala, Nebraska, after about three months' straight drive, passing through some hard country and often forced to go long distances without water.

Food was an object, but we, of course, managed to get by. In all my trail driving I was fortunately never molested by bandits or thieves. I had men with me that were dependable and, with their assistance, I made what I called a success. Our meals consisted of just whatever we could find that would do to eat.

In 1878 I took a herd from Bob Stafford's ranch near Columbus to Dakota, this time for Ellison & Sherrill, and my experience was about as is usually encountered on such drives. Then, in 1879, I took an interest in a herd and drove over the same ground. Was successful beyond my fondest expectations. The profits were not much, but it was in the days when a little money looked like a whole lot.

After that I bought and sold cattle in a small way in and around East Texas, often shipping to West Texas and selling cattle to stock the western range. In 1880 I went into the ranch business in Tom Green County and ranched there for about two years, being associated with W.D. Kincaid. In 1882 we moved to Haymond, in Brewster County, where we ranched until 1898.

The greatest pleasure I have is in thinking of many of my experiences and in meeting and remembering the cowmen of Texas. My association with them has always been a real pleasure, and when I have the good fortune of attending the annual roundup, the pleasure it gives me to meet the familiar faces and shake hands with the boys is worth a great deal more than it costs any of us to keep the association alive.

# Experiences of the Trail and Otherwise

### by M.J. Ripps, San Antonio, Texas

THERE ARE "A GREAT MANY WAYS OF KILLING a dog without choking him with butter," as the old saying goes. In handling cattle there are also many different ways, which may lead to the same result; and, again, one way, or cause, may lead to many and varied results.

No doubt many of my old-time friends and cattle punchers have here related their experiences handling cattle on the trail in a graphic and interesting way; but as there are so many "spooks and ghosts" to play Hail Columbia with cattle, I shall take the liberty of adding a few of the experiences that I was privileged, or "forced," to go through with, for the benefit of the younger set of cowboys and our dear friends, the readers.

A river changes its course in the course of time; likewise, the channels of trade are changed with the passing of the days, which the following trip will illustrate.

I think it was about Feb. 10, 1876, that J.W. Schelcher, Dick McRae, Manuel Cuero and I, with Louis Enderle as our foreman, went into Frio County, Texas, and gathered about 1,000 head of cattle and brought them up to the True-Heart Ranch on the San Antonio River. Here we finished the herd by adding another 800 head.

This herd was the Joe Shiner property, and right here will state how these cattle were bought. Cattle were always bought by the head, and the price per head varied according to the age and class of the animal. There were no cattle sold "over the scale," and platform scales for this purpose were not even dreamed of as a medium in the sale of cattle.

Now, in gathering these cattle on different ranches we came across cattle that had strayed from other ranches, and their owner not being present, we would send him word that we had one steer, a cow, or a number of his cattle, as the case may have been, and paid him the prevailing price. This was within the law and in use quite generally.

Cattle that had no brand or mark – well, that was not our fault. But it is remarkable the way these cattle persisted in following the herd. Naturally, our sympathy was with them. The ranches where we gathered the cattle had some very wild stock – outlaws – and to get them called for strategy and cunning.

These outlaw cattle would generally graze to themselves and come to water at night, especially if they scented danger or having seen a human being. There was a price on their head of two dollars for a big steer, one dollar fifty cents for a cow, and from there on down to fifty cents per head delivered in the herd.

To accomplish this we would watch around the watering places on moonlight nights and rope them. This netted us more money than we were able to make "by the month."

After we had roped an animal we would lead or drag him into the herd, or otherwise , we would tie the animal down, and after we had several of them tied we would bring a bunch of cattle and, with the bunch, bring them into the main herd. This was great sport, and it was very dangerous as well.

We started the 1,800 head and got as far as Goat Creek, north of Kerrville, without any serious trouble. We herded them at night in three reliefs, and generally kept five horses under saddle all night in case of emergency.

One night I was herding, and about midnight a bunch of wild hogs ran into the herd and stampeded the cattle. We were camped near a field close to a big flat, or prairie. The cattle headed for a lane, with me in the lead unable to hold them. The boys at camp heard the noise and came to my assistance, and were able then to control them. We lost only one steer, which was crippled in the back.

At the head of the Pedernales River we killed a calf for fresh meat for the men in camp. An old bull smelled the blood and started bellowing and pawing the ground. He made a great to-do about it, and it acted as a "war whoop does to the braves."

In the stampede that followed some 300 head got separated from the main herd and ran about a mile. We overtook them toward morning and brought the whole herd together without losing any. From there on to Fort McKavett we did not have any more trouble. Here I quit the herd, as I was offered a better proposition.

A second herd was started by Joe Shiner in 1878, with Louis Enderle as foreman and the same crew as on the previous trip; besides he had three or four darkies with the herd. I joined them at San Antonio, bound for Kansas City. We had a stampede on a creek near Kerrville, and it took us half of the next day to round up the 100 head that had scattered. In Coleman County Joe Shiner sold the herd to Bill Fraser and we delivered the cattle at Wichita, Kansas.

Another trip in 1898, I recall, when Manuel Lopez, Little Pete Tafolla and I, and a little boy leading the pack horse, went to Wetmore, Texas, and, with the assistance of the Classen Bros., rounded up 300 head of steers. We were to meet a bunch of 600 steers en route overland from Hondo, throw the two bunches together and take them to the feed pens at Seguin, Texas, for Short & Saunders.

However, after I had my 300 head gathered I received word to take them to Austin and deliver to John Sheehan, as he had bought them. The first night we made New Braunfels, Texas, but could get no pens. An old German sold us a load of corn fodder and some corn for our horses, so we herded all night in the open.

The second night we penned them in the railroad pens at San Marcos and took them out on the prairie next morning. Our cattle stampeded, running across a cornfield, but, being in November, did not do any damage. The herd reached Kyle, Texas, about noon and we stopped to cook a meal. A man rode up and asked if we needed any help. We were more than glad to hire him, and asked him about a pen for the night at Buda, Texas.

He said there was only one pen, and it was engaged for the night. This made us feel bad, and we were thinking of sending a man ahead to arrange for some place for us to stop. Our visitor spoke up and said that he had engaged the pen he spoke of, and that he had been sent out by John Sheehan to meet us.

That afternoon a passing train stampeded our herd, but we checked them in a lane. We penned at Buda that night and next day headed for Austin. When we got to the Colorado River we found it on a rise. We were not allowed to cross cattle on the bridge, so we had to swim for it. Two of my men stayed with me and the third, a "cold-footer," crossed on the bridge. The cattle swam across all right and were delivered as ordered, without being any short.

One winter George Saunders and Ripps were feeding 1,800 head of cattle in their pens at San Antonio, and these cattle had to be guarded at night. One night a Mexican named Victorian and myself were herding when the cattle broke the fence for a distance of 100 yards.

The cattle ran in a southerly direction, sweeping Victorian's horse with them. The cattle ran some five miles, with me in the lead and unable to check them. They finally broke into a pasture where I was able to turn them, and stayed with them until daylight, when relief came. The other relief man, who did not stampede with the cattle, did not show up until next day. Twelve men came out to help me bring back the cattle and it was some job. There were seven head missing next morning.

In 1880 and 1881 I went on a trail of a different nature by becoming a member of a surveying outfit to blaze the right of way for the Southern Pacific Railway from San Antonio west to the Rio Grande River. Two men joined the outfit with me at San Antonio, and the crew consisted of seventeen men.

We surveyed as far as Uvalde, when we got orders to arm ourselves and keep our eyes peeled for Indians. This was too much for the two men who had joined with me, and so they quit. We continued the survey, and were about 128 miles west of San Antonio, when the government sent twenty soldiers to us as an escort.

At the Nenecatchie Mountains we had our first experience with the redskins. They came in the night and tried to steal our mules and horses by stampeding them. We had our guards, or outposts, stationed some distance from camp and they exchanged shots, but none of our men were hurt.

At San Felipe, on the Rio Grande, Rangers took the place of the soldiers and acted as our protectors. While we were camped at the McKenzie Crossing on the Rio Grande, the Indians made another attempt to get our horses, but were routed by the Rangers. From there on we did not see any more Indians until we came to Eagle's Nest, on the Rio Grande.

We were camped some 350 feet above the level of the riverbed, and were cutting out a trail wide enough for a burro to pass with a cask, or small barrel on either side, to transport water from the river. We had stopped for the noon hour when we noticed nine Indians, seven bucks and two squaws.

They had evidently descended to the river bottom some miles above and were wending their way to a point directly in front of us, where they could get to the water.

They were coming in single file, some ten feet apart, and were in full war paint, the Indian in the rear being the guard. The eight went to water to satisfy their thirst, while one stood guard. Then the guard went to drink while one of the squaws stood guard, and she spied us, as we could tell from her gestures. When she gave the alarm they took to their horses and disappeared up the river. As we were not looking for trouble, we did not fire at them, but doubled our guards to protect against an attack from the rear.

Our next camp was at Painted Cave. One night we sent our mules and horses out to grass with two guards in charge. Indians crept up and tried to scare the animals. One of the guards, finding that something was not right, gave the alarm, and the fireworks started.

We fired some thirty or forty shots, and one of the guards claimed he got an Indian. This Painted Cave is worth a trip to see. It is a big opening under a protruding boulder, large enough for ten men to ride into on horseback at one time.

Its inner walls are decorated with Indian paintings of wild animals, lions, tigers, buffaloes, etc., and all the sign language on the walls – some of which we would not understand if they were played on a phonograph.

Besides this it contains the autographs of some of the pioneers carved in the rock, whose carvers have long since started on the "long trail." I was told by a friend of mine the other day, who had been there lately, that he ran across my name, carved there at that time – forty years ago.

I was born Dec. 5, 1858, in the old Ripps homestead in the western part of San Antonio on the property where George W. Saunders fed cattle for many years.

The only thing that is left to remind us of the olden days is the barbecue. In preparing barbecued meats I gained some proficiency, and have been, and am, called on a number of times a year to superintend these honest-to-goodness barbecues. What is there nicer than a nice slice of barbecue and a – (if Volstead wasn't so bad in figuring percentage) little of 2.75 plus—?

If a bunch of stockmen get together, you can rest assured there is going to be a barbecue somewhere. A number of times at their different conventions and gatherings I have had from 1,500 to 2,000 pounds of meat roasting over the hot coals and, I believe, to their satisfaction.

# Sixty-Eight Years in Texas

*by Pleasant Burnell Butler, Kenedy, Texas*

I WAS BORN IN SCOTT COUNTY, MISSISSIPPI, in 1848, being the eleventh child of Burnell Butler, who was born in Kentucky in 1805, and Sarah Ann Ricks, born in North Carolina in 1811.

In 1849 my oldest brother, Woodward, then a youth of twenty years, left the home in Mississippi to seek out a new location for the family. He crossed the Mississippi River into Louisiana, where he remained long enough to make a crop and, selling out, journeyed on until he reached Karnes County, then a part of Goliad County, in 1850, where he stayed on a tract of land that is now the Pleasant Butler homestead, near the San Antonio River.

In September 1852, father sold out in Scott County, Mississippi, and started to join my brother in Texas. I was at that time four years old, but remember distinctly the start for Texas, father and mother, twelve children, and seven Negro slaves, traveling in covered wagons, each drawn by two yoke of oxen, mother driving a hack with a team of big horses and father riding a fine saddle horse.

I recall clearly a stop made near Jackson, Mississippi, to bid good-bye to my aunt, Mrs. Porter, and how my aunt drove down the road with us in a great carriage with a Negro driver on a high seat in front – a barouche of the real old South.

We crossed the Mississippi River at Natchez, where the high red banks, down which they drove to the ferryboats that carried us across the great river, made an impression on my childish mind that has never been effaced.

When the family reached the spot on the wild prairie lands where the town of Nordheim now stands, we camped under a great live oak tree, the only tree in miles to break the prairie lands about us. Father and mother drove ahead in the hack to find Woodward in his camp on the San

Antonio River and to send him back to meet us as we came on with the wagons. He met us the next evening, Dec. 24, 1852, on the banks of the Eclato.

The new country, with its wide prairies, its wonderful grasses and abundance of game, became the home of the Butler family. I recall that my brother could go out in the evening when the sun was a quarter of an hour high and bring in a deer by nightfall. Turkeys also were plentiful.

In the spring of 1853 father cleared fourteen acres of brush land, pushing the brush back to make a fence, and planted corn. He harvested 700 bushels of corn, or fifty bushels per acre.

Also that spring he leased a part of the Stafford & Selmer tract of land and bought cattle. He gave a small heifer to me, from which, up to the year 1862, I raised eighteen head. But in 1863 came a great drought and my cattle diminished to one small steer.

In November 1863, Woodward, who had led the family into the new home and blazed the trail for their future prosperity, drove to Port Lavaca to bring the winter's supply of groceries. While there he contracted yellow fever and died.

The years wore on and the Great War between the North and the South shook even this remote corner of the country. I remember seeing great wagons, drawn by twelve steers, hauling cotton to Mexico, where it brought fifty cents a pound.

Flour was not available at $26 per barrel, and corn in various ways became the staple diet.

In 1862 my brother, W.G. Butler, who had joined the army, was sent home to gather a bunch of cattle for the Arkansas post. I was then a youth of fourteen and went along to the Hickok pens, near Oakville, where the cattlemen had assembled 500 head, which were headed at once for Arkansas. I helped to drive them as far as Pecan Springs, near the present town of San Marcos, where I bade my brother goodbye and returned home.

In 1863 came the great drought. The Nueces and San Antonio Rivers became mere trickling threads of water with here and there a small pool. The grass was soon gone and no cattle survived except those that had previously drifted across the Nueces River on to a range that was not so severely affected by the drought. In 1864 came rains and plentiful grass, and a search for drifted cattle was organized.

All the young, able-bodied men were in the army, so a party of forty-five young boys and old men, headed by Uncle Billy Ricks, of Oakville, went to San Diego to the ranch of Benito Lopez, from which point they worked for a month rounding up cattle and cutting out those of their own brands.

Every week a herd was taken across the river and headed for home, and in this way 500 head were put back on the ranges of Karnes County, where thousands had grazed before the drought. My steer was luckily among the 500.

In 1868 W.G. Butler, home from the war, drove a herd to Abilene, Kansas, to market, and I went along as far as Gonzales. This fired in me an ambition to ride the whole trail, and in 1870 I made my first trip through to Abilene in the outfit of my brother.

The trail then followed lay along the line from Austin to Belton, Valley Mills, Cleburne to Fort Worth, which at that time boasted of a livery stable, a courthouse and a store operated by Daggett & Hatcher, supply merchants, on the public square, through which we swung our great herd of cattle.

At Fort Worth it was necessary to take on supplies for a month, there being no big stores between Fort Worth and Abilene, Kansas, so at Daggett & Hatcher's we purchased flour, coffee, bacon, beans and dried fruit, three-quarter pound of bacon and the same of flour being allotted to each man for each day.

From Fort Worth the trail ran on to Gainesville, crossed the Red River and from there our outfit went up Mud Creek to the house of Bob Love, a Choctaw Indian, from whom we had to obtain passports through the Indian Territory.

I remember that Love demanded 10 cents a head for the 500 head in the herd, and that after considerable business talk we compromised, Love accepting a $20 gold piece, and in return gave the necessary papers. From Love's we traveled the Chisholm Trail, crossed the South Fork of the Arkansas, through the Osage country into Kansas.

Along the trail the Indians showed great interest in our party, particularly the chuck wagon. Hospitality had to be limited, and little grass grew under our feet through this part of the country.

Buffalo were very plentiful, so numerous in fact that it was necessary to ride ahead of the cattle to prevent them from cutting into the herd. I killed four buffalo on this trip, using only my six-shooter. I had little use for the sights on a gun and shot just as true when on horseback and on the dead run as when on foot.

In 1871 I started for Abilene in charge of an outfit of my own and was joined at Gainesville by several other herds, one belonging to Columbus Carroll, of Gonzales, in charge of Jim Cox; one of Murphy of Victoria, in charge of Capt. Lynn; and one of Clark & Woodward, in charge of Judge Clark. This time we were to travel a new trail, through a more open country, but where there had been no previous travel.

We crossed the river at Red River Station, seventy-five miles above Gainesville, where an Indian named Red Blanket waited to pilot us through the new country.

The herds traveled ahead in turn, a day at the time, the first herd breaking the trail for those following. For some time the trail ran along Line Creek, which lay between the Osage and Comanche nations. Red Blanket warned us that if we got above the creek the Comanches would surely kill us.

After this there was little discussion of which side of the creek made the best trail. Reaching Kansas in May, our outfit made camp on the Smoky River, twenty miles from Abilene, where the cattle grazed until September, when they were ready for market.

I made four trips over the trail to market my steers, and saw many miles of splendid country, but nowhere could I see the prosperity and the future that lay in my own part of Texas.

So in 1874, when Capt. Tom Dennis bought the 7,000-acre Jim King Ranch, now known as the Wilson Ranch, I bought from him the north half of the ranch and paid ten-percent interest on the debt until it was paid. The next year I bought one-half interest in the Burris cattle and worked them on the range.

During the years 1874, 1875 and 1876 W.G. Butler and I operated on the range together. During this time we sold 600 head to John Belcher, and delivered them at Fort Worth.

In the fall of 1876 I sold my interest in the Wilson Ranch to Coleman and Stokely, also all my cattle I had on the range at that time, range delivery.

In the year 1877 Coleman and Stokely delivered to me 2,200 head of steers, yearlings and two's, for payment of the cattle I sold them on the range. These cattle I rounded up and started up the trail, but on my arrival at Fort Worth I found a buyer and sold out to him.

In 1878 I finished receiving cattle from Coleman & Stokely and bought more from Sullivan & Skidmore to make out a herd, of 3,500 head, and again started up the trail to Dodge City, Kansas, going through several storms and enduring lots of hardships, and then, last, but not least, could not find a market for the cattle at Dodge City, so I was compelled to make the drive to Ogallala, Nebraska, where I sold out.

Arriving home in September 1878, I began laying my plans for another drive up the trail.

In February the following year (1879) I began receiving 3,500 from Jim Upton and others, getting everything in readiness for the drive. I started back to the prairies of Nebraska in March, and it took me three months to make the drive. I kept my cattle under herd, between the North and South Platte Rivers, until sometime in August, when I sold out.

I then started my camp outfit toward good old Karnes County, Texas, arriving home in September.

# My First Five-Dollar Bill

*by J.L. McCaleb, Carrizo Springs, Texas*

I WENT UP THE TRAIL IN 1868 with a herd for Mitchell Dixon of Hays County. We were holding our herd alongside of an old rail fence at the Red River Station crossing, waiting for a herd to cross.

I was in front (by the way, my place was always in front) on the left, and a good place compared to the boys further back, where they had to ride back and forth, as there was always a muley or a one-eyed steer leaving the herd, and further back, especially the rear, you had the lazy and sore-footed cattle to keep moving.

The best place around a herd while on the move – that is, if you want to keep well posted in cuss words – is the tail. At times the boys will not only cuss the cattle, but cuss each other and everything else in sight or hearing.

Now about my first five-dollar bill. I saw a small piece of paper in a fence corner, and as the cattle seemed quiet, I got down and picked it up, simply because I was hungry for something to read, if not more than one or two words. We did not have papers forwarded to us while on the trail.

Well, I read that it was good for five dollars. I had never seen one before, so after crossing our herd, and when we struck camp for dinner, showed it to the boss. He said that it was sure enough good money, so I rolled it up stuck it away down in the pocket of my leather leggins.

Money was of no value on the trail, as there was no place to spend it, but I valued that five dollars more than any five dollars I have ever had since.

One day while at dinner the Negro cook offered to bet me a two-year-old heifer he had in the herd against my five dollars that he could beat me shooting, only one shot each. I was good with a pistol, but I knew the cook was hard to beat. But I did not get nervous, as the two-year-old was about six to one if I won.

One of the boys got a little piece of a board, took a coal out of the campfire, made a black spot about the size of a twenty-five-cent piece, stepped off fifteen steps (about forty-five feet) and yelled, "All ready, shoot."

I was to shoot first. I jerked my old cap and ball Navy out and just about one second before I pulled the trigger I saw the heads of six Indians just over a little rise in the ground coming toward the camp. This excited me so that I did not hit the spot, only about one-half of my bullet touched the board just to the right of the target.

I yelled to the Negro, "Shoot quick! Look at the Indians!" By that time we could see them plainly on top of the rise. He fired, but never touched the board. So six big Osage Indians saved me my valuable find the five-dollar bill.

We bedded our cattle for the last time near Abilene, Kansas.

The boss let myself and another boy go to the city one day. As it had been a long time since we had seen a house or a woman, they were good to look at. I wore a black plush hat, which had a row of small stars around the rim, with buck-skin strings to tie and hold on my head.

We went into town, tied our ponies, and the first place we visited was a saloon and dance hall. We ordered toddies like we had seen older men do, and drank them down, for we were dry, very dry, as it had been a long ways between drinks.

I quit my partner, as he had a girl to talk to, so I went out and in a very short time I went into another store and saloon. I got another toddy, my hat began to stiffen up, but I pushed it up in front, moved my pistol to where it would be handy, then sat down on a box in the saloon and picked up a newspaper and thought I would read a few lines, but my two toddies were at war, so I could not very well understand what I read.

I got up and left for more sights – you have seen them in Abilene, Dodge City and any other place those days. I walked around for perhaps an hour. The two toddies were making me feel different to what I had felt for months, and I thought it was about time for another, so I headed for a place across the street, where I could hear a fiddle. It was a saloon, gambling and dance hall.

Here I saw an old long-haired fellow dealing monte. I went to the bar and called for a toddy, and as I was drinking it a girl came up and put her little hand under my chin, and looked me square in the face and said, "Oh, you pretty Texas boy, give me a drink." I asked her what she wanted and she said anything I took, so I called for two toddies. My, I was getting rich fast – a pretty girl and plenty of whiskey.

My old hat was now away back on my head. My boss had given me four dollars spending money and I had my five-dollar bill, so I told the girl that she could make herself easy; that I was going to break the monte game, buy out the saloon, and keep her to run it for me when I went back to Texas for my other herd of cattle.

Well, I went, to the old longhaired dealer, and as he was making a new layout I put my five on the first card (a king) and about the third pull I won. I now had ten dollars and I thought I had better go and get another toddy before I played again.

As I was getting rich so fast, I put the two bills on the tray and won. Had now twenty dollars, so I moved my hat back as far as it would go and went to get a drink – another toddy, but my girl was gone. I wanted to show her that I was not joking about buying out the saloon after I broke the bank.

After this drink things did not look so good. I went back and it seemed to me that I did not care whether I broke him or not. I soon lost all I had won and my old original five. When I quit him my hat was becoming more settled, getting down in front, and I went out, found my partner and left for camp.

The next morning, in place of owning a saloon and going back to Texas after my other herds, I felt – oh! what's the use? You old fellows know how I felt.

The winter of 1868 was spent having a good cowboy time. Wherever my horse, saddle and hat were I was there, spending my trail money. When spring came on I helped to get together one herd, branded a lot of mavericks and sleepers.

But there was a little freckled-face girl that I had danced a lot with in the winter months, so I made up my mind that I would stay in Texas that year, 1869. I fiddled, danced and worked cattle over a territory as big as the state of Maine.

A ranch fifty years ago was not measured by acres or miles – they were boundless. Schools and churches back in the wild days were not handy and most of the ranchmen and cowboys did not care. No mails, no papers, neighbors miles apart, what could one expect from such a wild life?

We would civilize up a bit when we went to a dance; that is, we would take off our spurs and tie a clean red handkerchief around our neck.

I drove beeves from the W.B.G. Grimes pens on the Leona to Matagorda Bay in the winter of 1869, then hired to John Redus on the Hondo, where I finished the winter.

In the early spring of 1870 I helped him get together 2,000 of the wildest longhorns that was ever started up the trail. They were travelers when strung out, but were inclined to stampede in front, the middle or rear. It did not take us long to mill them if in an open country, but in timber that was different.

I took sick this side of Waco and left the herd horseback for the Redus Ranch on the Hondo.

I punched cattle, fiddled and danced some years after, getting wilder all the time, until I met a curly-headed girl from Atascosa County, fell in love and married.

It took her a long time to tame me. But she did, and for the last fifteen or twenty years I do not have to be tied. Just drop the reins on the ground, I'll stay there.

# Some Thrilling Experiences of an Old Trailer

*by L.D. Taylor, San Antonio, Texas*

IN THE SPRING OF 1869 my two brothers, Dan and George Taylor, with Monte Harrell, rounded up 1,000 longhorn beeves, four to twelve years old, and started them to Kansas. I had never been out of our home neighborhood before, so I went along to get some experience on the trail.

The herd was rounded up in Gonzales County, about where the town of Waelder is now located. We swam the Trinity at Dallas, where our herd stampeded and ran through the streets of the town, creating quite a commotion. The damage they did cost us about $200.

When we reached Waco, the Brazos River was level with its banks, and we had to swim the herd across. It is a wonderful sight to see 1,000 steers swimming all at one time. All you could see was the tips of their horns and the ends of their noses as they went through the water.

Near Waco I learned some law, by taking two rails off a fence for firewood with which to cook supper. Was glad to get off by paying two dollars for those rails. We proceeded on to the Red River, which we crossed and traveled several days in the friendly Indian Nation. The first night there we rounded up the herd, but next morning they were gone, for they had been stampeded by Indians shooting arrows into them, and it required several days to get them all together again.

The Indians resorted to that kind of a trick to get pay for helping to get the cattle back again. When we left this section of the Indian Territory we turned our backs to civilization, for the remainder of the trip was to be made through a wild, unsettled, hostile country.

After a few days' travel we struck the Chisholm Trail, the only thoroughfare from Texas through the Indian Territory to Kansas, and about this time two other herds fell in with us, and, not knowing the country we were going through, the three outfits agreed to stick together, stay and die with each other if necessary. Ours was the third herd that had ever traveled that trail.

We had plenty of stampedes, and one day we had a run just after crossing a swollen stream. I was with the chuck wagon, and was left alone, so I just kept right on traveling. Late that evening, after I had turned out and struck camp for the night, my brother George came up and told me the herds and other wagons were ten miles behind. He gave me his pistol and went back to the herd, and I stayed there alone that night. The next day the herd overtook me, and I felt somewhat relieved.

One night the herd was rounded up about a half mile from camp, and during the night I was awakened by the shaking of the earth and an awful noise, and found the whole herd coming down upon us in a furious run.

I was bunking with Monte Harrell, and when I jumped up Harrell tried to hold me, but I jerked loose and ran around to the other side of the wagon. I soon had Mr. Harrell for company. I think every beef must have jumped over the wagon tongue, at least it seemed to me that every steer was jumping it.

From here on we had considerable trouble crossing the creeks and rivers, having to float our wagons across. When we reached one of these streams that was on a rise three or four men would swing on behind each wagon to hold it down until we got into the water, then the men would swim alongside the oxen and guide them across.

After going about 300 miles without seeing anyone or knowing our exact location, we came to the old military road running north. That day about noon two Negro soldiers came to our camp mounted on two big fine government horses. They asked me for grub and I told them I had none cooked, and as brother George spoke rather harsh to them, they rode away, going by one of the other herds.

After they had passed on, two young men with one of the other outfits decided to follow these Negroes and take their horses away from them, suspecting that they were not in rightful possession of the animals.

When they overtook the Negroes a fight ensued in which one of the boys was killed. The other boy returned to us one of the government horses and told us of the affair. We went out and found the body and buried it there on the trail, using axes and knives to dig the grave with. I have forgotten the murdered boy's name, but he was from Texas.

The Negroes, we learned afterwards, were deserters from the army. We found the other government horse grazing near where the fight took place, the Negroes having secured the horses belonging to these two boys and made their escape on them.

The next day I was about a mile behind the herd with the chuck wagon and four Indians came up. They grunted and asked for "tar bucket," so I grabbed the tar bucket and gave it to them, but they shook their heads and put their hands in my pockets, took all of my tobacco, gave another grunt, and went off with the tar bucket. In camp that night my brother asked why I permitted them to take our tar, but I replied that I was glad they did not take my scalp.

A few days later as we were traveling along we saw ahead of us something that looked like a ridge of timber, but which proved to be about 400 Comanches who were coming our way. They were on the warpath and going to battle with another tribe.

When they came up to our herd they began killing our beeves without asking permission or paying any attention to us. Some of the boys of our herd went out to meet them, but the boys of the other herds hid out in the grass, and only one man from the other outfit came to us.

They killed twenty-five of our beeves and skinned them right there, eating the flesh raw and with blood running down their faces, reminding me of a lot of hungry dogs.

Here I witnessed some of the finest horsemanship I ever saw. The young warriors on bareback ponies would ride all over the horses' backs, off on one side, standing up, laying down, going at full speed and shooting arrows clear through the beeves. We were powerless to help ourselves, for we were greatly outnumbered. Every time we would try to start the herd the Indians would surround the herd and hold it.

Finally they permitted us to move on, and we were not slow in moving, either. I felt greatly relieved, and they could have left us sooner without my permission. These Indians had "talked peace" with Uncle Sam, that is all that saved us. We heard a few days afterwards that they had engaged in battle with their foes after leaving us, and had been severely whipped, losing about half of their warriors.

In 1869 Col. John D. Miles was appointed Indian agent by President Grant and served in this capacity in Kansas and the Indian Territory, for the Cheyennes, Arapahoes, Kiowas and Comanches, which tribes frequently went on the warpath in those days, making it very dangerous for the trail drivers. We met Col. Miles the next day after the Indians had attacked our herd, and he made a note of the number of beeves they had killed belonging to us, and said he would report it to Washington, and we would receive pay for all we had lost. He was traveling alone in a hack on his way to some fort, and to me he looked very lonely in that wild and woolly country.

When we reached the Canadian River we found it on a big rise, so we decided to stop there a few days and allow our herd to graze while waiting for the river to go down.

While we were there a man came along one day and warned us to be on the lookout for Indians, saying they were liable to attack us at any time. He passed on, and the next day we crossed the river and after traveling about ten miles we came to a pool of water where we found this man's clothes on the bank. Investigation revealed that he had been stripped and dumped into the pool.

We reached the Arkansas River, where we had a little trouble getting across. There were a few houses on the Kansas side, and we began to rejoice that we were once more getting within the boundaries of civilization. Here we found a store and plenty of "booze," and some of the boys got "full." After leaving that wayside oasis we did not see another house until we were within ten miles of Abilene. We had several stampedes in that region.

One evening Monte Harrell said the prospects were good for a storm that night, and sure enough we had a regular Kansas twister. We had prepared for it by driving a long stake pin into the ground, to which I chained the wagon, and making everything as safe as possible.

At midnight the storm was on, and within a moment everything was gone except the wagon and myself. The cattle stampeded, horses got loose, and oxen and all went with the herd. The storm soon spent its fury and our men managed to hold the cattle until daylight and got them all back the next morning and we resumed our drive to Abilene, reaching there in a few days.

Abilene at this time was just a small town on a railroad, consisting of three saloons, one store and two hotels. Here we tarried to graze and fatten our cattle for market, and as several of the hands were not needed, they were paid off and allowed to return home, I being among the number.

While we were in Abilene, we found the town was full of all sorts of desperate characters, and I remember one day one of these bad men rode his horse into a saloon, pulled his gun on the bartender, and all quit business. When he came out several others began to shoot up the town. I was not feeling well, so I went over to the hotel to rest, and in a short time the boys of our outfit missed me and instituted a search, finding me at the hotel under a bed.

The next day we made preparations to start back to Texas, and went on the train to Junction City, Kansas, to get our outfit. It was the first train I ever rode on, and I thought the thing was running too fast, but a brakeman told me it was behind time and was trying to make up the schedule. We secured our outfit, took in several men wanting to come to Texas, elected a boss and started for home.

The second night out we camped in a little grove of timber and during the night a storm struck us, another one of those Kansas zephyrs that was calculated to blow hell off the range. I located a stump and anchored myself to it, while the boss, a long-legged fellow, had secured a death grip on a sapling near me.

During the progress of the storm his feet were constantly in my way, flying around and striking my shins and knocking the bark off the stump I was hanging to for dear life. I could hear him trying to pray, but I was so busy at that particular time that I did not pay much attention to what he was saying. The wind would pick us up and flop our bodies against the ground with great force, but I hung to that stump and got through all right.

We reached Fort Gibson, on the Arkansas, and here we were compelled to stay a week on account of high water. The boys chipped in and bought a lot of whiskey at this place, paying twelve dollars a gallon for it.

I opposed buying the whiskey because it was a serious offense to convey it into the Indian Territory, but they bought it anyway, and after we had started on our way again some trouble arose among the outfit.

One day an old Indian brought a horse and outfit to our camp and I bought this outfit, paying the Indian seventy-five dollars for it, so I left the bunch and pulled out alone through the Indian country. I reached Red River safely and made it through to my home without mishap, reaching there with only seventy-five cents in my pocket.

In conclusion I will say that I have seen cowboys who had been in the saddle for twenty-four hours without sleep or anything to eat, come into camp, lay down on a log and go to sleep almost instantly, and sleep sound with the rain pouring down and water four inches all around them.

All of the boys who were with me on this trip mentioned above are dead except one, William McBride. I was twenty years old when I made that trip; I am now seventy years old.

# Had Plenty of Fun

*by Gus Black, Eagle Pass, Texas*

I HAVE NO TIME TO WRITE BOOKS. If I gave all of my experience on the trail it would fill this book and then some. From 1875 to 1882 I suppose I had more experience, good and bad, than any one man on the trail, with Indians, buffalo, horse rustlers and cutthroats, and during that time I worked eighteen hours out of every twenty-four.

Wound up in 1882 without a dollar in hand, but in possession of several thousand dollars worth of fun. I am now seventy-one years old and can ride a horse just the same as of old.

I have been right here in Texas ever since the morning star first "riz," and when you publish your next book I hope to be a retired stockman, for my time will then be my own, and I will give you something good. However, since you insist, I will relate a few incidents and you can arrange them to suit yourself.

I went up the trail the first time with Ben Duncan and Jim Speed of Frio County, and the second time with Woodward & Oge of the same county. For many years I was boss for Lytle & McDaniel and Lytle & Schreiner.

One year while on the trail we found Red River out of banks at Red River Station, with fifteen or twenty herds there waiting to cross.

I was in charge of a herd of 3,500 cattle and was anxious to get across. The toll man was demanding $1.25 per head for crossing cattle at that point, but I was determined not to pay it, for the total amount seemed too high, so of two high things I decided to choose the river.

While my herd was stopped on the Texas side of the river, and the toll collector was absent, I swam across to the other side and made arrangements with a man over there to come and ferry my wagons over. Then I swam back and got from two to five men from each outfit there to help me. This gave me a bunch of some forty or fifty men and we pushed my cattle right into the raging river and rushed them across.

Just as we emerged on the other side the toll man appeared on the bank we had left and I yelled back to him: "You are too slow to collect from Gus Black."

I delivered many cattle for Lytle & Schreiner in Wyoming and Nebraska. One year this firm sold several herds to Gov. Bush of Wyoming. One trip Governor Bush came out to meet the herd in company with Capt. Lytle, and we entertained him in camp.

That morning I had found a couple of longhorns, which had slipped off the head of a dead cow on the trail, and in a spirit of fun I fitted them onto the just-sprouting horns of a dogie yearling with our drags. That little old yearling was a comic sight with those great longhorns on its head, and caused lots of fun for the boys.

When Governor Bush was looking over the herd he espied this "longhorned" yearling, and began to hurrah Capt. Lytle about the animal. I told the Governor that it was just a yearling, but he said it was a four-year-old, and would bet any amount of money on its age.

I told him I would bet $200 it was a yearling. He promptly covered the bet, saying he knew I was a hard-working man, and he hated to take my money, but he wanted to prove my ignorance and teach me a lesson.

At the same time he said he would just as soon bet me $1,000, but knew I could not afford to lose that much money. I told him to put it up, that I always "blowed in" my money anyhow and would just as soon let him win it as anybody else. So the bet was made, and then I roped the Bogie and took those horns off. Governor Bush was dumbfounded, and the laugh was on him.

When settlement came around I told him to keep his money, as he was so damned ignorant I just wanted to teach him a lesson. Then he sent up the whiskey and cigars to the outfit.

On another trip, after we crossed Smoky River we encountered a colony of grangers who made it a rule to charge every herd fifty dollars for permitting passage through their community. I rode into the village and consulted with their chief leader who informed me that the charge was made to pay for inspecting herds for contagious diseases, etc.

I told him I had no money but would give him a draft on Capt. Lytle, which he said would be satisfactory as Capt. Lytle's check was good anywhere in the world. He asked me to kindly add another ten dollars to the amount for tobacco for the villagers, which I did, and then put my herd through. The first telegraph station I reached I wired Capt. Lytle that

I had been buncoed out of sixty dollars and to refuse to pay the draft. Those fellows were skinning us and I figured that turn about was fair play.

I am glad George Saunders took the lead in the organization of the trail drivers of the early days, for such an association has long been needed to preserve the history of the rugged noble men who made the cattle industry.

I hope to live to see the day when that monument suggested by Mr. Saunders is placed on the old trail as a tribute to those who have gone their way and a reminder to oncoming generations that we "blazed the trail" and vouchsafed unto them peace, happiness and prosperity.

# Thrilling Experiences

*by Levi J. Harkey, Sinton, Texas*

I WAS BORN APRIL 6, 1860, at Richland Springs, San Saba County, Texas. My parents came from Yell County, Arkansas, (now laugh, you darn fools) in the year of 1853, and first stopped on Wallace Creek, about ten miles southwest of the town of San Saba. In 1856 they moved to Richland Springs, fifteen miles west of San Saba and there settled permanently.

My parents died in 1866, their deaths being about three weeks apart, leaving thirteen children, eight boys and five girls, the eldest being only eighteen years old, to fight it out with Comanche Indians, and believe me we had a time.

I have seen as many as seventy-five Indians in a bunch, and have been chased by them several times, but was too fleet on foot for them. You may talk about the Indian troubles experienced while going up the trail, but it was nothing to compare with the dangers we had to contend with.

They came into our immediate section every light moon and on one occasion they came down upon us seventy-five in number, all giving the Comanche yell.

Five of us little brats were about 200 yards from the house fishing. My sister Sarah thought it was cowboys, and she ran up a live oak tree to watch them, while we ran to the house. When I reached the house, the other children were inside and closed the door, and I never got inside until after the danger was over.

My two oldest brothers were in the field plowing at the time and when they came and got the old flintlock rifles the Indians fled. The Indians passed under the tree where my sister was but never discovered her. Another sister, Julia, now Mrs. C.T. Harmon, hid in the cornfield.

That Indian raid caused all the people on Richland Creek to fort up near the town of San Saba. The Indians and the U.S. soldiers stayed around there until the following spring, and left with all the cattle and horses in that section. A short time after the Indians left, the soldiers left, but not until they had destroyed all the log cabins in the neighborhood.

In 1876 I left Richland Springs with C.T. Harmon and wife, and landed at the Rocky Ammons Ranch, on the Atascosa River, eighteen miles west of the old town of Oakville, on Oct. 21, 1876. Ammons and Bill Harmon were partners in the cattle business at that time.

In 1877 I left the Ammons Ranch with a herd of 2,000 mixed cattle, cows and steers, belonging to C.C. Lewis and Nick Bluntzer, for Dodge City, Kan., Arkansas, Bill Harmon as road boss. I returned to the Ammons Ranch the same year and did general ranch work for Mr. Ammons until 1883. From 1883 till 1890 I speculated in Spanish horses in and out of San Antonio.

Many times have I ridden with our genial president, George W. Saunders, who in those days was a live-wire.

In 1891 the horse business took a tumble downward, and I went to Beeville, Texas, and ran a wet goods shop until 1906, when I sold that business, and went into a dry goods business. While retailing wet goods, I accumulated about $100,000 worth of property, but while I was in the dry goods business I signed notes at the various banks for a friend who speculated in cattle, and he broke me flatter than a pancake.

In 1911 I sold my business and moved to the Panhandle, to a place called Dickens, Texas. While up there I sold my land in Live Oak County and all of my Beeville property, and paid everything I owed. In 1912 I moved from Dickens to San Patricio County, and went to work in the Tax Assessor's office for Chris Rachal, who was assessor at that time. In 1916 I was elected tax assessor for San Patricio County, and am still holding it down, and hope I will be able to hold it down a few years longer.

Nov. 27, 1921, I took C.T. Harmon to San Antonio in my old reliable Ford, to attend the Old Time Trail Drivers' Convention with no intention whatever to attend myself, but Charlie persuaded me to go over to the hall with him, and I met so many of the old timers it made me feel good, so I walked right up and joined and paid my dues, received a badge, and was as happy as a lark, and am very proud I belong to the association.

I shall always take off my hat to the old timers of Texas. Too many people never give them credit for anything, much less for blazing the way for the development of the greatest state in the Union, Texas. May God bless them is my prayer.

## Lost Many Thousands of Dollars

### by C.S. Brodbent, San Antonio, Texas

IN THE EARLY DAYS OF THE TRAIL DRIVERS I lived in Summer County, Kansas. In that county was one of the chief herd rendezvous after running the gauntlet of the Indian Territory. From Caldwell the trail led north through Summer County to Wichita, Newton and Abilene, Kansas. There was no Wellington or Newton at the beginning, and Wichita was but a frontier hamlet.

We bought trail cattle and drove them to our farms and made good money, as we put up large quantities of hay and raised some corn. As winter came on, the trail cattle on the open range starved and froze by the thousands, and many owners met disastrous losses.

The prevalent idea that the trail days were halcyon days of easy money making is erroneous. Many a man in comfortable circumstances in Texas became impoverished, and many a Kansas farmer who thought he was getting cattle dirt cheap from the trail, found himself a loser before spring by not having prepared enough feed.

Living so near the trail I was near the center of this great industry and became acquainted with Texas cattle owners and cowboys and, I suppose, became somewhat fascinated with the life. And in 1875 I located in the Rio Grande Valley, in the Nueces and Devil's River Country and about the last year of the Overland Drive, put up two herds and drove from Val Verde County to Indian Territory.

Our cattle were dying from drought and the drive was our only recourse. The venture was not a success. There was almost no demand in the territory, and the constant expense and Indian tax made sad inroads. I got out of this mess with a loss of over $10,000; not all, however was legitimate loss, for I heard of my brands being sold on the Kansas market, for which I never received any pay.

There was some dishonesty in this trail driving. A trail boss who did not reach his destination with an equal or greater number than he started with was considered incompetent. Hence ranchers along the trail made bitter complaints of moving herders "incorporating" their stock. On the other hand many of the cattle lost from the herds were picked up by these ranchers, which partially recouped their losses thereby.

We had no Cattle Raisers' Association as we have now, and the business of the cattle trail was, in its nature, not such as encouraged a high standard of honesty, though many of the drivers and owners were of the strictest and loftiest moral character.

It is perhaps a surprising feature of the cattle drive that the owners of many herds that illegitimately increased the most on what they made a piratical journey north, went broke, and some of the most noted "cattle kings" became herdsmen or dropped into oblivion.

A considerable number of Texas home ranchers got pay for the cattle they had sold to drivers. In some cases losses were unavoidable – in other cases dishonesty.

The most fortunate ranchers in the increase of herds in those open range days, were, I think, those bordering on the Gulf Coast. Cattle drifting from the north before winter storms, could drift no further, and I have often been told that some of the greatest fortunes there were based on drift cattle.

The Texas fence law and railroads obliterated the Texas cattle trail, and in its passing there should be no cause for regret.

The old-time cowboy had heroic attributes, was generous, brave and ever ready to alleviate personal suffering, share his last crust, his blanket and often more important, his canteen.

He spent his wages freely and not always wisely, and many became an easy prey to gambling and other low resorts.

Some among them became leading men in law, art and science even in theology, proving again that it is not in the vocation but in the man, that causes him to blossom and bring a fruitage of goodness, honor and godly living.

This screed is not much of a story of the trail, but you will have enough recitals of hairbreadth escapes from Indians, floods, lightning and accidents, enough of suffering from cold, heat, hunger, thirst and dust, and this variety may be one of the species of your book.

You will also hear many amusing incidents for fun and frolic formed a part of the cowboy's life – many pathetic stories, too, for sickness and death followed the trail. But I had seen such before trail days when wearing a soldier's uniform, and I do not care to dwell thereon. Paraphrasing a favorite stanza:

*Cowboy rest, thy labor o'er.*
*Sleep the sleep that knows no breaking;*
*Dream of cattle drives no more,*
*Days of toil and nights of waking.*

# The Latch String Is On the Outside

*by R.T. Mellard, Eddy County, New Mexico*

I WAS BORN IN MISSISSIPPI in Lawrence County, July 10, 1849. My father and mother were slave-holders and wanted to enlarge their holdings, so my father, in 1855, visited Texas, and was so impressed with the vast possibilities that he sold his farm on Pearl River, loaded his family and slaves in buggies and wagons and started to Texas.

He arrived in Walker County in the latter part of 1856, and bought 880 acres of rich bottom land on the Trinity River and immediately began to improve the same, until December 1860, when he was assassinated.

My mother's brother in Mississippi heard of the tragedy and came to Texas in March 1861, and persuaded my mother to let me go back to Mississippi with him. We took the little steamboat, Mary Leonard, went down the Trinity River to Galveston, thence by steamer to New Orleans, Louisiana, and went up to his plantation on Pearl River.

In April, 1861, when war broke out he put me in school in Brook and immediately went to Virginia where he was engaged in some of the bloodiest battles of the Civil War, and I never saw him until the latter part of 1865, and I only heard from my mother once during the entire war.

I remained with Mr. and Mrs. Larkin, who were both father and mother to me, and I attended school until the Yankees burned our school building in 1864, and practically wrecked the town. In October 1865, my uncle furnished me funds and I started for home, not knowing whether my mother and two sisters were alive or not.

I went to New Orleans, stopped there for a few days with relatives, then took a steamer for Galveston, from there by rail to Navasota, where I bought a horse and went to Huntsville, a distance of fifty miles, and thence fifteen miles to where I found my mother and two sisters.

The Great War had practically broken her up, since the property consisted mostly of slaves. With a little money that was left to us children, I took my share (a few hundred dollars) and entered Austin Male College at Huntsville, in 1866, where I remained until the fall of 1867. I rented a small farm on the Trinity River in 1868 and worked that until the spring of 1870.

Not being impressed with farming very much I saddled my horse and in company with a young friend left there and rode to Wrightsboro in Gonzales County where I arrived in May, 1870, and began my career as a cowboy.

Fortunately for me I met and worked for A.B. Johnson, one of the finest men I ever knew. I also got acquainted with Mr. Crawford Burnett, a better man Texas never produced, and to him I owe my success in life. In the spring of 1871 he made a contract with P.D. Armour & Co. of Chicago, to road-brand and put on the trail 10,000 big steers, four-years-old and up.

The price of these steers was twelve dollars in gold. They were to go 1,000 in a herd. I made a deal with Mr. Burnett to go up the trail for fifty dollars per month, to be paid in gold. I think the ratio between gold and greenback at that time was $1.25.

On April 10, 1871, I bade my sweetheart, Miss Sallie Wilson, the charming stepdaughter of A.B. Johnson, farewell and together with T.V. DeWoodey, Jack Harris, John and Bill Fullerton, and other boys whose names I can't recall, went over to Sandies Creek, where we met our boss, Ischam Finche.

The next morning with a little pair of dun oxen we left for San Antonio, where we met Mr. Burnett. We fitted up our outfit and left for Mason County on the Llano River, where we were to receive the steers. There had already been constructed huge corrals made of big logs, so we at once began putting the famous "Flower de luce" road-brand behind the left shoulder.

When we had branded about 800 steers the Germans began pouring the cattle in so rapidly we had to give up the pens. I think at that time we had about fifty men in camp, it being the intention to put ten men with each herd, besides the boss and cook. The first night out, Mr. Burnett selected about twenty men who had had some experience in cow driving, but none of whom were ever around a herd of big steers on a dark night.

I was one of the twenty selected and I shall never forget the first night. Any old driver can tell how hard it is to hold a bunch of big steers on the range where raised, and among timber on the banks of the Llano. About midnight there was an old cow that kept bawling around and trying to get in the herd.

One of the boys chased her off, and thinking he had her a half a mile away pulled his pistol and fired it to scare her. It being very dark he did not know he was in the edge of the herd, and at the report of the pistol business began to pick up.

Those steers got up "some speed." A part of them broke away and ran into our remuda and business also picked up with them. Some of the ponies are going yet. And it is said that one of our bosses and some of the boys were up in live oak trees, trying to pull their horses up too. However, we succeeded in holding the largest part of our herd and in a day or two we had the 1,000 steers ready for the trail.

Mr. Burnett asked me to go with the first herd. First I want to mention the fact that there were no banks in that part of the country and the gold to pay for the steers was brought from San Antonio in a hack in a very heavy sack and was kicked out into camp and lay there like a sack of oats, $20,000 to the sack, until it was paid out.

Mr. Burnett informed me years later that if he ever lost a dollar he never knew it. Any of the boys that were with me could vouch for this statement. We crossed the Colorado River and got on the prairie near Lampasas where we waited a few days for the next herd. Riley Finch was our boss.

It was Mr. Burnett's plan to have two herds travel in close proximity and when it arrived we started north up the old Chisholm Trail. The grass was fine and we moved along without mishap until we were crossing the Bosque River at Clifton, where a drunken Mexican, who was cooking for another outfit, let his oxen run into the tail end of our herd and two of the boys engaged in a little cussing scrape.

Late that afternoon when they met the Mexican alone, his boss having turned him off, they shot him and threw his body into a clump of prickly pear, where it was discovered by the civil authorities a few days later.

While we were between the Bosque and Brazos it began raining and we were delayed quite awhile and had several stampedes. In the meantime all of the men of both herds were arrested, and taken to Meridian by the sheriff, not all at once, however; there were enough left to take care of the herds.

When the sheriff became satisfied that the two men who had done the killing had left he permitted us to go on. I have never heard of those two men since. I knew them quite well. This was the only killing that ever occurred in our outfit.

When we arrived at the Brazos it was running bank full. Jack Harris and myself, being expert swimmers, plunged into the river and pointed the steers to the other side. When we would become a little tired we would swim up and catch a big steer by the tail and you ought to have seen him move.

We finally got both herds across and swam the ponies, then crossed the chuck wagon on a little ferry boat and resumed our journey. The rains had been abundant and the grass was never better.

We arrived in Fort Worth, then just a very small fort, where we purchased supplies and moved across the Trinity River; thence to Doan's Store on the Red River, where we got supplies enough to cross the Indian Territory.

We then proceeded across the North Fork of the Red River, and on to Wichita, Kansas, and crossed a number of streams between the North Fork and the Arkansas River, including the North and South Canadian. When we arrived at Wichita, Kansas, there was no railroad there, just a small village springing up in anticipation of the Santa Fe Railroad coming.

We proceeded from there to Abilene, Kansas, then north across at Solomon River and on about seventy-five miles to the northern line of Kansas, where P.D. Armour & Co. had erected a large plank corral, on a beautiful creek, with large cottonwood trees and rolling hills where no cow had ever been. A few buffalo were still there.

This was about the first of August and we had been on the trail since April. The first night after our arrival at the corral, the boss had us to pen those steers, the first pen they had seen since they left the Llano River.

The boss told us to go to the camp and informed us that we were through night herding, which was music to our ears, but while we were sitting around the campfire that night spinning yarns, those steers stampeded and tore down about one-half of the plank corral.

A few of us ran and with our coats succeeded in cutting a part of them off, and held the gap until daylight. Those steers, which got out of the pen were at a loss to know where to go, and were nearby the next morning, minus a lot of broken horns.

I remained there about a week and as I had an engagement in Texas I left with one companion for home. We took the Union Pacific train to St. Louis; from thence to New Orleans; across the Gulf of Mexico to Galveston; to Columbus on the Colorado River; then the Southern Pacific railway; by stage to Gonzales; on horseback to Wrightsboro, where I had bidden my sweetheart goodbye. On the 17th day of August, 1871, Miss

Sallie L. Wilson and I were married.

In the spring of 1872, my wife's half-brother bought a mixed herd of cattle, and I went into the Indian Territory with them, over the same trail, and I think J.B. Wells, of Gonzales, is the only one living at present who went with us.

I returned home and began to accumulate some cattle of my own, until 1876, I moved my herd to San Saba County on account of range. Later, in 1877, I moved them back to Gonzales County, and in 1879, together with John Putman, Della Shepard and Desmuke we pooled our cattle and started the herd to Albany in Shackleford County where I cut my cattle, the range not being good, and drove them west of Oak Creek, in Tom Green County.

In the fall of 1880 I turned them over to my wife's half-brother, W.A. Johnson, on shares for a period of five years.

In the latter part of 1880 I returned to Gonzales County and in 1881 began driving cattle again for Crawford Burnett, driving to Colorado and Wyoming and continued until the railroads took them away from us, driving in 1887, the last herd that left Gonzales County and delivering on the Platte River in Wyoming.

I have been engaged in the cattle business all of these years, having ranched in the Panhandle and Western Texas. I sold my ranch and cattle in El Paso County because the youngest of my five sons, being interested with me, had to go into the army. I sold this ranch and cattle in 1917, except the registered part of the herd, and bought an irrigated farm and small ranch in Eddy County, New Mexico, where I am now engaged in raising Hereford cattle, alfalfa hay and red apples.

On the 17th day of August my loving wife and I celebrated our golden wedding, surrounded by eight living children, one grandson, and a host of relatives and friends. On the grassy lawn there was an old-fashioned barbecue prepared by the children. We were recipients of many nice presents.

My advice to all young people is to marry early and live an active outdoor life. I am now seventy-two years old, hale and hearty, and can rope and tie down, single-handed any steer in Texas or New Mexico. I am a Baptist, a Democrat, a 32nd degree honorary member of the Amarillo Lodge No. 731 and past master of same lodge. I have two sons who are 32nd degree Masons. The youngest became Scottish Rite and Shriner before reaching the age of 22 years, and one among the youngest Scottish Rite who faced the German firing line.

My wife and I would be glad to hear from any of the boys, and should any of them pass this way the latchstring is always on the outside of my door.

# A Faithful Negro Servant

### by J.E. Folts, Columbus, Texas

IN THE SPRING OF 1870 my uncle, R.B. (Bob) Johnson, drove a herd of cattle up the trail to Abilene, Kansas.

He took with him as one of the cowhands a young Negro whom he raised on his ranch, and whose picture accompanies this sketch. The herd was started from Colorado County, crossing the Colorado River at La Grange and intersecting the Chisholm Trail near the Red River, and passing across the Indian Territory.

Soon after reaching Abilene my uncle became ill and died. His body was embalmed, put in a metallic casket and temporarily buried at or near Abilene about the last of July of that year. The following September the body was disinterred and placed in a Studebaker wagon and the Negro cowhand, George Glenn, as driver, started on the long trip back to Texas.

It was impossible at that early date to get a dead body shipped back by rail, as there were no railroads, at least none leading from Abilene, Kansas, to Texas. This faithful Negro brought his old master's body back, being forty-two days and nights on the road, sleeping every night in the wagon alongside the casket.

He carried the body to the cemetery at Columbus where it was laid to rest by the side of the wife who had died some years before. Of such stuff were the old trail drivers, white and black, made of.

The badge on the Negro's coat is the road brand of the trail herd and is called "scissors."

# Grazed on Many Ranges

### by T.J. Garner, Loveland, Colorado

I WAS BORN IN TENNESSEE IN OCTOBER, 1853. My parents. died when I was a small boy, and I lived in Caldwell County until I was large enough to ride a horse into the brush after those wild cattle, which were not looked after during the Civil War.

In 1850 I made my first trip up the trail for Peck & Evans. We left Gonzales about the first of March and got along fine until we reached Fort Worth. There we had four inches of snow and very cold weather. Went to Gainesville, crossed Red River and went out by Fort Arbuckle, on to Wichita and Abilene, Kansas. We saw a great many buffalo and lots of Indians, but had no trouble with them. We delivered our herd and went home.

In the fall of 1870 I joined the Texas Rangers at Gonzales, and was mustered in at San Antonio. Went to Montague County and fought Indians that winter and also the following spring and summer. Had some close calls but came out without a scratch.

In 1872 I went with a herd of cattle from Lockhart, Texas, to Salt Lake City, Utah, with Mack Stewart as boss. We had a very good trip and only a few stampedes. Reached Salt Lake about the first of October. When we left this place we took a stage for Ogden and boarded cars for Kansas City, and from there came to Austin.

In 1873 I went with a herd for Jack Meyers from Lockhart to Ellsworth, Kansas. Coleman James was boss. We had a fine trip. Went back to Texas with the horses, and there worked on the range for a number of years.

In 1877 I again hit the trail, this time with a herd for Hood & Hughes, from Uvalde to Caldwell, Kansas. They sold out there and I took 640 of those old mossheads down to the Kaw Nation for Smith & Leedy. We held them there until the 10th of October and then started for the feeding pens. Swam them across the Arkansas River a few miles below Arkansas City, and went along the Flint Hills to the head of Elk River, near Eureka, Kansas.

When we reached a point within about a mile of the pens ten French ranchers came out of a gulch and were going to give Hank Leedy a grass necktie. Hank was scared almost to death, and his face went as white as my hair is today when they caught his horse by the bridle and began to curse and abuse him.

I said: "Don't get scared, Hank, I am Johnny on the spot," and I lit off old Gray Eagle alongside of a rock that stood about four feet high and prepared for action.

Bringing my Winchester into position I started in to make those fellows a speech, but they did not wait to hear it, and went back into the gulch faster than they had come out of it. Hank said: "Jack, you must have lots of gall to talk that way to those fellows."

I told him it was not what I said that turned the trick, it must have been my looks or my Winchester that caused them to scamper away.

While I was at Uvalde, Texas, a Mexican gave me his hat and what money he had because I was better at monte than he was. I was still wearing the hat and I had not been in a barber shop for several months, so I did not look like a band-box boy, and my looks may have had a great deal to do with their sudden departure. We were three days too early with our cattle, and that was the reason those ranchmen got so "riled" up.

We put the steers in a pen about fifteen acres in size. It was located in a canyon, which had been walled up at both ends, except a space of about twelve feet for the entrance. This space was closed by pole bars.

We went to Hank Leedy's house and he introduced me to his good wife and told her to prepare a good supper for us. And when it was ready I promptly got on the outside of six or seven hot biscuits and boiled eggs. It was the best meal I had had for six months.

Hank's house was on a bluff overlooking the pens where we had put the cattle, and that night a great hail and rainstorm came up. When the lightning flashed I could see those old steers run from one end of the corral to the other, but they could not get out. That was the only stampede I ever enjoyed.

Hank insisted on us staying with him a few days to rest up, telling us our pay would continue as long as we remained there, and we stayed there several days. I don't think Hank cared so much for our "rest" as he did about something else.

One day one of the boys and myself were out in the hills a few days later and met four men driving a bunch of cattle. We rode up to them and talked awhile and learned that they were among the crowd that had stopped our cattle and threatened to lynch Hank.

I told them there was no danger of Texas fever affecting their cattle as there had been so much weather and frost, and they seemed satisfied, and we parted friendly and wished each other good luck and goodbye.

I remained with old Hank a few days longer, then told him I thought he was safe and I would go to Eureka, and sell my horses and go back to Texas. He wanted me to give him my Winchester and pistol, but I could not part with both of them so I gave him the Winchester only, and bade him and his excellent wife goodbye.

I went to town, sold out and then hired a farmer to haul me to Humboldt, a distance of sixty miles, where I hit the cars for Texas. Went by way of Sherman, Dallas, Houston and San Antonio. Remained in San Antonio a few days and then went to Bell County and wintered.

In 1878 I went from Round Rock to Allen's ranch on the Colorado River below Columbus, for Dudley and John Snyder, and got 2,700 one, two and three year old steers, and drove them by way of Gonzales to Lockhart, through Austin, Round Rock, Fort Worth, Red River Station, on to Dodge City, Ogallala and Julesburg, where they were branded and turned loose on the range. All of the hands were tenderfeet except two.

The cattle would get to drifting in the fog and stampede and run all night long. For three weeks I did not unroll my bedding, and did not get more than an hour's sleep each night. Finally they got settled down and we made it through with but little loss.

I worked on the L L Ranch at Julesburg until November, shipping out beeves, then went back to Ogallala, and from there to the Spotted Agency in South Dakota. Stopped at Bill Shope's ranch a few days and he wanted me to go back to Ogallala with him and help ship out beeves from his North Platte ranch. When I finished this job I went to Denver and wintered there.

In 1879 I went to work on the range at Hugo, Colorado, for Frank Cochrane. Worked for him four years.

While on this job I went to the Blue Mountains near Durango and gathered a herd of mixed cattle, drove them to Rocky Ford, shipped the beeves to Kansas City, drove the stock cattle to Brush Station on the South Platte, cut out the dry stock and put 4,000 cows with their calves and 2,500 yearlings in one herd and drove them down the river twenty-four miles to Bush's Ranch and delivered them, then returned to the station and drove dry stock to Cheyenne and sold then to Richie Brothers. I delivered them on Powder River near the Montana line and came back and spent the winter in Denver.

In 1883 I went to the Black Hills in South Dakota and worked on the range there and in Northern Wyoming and Montana for a few years, and then started a cow ranch of my own.

I got married in 1891 to one of the finest little seventeen-year-old girls in that country, and we held down the ranch for a few years, but you know the old saying about the big fish eating up the little fish, so I sold out what I had left and came to Loveland, Colorado, and have been running a shoe shop here ever since.

I have a few cattle up on the Thompson River near Loveland, and am at present raising milk goats here. Also I have a ranch in Texas, with my nephew as partner and manager.

I see in the first volume of the Trail Drivers' book a sketch wherein one of the old boys stated that he would like to make the drives again. I would not care to do so, for I would not again take some of the chances I took then for all the money in these United States.

I had enough of three- to seven-months' work, night and day, in hail-storms, stampedes, blizzards, and the like. And then when the cattle were delivered and we would go to town to find lead whizzing around too close to be comfortable, and see poor fellows falling to rise no more. I do not want any more of the old life.

I see some of the old trail drivers are living on Rough Row, and my sympathies go out to them. My little wife and I are living on Easy Street, and would be pleased to have any of the old trail boys call on us if they should ever come to Loveland, Colorado.

# An Eventful Career

*by William B. Krempkau, San Antonio, Texas*

WILLIAM B. KREMPKAU, THE SUBJECT OF THIS SKETCH, was born in a house on Salinas Street, three blocks from the San Fernando Cathedral, San Antonio, Texas, March 9, 1863.

His parents came from Ransbach, St. Arnin, Alsace, with the Castro colonists in 1844, and located in San Antonio. At that time the principal trading done by the early settlers was with Indians and Mexicans, very few white people living in San Antonio.

Money was very scarce and trading was done by exchanging goods for buffalo robes, furs, gold and silver ore, which the Indians and Mexicans brought in. Wood and prairie hay was transported on burros. Water was hauled on skids, or rolled in barrels from the river, creeks and ditches; there were only a few wells in the town. In relating his experiences Mr. Krempkau said:

"My grandfather joined Napoleon's army in 1808 and served until 1815, and was promoted to be a captain. He was wounded three times, and decorated several times for bravery. One of my uncles was killed at the Battle of Manassas the same day Gen. Albert Sidney Johnson fell.

"The call of the wild became so strong, however, that I left school and divided my time between the cow camp and the freighter's camp. Mr. Monier was a neighbor to our family and was one of the most extensive freighters out of San Antonio to government posts in Texas and to different points in Mexico.

"I often lounged around his corral, which was always full of wagons, teams and teamsters, and made myself useful in assisting the freighters in every way possible with the result that I soon became a favorite with those old grizzly teamsters, and they encouraged me to take up their line of work. Mr. Monier took contracts to break wild mules for the government to use as pack mules. He often received fifty or a hundred mules at a time, and had a novel way of breaking them in. His hands would rope each animal in the corral, and securely tie bags of sand on their backs, and then lead or drive them around for quite awhile, repeating the performance every day, until the mules were gentle.

"At first they would buck and cavort around pretty lively, but a mule is quick to learn, and after two or three days they would be easily handled. In this kind of work I soon became an expert, and learned to throw the lasso as good as any of the men. I could throw the rope and catch a wild mule by the foot or head with perfect ease.

"Mr. Monier needed hands that were quick with rope or gun, and soon employed me to accompany him on his perilous journeys to Mexico. I remained with him several years, often going to Chihuahua, San Luis Potosi, Saltillo and other points, and I experienced all the thrills and excitement incident to those early days, with Indians, high water, Mexicans, dry weather, and crossing deserts. For protection against attack by Indians we always corraled the wagons at night, and in making a corral I could swing the wagons around as quick as anyone.

"I was with Mr. Monier on the last trip he made to Mexico, in 1880. This was a cotton train, twenty bales to the wagon, and it was delivered at San Luis Potosi.

"In 1882 I went up the trail to Dodge City, Kansas, for Smith & Elliott of Springfield, Illinois. The herd was bought in Mason, Gillespie and San Saba counties, and delivered to my boss, Charlie Baldo of Uvalde County. Baldo was one of the best trail bosses I ever knew.

"He treated us all fine, and was liked by every man in the outfit. We went the western trail and had all sorts of exciting experiences on the trip, thunderstorms, swollen streams, stampedes, Indians, long dry drives, wild animals, loss of sleep, and a frequent hankering for the chuck wagon when kept in the saddle for twenty-four hours or longer.

"We delivered the cattle at Dodge City, and there I met many of my old friends from Texas. As soon as I could get loose from the herd I took a bath in the river, went to a barber shop and got my face beautified, put on some new clothes, and went forth to see the sights in the toughest town on the map – and I saw 'em.

"I came back home on the train, my first railroad experience, and was surprised to find when I reached San Antonio that my baggage had arrived also."

# No Room in the Tent for Polecats

*by W.B. Foster, San Antonio, Texas*

I WAS BORN JAN. 6, 1849, one mile from Foster Cross Road, Sequado Valley, East Tennessee. I lost my mother when I was seven years old. One year later my father married Mrs. Julia Morris and moved to Hickory Hill, Gallatin County, Illinois.

I stayed there until I was eighteen years old, then I went to East Tennessee, staying there three years and then drifted over to Trotters Landing, Mississippi, and from there came to Texas. I landed in San Antonio April 6, 1871. Killed my first wolf on Dignowity Hill, now being in the city limits.

I was there only a short time until I hired to W.M. Todd to go north with cattle. Wade Hampton of Seguin had charge of the herd. Todd bought horses for himself. Major George of Seguin and Monoy & Wilbert of Nevada also hired men for Todd's three outfits. We camped for several days under a big hackberry tree that now stands on Roosevelt Ave. in San Antonio.

From there we went to Guadalupe River. Major George took one outfit to Seguin. We camped in a little pasture belonging to Mr. Braners just north of Youngford.

While there Col. Todd bought a fine pair of steers from Edwards & Ervin. He wanted them broke to work so we drove them out on the prairie, roped and tied them down, yoked them and tied their tails together, tied the bed to the wagon, put a rope around their horns, put a half hitch in their mouths and then hitched them to the wagon.

Al Meyers and myself got into the wagon to drive, the boys untied their legs and other men rode on each side to keep them straight, and if you don't think we had a ride over those hog wallows, you have another thought coming. We could handle them when we went to receiving cattle.

We next moved to Cordova Pens, four and a half miles northwest of

Seguin, where we road-branded the cattle TOD that we had received from J. Plumer at the May pasture, two miles from the Sutherland Springs, the ranch brand being AT. We received 1,300 head in four herds. In coming from the May pasture to the branding pens, we came by Sutherland Springs, crossed the Guadalupe River at Sheffield Ford below Seguin, and passed north of Seguin.

Just as we started on the trail, W.M. Pusey came from Denver, Col. Todd let him have Wade Hampton to help him gather a herd. Pusey was Todd's son-in-law. Todd then hired Col. G.W. Nail of Hunter to boss his herd.

We crossed the San Geronimo Creek at the Austin Crossing, the San Marcos at the McGee crossing by the Manchaca Springs; here I witnessed the densest fog I ever saw. We crossed the Colorado River west of Austin, left Round Rock to the left, and crossed the Gabriel River some distance east of town. Little River was up, as it had been raining and everything crossed but one steer. I roped him and got him in the water and he swam across.

Todd had a very fine mare, which he had bought from Nick Crenshaw at Seguin. A man by the name of Thompson, who was riding her, went around a bend of the river here and we never heard or saw anything of him or the mare after that.

We crossed just above the suspension bridge at Waco. At Hillsboro the cattle stampeded around a school house. The young lady teacher was quick to close the door, but the kiddies were scared just the same. I rode a big horse that I called "Jack Moore" and he was some horse.

We had just left Hillsboro, when the cattle spied a little girl going to school with a red shawl on her head. Each corner of the shawl was blown by the wind and this was more than the cattle could stand. I was behind the herd and saw what was exciting the cattle so I got all there was in "Jack Moore" and picked her up just in time.

At Cleburne a bad man beat up Tony Wilder, a seventeen-year-old boy who belonged to our outfit. Al Meyers tried his hand on the bad man, using his quirt. Wilder never carried arms of any kind; he was more like a girl than a boy and everyone in the outfit loved him. He and myself were the only ones out of an outfit of twenty-two men that had not killed a man.

At Fort Worth the river was up. We went up about ten miles west of town and cut brush to build a chute to the river in order to force the cattle into the water, the bank being about eight or ten feet higher than the water.

I always led the cattle across all streams and on this occasion I went down that chute in front of a stampeded herd. On the north bank my horse bogged, I jumped off him and as I did so I discovered several Indians sitting on a log nearby. I shouted back to the men on the other side that there were Indians there.

It was some time before the other men crossed on a ferry just below the mouth of the Clear Fork of the Trinity River, and when they got there the Indians were gone.

At the Trinity River we wound up a wild drive of one-hundred miles in four days with stock cattle. Col. Todd was drinking all the time and was very disagreeable, which caused Col. Nail to leave us. Everyone in the outfit was sorry to see him leave as he was a fine man and one of the best cowmen I ever saw.

As we neared the Red River Canyon, we were strung out on the trail, a small herd to our right tried to rush to the mouth of the canon. When they got close and were about to pass us, Al Meyers commenced to shoot in front of them. They had business the other way, and like they were in a hurry to get there.

Red River Canyon is about twenty-five miles through and only one place where a herd could be bedded. When we camped near the Red River Station, I quit and went to town ahead of the herd. The river was very high.

People tried to get Todd to wait until the water went down. None of the men would lead the herd. The cattle got about the middle of the stream and then went to swimming in a circle. Todd began calling for me. He had long white hair and was wild for short time. He turned to Al Meyers and said: "You know where my son Foster is? Tell him I will give him anything in the world if he will save my cattle for me."

I stripped to my underclothes, mounted "Jack Moore" and went to them. I got off the horse and right on to the cattle. They were so jammed together that it was like walking on a raft of logs. When I finally got to the only real big steer in the bunch I mounted him and he pulled for the other side.

When he got near the bank I drifted down the stream to the horse. It must have been about nine o'clock in the morning, on the 8th day of June, 1871, so I kept the herd together all day until nearly sundown; no hat, no saddle – just my underclothes.

At Monument Rock some of the boys put the Colonel's tent over a bed of polecats and when he went to bed they tied the front of the tent. In trying to get out a little later the Colonel tore down the tent.

The next morning the Colonel sent me to Fort Sill after the mail. It was thirty-five miles to Fort Sill and the Indians were on the warpath, but I did not see any. I caught the herd again at the old stage stand.

I had a letter for Al Meyers, and in thirty minutes he was on his way to Philadelphia, Pennsylvania, to get married. Jimmie Billings also got a letter telling him that he could return to New York City, his old home. He had been a bounty jumper during the war.

The next day Col. Nelson and I were near the trail when the stage came along. The driver told Nelson that the officers had learned where he was and that they would be after him soon; he then rode around the herd and was gone. Nelson was the right-hand man to John Morgan, the raider, during the war between the states. He had been bootlegging in Indian Territory.

We crossed the Washita River where the McDonald Ranch is now and crossed the Canadian River at Billie Williams' store. That night Col. Todd and I fell out and I quit. He talked a long time to me before I would agree to stay with the outfit until he got out of the Indian country.

The next morning when I went out to try to get a wild turkey, I rode into a bunch of Indians. Jack Moore carried me from them and when I got to the herd, I had been struck with several arrows, so was Jack Moore.

Jimmie Billings cut the arrows out of both of us with a pocket knife. I lost quite a lot of blood. While they were at work on me, William Packer rode up and had me put in his wagon and in a few days I was in the saddle again. But "Jack Moore" and I parted forever. I finished my trip with Harrow & Packer, who had 300 head of butcher cattle, which they were taking to Bloomington, Illinois.

We passed Caldwell, Kansas, and were in Wichita Falls on the 4th day of July, 1871, just two years after the first peg was driven into the ground to lay out the town. The cattle were shipped from Florence, Kansas.

William Slaughter and I went across the country to Abilene. Wild Bill, or I should say William Hickok, was city marshal. He was very kind to me and I thought a great deal of him.

I shipped cattle from Abilene to St. Louis for Jim Reed, a one-armed man. One day while I was asleep at the Belle Hotel in St. Louis, Zack Mulhall called and asked what I was dreaming. I told him of "home." He then asked me why I did not go home. I told him to go to the ticket office with me and the first train that went out I would go on it. The train went east just one hour before the one went west.

I found things changed from what they were when they left.

# Harrowing Experience with Jayhawkers

*THE FOLLOWING ACCOUNT IS BY J.M. DAUGHERTY, of Daugherty, Texas, a charter member of The Old Trail Drivers. He is better known to all cattlemen as Uncle Jim Daugherty, and is one of the best-known Texas cattlemen still in the business.*

*At present he is sole owner of the Figure 2 Ranch, located in Culberson and Hudspeth Counties, Texas, estimated to be the largest and best equipped ranch in Texas. He maintains his headquarters at Daugherty, Texas. Uncle Jim has made many trail drives, starting as a boy in his teens in 1866 and continuing until 1887, during which time he has driven many trails and delivered many herds to all parts of Kansas, Nebraska, the Dakotas, Montana, Wyoming, Utah and Colorado:*

In the spring of 1866 I made my first trail drive. Starting from Denton County, Texas, with a herd of about 500 steers and five cowhands and myself, I crossed Red River at a crossing known at that time as Preston. From there I drove to Fort Gibson, Indian Territory, and from Fort Gibson I drove to Baxter Springs, Kansas, close to the Kansas and Indian Territory line. I had started to Sedalia, Missouri, where I intended shipping the cattle by rail to St. Louis.

On arriving at Baxter Springs I found that there had been several herds ahead of me that had been disturbed by what we called at that time Kansas Jayhawkers, and in one instance the Jayhawkers had killed the owner, taken the herd, and ran the rest of the cowboys off. This herd belonged to Kaynaird and was gathered in the southern part of the Choctaw Nation in the Indian Territory.

"After hearing this news I decided to stop and lay up for awhile, and stopped with the herd on what was then known as the Neutral Strip, a strip of land about twenty miles wide that ran across the northern part of the Indian Territory, next to the Kansas line. Here I left the herd and my cowboys and I started to ride alone up the trail to investigate conditions.

"I rode as far as Fort Scott, Kansas, and there I met a man by the name of Ben Keys, whom I told I had a herd on the Neutral Strip I would like to sell. He agreed to buy them if I would make deliverance at Fort Scott, Kansas.

I returned to the Neutral Strip and we started driving the herd north along the Kansas-Missouri line, sometimes in the state of Kansas and sometimes in Missouri. From the information that I had received regarding the big risk we were taking by trying to drive through, we were always on the lookout for trouble.

"Some twenty miles south of Fort Scott, Kansas, and about four o'clock one afternoon a bunch of fifteen or twenty Jayhawkers came upon us. One of my cowboys, John Dobbins by name, was leading the herd and I was riding close to the leader.

"Upon approach of the Jayhawkers, John attempted to draw his gun and the Jayhawkers shot him dead in his saddle. This caused the cattle to stampede and at the same time they covered me with their guns and I was forced to surrender. The rest of the cowboys stayed with the herd, losing part of them in the stampede.

"The Jayhawkers took me to Cow Creek, which was nearby, and there tried me for driving cattle into their country, which they claimed were infested with ticks that would kill their cattle. I was found guilty without any evidence, they not even having one of my cattle for evidence. Then they began to argue among themselves what to do with me. Some wanted to hang me while others wanted to whip me to death.

"I, being a young man in my teens and my sympathetic talk about being ignorant of ticky cattle of the south diseasing any of the cattle in their country, caused one of the big Jayhawkers to take my part. The balance were strong for hanging me on the spot, but through his arguments they finally let me go.

"After I was freed and had joined the herd, two of my cowboys and I slipped back and buried John Dobbins where he fell. After we had buried him we cut down a small tree and hewed out a head and footboard and marked his grave. Then we slipped back to the herd.

"This being soon after the close of the Civil War, the Jayhawkers were said to be soldiers mustered out of the Yankee army. They were nothing more than a bunch of cattle rustlers and were not interested about fever ticks coming into their country but used this just as a pretense to kill the men with the herds and steal the cattle or stampede the herds.

"After rejoining the herd I found that during the stampede I had lost about 150 head of cattle, which was a total loss to me. I drove the balance of the herd back to the Neutral Strip, and after resting a day or two, went back to Fort Scott, and reported to Mr. Keys what had happened. Mr. Keys sent a man back to the herd with me to guide us to Fort Scott.

"On my return to the herd with the guide we started the drive to Fort Scott the second time. The guide knew the country well, which was very thinly settled. We would drive the herd at night and would lay up at some secluded spot during the day.

"After driving in this manner for five days and five nights we reached Fort Scott about daybreak of the fifth night and penned the cattle in a high board corral adjoining a livery stable, which completely hid them from the public view.

"We put our horses in the livery stable, and went to a place Mr. Keys had provided for us to sleep and get something to eat, as we had left our chuck wagon a day behind us on the trail. As soon as the cattle were penned Mr. Keys paid me for them. Then we ate our breakfast and slept all day. When darkness fell we saddled our horses and started back over the trail to Texas.

"I returned to Texas without any further incident worth noting, and continued to drive the trail, rarely missing a year that I did not make a drive."

# Reminiscences of the Old Trails

*by C.F. Doan of Doan's*

I AM NOW 74 YEARS OLD and looking back over my life I find the main part of it has been spent near the Old Chisholm Trail, or on the Dodge City, Kansas trail.

My first introduction to the Old Chisholm Trail was in 1874 when in company with Robert E. Doan, a cousin, and both of us from Wilmington, Ohio, we set out for Ft. Sill, Indian Territory, from Wichita, Kansas. We made this little jaunt by stagecoach of 250 miles over the famous trail in good time.

In 1875, very sick, I returned to my home in Ohio from Fort Sill, but the lure of the West urged me to try my luck again and Oct. 10, 1878, found me back in the wilds and ever since I have lived at Doan's, the trail crossing on Red River known far and wide by the old trail drivers as the jumping off place into the great unknown the last of civilization until they hit the Kansas line.

While sojourning in the Indian Territory in 1874 and 1875 with Tim Pete, Dave Lours and J. Doan, I engaged in trading with the Indians and buying hides at a little store on Cache Creek, two miles from Fort Sill.

Our life at this place was a constant thrill on account of Indians. During the month of July, 1874, the Indians killed thirteen hay cutters and wood choppers. Well do I remember, one day after a hay cutter had been killed, a tenderfoot from the east with an eye to local color decided to explore the little meadow where the man had been killed expecting to collect a few arrows so that he might be able to tell the loved ones at home of his daring.

But the Indians discovered the sightseer and with yells and his collection of arrows whistling about his ears, chased him back to the stockade. Terror lent wings to his feet and he managed to reach safety but departed the next day for the East, having lost all taste for the danger of the West.

Jan. 8, 1875, found me caught in a blizzard and I narrowly escaped freezing to death at the time. Indians around Fort Sill demanding buckskin, as their supply had run low, I was sent by the firm on horseback to the Shawnee tribe to buy a supply. This was my second trip.

Soon after my departure the blizzard set in and I was warned by the mail carrier, the only man I met on the trip, to turn back or I would be frozen. But the thoughts of the buckskin at four-dollars per pound caused me to press on. I managed to reach Conover Ranch badly frozen, I was taken from my horse and given first-aid treatment.

I was so cold that ice had frozen in my mouth. The mail carrier, who had advised me to turn back, never reached the fort, and his frozen body was found some days after the storm.

For two weeks I remained in this home before I found strength to continue the journey. I was held up another week by the cold near Paul's Valley, but I got the buckskin, sending it back by express-mail carrier and returned on horseback.

Indians during this time were held in concentration camps near the fort, both Comanches and Kiowas, and beeves were issued twice a week.

A man by name of Conover and myself did the killing and about seventy-five or eighty head were killed at one time. The hides were bought from the Indians and shipped to St. Louis.

After the bi-weekly killings, the Indians would feast and sing all night long and eat up their rations and nearly starve until the next issue day came.

It was at this time that I met Quanah, chief of the Comanches, who was not head chief at that time, and Satanta, chief of the Kiowas. I was warned during that time by Satanta that the Indians liked me and they wanted me to leave the country because they intended to kill every white man in the nation.

I rather think that the friendly warning was given me because I often gave crackers and candy to the hungry squaws and papooses and of course Satanta's family received their share.

Satanta escaped soon after that and near where El Reno now stands, at the head of his warriors, captured a wagon train and burned men to their wagon wheels. He was captured again and taken to the penitentiary where he committed suicide by opening a vein in his arm.

After moving to Doan's of course I saw a great deal of Quanah, who at that time had become head chief. He told me that he had often been invited to return to his white relations near Weatherford but he had refused. "Corwin," he said, "as far as you see here I am chief and the people look up to me, down at Weatherford I would be a poor half-breed Indian." Perhaps he was right.

Big Bow, another Kiowa chief, often followed by his warriors, rode up to the little store on Cache Creek one day and arrogantly asked, would we hand over the goods or should they take them? We told them we would hand over the goods as he designated them.

Later when Big Bow and I became good friends, he said, "Us Indians are big fools, not smart like white men. 'Cause you handed over the goods that day, but Washington (Uncle Sam) took it out of our pay." It was quite true for as soon as the wards of the government had departed, the bill was turned into their guardian, Uncle Sam.

We had but one bad scare from the Indians at Doan's, and that date April, 1879, is indelibly fixed on my memory. The Indians came close enough to the house to be recognized by the women and they ran our horses off. I was up in the woods hunting at that time and reached home at dusk to find three terror-stricken women, a baby and a dog for me to defend.

All the other men had gone to Denison for supplies and our nearest neighbor was fifty miles away; so thinking discretion the better part of valor, we retreated to a little grove about half a mile from our picket house and spent the night, expecting every moment to have a "hair-raising" experience.

The Indians proved to be a band of Kiowas returning from near where Quanah now stands, where they killed and scalped a man by name of Earle. Three days later the soldiers came through on the trail of the Indians expecting to find our home in ashes and the family exterminated.

The Indians had returned to the reservation. The Kiowas told me afterward quite coolly that they would have attacked us that night but believed us to be heavily garrisoned with buffalo hunters – a lucky thing for us. This was the last raid through the country. The Indians after that became very friendly with us and told me to go ahead and build a big store, that we would not be molested. They had decided this in council.

The spring and summer of 1879, I saw the first herds come up the trail, though the movement had started two years before. My uncle, J. Doan, who had been with me the two years in Fort Sill, had established this post at Doan's, April 1878, and we had arrived, that is, myself, wife and baby and the judge's daughters, that fall.

So we had come too late to see the herds of 1878. One-hundred-thousand cattle passed over the trail by the little store in 1879. In 1881, the trail reached the peak of production and 300,000 were driven to the Kansas shipping point.

In 1882 on account of the drought, the cattle found slim picking on their northern trek and if it had not been for the "butter weed" many would have starved to death as grass was all dead that year. Names of John Lytle, Noah Ellis, Ab and John Blocker, Harrold and Ikard, Worsham, the Belchers, Ligon and Clark, Wiley Blair, the Eddlemans and others come into my memory as I write this, owners and bosses of the mighty herds of decades ago.

One man, Dubose, with whom we would go a piece, like school kids, up the trail, complained plaintively that he never in all those summers had a mess of roasting ears, of which he was very fond, as the corn would be about knee high when he left Corpus Christi and as he came slowly up the trail he would watch the fields in their various stages but by the time he left Doan's and civilization it was still too early for even a cob.

Capt. John Lytle spent as high as a month at a time in Doan's preparing for his onward march. Accompanied by his secretary he would fit out his men and everything would be shipshape when he crossed the Red River. He was a great man and his visits were enjoyed.

Wichita Falls failing to provide suitable branding pens for the accommodation of the trail drivers, pens were provided at Doan's. Furnaces and corrals were built and here Charley Word and others fitted with cartridges, Winchesters by the case, sow bosom and flour, and even to Stetson hats, etc.

This store did a thriving business and thought nothing of selling bacon and flour in car-load lots, though getting our supplies from Denison, Sherman, Gainesville, and later, Wichita Falls.

The post office was established here in 1879 and I was the first postmaster. It was at this office all mail for the trail herds was directed as, like canned goods and other commodities, this was the last chance.

One night while a crowd sat around the little adobe store someone struck up a lively air on a French harp and the door opened and in sailed a hat followed closely by a big black fellow who commenced to dance. It was one of Ab Blocker's niggers who had been sent up for the mail, giving first notice of the herd's arrival.

Many a sweetheart down the trail received her letter bearing the postmark of Doan's and many a cowboy asked self-consciously if there was any mail for him while his face turned a beet red when a dainty missive was handed him.

The old trail played a part in the establishment of the Doan's picnic. For in 1884 when grass had risen and the cowmen had gone up the trail or out to the spring roundups; the women of course were playing the role of "the girl I left behind me," so a picnic of five women and one lone man was inaugurated.

I have never missed a picnic from that day. Now the crowd is swelled to thousands, the dinner is a sumptuous affair and every two or three years the state and county candidates for offices plead with the people to give them the other fellow's job or one or more chance as the case may be.

The first house at Doan's was made of pickets with a dirt roof and floor of the same material. The first winter we had no door but a buffalo robe did service against the northers. The store, which had consisted mainly of ammunition and a few groceries occupied one end and the family lived in the other.

A huge fireplace around which Indians, buffalo hunters and the family sat, proved very comforting. The warmest seat was reserved for the one who held the baby and this proved to be a very much-coveted job. Furniture made with an ax and a saw adorned the humble dwelling.

Later the store and dwelling were divorced. An adobe store, which gave way to a frame building was built. Two log cabins for the families were erected. In 1881 our present home was built, the year the county was organized. This dwelling I still occupy.

Governors, English lords, bankers, lawyers, tramps and people from every walk in life have found sanctuary within its walls. And if these walls could speak many a tale of border warfare would echo from its gray shadows.

Here, my old adobe house and I sit beside the old trail and dream away the days thinking of the stirring, scenes enacted when it seemed an endless procession of horses and cattle passed, followed by men of grim visage but of cheerful mien, who sang the "Dying Cowboy" and "Bury Me Not on the Lone Prairie" and other cheerful tunes as they bedded the cattle or when in a lighter mood danced with the belles of Doan's or took it straight over the bar of the old Cowboy saloon.

# Why I Am a Prohibitionist

*by George F. Hindes, Pearsall and Hindes, Texas*

I WAS BORN IN ALABAMA, SEPTEMBER 1844, and graduated in a little home-made school house in the piney woods of Lauderdal County, Mississippi, near where the city of Meridian now stands. I graduated at the age of eleven years, and moved with my parents in wagons from there to Caldwell County, near Lockhart, Texas, that fall.

I visited Lockhart on Christmas day for the first time, and in those days Lockhart was wild and woolly, a wide-open town, where whiskey and every other kind of "blue ruin" flowed freely.

That day I saw a Mr. Perry kill a Mr. Cabaniss with a knife. To me it was a frightful experience. My curiosity caused me to ask what caused the trouble, and I was told it was whiskey. Then I went strong for prohibition, and was never intoxicated in my life.

We lived in Caldwell County until the fall of 1856, when my father sold a likely Negro woman to Major Fields for stock cattle, and we started west with the cattle to grow up with the country, as per Horace Greeley's advice.

I was "herd boss" on the trip. We drove our herd through San Antonio, from Alamo Plaza to Commerce Street, and down Commerce Street to South Flores Street, and on to Atascosa County. This was before the county was organized, and my father served on the first jury impaneled in the county. We settled on the San Miguel Creek, where the town of Hindes is now located, and where we had a world of free range, with great abundance of wild game of every kind, even wild mustang cattle and mustang horses.

I soon got to be an expert shot with rifle and pistol, a good roper, and a fast and fearless rider, and soon made friends with all the mustangers and hunters. We killed the native wild cattle for their hides and tallow, and the meat we could save. I caught and tamed lots of mustang horses, mostly young stock.

In the pioneer days of danger and adventure, and with no other or better job, I learned to be so fond of hunting and the chase, that I have never gotten over it, and can still ride a horse and shoot a rifle as good as anyone.

On two occasions, the Indians rounded me up. Once, with a Mr. Seals on the San Miguel, when we stood them off half of one night, and another time with a Mr. Atkins, when they kept us surrounded half of one afternoon at Charco Largo. A good run always suited me better than a doubtful stand, but either one is lonesome and frightful.

In August, 1865, twenty-eight redskins gave me a hard race, but I beat them to the river bottom and got away. Another time fifteen of them gave me a close chase and would have caught me, but in their trying to cut me off from the river, they ran on to a steep bluff bank and could not get down.

On one occasion three friends and myself went on a hunting trip south of the Nueces River for a week's hunt. Had a good time, but in a short time thereafter all of the three were killed and all dying with "their boots on."

At another time, my father, a Mr. Wheat, and myself had a good and successful hunt on the San Miguel; and in a short time the Indians killed Mr. Wheat in Medina County, and my father was killed by the Indians at his home in McMullen County.

The pioneers that were on the frontier before and during reconstruction days suffered many privations and hardships, and half of them did not live to tell the story.

But during these times, as dreary and dull as they were, there was a man whose life was as brilliant as a ray of sunshine following the dark and tempestuous clouds. That man was Jim Lowe, who was one of the first settlers in McMullen County, and who was the best fixed man in that section. He was truly one of God's noblemen – a philanthropist of the first order. He made it possible for many poor families to have bread in their homes, who, otherwise, would have had to live on meat alone. I was truly benefited by his wise counsel and good backing.

In March, 1865, about the close of the Civil War, I married the best little girl in the world, and she lived to bless my life for fifty-six years to a day, and passed on to her reward in March 1921.

*"When musing on companions gone,
We doubly feel ourselves alone."*

The year 1865 was an eventful one in my life. Married in March (I was promptly notified that I must "quit my meanness"), the war closed in May, and the Indians killed my father in August.

However, with all the energy and determination I possessed I went to work on the "wreck," for we lost practically everything we possessed during the war.

I proceeded under difficulties too numerous to mention, but by the spring of 1872, had gotten together a pretty good little herd of mixed cattle, and drove them to Kansas that spring. I had about the usual amount of trouble that a man has on his first drive over the "trail." Was compelled to swim swollen streams, had storms at night, and several stampedes.

Finally I bumped into the Osage tribe of Indians, and they gave us an exhibition of what they could do to a Texas herd, shooting and yelling the regular Indian war-hoop. They killed about one hundred beeves right there on the prairie, in sight, and scattered the others to the four winds, causing Mr. Redus great loss and trouble.

I drove my herd to Wichita, Kansas, and held them there on fine grass until fall, and sold out at good prices. When I got home that fall, I had more than $15,000 cash, in gold, $10,000 life insurance policy, a remnant of cattle and a good bunch of horses that I had left in Texas. I did not owe a dollar, and felt chesty as Croesus, in his palmiest days, ever dared to feel.

I handled several herds after that in Kansas and Wyoming, and always made a little money. I never bossed another herd all the way from start to finish, but I knew the game, and if a man made good, it was indeed a hard trip.

At another time I delivered 2,500 head of cattle in Wyoming, on the tenth day of September, in an all-day snowstorm; and while it was indeed something different to what I had been accustomed to, I could not enjoy it at all.

I kept buying, selling and trading cattle until 1882, when I made the best money in my life by buying about 40,000 acres of San Miguel land where the town of Hindes is now located on the San Antonio, Uvalde and Gulf Railroad, at a very low price.

I have watched it go up in value in these forty years while I was using it for pasture until I have sold some of it for one-hundred dollars an acre;

some at seventy-five dollars an acre, and have never sold any for less than twenty dollars an acre. I allotted my children sufficient land that if used and managed with prudence and care, will provide them liberally with life's needs, still have a good block of it left, and expect to develop an oil field in the near future.

In the fall of 1903 I helped organize the Pearsall National Bank at Pearsall, Texas, and have served continuously on its board of directors. For the past ten years I have been its president, resigning just recently in order to enable me to give my personal business the attention it deserves.

In 1909 I also helped to organize the Atascosa County State Bank at Jourdanton, Texas, and served as its president for six years, relinquishing my post of duty only after the bank was thoroughly established and was doing a nice business. However, I am still one of the largest stockholders in the Atascosa County Bank, and a large stockholder and director in the Pearsall National Bank.

Looking back now it seems that providential guidance has been instrumental in my living through the many harrowing experiences of the early days, when Indians roamed the country, and later, especially after the war, when outlaws gave so much trouble to the pioneers of the southwest.

It gives me much pleasure and consolation in having been spared to see the great southwest transformed from pioneer to the modern stage; where folks mingle with one another in security and all friendliness, and where now exists a spirit of democracy and helpfulness that makes the country a desirable place to live, grow and prosper.

I do not say boastingly, but there is a great deal of personal satisfaction in knowing that I was permitted to have a part in the up building of this section of our wonderful state.

# Played the Fiddle on Herd at Night

*Lake Porter, Falfurrias, Texas*

I WAS BORN JAN. 5, 1854, IN CHICKASAW, MISSISSIPPI, and came to Texas with my parents before my eyes were open, landing at Seguin, Guadalupe County, where we lived three years, then moved to Goliad County and settled on the Maha Rayo Creek, where we were living when the Civil War broke out.

We moved to the town of Goliad while the Civil War was going on, living there until its close, at which time my father, S.P. Porter, was killed in the town of Gonzales. My mother was left with eight small children, one pair of twins in the bunch. I was about the middle of the bunch, being at that time about nine years old.

As father was taken from us suddenly, leaving mother without means, it was "root, hog, or die" with us little fellows, so your humble servant went to work for R.T. Davis for my grub and clothes, and, bless your life, the clothes did not consist of any broadcloth suits either.

I worked for Davis one year and was then employed by A.C. Jones, Sr., of Bee County, who had a small horse ranch on the extreme head of Blanco Creek, then known as the Coleman Ranch and now owned, I think, by the McKinneys of Bee County.

I spent some lonesome days on this ranch, but I was getting well paid, as I was drawing the enormous salary of five dollars per month and my feed. I worked two years at this price and while the wages look small, I had more ready cash when the job ended than I had many times since, working for much larger wages.

When I left the Jones Ranch I went back to my dear mother, who still lived at Goliad. At that time she was in poor health and confined to her bed a great deal of the time, so I did the cooking and sometimes the washing for the family, while my two older brothers, Dave and Billie Porter, made a crop on land rented from R.T. Davis, my first employer.

In the fall my mother traded her place at Goliad for what is known as the old Reed place on Goat Creek in Goliad County, where I grew to manhood, and where the happiest days of my life were spent. I was barely in my teens when the big Kansas cattle drives started, and, like other boys of that time, I wanted some of the experience of outdoor life, so in the spring of 1871, with a herd belonging to one-armed Jim Read, I bade adieu to the southern climate for a season and headed northward, finally winding up at Abilene, Kansas.

After remaining there for a short time we got rid of our encumbrance, the longhorned steers, and turned our faces southward and in due time arrived safely at our starting point in Goliad County. Nothing apart from the usual happenings of the trail life took place on this trip.

Abilene was a wild and woolly town in those days, at least it seemed to be to a country boy out on his first jaunt.

There was plenty of game on the trail, Indians, buffalo, deer and antelope. The principal hotel in Abilene was the Drovers' Cottage, Mrs. Lou Gore, proprietress, which was general headquarters for all cattlemen.

After a five-months' trip I arrived at home pretty well hooked up, my earthly possessions being a suit of clothes, a pair of star-topped boots and $2.50 in cash for my trip. Well done, good and faithful servant!

I went up the trail three years for Jim Read and one year for W.G. Butler of Karnes County. When I was growing up I learned to play the fiddle, but there were only two tunes that I could play to perfection, one of which was "Seesaw," and the other was "Sawsee."

Often I have taken my old fiddle on herd at night when on the trail, and while some of my companions would lead my horse around the herd I agitated the catguts, reeling off such old time selections as "Black Jack Grove," "Dinah Had a Wooden Leg," "Shake That Wooden Leg, Dolly Oh," "Give the Fiddler a Dram," "Arkansaw Traveler," and "The Unfortunate Pup." And say, brothers, those old longhorned Texas steers actually enjoyed that old time music. I still have the old music box, which I used to play in those care-free, happy days.

My last drive up the trail was in 1875, after which I quit the trail, but never quit the cow-punching job until many years later.

Sweet is the memory of the old bygone days. Many of the old trail boys have passed over the Divide, and it will not be long until we, too, will pass out, to give our places to those coming on. My associates on the trail, as I recall them now, were Emory Hall, Babe Moyer, Young Collins, Bud Jordan, Bill White, Hiram Reynolds, John Reynolds, John Naylor,

Dave Porter, Bud Lansford, Ysidro Morris, John Young, Jack Best, and others.

I was married Dec. 10, 1878, to Miss Nelia Williams of Refugio County, daughter of Judge J. Williams, who for many years was sheriff of Refugio County.

Three children were born to us, two boys and one girl, all of whom are still living. In 1882 I moved my family to Atascosa County, settling one mile south of Pleasanton, near the Tilden Road, where we remained fourteen months, then moved to McMullen County, where we resided until 1912, then we moved to Brooks County, our present home.

While a resident of McMullen County I served as sheriff there for eight years, and I am now serving my second term as sheriff of Brooks County.

# Packsaddle Mountain Fight

*from a Sketch by N.G. Ozment, in* San Antonio Express

JAMES R. MOSS WAS BORN IN FAYETTE COUNTY, TEXAS, Jan. 24, 1843. When he was a small boy, his parents moved to Travis County, settling near Lake Brushy, some twelve miles northwest of Austin. In 1857 he moved with his parents to Llano County. It was this year that the town of Llano was laid off.

John Oatman erected the first store ever built in the town. His father donated fifty acres of land on which to build the town. In an election held to locate the county seat, Llano was selected. When but a youth, young Moss took his place as one of the defenders against the incursion of the Indians.

In February 1862, a volunteer company of 700 men, including young Moss, was formed in the town of Llano to fight for the defense of the Confederacy.

From Llano the company went to Camp Terry, southeast of Austin. Mr. Moss was in Company E, 17th Infantry, McCulloch's brigade, Walker's division. He was in the battle of Milliken's Bend. The day before the capture of his company he was transferred from the Infantry to the Third Battalion, Texas Cavalry, on account of a crippled ankle. He remained with the cavalry through the succeeding period of the war.

When young Moss returned from the war he was broken in health and without as much as a full suit of wearing apparel. With that indefatigable energy and purpose, characteristic of the man, he at once began to lay a foundation for the future.

In the absence of the young men during the war the Indians had driven away many horses and driven their owners back further east. The elder Moss had taken the precaution to have his sons move the horses down on Barton's Creek, near Austin, before young Moss joined the army. A year after his return, James and his brother, Charles, took charge of their father's cattle on shares.

Week after week, after working all day, they, with some hands working for them, would take the horses to some favorable grazing place and take shifts in guarding them through the night.

The moon nights increased the vigilance of these young cattlemen, for they well knew these were the nights the Indians were most likely to swoop down after the ponies.

Besides the cattle, the two young men raised many hogs. As there was no local market for these, they killed and baconed about 200 head one winter and the next summer loaded the meat into ox wagons and took it to Austin, Bastrop, LaGrange and as far as old Washington to secure markets for same. The weather became so hot that the boys drove at night and rested through the day.

Watching every chance to turn time into money, after the spring work with the cattle, young Moss took the contract to harvest the wheat crops of Cadwell and Saeter. He hired a Negro man to help him. The wheat was cradled and hand-bound. The shocking was done at night.

In the later sixties he, with others drove cattle through to Louisiana and sold them to a United States contractor, delivering on board a steamboat on the Mississippi River at Hogs' Point, below the mouth of Red River.

In April, 1869, Mr. Moss threw in with Damon Slater and started to California with about 1,400 head of cattle. The year before Mr. Slater found the market good out there, hence this trip. James had his brother Charles with him on this trip. The entire outfit was composed of nine cow hands, two horse herders, two wagoners and the cook.

Here is, in brief, the route taken : From Llano to Concho, thence up the Pecos River, and Rio Hondo, up San Benito, a branch of the Hondo, thence across the Divide to Tula Rosa, New Mexico, thence to Rio Memphis. Here they saw the first white woman they had seen since leaving Llano. She seemed perfectly happy with her husband in those wilds.

From there they drove to Apache Pass, Arizona, through Tucson, and on to Gila River, crossing the Colorado below the mouth of the Gila, at Fort Yuma. They drove into old Mexico and traveled ten or fifteen miles in this country, thence across what is now the Imperial Valley in California.

From here they turned southwest toward the mountains. Entering these, they drove up to the old Warner Ranch. Here they struck the Immigrants' Trail, finally arriving at Williamson Port, on the Pacific, where they wintered. The following spring the cattle were delivered some twenty-five or thirty miles from Los Angeles.

On Aug. 4, 1873, a band of redskins were depredating in Llano County. A company of eight men, consisting of S.B. Harrington, Arch Martin, Robert Brown, Pink Ayers, Eli P. Lloyd, W.B., S.B., and J.R. Moss, struck their trail in the early morning and followed it for thirty-five or forty miles, locating the Indians on Packsaddle Mountain about noon.

The red men had gone up the mountain from the south side and when discovered by the settlers most of them were sitting around eating some of the beef, which had just been roasted. One or two were lying on the ground, either asleep or resting. There were seventeen bucks, two squaws and a boy.

Before giving an account of the battle it will be noted that the Indian who was supposed to be on guard was guilty of negligence that proved fatal to some of his comrades, if not himself. Had he been watching he could have seen the approaching Texans a mile away, which possibly would have changed the result of the conflict.

When the settlers rode up the mountain they observed twenty or more horses stolen by the Indians but a short distance away. Beyond the horses the Indians were seen eating and resting. The white men by a quick dash ran in between the enemy and the horses. By this time the red men were up and armed. Their weapons were Winchesters, breech loaders, muskets, pistols, and bows and arrows, though the latter was not used.

The Texans all used Winchesters save W.B. Moss, who used a Colt Ranger pistol. W.B. Moss began firing at the Indians before dismounting. Firing two shots, he dismounted and joined his comrades, all of whom save Pink Ayers had dismounted. Ayers was shot in the hip. The mule he rode was also shot, and the rider did not reenter the fight. So it was seventeen to seven against the whites.

The Indians retreated to a ledge of rocks behind some blackjack timber, where they quickly formed a line of battle and rushed at the Texans with a vengeful determination to make quick work of them, but they found the settlers ready for them.

W.B. Moss emptied his pistol at them and was bending over to knock the shells from it when a bullet crashed into his body near the right shoulder, and passing through his lungs, lodged in his left side dangerously near the heart.

The battle was now on in earnest. James Moss saw his brother fall and thought at first that he had down to reload, but noticed later he was struggling. He ran to him and asked him if he was hurt badly. The brother spit out a mouthful of blood before he could speak, then said: "Yes, I think they have killed me. I wouldn't hate it so bad if I could have fought till the battle is over."

James gently turned the wounded brother over, then renewed the battle with the foe, some of whom had now rushed within six feet of the white men. Arch Martin threw his gun into position to fire. At the same instant a bullet from an Indian's gun struck the guard of his Winchester, glancing downward and went into his groin.

The Indians were putting up a hard fight. Mr. Moss says that some of them were game and seemed to fear nothing. Though they were game, they soon found they were having no walkover in this fight.

One fellow rushed toward James Moss, shooting over his shield at him. The Indian covered his chest with precision while he was firing. The Texan aimed just below the shield and fired and a bullet crashed into the red man's bowels. Moss then turned on another Indian who was getting too close for it to be comfortable.

The savages now retreated once more to the ledge, reformed line and came at their foemen again, but showed more precaution this time, for they kept at a greater distance. When Mr. Moss had a chance to take his eye for a moment off the foe he glanced toward where the Indian he had shot fell, but he was gone.

One buck who seemed determined to make his way to the horses advanced alone some distance to the right of the others. With gun raised he came within a few feet of the Texans, some of whom fired at him, then he suddenly retreated to the edge of the timber and fell forward, dead. When found he still grasped his gun. The Indians were now retreating. Some four or five of them started up a chant as they retreated, leaving three of their number dead on the ground.

One of the three had moved some distance away from the fight when found. He had a bullet hole in the bowels and one in the chest. This was likely the Indian Mr. Moss shot below the shield. Eli Lloyd was shot in each arm and also had a bullet to cut the skin between his fingers.

W.B. Moss' wound proved to be a serious one, as he lay for weeks before he was able to get around. The bullet was never extracted from his body. The Texans recovered the stolen horses by the Indians.

In September 1877, Mr. Moss was married to Miss Delia Johnson, daughter of Capt. A.J. and Martha Johnson. The following sons and daughters were reared in this home: Zella, bookkeeper and cashier of the Moss Mercantile Company of Llano; Matthew, president of the Llano

National Bank; Edgar, a well known and prosperous stockman of Llano County; J. Ray, manager of the Moss Mercantile Company, Llano; Mrs. J.B. Gage, Austin; Inez, teacher in Dallas; W.R., engaged in oil business at Rockdale; A.J., deceased; Mary, a student in the School of Arts in Chicago; Otilla, an ex-teacher, now with her father in Llano; Richard Olney, assistant cashier of the Llano National Bank.

Mr. Moss by habits of industry and thrift rose from cowboy to cattle king. He bought ranch property in Legion Valley, Llano County, amounting to 8,000 acres of land. He was one of the pioneers of this section in raising Durham cattle. Some years ago he moved from the ranch to Llano. His faithful companion, who shared with him the hardships and privations incident to an earlier day in Texas, passed peacefully to rest Dec. 3, 1918.

### The Cowboy's Prayer

*O Lord, I've never lived where churches grow;*
*I love creation better as it stood*
*That day You finished it so long ago*
*And looked upon Your work and called it good.*
*I know that others find You in the light*
*That's sifted down through tinted window-panes,*
*And yet, I seem to feel You near tonight*
*In this dim, quiet starlight, on the plains.*
*I thank You, Lord, that I am placed so well;*
*That You have made my freedom so complete;*
*That I'm no slave of whistle, clock or bell,*
*Or weak-eyed prisoner of wall and street.*
*Just let me live my life as I've begun,*
*And give me work that's open to the sky;*
*Make me a pardner of the wind and sun*
*And I won't ask for a life that's soft or high.*
*Let me be easy on the man that's down,*
*And make me square and generous with all;*
*I'm careless sometimes, Lord, when I'm in town,*
*But never let them say I'm mean or small,*
*Make me as wide and open as the plains,*
*As honest as the horse between my knees,*
*Clean as the wind that blows behind the rains,*
*Free as the hawk that circles down the breeze.*

*Forgive me, Lord, when sometimes I forget;*
*You know about the reasons that are hid,*
*You know about the things that gall and fret,*
*You know me better than my mother did.*
*Just keep an eye on all that's done and said,*
*Just right me sometimes when I turn aside,*
*And guide me on the long, dim trail ahead,*
*That stretches upwards toward the Great Divide.*

—Chas. Badger Clark, Jr.

(The above was recited by Mike H. Thomas, Grand Master F. & A.M., at the funeral of Thomas A. Coleman, who died in San Antonio in March, 1923.)

# Where They Put the Trail Boss in a Jail

### by W.T. (Bill) Jackman, San Marcos, Texas

I WAS BORN IN HOWARD COUNTY, MISSOURI, on the 19th day of April 1851, and remained there until the year 1859, when my father removed to Bates County, near the Kansas State line.

We were here until the Civil War began, when the depredations, murders and all kinds of lawlessness became so numerous by organized bands of outlaws that we were compelled to go north of the Missouri River where better protection could be had. The atrocious deeds of these marauders became so rife that this section of the country became almost depopulated, the men all having gone to the army and the families fleeing for protection.

Afterward, these outlaws came into our section, burning residences and property of all kinds, taking with them stock or other valuables found. After enduring all kinds of hardships for about two years, my mother and the family of children were banished by the federal authorities and sent to the Confederate lines in the state of Louisiana.

Our trip was first to St. Louis, Missouri, thence down the Mississippi River to Natchez, Mississippi, then across the country to Alexandria, Louisiana, under guard of twenty-five soldiers.

From this place we went across the country by stage line to Shreveport, La. We remained one year, our father then being in the army of Missouri and Arkansas with Gen. Sterling Price.

At this time, by some means unknown to me, my mother received instruction from my father to remove to Red River County, Texas, near Clarksville. We arrived there late in the fall of 1864 and immediately afterward rented a small piece of farmland.

After Lee's surrender, father came and we started south with the intention of going into old Mexico. About 200 officers and soldiers of the army, father being among this number, anticipated going into Mexico or other foreign countries to avoid the oath of allegiance to the federal government.

On our arrival at San Marcos my father talked with some of the old settlers and was advised not to go into Mexico with his family. This advice was accepted and father proceeded on the trip alone, leaving the family in a tent on the Blanco River.

We were in destitute circumstances, having but a few dollars on which to subsist. I rented land again and started a crop the following spring. Being among strangers and almost penniless I and my little brothers began the struggle for a living.

The citizens were kind in assisting us in many ways, besides advising us how to cultivate the land. Such advice was very helpful, I being perfectly ignorant of the mode of cultivating cotton, never having seen any raised in my native state. The friends found here have all passed away without an exception, and the younger generation have taken their places.

I will mention a few of the old friends as, I think their names should be perpetuated. Among them were: Maj. E. Nance, Capt. G. Story, Shady Dixon, Dr. P.C. Woods, Felix Kyle, Jas. L. Malone, John and Joe Brown, Nestor Boon, C.R. Johns, Ed Burleson, Ferg and Curran Kyle and many others.

Father returned from Mexico, not being satisfied with the country. He surrendered to federal authorities in San Antonio and was taken to New Orleans and delivered into the hands of Phil Sheridan, who was in charge.

After a few months he was discharged; he came home to the family and found us trudging along with our little farm project. We continued to live on the Blanco until we made the fourth crop, when father bought the property on Blanco River and there spent the balance of his life, passing away at the age of 60 years.

I remained with the family until I was twenty years of age. I then tried to farm one year in my own interest. I did not succeed financially, being overcome by drought and other misfortunes.

Dissatisfied with farming I decided to change occupation, so I saddled my horse and drifted to the West. After three or four days travel I found myself in Uvalde, Texas, ninety miles from San Antonio. Here I met Cood Adams, a member. of the firm of Adams Bros. in the ranch business on the Leona and Frio Rivers, some fifteen miles from Uvalde.

Cood and Mart Adams composed the firm of Adams Brothers, though John Adams who lived fifteen miles west of San Antonio on the Castroville road, James Adams who lived at San Marcos and Bill Adams of San

Antonio, worked some on this ranch while I was there.

Cood Adams agreed to give me employment. I asked the amount of wages to expect and he replied, "I am getting Mexicans for twelve dollars and board," and with this understanding I commenced to work.

I had worked about four months when I decided to go home and spend the Christmas holidays. When ready to start Mr. Adams gave me a check for eighty dollars and asked if I intending returning. I replied that I would if the price would justify. He made me an offer of one-hundred dollars per month and in one minute he had my reply, "I will be here."

On my return he stated that he intended making a drive to the northern markets in the spring of that year and must commence gathering cattle on the range and placing them in pastures until ready for the drive. I started preparations with seven Mexicans, about 30 horses, and a pack horse. The Mexicans could not speak English and I could not speak Spanish.

I did not know any of the range and thought I was up against a hard proposition but, believe me, we brought home the goods.

When I asked the particular brands to gather, he said, "Bring everything you find, regardless of brand." There was a custom among the ranchmen to use each others' cattle and the other fellow got the credit on the book. A thoroughly educated gentleman by the name of Capt. Cooper was the bookkeeper and lived on the Frio Ranch at that time. I never saw him again and do not know what became of him afterward.

When the cattle were gathered from the range we commenced branding and putting them in shape for the trail. Afterwards I was assigned the task of driving one of the herds.

This was in 1870 and my first experience in handling cattle. I walked into the harness without flinching, though my experience on this trip was in many respects very trying, there being so many new lessons for me to learn.

The country through which we traveled was rough and brushy, making the work heavy on the men and very trying on the horses and cattle. We passed from Uvalde county through Bandera, Mason, Llano and Coleman counties, keeping our general course to the north.

About four miles before reaching the town of Bandera, one day about noon, while dinner was being prepared, I had the herd rounded up to brand a few head, which had been overlooked at the ranch.

After finishing the work and eating dinner we were drifting slowly along when a young cowman rode up beside me. He was very talkative and seemed to be a nice fellow. After conversing some time in a general manner he asked, "Where did you get that yearling?" referring to the one I had just branded.

"At the ranch," I replied. He said, "I would be sorry to see you get in trouble, but that yearling belongs to an old Dutchman who lives down the creek and he is as mean as hell. There is one trail boss in jail at Bandera now for driving one of his yearlings."

The young fellow rode away and I felt that he was telling facts so I commenced thinking fast. I could almost feel the cold bars of the jail in company with the other boss, but the yearling disappeared right now and so did Bill.

I caught a good horse and just kept on high places near the herd for several days. At our next reunion I would be pleased if the trail boss who was in jail would speak out and give his experience. I would be glad to meet him.

We moved on slowly to a point near where we crossed the Llano River. Here a young fellow applied to me for work. He was probably thirty years of age, rather small in stature, roughly dressed, wearing long yellow hair, which hung gracefully down over his shoulders, giving him the appearance of a very tough character.

Needing help I looked the gentleman over while I talked; he finally said, "Hire me, I know all about cattle and will make you a damned good hand."

I decided to hire him and asked his name to record the date. He said, "Just put me down as Rusty," which I thought very appropriate and used it all the time when addressing him. He gave fine satisfaction in his duties.

When we had reached a point twenty miles west of Fort Griffin on what is known as Elm Creek, we made camp for the night. Next morning on looking over the herd, I found a cow was gone and I knew she would return to our last bed ground some fifteen miles back on the trail, and I went back and found the cow and returned to camp with her.

On my arrival at camp I found that "Rusty" had shot John Rice, one of my hands. The weapon used was an old model brass mounted .44 Winchester rifle, which he carried on his saddle at all times. The bullet had passed entirely through the body on the opposite side of the spine from the heart and blood was flowing from both front and back.

I sent at once to Fort Griffin for a doctor, also giving instructions that a hack be brought for the purpose of conveying the wounded man to the hospital.

The doctor came and pronounced the case almost hopeless, though we rushed for the hospital as speedily as possible. I arranged with those in charge to keep me posted as to his condition and on my arrival at Dodge City, Kansas, received a letter stating that he had recovered sufficiently to return home, and that he would entirely recover in a short time.

I never heard of him again and I hope to find someone who can give me information regarding his whereabouts. Rusty took one of my best horses and I have not seen him since. Should he be a member of this association under another name, I would like to hear from him, as all offenses are now barred by statute of limitations.

I never saw Cood or Mart Adams after the drive. One of the brothers, Bill, received the herd at the point of destination and I returned home, thinking my aspirations in this line of work were satisfied in the extreme, though in 1877 Col. J.F. Ellison, who then lived at Martindale, Caldwell County, prevailed on me to drive a herd for him, which I delivered at Ogallala, Nebraska.

During 1878 I drove for Ellison & Sherill. This firm was composed of Jas. F. Ellison and Jas. H. Sherill, who had formed a co-partnership for the purpose of conveying one herd to the northern markets over the trail.

During one of these drives Givens Lane and I were driving a herd each, and were traveling near each other. The country was dry, grass scarce and watering places for two herds at one time was hard to find. We were then near Buffalo, Kansas and were having hard times. Givens and I had gone to the front hunting grass and water.

A creek, some distance north of Buffalo, had nice running water, but the nesters of that section had plowed a furrow on each side of the trail and posted signs reading about as follows: "Keep your cattle inside these furrows or be prosecuted." The creek north of the trail had the finest water sufficient to swim a good sized steamboat and the grass was excellent.

We had become enraged on reading these warning signs and Givens said, "Bill, suppose we put our herds into that fine grass and water and take the chances," to which I agreed. The cattle were now in sight and looked as though the two herds were strung out for a distance of three miles.

My herd came first, and Givens and I rode in front of the cattle until the water was scented and the cattle began running.

The nearer the water, the faster they got, but now came the nesters, who were living in dugouts and could not be seen until they all mounted their old mares, barebacked. They were bare-footed, bare-headed and all carrying double-barrel shotguns, yelling and demanding that we turn the cattle back to the trail.

We said, "We cannot stop them – you boys stop them if you can." You never saw such maneuvers in your life, but the cattle went to the water just the same. The nesters went for the officers and we had to keep on the dodge for several days by riding on the high grounds and keeping a close look out over the country for officers.

On another occasion I did not get out so well. I made camp about 4 p.m.. There was not a house or farm to be seen near us and we supposed we were not trespassing. A Dutchman suddenly rode into camp and said, "You must move these cattle. This is my land and you cannot camp here tonight."

I reasoned with him, saying that it was late and danger of stampeding the cattle and I thought I made him a first class argument, but it didn't work. He still said, "You must move this tam cattle right now and do it quick, you shall not stay here." Then I said, "You move right now and do it quick," and he did so.

But the next morning the constable came with a warrant of arrest and said I must go to justice court with him. When we arrived the High Court was on his rostrum and the Dutchman was on hand also.

As the constable and I walked into the court, the judge looked as knowing as any man I ever met and the constable acted as if he had arrested one of the worst criminals on earth. I shall never forget this deal.

As I walked into the room the Dutchman said, "Judge, there is the fellow vot told me to go to hell mit a pistol." After parleying a little, his majesty said, "This seems to be a very aggravated case, I fine you $100.00 and costs." The fine and costs totaled $130.00, which I paid.

You will notice that the pleasures on the trail were mingled with troubles and hardships. During the spring of 1878 Mr. Ellison engaged me to take a herd to Ogallala, Nebraska. I did not know either the men, the horses or the cattle. All the stock were poor but this was an exceptionally good year, there being plenty of grass and water, I made the trip in good time with all horses and cattle looking fine.

When I delivered this herd and was ready to start home Mr. Ellison made me a proposition to take charge of his ranch, to buy cattle through the fall and winter and make preparations for another drive the following spring.

This class of work continued with me in the same manner for several years, buying each fall and winter and making the drive afterward.

My early spring work was to get all the cattle properly branded and start the first herd with the earliest grass and continue to send them each ten or twelve days until the last herd, which I would take myself. The first herds were generally over one-half of their journey before I got started from the ranch.

Many of my readers will remember Mr. Ellison perfectly well, his acquaintance extending entirely over Texas and many other states. I would like to say that he was one of the best men I ever knew, honorable and upright in all his dealings and greatly loved by those who knew him best.

Well do I remember his admonition to me when I commenced work; "Bill, do all you can to save my cattle under any and all circumstances and I will protect you with my money to the last, but do not handle cattle belonging to others, I want nothing but my own." I remained with him until he discontinued the cow business.

I made nine of these trips over the trail, beginning in 1870 and ending in 1890. I learned to love the work, though many hardships attended each trip. Finally barbed wire came into use, agricultural pursuits became of great interest to the people, and the trail country was closed by farms and pastures.

The successful trail boss or cowboy was happy when he found plenty of grass and water, and prouder still when he would reach the market with his horses and cattle in nice condition.

The number of men necessary in handling a herd of 3,000 head of cattle was the boss, eight men with the cattle, a cook, and one man with the horses called the "remuda man," making eleven in the outfit.

About sixty horses were furnished to each herd, or six to each man, excepting the cook. The best horse of each mount was selected for his night horse and was used for no other purpose.

This horse was supposed to be perfectly gentle, easily handled, clear footed, of good sight and to have all qualities of a first-class cow horse. His other five horses were used each one-half day until all had been used, then he commenced over again with the same process.

A first-class new wagon was furnished each outfit and the same was generally drawn by four mules or two yoke of oxen, mules being preferable.

Thirty days' provisions or more could be handled in addition to the bedding, slickers, clothing, etc. belonging to the men.

A barrel was placed inside the wagon bed, generally between the wheels, fastened securely and with a faucet running through the bed outside, where water could easily be drawn. One barrel of water could be made to last for two days or more.

A box was made into the front part of the bed on the outside and fastened securely for the purpose of carrying different trinkets, which could be used in case of trouble. The chuck box was made into compartments for holding the cooking utensils, a lid was fastened by hinges to the back to the box, which could be lowered to make a table for the cook.

The most important addition to the wagon was the "cooney," which consisted of a cowhide placed under the wagon loosely and fastened to each side of the wagon securely, making a place to hold the wood for cooking purposes.

The cook was furnished all necessary utensils to make his part of the work easy, and better still, was supplied with provisions, which would enable him at all times to furnish a good and wholesome meal.

Plenty of good chuck brought plenty of good work, and satisfaction among the men. The best cook was paid the best price for his services.

The trail men all dressed in about the same manner, their costume consisting of a substantial suit of clothing, fine Stetson hat, the best shop-made boots with high heels, spurs of the best make, red bandana handkerchief for the neck, a good pair of leather leggings, and quirt and a good fish-brand slicker.

All used splendid saddles and bridles, the bridle bit generally shop or home-made. When diked out in this garb a man was supposed to be ready for all kinds of weather and all kinds of emergencies. The outfit was then worth about $100 but would now easily cost $250.

In Kansas and Nebraska were many nesters and farmers who had taken up claims of land under the laws of those states were scattered over the whole country, and these people often came to the herd and asked if they might have the calves, which were born on the bed grounds, as the drovers generally killed them.

On one occasion, one of these fellows came in a two-horse wagon just about dusk. One of the boys met him and claiming to be the boss made a trade with him to the effect that he should stand guard, for which he was to receive any calves that might be found next morning.

This fellow was put on first relief and the boys let him remain on guard all night. To the shorthorn's astonishment when daylight came the herd contained nothing but steers.

The boys gave him the "horse laugh" and he pulled out for home.

At Ogallala in 1879, I met a man by the name of George Knight. I do not know from what part of Texas he came, but I think he was owner of a herd and drove them in person over the trail. He was a great talker and had much to say about the hardships endured on his trip.

Said he was almost killed by hail on one occasion and was only saved by turning his horse loose and putting the saddle over his head.

Another time the rain fell in such torrents that he had to swim two miles in making his escape from high waters; again during a severe rain and hail storm accompanied by the most terrific thunder and lightning he decided to turn his herd loose, go to camp and get under the wagon. The storm still raged and he took from his pocket a memorandum book and by the light of his lantern wrote, "George Knight, struck and killed by lightning 20 miles south of Ogallala on July 20, 1879."

After my trail work was over I embarked into the ranch business and was quite successful for several years, but droughts came, low prices of cattle and other misfortunes and so this adventure was a financial failure.

During 1892 I became a candidate for sheriff of Hays County; was elected by a fine majority and held this position for twenty years. Afterwards was marshal of San Marcos and now I find myself postmaster of this place, a position I have held for eight years.

My father was Col. S.D. Jackman of fame in the Confederate army with Gen. Sterling Price and Joe Shelby. He did much recruiting in the state of Missouri, was severely wounded on one of these trips and never entirely recovered.

He was born in Kentucky and removed with his father and family at the age of four years to the state of Missouri. He served two terms in the Texas Legislature and was U.S. Marshal of the western district of Texas at the time of his death in 1886, at the age of 60 years.

# Relates Incidents of Many Drives

*by William Baxter Slaughter, San Antonio, Texas*

MY PARENTS, SARAH JANE and Rev. George Webb Slaughter, a Baptist minister, came from Alabama in 1830, crossed the Sabine River, settling in what was then Mexican territory, Coahuila, now Texas.

The Mexican government at that time was enforcing in such tyrannous manner the regulations of adherence to the Catholic church that armed resistance was made by the settlers and my father, then a young man, joined in the resistance. He was closely connected, with the Independence of Texas from that time on, a full account of which is recorded in John Henry Brown's "History of Texas."

My parents moved from Sabine county to Freestone county in 1850 and settled near the old town of Butler, at which place I was born in 1852.

In 1857 my father moved to Palo Pinto County and engaged in the cattle business. In 1861 he moved part of his cattle into Young County, Texas, and during the Civil War furnished the Tonkaway Indians with beef under a contract with the Confederate government.

An older brother, J.B. Slaughter, now of Post, Texas, and I with our father gathered the steers each week and delivered them at the Agency. This was continued until the close of the Civil War and two of my older brothers, Col. C.C. Slaughter and P.E. Slaughter, were rangers under Capt. Jack Cureton, grandfather of the now Chief Justice of the Supreme Court of Texas.

Upon return of my oldest brother, Col. C.C. Slaughter, we found the Confederate money received in payment for the cattle furnished to the government for the Indians during the Civil War had no value.

It was turned over to the children attending the school to use as thumb paper for the old Blue Back Spellers of those days.

Hence we had no money, but plenty of cattle and Col. Slaughter suggested to my father that we gather a herd of steers and drive to Shreveport,

La., and ship to New Orleans in order to get ready cash.

In the fall of 1867, my father, my oldest brother, and myself, with three other hands, left Palo Pinto with 900 steers, our destination being Shreveport, Louisiana. When we reached Rockwall County, we met Col. T.H. Johnson, who had made a contract to deliver 1,500 steers at a small packing plant just east of Jefferson, Texas, situated on a little bayou.

With the 600 head of steers he had gathered and the 900 we had, it was possible to complete the contract. The time for delivery was short and a trade was made with him.

My brother, Col. C.C. Slaughter, and Mr. Johnson left in a buggy for Jefferson immediately after closing the trade, being followed up with a herd of 1,500 steers in charge of my father.

As soon as we struck the piney woods we would place the herds in the fields overnight in order to get crop grass for them and the rainy season being on we were continually having to pull them out of the quicksand in the mornings.

When we arrived at the packery we held the cattle there about two weeks until they were all killed. My father received $24,300 gold, or $27 per head, for the steers and we immediately went back to Jefferson and loaded the wagon with merchandise, including some oranges, the first I ever saw.

He bought a pair of old-fashioned saddle bags and packed $20,000 in gold and put it across the rear of my saddle. I rode the pony with the gold back to Palo Pinto. This was the first drive I ever made.

In 1869 I went with a herd of cattle to Abilene, Kansas, my brother, P.E. Slaughter, being in charge.

We crossed the Red River at the old Gaines crossing about 15 miles north of Gainesville, Texas, and went on by what is known as the Old Love Ranch, in the Indian Territory and then turned northwest, keeping on the south side of Paul's Valley, on the Washita River, crossing at Washita Springs and on through Indian Territory, entering Kansas on Bluff Creek where Caldwell, Kansas, is now situated. Then we went on north across the Arkansas River where Wichita is now located.

I remember an old fat merchant by the name of McClain who had a store made of cottonwood logs on the south side of the river with the sign to the south reading, "The First Chance" and the one to the north, "The Last Chance" to get supplies. We crossed the broad prairies from there to Abilene. This herd of cattle was sold to Lem Hunter of Illinois, by my brother, Col. C.C. Slaughter.

The third drive was in 1870. I went this time as foreman, with a herd of 1,800 head of steers, which was turned over to me on the head of Bear Creek, now known as the Corn Ranch in Parker County.

I went over the same route as we had gone the year before, everything moving nicely until I came to the Red Fork of the Arkansas River, where I came in contact with the Little Osage Indians, who were out under a permit from the agent of the Little Osage Agency, telling what a fine civilized tribe they were and saying that they would harm no one. Their only object was to kill some buffalo and deer.

They played havoc with W.B. Grimes' herd, which was just ahead of me. Two of Grimes' cowboys, who had quit, were returning to Texas gave me the information that if I went on I would lose my herd, and advised me to change my routing.

This herd had been contracted to Lem Hunter of Illinois, Jack Gillespie, and Billy Rogers of Kansas City, and I knew that I could not turn back and get them to Abilene in time to comply with the contract, as there was a forfeit with the Chick Bank at Kansas City of $10,000 by Hunter and his associates and a like amount by my brother, that the herd would reach Abilene on time specified by the contract.

As the cattle had been sold for thirty-five dollars per head, a fancy price in those days, I made up my mind to follow the instructions I had always received from my father to never turn back or to think of the bridge that I was to cross until I came to it and then go over.

Being familiar with the habits of the Tonkaway Indians, to whom my father had supplied beef during the Civil War, I knew what they admired.

I had one cowboy who had what we call a "desperado" or "Mexican sash." It was made of silk, about six-feet-long, three- to four-feet wide, very gaudy, each end having silk tassels, I also had three bandana handkerchiefs, two red and one blue. I made up my mind this was the bridge that would get me by, if I came in contact with the Indians, as stated by Grimes' two cowboys.

The next day when we reached the south side of Red Fork, and where the city of Kingfisher is now located, I found the statements made by these cowboys were true. I discovered the village made by the Indians; it was a city of tepees made out of buffalo hides, which had been thoroughly dressed and smoked.

As soon as we discovered them, we halted and had our dinner. The herd had not been watered and could not get to the river as the high bluffs on the south side were impassable and extended up to where we were to cross the river.

I instructed the cook to separate some flour, coffee and bacon, enough for three meals, and cache it in the cowhide stretched under the wagon, where we used to carry the old Dutch oven, camp kettle and the wood, picked up along the trail. I told the cook if the Indians came up and asked for flour, bacon and coffee, to throw out all the bedding and let them have it.

We looked and saw about thirty Indians coming. The chuck wagon was in the rear of the herd and the horses in front, leading the herd.

The chief asked for the foreman and I told him I had charge of the herd. He had three squaws with him. He had his Indian war paint on, and had a shield fastened to the back of his hair, ornamented with all kinds of feathers, which extended about ten feet back, and two of the squaws were riding in the rear of the chief holding his head gear to keep it from dragging on the ground.

The chief called for flour, bacon, sugar and coffee and the cook threw it out on the ground and it was put on a pony and two of the Indians returned to the village with it. The Indians immediately commenced whipping the cowboys' horses but I had told the cowboys to pay no attention to this.

About this time the wind commenced blowing from the south and my herd could smell the Indians and I saw they were getting very restless, I said to myself, "Now is the time to cross the bridge."

I pulled the desperado sash and the three handkerchiefs, which I had hid in the bosom of my cowboy shirt, spread the sash over the chief, handed each one of the three squaws the handkerchiefs and you would have thought I was a little god for a little while, for they had a great talk in their own language, making much of me.

This gave a chance for the herd to get to the crossing and as the front cattle were following the horses across, we rushed up behind the rear cattle and the scent of the Indians made them cross quickly. They demanded beef so I cut out three large steers that had sore feet, caused by wet weather.

They had these steers killed in less time than I can say it and took the hide off and went into the little manifold or maw, scraped the grass back off of it and ate it raw while it was warm. But I could not understand why they wanted beef while there were thousands of buffalo in sight.

When the herd was across the river, they bantered us for horse races. I had eight of the horses brought back to the south side of the river, myself and two of my cowboys ran races with them all that afternoon.

I had about thirty dollars in silver and they had some very handsome dressed buffalo hides, I would put up about two dollars or three dollars against those beautiful hides, and allowed them to use their warriors as judges – and they were honest.

When I won they gave hides up and when they won I gave them the money.

I had about five hides when the sun was about down. I sent all the horses except the one I was riding and the cowboys were riding across the river and put up the twenty dollars I had on the last race and instructed the boy that was going to run it, as he was riding the best horse I had, to jockey with them about fifteen minutes after I left, before running and turning the horse loose and he would be across the river before they knew it, directing him that when he crossed the river to turn to the left and follow the big hollow up to the high hills and I would wait there, which he did.

The Indians shot at him several times but I think only to scare him. I had "crossed the bridge" with the Mexican sash. It saved my herd I feel sure.

We turned west at the point of the Blackjacks, ten miles north of Red Fork, and camped between two deep bluff hollows that night and did not unstop the bells on the oxen.

Early next morning we pulled the herd across to the west side of Turkey Creek and kept up Turkey Creek on the west side, which runs due north until we came to Sewall Branch Supply Station where we secured enough supplies to carry us to Bluff Creek where Capt. Stone had a large store.

All of the old trail men knew Capt. Stone, who in the later years was one of the great buyers for our Texas cattle, when they reached Kansas. We had no more trouble and reached Holland Creek, near Abilene, three days before the expiration of the contract for the delivery of the cattle.

As soon as we reached Holland Creek, my cowboys all wanted to go to Abilene.

I divided them into squads and picked up two straws, one long and one short, and informed them that the ones that got the long straw would be allowed twenty-four hours in Abilene, when they would return and let the others go.

The young man, Wash Wolf, who furnished me the sash that saved my herd, was in the first squad and never returned. He immediately got on a spree on arriving in Abilene and was killed in a dance hall there and I saw him no more.

The herd was delivered and I received instructions from my brother to return to the Young County Ranch with the outfit.

My fourth drive was in 1871. I had charge of the herd as in the previous year. I went from Young County where Graham is now situated, through Lost Valley, known as the old J.C. Loving Ranch, on due north by Buffalo Springs, out by Victoria Peak, where Stephens & Worsham had a cattle ranch, about 20 miles north to the upper sand timbers.

It commenced raining, about the time to bed the herd. We noticed northeast of us in another grove of timber a fire, which later proved to be a band of Indians.

Our herd stampeded that night. Next morning we counted the herd and found we were short 200 cattle. We soon found the trail, which went southwest about two miles and split into two parts, part of them going south and part going west.

Myself and another man followed the trail south about ten miles and found part of the cattle and brought them back to the main herd.

We waited on the other two men to return until the next morning and as they did not return we went to where the cattle had separated and took the trail of the two horses, following the ones that went west about eight miles and found the two men had been murdered by the Indians, scalped and their bodies badly mutilated.

We buried them there and returned to our herd and moved rapidly until we reached Red River Station, getting on the old Chisholm Trail.

# The Killing of Oliver Loving

*by Charles Goodnight, Goodnight, Texas*

OLIVER LOVING, SR., IS UNDOUBTEDLY the first man who ever trailed cattle from Texas. His earliest effort was in 1858 when he took a herd across the frontier of the Indian Nation or "No Man's Land," through eastern Kansas and northwestern Missouri into Illinois.

His second attempt was in 1859; he left the frontier on the upper Brazos and took a northwest course until he struck the Arkansas River, somewhere about the mouth of the Walnut, and followed it to just about Pueblo, where he wintered.

In 1866 he joined me on the upper Brazos. With a large herd we struck southwest until we reached the Pecos River, which we followed up to Mexico and thence, to Denver, the herd being closed out to various posts and Indian reservations.

In 1867 we started another herd west over the same trail and struck the Pecos the latter part of June. After we had gone up this river about one hundred miles it was decided that Mr. Loving should go ahead on horseback in order to reach New Mexico and Colorado in time to bid on the contracts, which were to be let in July, to use the cattle we then had on trail, for we knew that there were no other cattle in the west to take their place.

Loving was a man of religious instincts and one of the coolest and bravest men I have ever known, but devoid of caution. Since the journey was to made with a one-man escort I selected Bill Wilson, the clearest-headed man in the outfit, as his companion.

Knowing the dangers of traveling through an Indian-infested country I endeavored to impress on these men the fact that only by traveling by night could they hope to make the trip in safety.

The first two nights after the journey was begun they followed my instructions. But Loving, who detested night riding, persuaded Wilson that I had been overcautious and one fine morning they changed their tactics and proceeded by daylight.

Nothing happened until two o'clock that afternoon when Wilson, who had been keeping a lookout, sighted the Comanches heading toward them from the southwest.

Apparently they were 500 or 600 strong. The men left the trail and made for the Pecos River, which was about four miles to the northwest and was the nearest place they could hope to find shelter.

They were then on the plain, which lies between the Pecos and Rio Sule, or Blue River. One-hundred-and-fifty feet from the bank of the Pecos this bank drops abruptly some one hundred feet.

The men scrambled down this bluff and dismounted. They hitched their horses (which the Indians captured at once) and crossed the river where they hid themselves among the sand dunes and brakes of the river.

Meantime the Indians were hot on their tracks, some of them halted on the bluff and others crossed the river and surrounded the men. A brake of carrca, or Spanish cane, which grew in the bend of the river a short distance from the dunes was soon filled with them.

Since this cane was from five- to six-feet tall these Indians were easily concealed from view of the men; they dared not advance on the men as they knew them to be armed.

The Indian on the bluff, speaking in Spanish, begged the men to come out for a consultation. Wilson instructed Loving to watch the rear so they could not shoot him in the back, and he stepped out to see what he could do with them.

Loving attempting to guard the rear was fired on from the cane. He sustained a broken arm and bad wound in the side. The men then retreated to the shelter of the river bank and had much to, do to keep the Indians off.

Toward dawn of the next day Loving, deciding that he was going to die from the wound in his side, begged Wilson to leave him and go to me, so that if I made the trip home his family would know what had become of him.

He had no desire to die and leave them in ignorance of his fate. He wished his family to know that rather than be captured and tortured by the Indians, he would kill himself.

But in case he survived and was able to stand them off we would find him two miles down the river. He gave him his Henry rifle, which had metallic or waterproof cartridges, since in swimming the river any other kind would be useless.

Wilson turned over to Loving all of the pistols – five – and his six-shooting rifle, and taking the Henry rifle departed. How he expected to cross the river with the gun I have never comprehended for Wilson was a one armed man. But it shows what lengths a person will attempt in extreme emergencies.

It happened that some one-hundred feet from their place of concealment down the river there was a shoal, the only one I know of within one hundred miles of the place. On this shoal an Indian sentinel on horseback was on guard and Wilson knew this. The water was about four-feet deep.

When Wilson decided to start he divested himself of clothing except underwear and hat. He hid his trousers in one place, his boots in another and his knife in another all under water. Then taking his gun he attempted to cross the river. This he found to be impossible, so he floated downstream about seventy-five feet where he struck bottom.

He stuck down the muzzle of the gun in the sand until the breech came under water and then floated noiselessly down the river.

Though the Indians were all around him he fearlessly began his "get-away."

He climbed up a bank and crawled out through a cane brake, which fringed the bank, and started out to find me, bare-footed and over ground that was covered with prickly pear, mesquite and other thorny plants.

Of course he was obliged to travel by night at first, but fearing starvation used the day some, when he was out of sight of the Indians.

Now Loving and Wilson had ridden ahead of the herd for two nights and the greater part of one day, and since the herd had lain over one day the gap between us must have been something like one hundred miles.

The Pecos River passes down a country that might be termed a plain, and from one to 200 miles there is not a tributary or break of any kind to mark its course until it reaches the mouth of the Concho, which comes up from the west, where the foothills begin to jut in toward the river.

Our trail passed just around one of these hills. In the first of these hills there is a cave, which Wilson had located on a prior trip. This cave extended back into the hill some fifteen or twenty feet and in this cave Wilson took refuge from the scorching sun to rest.

Then he came out of the cave and looked for the herd and saw it coming up the valley. His brother, who was "pointing" the herd with me, and I saw him at the same time. At sight both of us thought it was an Indian as we didn't suppose that any white man could be in that part of the country.

I ordered Wilson to shape the herd for a fight, while I rode toward the man to reconnoiter, believing the Indians to be hidden behind the hills and planning to surprise us. I left the trail and jogged toward the hills as though I did not suspect anything.

I figured I could run to the top of the hill to look things over before they would have time to cut me off from the herd. When I came within a quarter of a mile of the cave Wilson gave me the frontier sign to come to him.

He was between me and the declining sun and since his underwear was saturated with red sediment from the river he made a queer-looking object. But even when some distance away I recognized him. How I did it, under his changed appearance I do not know.

When I reached him I asked him many questions, too many in fact, for he was so broken and starved and shocked by knowing he was saved, I could get nothing satisfactory from him.

I put him on the horse and took him to the herd at once. We immediately wrapped his feet in wet blankets. They were swollen out of all reason, and how he could walk on them is more than I can comprehend. Since he had starved for three days and nights I could give him nothing but gruel. After he had rested and gotten himself together I said :

"Now tell me about this matter."

"I think Mr. Loving has died from his wounds, he sent me to deliver a message to you. It was to the effect that he had received a mortal wound, but before he would allow the Indians to take him and torture him he would kill himself, but in case he lived he would go two miles down the river from where we were and there we would find him."

"Now tell me where I may find this place," I said. Then he proceeded to relate the story I have just given, of how they left the Rio Sule or Blue River, cutting across to the Pecos, how the Indians discovered them and how they sought shelter from them by hiding in the sand dunes on the Pecos banks; how Loving was shot and begged Wilson to save himself and to tell his (Loving's) family of his end, how Wilson took the Henry rifle and attempted to swim but gave it up, as the splashing he made would attract the Indian sentinel stationed on the shoal.

Then Wilson instructed me how to find his things. He told me to go down where the bank is perpendicular and the water appeared to be swimming but was not.

"Your legs will strike the rifle," he said.

I searched for his things as he directed and found them everyone, even to the pocket knife. His remarkable coolness in deliberately hiding these things, when the loss of a moment might mean his life, is to me the most wonderful occurrence I have ever known, and I have experienced many unusual phases of frontier life.

This is as I get it from memory and I think I am correct, for though it all happened fifty years ago, it is printed indelibly in my mind.

OLIVER LOVING, a rancher and cattle drover, developed the Goodnight-Loving Trail with Charles Goodnight. He was mortally wounded by Indians while on a cattle drive in September 1867.

# W.J. Wilson's Narrative

IN THE SPRING OF 1867 I bought a bunch of cattle on the Clear Fork of the Brazos, started up the river with them and fell in with Charles Goodnight and Oliver Loving.

They had had some trouble with the Indians, and we considered it safer to all travel together.

We went on to the Pecos River on the old Butterfield trail. It never failed to rain on us every day until we reached Horsehead Crossing.

The night we arrived at this crossing the cattle stampeded and all got away. Next morning we started to round them up. After hunting for three days we still had about 300 head of our big cattle missing. The rain had made all of the trails look old and we couldn't tell a new trail from an old one.

We concluded to go back to China Pond and take a circle from there and try to cut the cattle off. China Pond was about twenty-five miles back on the trail.

So seven of us, made up from different cattle outfits, went back, and when we reached China Pond we decided to go east, and many miles out we found the trail of our cattle, and the signs showed that Indians had captured them and were driving them to their camp up the river.

They had evidently expected us to come down the river looking for the cattle, and they did not discover us until we were within 150 yards of them.

Seeing we were greatly outnumbered, and as it was about sundown, we decided to turn back and go to our camp, which we did, arriving there the next day.

When I returned from this cow-hunt, Mr. Loving asked me to go to Fort Sumner, New Mexico, with him. We had a verbal contract with the people who were feeding the Indians there, and we wanted to hold that contract.

The distance to Fort Sumner was about 250 miles, and we were supposed to travel at night and lay up in the daytime so the Indians would not attack us.

The second day of our journey we stopped on a stream we called Black River, and stayed there two or three hours, rested up our horses, then concluded to go on to the point of a mountain where the road ran between the mountain and the river, and stay there that night.

As we neared this mountain we discovered several Indians.

They saw us about the same time, and we knew we were in for trouble, but we reached the river all right, and I picked out a little mound next to the river where I could see all around me, except one little spot where the polecat brush had grown up about three feet high, and that brush obscured my view of the river for a distance of about 100 yards.

I told Mr. Loving if he would stay down at that little clump of bushes and keep the Indians from crawling up on us from the river I would keep them off from above. These Indians had increased in numbers until there were over a hundred of the red rascals.

I think they had been hunting south of the river and were going back to their old ground.

After staying in the brush a little while Mr. Loving came to where I was, and I urged him to go back there and prevent the Indians from coming in on us from the river.

He started back down there carrying a pair of holster pistols over his left arm. The bushes were about forty yards from where I was standing, and I kept my eyes on this spot for I knew if a demonstration was made from that direction the Indians would charge us from the hill.

When Mr. Loving had almost reached the bushes an Indian rose up and I shot him, but not before he had fired on Mr. Loving. The Indian's shot went through Loving's holsters, passed through his wrist and entered his side. He came running back to me, tossed his gun to me and said he was killed and for me to do the best I could.

The Indians at this time made a desperate charge, and after I had emptied my five-shooting Yarger, I picked up Mr. Loving's gun and continued firing. There was some brush, only a few inches high, not very far from where I was, and the Indians would run to it, crawl on their bellies, and I could not see them.

I managed to get Mr. Loving down to the river and concealed him in a sandy depression, where the smart weeds grew about two-feet high and laid down beside him. The Indians knew we were down there somewhere, and used all sorts of ruses to find our exact location. They would shoot their arrows up and some came very near striking us.

Finally an Indian with a long lance came crawling along parting the weeds with his lance as he came, and just about the time I had determined to pull the trigger, he scared up a big rattlesnake.

The snake came out rattling, looking back at the Indian, and coiled up right near us. The Indian, who still had not seen us, evidently got scared at the rattlesnake and turned back.

We lay there until night. Mr. Loving's wounds had thrown him into a high fever, and I managed to bring up some water from the river in his boot, which seemed to relieve him somewhat.

About midnight the moon went down, but the Indians were still around us. We could hear them on all sides. Mr. Loving begged me to leave him and make my escape so I could tell his folks what had become of him. He said he felt sure he could not last until morning, and if I stayed there I would be killed too. He insisted that I take his gun, as it used metallic cartridges and I could carry it through the water and not dampen the powder.

Leaving with him all of my pistols and my rifle, I took his gun and with a handclasp told him goodbye, and started to the river.

The river was quite sandy and difficult to swim in, so I had to pull off all of my clothes except my hat, shirt and breeches.

The gun nearly drowned me, and I decided to get along without it, so I got out and leaned it up against the bank of the river, under the water, where the Indians would not find it. Then I went down the river about a hundred yards, and saw an Indian sitting on his horse out in the river, with the water almost over the horse's back. He was sitting there splashing the water with his foot, just playing.

I got under some smart weeds and drifted by until I got far enough below the Indian where I could get out. Then I made a three days' march barefooted. Everything in that country had stickers in it. On my way I picked up the small end of a tepee pole, which I used for a walking stick.

The last night of this painful journey the wolves followed me all night. I would give out, just like a horse, and lay down in the road and drop off to sleep and when I would awaken the wolves would be all around me, snapping and snarling.

I would take up that stick, knock the wolves away, get started again and the wolves would follow behind.

I kept that up until daylight, when the wolves quit me. About 12 o'clock on that last day I crossed a little mountain and knew the boys ought to be right in there somewhere with the cattle.

I found a little place, a sort of cave, that afforded protection from the sun, and I could go no further. After a short time the boys came along with the cattle and found me.

Charles Goodnight took a party of about fourteen men and pulled out to see about Mr. Loving. After riding about twenty-four hours they came to the spot where I had left him, but he was not there.

They supposed the Indians had killed him and thrown his body into the river. They found the gun I had concealed in the water, and came back to camp.

About two weeks after this we met a party coming from Fort Sumner and they told us Loving was at Fort Sumner. The bullet, which had penetrated his side, did not prove fatal and the next night after I had left him he got into the river and drifted by the Indians as I had done, crawled out and lay in the weeds all the next day.

The following night he made his way to the road where it struck the river, hoping to find somebody traveling that way.

He remained there for five days, being without anything to eat for seven days.

Finally some Mexicans came along and he hired them to take him to Fort Sumner and I believe he would have fully recovered if the doctor at that point had been a competent surgeon.

But that doctor had never amputated any limbs and did not want to undertake such work.

When we heard Mr. Loving was at Fort Sumner, Mr. Goodnight and I hastened there. As soon as we beheld his condition we realized the arm would have to be amputated. The doctor was trying to cure it without cutting it off.

Goodnight started a man to Santa Fe after a surgeon, but before he could get back mortification set in, and we were satisfied something had to be done at once and we prevailed upon the doctor to cut off the affected limb. But too late. Mortification went into his body and killed him.

Thus ended the career of one of the best men I ever knew. Mr. Goodnight had the body of Mr. Loving prepared for the long journey and carried it to Weatherford, Texas, where interment was made with Masonic honors.

# On the Fort Worth and Dodge City Trail

### by T.J. Burkett, Sr., Waelder, Texas

WHILE STATIONED IN A LINE CAMP on the south line of the R2 Ranch in Walbarger County during the month of May 1883, a message came stating that I was wanted to go up the trail, and at once to go to the R2 headquarters situated on Mule Creek, a tributary to Red River.

Within three days every employee and the herd was ready to hit the Fort Worth and Dodge City Trail. The herd was owned by Stephens & Worsham, and was bossed by Daniel P. Gipson.

The first night out a thunderstorm came up and the cattle stampeded and we ran them all night. I held between 400 and 500, and Billie Gatling held about 600 until after daylight, when several of the boys helped us bring them back to camp. We had 1,800 steers in that herd and it took several days to gather all of them up.

We crossed near Doan's, where the Dodge City trail crosses Red River, and resumed our long and tiresome journey in the direction of the north star.

Hour by hour, step by step and day by day we pursued our way, not knowing the hardships that were in store for us. We had from one to three rains a week. Our route lay through the Indian Territory, where the range was a paradise for the longhorn.

One night we had a stampede in the Wichita Mountains, and when the sun rose on the bed ground the next morning there was not a steer in sight. After three days' hard work we again had them ready to wend their way to a distant clime beyond the sands of the Cimarron.

One day Quanah Parker, accompanied by another Indian came to me and wanted "wohaw, plenty fat, heap slick." I pointed to Gipson and told Quanah he was the wohaw chief, but the little Indian shook his head and said Gipson was *"no bueno."*

Gipson told me to ride into the herd and cut them out a yearling, and they went off with it. There were about 500 Indians camped near the trail, and nearly every herd that passed gave them a beef.

Hundreds of cowboys knew Quanah Parker, and he had scores of friends among the white people.

After we passed out of the Indian Territory we soon discovered that we had arrived at a Sahara in America.

The grass was burned to a crisp, stock water was scarce, provisions were high and everything in the vegetable line was scarce. Irish potatoes the size of a hickory nut were $2.50 per bushel. Sometimes the boss had to pay $10 to water the herd.

People there informed us that it had not rained there in seven months, and it looked to me like it had not rained in seven years.

Holding one foot on the Kansas soil and the other on Territory soil was like having one foot in the submerged alluvial soil of the Nile and the other out in the desert where it had not rained enough to wet a pocket handkerchief in a hundred years.

The cool nights and almost unbearable heat in the daytime about got the best of the cowboys.

Two days after we struck camp southwest of Dodge City several of the cowboys were excused by the boss to go to town for supplies.

Soon after they arrived there they began to "tank up" on mean whiskey and proceeded to shoot up the town. As they came out at a high rate of speed one of them, John Briley, was killed by the marshal of Dodge City. I was in Dodge City the next day and saw that he was buried. Associating with bad company has cost many a man his life.

Man dieth and goeth to his long home, and the mourners go about the street. At the cemetery in Dodge City I noticed a number of fresh mounds, and I said to the sexton there that an epidemic of some kind must have struck that place, but he said the graves were those of desperadoes who had died with their boots on.

While looking around I noticed on a small tombstone the following inscription: "Here rests Mary Hamilton, aged 14."

Then came the following lines:

"Weep not for me my parents dear, I am not dead, but only sleeping here. I was not yours alone, but God's who loved me best, and took me home."

Before we reached Dodge City, Mr. Gipson received a message that Stephens & Worsham had 1,500 steers on the trail and to wait until they arrived, as they wanted to put both herds together.

When one herd was made out of the two, making 3,350 head, all of the scrub employees were turned off and all of the stout, able-bodied men were selected to go on with the herd.

Mr. Gipson returned to Texas and Frank Watson took charge of the outfit, and we proceeded on our way.

An old trail driver told me that after a herd crossed the Arkansas River they would never stampede again. I was only pleased to find that his statement was true, for they did not stampede again.

Solve this mystery if you can.

After we crossed the Kansas and Nebraska line we had a lovely range and plenty of water through Nebraska.

When we crossed the plains of that state for a distance of seventy-five miles we did not see a stick of timber as large as a hoe handle and there was not a single house on this immense domain, not a creek or a river.

Luckily for us heavy rains had fallen over the entire plains, and we had water. Old cowmen claim that on this stretch of plains the mercury often drops to thirty degrees below zero, and it is snow-bound for several weeks at a time. During severe winters it is impossible for anything to live there in the open.

After leaving the Nebraska line we crossed over into Colorado, and there had the pleasure of feasting our eyes on the most beautiful range that was ever beheld by a cowboy.

The gramma grass was half a knee high, and was mixed with nutritious white grass that was waist high, waiving in the breeze like a wheat field.

We drove up the Arickaree, a distance of about 100 miles, and had a picnic along this bubbling stream every day. The Arickaree was a tributary of the Platte River.

We delivered our cattle near Deer Trail, Colorado, fifty miles southeast of Denver, and sixty-five miles east of the foot of the Rocky Mountains, on Sept. 25, 1883, to a man named Fant, who had bought them on the trail a few days before their arrival.

After four long and lonesome months on the trail we at last reached our destination safe and sound, and after spending three days sightseeing in Denver we pulled out for our homes in Texas. The old R2 boys are scattered today from the Black Hills in Dakota to Buenos Ayres in South America.

*Gone to rest beyond the stormy seas,*

*To mingle with the blest on flowery beds of ease.*
*This world is but a bubble, there is nothing here but woe,*
*Hardships, toils and troubles wherever we may go;*
*Do what we will, go where we may, we are never free from care,*
*For at best this world is but a castle in the air.*

# Character Impersonation

AMONG THE DIFFERENT FORMS of entertainment provided for the Old Time Trail Drivers at their reunion in San Antonio in Oct. 1922, the character impersonations by Miss Elizabeth Slaughter were considered the best by the old cowboys in attendance.

Miss Slaughter is a granddaughter of Mr. and Mrs. W.B. Slaughter, and as an entertainer she capped them all when she appeared before the audience garbed as a cowboy and recited a poem titled, "The Chisholm Trail," from John A. Lomax's book.

She gave the gestures and the emphasis necessary to make it true to life, and did not hesitate to use the cowboy slang wherever it occurred in the poem:

## The Old Chisholm Trail

*Come along, boys, and listen to my tale,*
*I'll tell you of my troubles on the old Chisholm trail.*
*Coma ti yi youpy, youpy ya, youpa ya,*
*Coma ti yi youpy, youpy ya.*
*I started up the trail October twenty-third,*
*I started up the trail with the 2U herd.*
*Oh, a ten-dollar hoss and a forty-dollar saddle —*
*And I'm goin' to punchin' Texas cattle.*
*I woke up one morning on the old Chisholm trail*
*Rope in hand and a cow by the tail.*
*I'm up in the mornin' afore daylight*
*And afore I sleep the moon shines bright.*
*Old Ben Bolt was a blamed good boss,*
*But he'd go to see the girls on a sore-backed horse.*
*Old Ben Bolt was a fine old man*
*And you'd know there was whiskey wherever he'd land.*

My hoss threw me off at a creek called Mud,
My hoss threw me off round the 2U herd.
Last time I saw him he was going across the level
A-kicking up his heels and a-running like the devil.
It's cloudy in the West, a-looking like rain,
And my damned old slicker's in the wagon again.
Crippled my hoss, I don't know how,
Ropin' at the horns of a 2U cow.
We hit Caldwell and we hit her on the fly,
We bedded down the cattle on a hill close by.
No chaps, no slicker, and it's pouring down rain,
And I swear, by G—d, I'll never night herd again.
Feet in the stirrups and seat in the saddle,
I hung and rattled with them longhorned cattle.
Last night I was on guard and the leader broke ranks,
I hit my horse down the .shoulders and I spurred him in the flanks.
The wind commenced to blow, and the rain began to fall,
Hit looked, by grab, like we was goin' to lose 'em all.
I jumped in the saddle and grabbed holt the horn,
Best blamed cow-puncher ever was born.
I popped my foot in the stirrup and gave a little yell,
The tail cattle broke and the leaders went to hell.

I don't give a damn if they never do stop;
I'll ride as long as an eight-day clock.
Foot in the stirrup and hand on the horn,
Best damned cowboy ever was born.
I herded and hollered and I done very well,
Till the boss said, "Boys, just let 'em go to hell."
Stray in the herd and the boss said kill it,
So I shot him in the rump with the handle of a skillet.
We rounded 'em up and put 'em on the cars,
And that was the last of the old Two Bars.
Oh, it's bacon and beans most every day—
I'd as soon be a-eatin' prairie hay.
I'm on my best horse and I'm goin' at a run.
I'm the quickest shootin' cowboy that ever pulled a gun.
I went to the wagon to get my roll,
To come back to Texas, dad-burn my soul.

*I went to the boss to draw my roll,*
*He had it figured out I was nine dollars in the hole.*
*I'll sell my outfit just as soon as I can,*
*I won't punch cattle for no damned man.*
*Goin' back to town to draw my money,*
*Goin' back home to see my honey.*
*With my knees in the saddle and my seat in sky*
*I'll quit punching cows in the sweet by and by.*
*Coma ti yi youpy, youpy ya, youpy ya,*
*Coma ti yi youpy, youpy ya.*

# A Log of the Trails

*George W. Saunders, San Antonio, Texas*

THE QUESTION OF THE LOG of the Chisholm and other trails leading to the Northern markets has more versions than any question connected with the early trail days because no one, it seems, gives this phase of the game more than a passing thought.

Most everyone has heard of the Chisholm Trail, the Goodnight Trail and the Loving Trail but as a matter of fact most of the trail drivers did not care anything about the name of the trail they were traveling, as they were generally too busy to think or care about its name. In conversation I have heard men say: "I took the Chisholm Trail at Goliad, Lockhart, Corpus Christi, San Antonio and many other Texas points."

Some of the sketches in Volume One of *The Trail Drivers of Texas* speak of the Chisholm Trail starting at San Antonio, Texas; some at other places. The writers of these sketches were honest. They had probably heard this and had not taken the trouble to investigate the real routing and commencing point, until after the organization of The Old Trail Drivers' Association in 1915.

At that time our secretary was instructed to write to old trail drivers all over the country for information on this subject. We received many letters, each one giving his version, which differed somewhat.

W.P. Anderson, who was railroad agent at Abilene, Kansas, in the late sixties, and had to do with the first shipments of cattle out of that place, gives us a satisfactory description of the Chisholm Trail, laid out by Jesse Chisholm, a half-breed Cherokee Indian, from Red River Station to different points in Kansas.

Quoting from Mr. Anderson's letter to the Secretary, which is recorded in the minutes of the first reunion and to be found on page 13 of the first volume of *The Trail Drivers of Texas*:

"In reference to Mr. Goodnight's allusion to my 'blazing' the trail for the Joe McCoy herd, my recollection of the first herd that came to Abilene, Kansas, was that of J.J. Meyers, one of the trail drivers of that herd now living at Panhandle, Texas. A Mr. Gibbs, I think, will ascertain further on the subject.

"The first cattle shipped out of Abilene, that I recollect, was by C.C. Slaughter of Dallas, and while loaded at Abilene, Kansas, the billing was made from Memorandum slips at Junction City, Kansas. The original chapters of Joe McCoy's book were published in a paper called *The Cattle Trail*, edited by H.M. Dixon, whose address is now the Auditorium Building, Chicago.

"It was my connection with this publication that has probably led Mr. Goodnight into the belief that I helped blaze the trail with McCoy's cattle herd.

"This was the first paper that I know of that published maps of the trails from different cattle shipping points in Kansas to the intersection of the original Chisholm Trail, one from Coffeyville, Kansas, the first, however, from Baxter Springs, then from Abilene, Newton, then Wichita and Great Bend, Dodge City becoming so famous obviated the necessity for further attention in this direction."

One of the greatest developing projects ever known in the United States was done by this industry in taking the wilderness from the Indians and wild animals, stocking, peopling and developing sixteen states and territories in 28 years, namely; Western Indian Territory, Western Kansas, Nebraska, Montana, North Dakota, South Dakota, Colorado, Idaho, Nevada, Oregon, Washington, New Mexico, Arizona, Wyoming, Utah and Northwest Texas.

We all know that this entire domain was a wilderness in 1867 and only a few trappers and miners had penetrated them.

However, the Government's Immigrant California Trail crossed this wilderness, as did a few prospecting expeditions, but up to this date habitation was confined to a few trading posts and forts.

Compare this condition with the condition in 1890. All of the Indians were on reservations, the millions of buffalo were replaced by herds of fine cattle, horses, sheep and hogs; the iron horse rumbled through these lands, bringing happy, prosperous people, who built towns, schools, churches and tilled the rich soil that was waiting for them.

The government and other interests did their part and did it well, but to the old trail drivers belongs the glory and honor for having blazed the way that made this great development possible. They did more toward development in twenty-eight years than was ever previously done in one hundred years by our ancestors.

The trail to the North from Texas was started in 1867 and closed in 1895, but most of this great development was done in twenty years, from 1870 to 1890.

It is conservatively estimated by old trail drivers that there were 98 million cattle and 10 million horse stock driven over the Northern Trails during the 28 years of trail days and that there were 35,000 men employed to handle these herds.

Many of them are dead. Those surviving are identified in all lines of business, from high finance to day laborers. The majority of them belong to Texas.

One-thousand-two-hundred of them belong to the Old Trail Drivers' Association, which holds its annual reunions in San Antonio in October of each year, when they live over the bygone days.

From Red River to Abilene, Kansas, as I remember, the streams in 1871 were: Big and Little Washita, Turkey Creek, South and Northern Canadian, Cimarron, Bluff Creek on the line of Kansas.

Here we found the first civilized settlement of English-speaking people. The next streams were Pond Creek, Salt Fork of the Arkansas, North Fork of the Arkansas, at Wichita, Kansas.

The next town, Newton, Kansas, was a railroad camp as we went north and a big town when we came back through two months later, that being the terminus of the railroad at that time.

Next stream was Smoky River, on which was located Abilene, Kansas, the great Texas cattle market at that time. My experiences at Abilene, and full details of this trip from Texas and return over the trail in 1871, and my trail experiences up to 1886 are fully described in volume one of *The Trail Drivers of Texas*.

Some herds left the main trail in Wilson County, passed through Bexar County via San Antonio, to get supplies, then through Comal County, intersecting the main trail in Hays or Caldwell counties. All of these trails zigzagged and touched lots of adjoining counties not mentioned in my log.

The thousands of herds that were bought at Abilene, Wichita, Dodge City, Ogallala and other markets were driven to ranches all over the northwest, some as far as the Canadian line.

Here is a correct log of the cattle trails from Texas to Kansas and the northwestern states and territory beginning at the Rio Grande in Cameron County and giving the names of all the counties in Texas these trails passed through:

Starting at the Rio Grande, the trail passed through Cameron, Willacy, Hidalgo, Brooks, Kenedy, Kleberg, Nueces, Jim Wells, San Patricio, Live Oak, Bee, Goliad, Karnes, Wilson, Gonzales, Guadalupe, Caldwell, Hays, Travis, Williamson, Bell, Falls, Bosque, McLennan, Hill, Johnson, Tarrant, Denton, Wise, Cook, Montague, to Red River Station, or crossing where the Texas trail intersected the Chisholm Trail.

In the late seventies it became necessary to move the trail further west, as the old trail was being taken up by farmers. The trail was changed to go through Wilson, Bexar, Kendall, Kerr, Kimble, Menard, Concho, McCulloch, Coleman, Callahan, Shackleford, Throckmorton, Baylor and Wilbarger to Doan's Store or Crossing on Red River.

Later on the Southern herds quit the old trail in San Patricio County and went through Live Oak, McMullen, La Salle, Dimmit, Zavala, Uvalde, Edwards, and intersecting the Western trail in Kimble County, from where all followed the well defined and much traveled Western trail to Doan's Crossing on Red River.

As I remember the trail to Dodge City from Doan's Crossing it passed up North Fork Red River, Croton Creek, crossed North Fork Red River at Wichita Mountains, up North Fork to Indian Camp, Elm Creek, Cash Creek, Washita, Canadian, Sand Creek, Wolf Creek, Otter Creek, Beaver Creek, Wild Horse and Cimarron where Red Clark conducted a road house called "Long Horn Roundup," on up Bear Creek, Bluff Creek, at Mailey's road house, Mulberry Creek and Dodge City.

Now, my gentle readers, you have the log of old northern cattle trails, through Texas, and by looking at a map of Texas you can locate any part of the trail by the counties touched, but remember several of the Texas counties were not organized at that time and none in the Indian Territory.

You will recall it has been fifty-five years since the trail started and twenty-four since it closed. I personally drove over all these trails described and there are hundreds of men yet living that will vouch for the correctness of this log.

John Chisum of Denton County, drove lots of cattle to the head of the Concho in the late sixties, and on to the Pecos later. Oliver Loving, Chas. Goodnight, John Gamel, and others drove some herds from the head of the Concho to Horsehead Crossing on the Pecos in the sixties, on up the Pecos to Fort Sumner and on to Pueblo, Colorado.

There was a trail called the Goodnight Trail that went from the Pecos by way of Tascosa to Dodge City and other Kansas markets, but I have been unable to get a true log of that trail.

For the information of readers who are not familiar with geographical Texas and its cattle industry, I will state that herds starting from ranches in all parts of the state would intersect the nearest of these Northern trails, coming in from both sides and I doubt if there is a county in the state that did not have a herd traverse some part of it during trail days.

Some of the sketches in both volumes of *The Trail Drivers of Texas* report trouble with the Indians on the trail and others report no trouble.

For your information I will say the Indians were not always in the same mood, as sometimes they would leave the reservations on hunting expeditions and change their plans to murder and stealing from the trailers, emigrants and settlers.

They were always ready to steal but they were not fond of the Texas cowboy's mode of dealing with them and were very friendly when there were several herds near each other on the trail, but a lone herd was most always imposed on. Few herds passed through the Indian Territory in early days without some trouble with the Indians.

I have gone several trips without any trouble more than having them beg for a few animals and some provisions; at other times I have had them steal horses, stampede the herd and molest us in every possible way, but the best remedy for them was to stand pat and they usually came to our terms.

The publication of this, the second volume of *The Trail Drivers of Texas* will complete a work I started many years ago, beginning with the agitation of, and the final organization of the Old Trail Drivers' Association.

Collecting data for the two volumes was a task that would have tested the patience of Job. I was like Davy Crockett – I knew I was right – and I went ahead. The work was tedious and slow, but I enjoyed it because I knew the organization should exist, and the books would be very interesting and would give facts that the rising generation should know.

The general matter of which these two volumes is made up depict a life of which the present generation knows very little. They deal with actual happenings that occurred in the days of trail driving, and these facts are much stranger than fiction. I started a campaign to raise $30,000 to build a monument in Brackenridge Park at San Antonio, on the old trail, to perpetuate the memory of those noble old trail drivers.

Donations are coming in regularly, and I believe we can build this monument in 1924. When it is completed my work is done.

The cowboys, or cowpunchers, sometimes called "waddles," were men who did all kinds of ranch and trail work with cattle. Whether he was a ranchman, owner of trail herds, son of a cattle king, or just a hand, his occupation gave him that name.

Right here I want to defend the cowboys, or cow-punchers, against the so-called "Wild West" fiction stories that purport to link them with elements of bad men.

There was a very small percent of them went wrong, as the temptations and influences they met at the northern markets after a long, lonesome, tiresome journey, could not be resisted and entrapped some of them, but no larger percent than would have fallen from the same number of college students.

It is not fair to besmear the name of the cowboy with the deeds of every outlaw in the country. I know the majority of these cowboys made the best citizens of Texas.

It is true they were light-hearted and carefree, but they never forsook a friend, or failed to respond to the call of distress.

Woman's virtue was their highest ideal, and their respect for womankind was unbounded. These cowboys stood the acid test, and I do not think a nobler set of men ever lived.

In this volume there are about 200 pictures of representative trail men. I claim that one hundred of them and their connections handled fully seventy-five percent of all the cattle and horses that were driven out of Texas to the Northern markets during the trail days. I am proud to say I was personally acquainted with ninety percent of these noblemen.

They are passing away fast, and I fear there will never be another set of men with such traits of character, home-loving, straight-forward and God-loving, as the old trail drivers were. They have all stood the acid test, and their memory will stand as a lasting monument to their many deeds and great achievements.

# Experiences of a Ranger and Scout

*by A.M. (Gus) Gildea, Deming, New Mexico*

I WAS BORN APRIL 23, 1854, in Dewitt County, Texas, my father, ranching at the time, having moved to Texas in 1852 from Mississippi.

J.E. Gildea was a soldier, under Gen. Scott in Mexico, 1846-47, having enlisted in New Orleans, returning there in 1848 after the Mexican War and married Mrs. Mary Adelaide Cashell, a widow with one young son, Augustus Lorraine Cashell who is living at this time, January 1922, in Pope County, Arkansas.

J.E. Gildea and his step-son, Cashell, were both in the Confederate Army and came out lieutenants, and after Gen. Lee's surrender both went to Mexico, my father from the lower Rio Grande where the Confederates under Brig. Gen. J.E. Slaughter had repulsed the Yankees in what is known as the battle of Casa Blanca and which was fought some time subsequent to Gen. Lee's surrender and my half brother Cashell, went as interpreter with Gen. Joe Shelby's men.

My father was with the French and Austrian army of invasion and Lieut. Cashell with the Mexican Republican army until the Confederates in this last fight of the Civil War were pardoned by proclamation of President Johnson, when they returned home and went to gathering their scattered stock of horses and cattle at the ranch on the Nueces river fifteen miles below Oakville, in Live Oak County, and here is where I began my cowboy work at twelve years of age.

From then, 1866 until 1906, I was more or less in the saddle on the frontiers of Texas, New Mexico, Arizona and in Old Mexico.

In 1868 I was sent to Louisville, Kentucky, to school and to study medicine and after a year's time I got lonesome and wanted to hear the wolves howl and the owls hoot back in the West, so I took "French leave" out of school and went up the Ohio River to Cincinnati and from there out in the country and down into Indiana and back to Kentucky, then into Tennessee, Arkansas, Mississippi and Louisiana until I again reached New Orleans, where I stayed several months.

Coming back to Texas in the fall of 1870 I was again sent to school to St. Mary's College in San Antonio and attended this school until 1872, when I went on to the frontier south and west of San Antonio, selling Grover & Baker sewing machines.

The first school I attended was the old "free school" on what is now Houston Street in San Antonio, Texas, taught by good old man Newton and Mr. Lacky in 1859 and 1860. The latter hiked North at the opening of hostilities between the North and South, and his place was filled by Mrs. Pryor.

At that time Houston Street was only a road through mesquite and huisache brush. In 1864-65 I attended the St. Mary's College and here I was taught those Christian principles that ever remained with me and encouraged me to overcome many temptations in after life.

In 1870-71 I again attended this college after my return from my "spin" over the range in the Southern and Eastern States as mentioned, and on this "spin" I rode with the Klu Klux Klan in Tennessee when there was no other law to protect Southern homes against the ravages of freed Negroes urged on by the carpetbaggers and protected in their nefarious practices by federal bayonets.

In 1866-67-68, when not attending school I was working cattle for my father in Live Oak County branding, gathering and driving to Bexar County, where we were then living on the Olmos Creek, five miles north of San Antonio.

In 1876 I left Dimmit County, where I owned a small bunch of cattle, which I sold, and started to Arizona, stopping awhile in Menard County where I had a sweetheart and here I joined Thomas W. Swilling to go with him to Arizona.

We left Menardville early in Sept. 1876, and pulled out via Fort Concho, fifty miles north, where we laid in a supply of grub, enough to last us until we reached Roswell, New Mexico, and again "hit the grit" for Arizona, every mile of it over an uninhabited country, infested with hostile Indians.

At Centralia, which was a stage station on the high plains guarded by Negro troops, we left the stage road and followed the old Butterfield route to Horsehead Crossing on the Pecos; thence up east of Pecos to New Mexico.

The Indians were raiding the country when we left and we saw their trails and camped on them quite often from Fort Concho until we got to Seven Rivers in New Mexico.

About twenty-five miles west of Fort Concho we met a company of cavalry escorting the telegraph operator at Fort Concho, a Mr. Milburn, who had been out repairing the line between Fort Concho and the Pecos River on the stage road, about three miles of which had been cut and destroyed.

Mr. Milburn, whom I knew when operator at Fort Duncan, advised us to return with them to the fort, stating that the country was "lousy" with Indians, and we would not be able to get through.

At Centralia the Negro sergeant in command of the guard advised us to go back. At the rifle-pits we nooned where the Indians had camped the night before; at Castle Gap the Indian trail split, the largest party keeping the trail westward and the smaller party going northwest.

The large trail was mostly horses and was about forty in number, no doubt going to the Mescalero Agency at Tularosa, New Mexico, crossing at Horsehead and thence northwest through the Guadalupe Mountains with a bunch of stolen horses. Another trail came in from the north and crossed our trail near Castle Gap, going southeast toward Camp Lancaster, at the mouth of Live Oak Creek. There were about ten on foot and three horses and they crossed the trail we were on about five hours before we came along.

We traveled until about midnight, hoping to strike the Pecos at Horsehead, water and get away in the dark hours as it was a bad place for Indians, but being sleepy and tired, we left the trail and went about 200 yards south and lay down to sleep, staking our horses on fine grass.

About 5 a.m. we saddled up and pulled out before day and reached Horsehead about nine o'clock, not many hours behind two bands of Indians.

About three o'clock the next afternoon we a saw dust ahead of us and not knowing but what it was Indians I sent Swilling with the pack horse into the cane brakes of the Pecos while I maneuvered up the river to see who was coming and found out that it was two white men, a Mr. Pearce, and Nath Underwood, driving a small bunch of cattle from New Mexico to Ft. Stockton, Texas.

They let us have a little corn meal and some "jerky" from their meager supplies and we went on about five miles to Pope's crossing on the Pecos, where we watered our horses and filled our canteens, then crossed our trail and went behind a butte about one-half mile from our trail and camped. Pearce and Underwood went about two miles farther on their road and camped, making the distance between our camps about seven miles.

They hobbled two saddle horses and one. pack-horse and staked the other pack horse, which was a beautiful black and white paint.

The Indians had no doubt spotted them before we had met them and had gone under the banks of the Pecos and hid until they went into camp and sometime during the night went after their horses, knowing that they had four and only finding the one staked and seeing the trail of our three horses naturally supposed that it was the other three belonging to the cattlemen going on the back track, which they followed and ran into us just at daybreak.

It was misting rain when we got up to make a fire next morning and we had rolled our shooting irons in our bed to keep them dry and we did not see the Indians until they were very close to us, nor could they see us until they reached the top of the butte.

We saw each other about the same time and they fired only one shot with a carbine and ran back toward the Pecos. When I got my gun they were 150 yards away and I fired four shots, wounding one horse and killed one Indian and wounding one.

They changed their course, going south down the river a half a mile, then turned east and went up on another butte about three-quarters of a mile from us and buried the dead Indian, then went north parallel to the river and crossed it next day where they were seen by a cowman.

We then made coffee and packed up and were about to leave when Nath Underwood rode into camp on their trail. I told him about seeing them with his paint horse. Two Indians were riding him. There were seven Indians and four horses, three horses carrying double. (Nath Underwood now lives in San Antonio and I had the pleasure of meeting him at the Old Trail Drivers' Convention in November 1921.)

Next day we got to Pearce and Paxton's camp and got enough "chuck" to last us to Seven Rivers. After resting our horses a few days, Mr. Paxton wanted me to locate land at Rattlesnake Springs, near the Guadalupe Mountains and he and I went to see it, leaving Tom Swilling in camp with the others whose names I do not remember.

We pulled out early in the morning, crossed the Pecos, then on up Delaware Creek on which we nooned, then went on to Rattlesnake Springs, only to find it in possession of other parties, three Jones brothers, with whom we spent the night, and started back next morning.

At noon we camped in the deep bed of the creek and while there we heard a racket and in peeping over the bank we saw ten Indians driving about twenty-five horses about fifty yards distant right on the trail. The loose herds ahead had obliterated our trail, but they were liable to see it any time and return to investigate.

When he got back to Paxton's camp that night we found all well, but the next day one of the Jones boys came to camp and reported that the Indians had passed their ranch just at night, and next day they were afraid we had been killed and came to investigate.

Tom Swilling and I continued our journey to Seven Rivers (Beckwith's ranch) where we met John Slaughter's outfit returning from a cattle drive up in New Mexico.

When we arrived at South Spring, the headquarters ranch of John S. Chisum, we camped on the ground where the Slaughter outfit had camped a few days before and saw where a Texas cowboy had been shot from his horse by one of Slaughter's men as he rode into their camp, his congealed blood lying in a pool on the ground where he fell and died.

His name was Barney Gallagher, and I knew him at Carrizo Springs in Dimmit County. He was generally known as "Buckshot," a typical cowboy character of those frontier days.

Chisum was putting up two herds of cattle when we arrived and we went to work gathering a mixed herd for Nebraska and one of wild old "moss-horns" for the Indian reservation at San Carlos, Arizona, John Chisum having the contract to furnish the government beef for more than 7,000 Indians on this and its sub-agencies.

While working the range, which included all the country from Anton Chico on the north to Seven Rivers on the south and the White Mountains on the west to the Canadian on the east, which John Chisum claimed as his range and over which grazed approximately 100,000 head of John Chisum's "rail" brand and "Jingle-bob" earmarked cattle, we had some tough work and adventures.

Two men were tried by "Judge Lynch" and executed; one at Bosque Grande Ranch, for murder and hung, and one near Narvo's Ben Crossing while bringing a herd down the river to Headquarters Ranch, for murder and shot. Both of these were for cold-blooded murder, which was witnessed by other cowboys who immediately arrested, tried, convicted and executed the murderers, and went on with their work as if nothing of so grim a nature had just happened.

The law of the range was "forget it" for discussions were likely to lead to trouble. In those days, cowboy law was enforced and every cowboy knew it, and I never knew of the subject again brought up around the campfire.

After the Nebraska herd had been gathered, cut and road-branded it took the trail via Trinidad, Colorado, with Si Funk in charge, and in about a week we were ready to hit the trail for Arizona with 4,000 head of wild "moss-horn" steers and 150 head of horses, including the wagon, teams and some private stock belonging to the boys.

It was now November and the weather was getting very cold. We had, as near as I can recall, twenty regular men in the outfit, the "big boss," "Big Jim," the Negro cook and the secretary; our night reliefs of four men three hours each and one man on relief three hours with the remuda.

The men had running guard relief and sometimes were justified in reducing the force on relief and at other times reinforcing it according to the foreseen danger of Indians, trail robbers or weather stampedes.

We camped one bitter cold, sleety night on the summit of the White Mountains and were to pass through the Mescalero Indian reservation next morning.

We had grazed our herd that day in the mountains where the grass was good and protected from the snow that had fallen heavy the day before and the previous night, and we thought that they would bed easily, but they were restless and wanted to drift, which necessitated putting on double guard and bunching the remuda under close guard, for we believed the Indians would try to stampede both cattle and horses as they were mad at Chisum's men, who had killed some of them the previous year on the reservation.

Every man not on duty that night had his horse saddled and tied up, as Chisum told us on the trail that ever since the Indians had been located on the Tularosa, through which his cattle trail led, that as toll, they would cut twenty head of the best beeves each trip, and they do the cutting themselves and they would not take "drags."

Every man in the outfit except "Old John" and old man Northrup, his private secretary, had a powwow and made "big medicine" and did not intend to let "big Injun" have any beef on this trip. There were with us twenty-one well armed men, with the cook, and more than 1,000 fighting Apache "bucks" five miles ahead of us, whom we had to encounter mañana, unless we submitted to their insolence.

We knew Chisum's men just a year before had ridden into the reservation after stolen stock and on getting no satisfaction from Godfroy, the agent, they attempted to drive the stock away and were attacked by the Indians and some of the Indians were killed and all driven into Ft. Stanton; that now they were not on Government reservation, having left it after the cowboy raid above mentioned and took refuge along the brakes of the Tularosa and Lost Rivers on the west side of the White mountain, therefore had no right to demand toll and we believed they would not attack us if we refused their demand for beef, we resolved to refuse and fight if it became necessary.

At 3 a.m. the cook was roused and told to "rustle chuck." We were not long in getting on the outside of some hot coffee, "pone" and "sowbelly" and at daylight every man was in his saddle at the herd.

The remuda was now thrown in the herd and we were looking for "Old John" to come and start the cattle, when old "Solomon," the Mescalero chief, and twenty painted warriors, well mounted and armed, came toward us. Frank Baker (afterward killed by Billy the Kid) and I rode out and met him and he not seeing Chisum whom he knew, ignored us and attempted to pass.

I signaled him to halt and with a scowl on his face he said, *"Captain Cheese-om? Queremos baka-shee,"* (all the Apaches called beef or meat baka-she, pronounced bah-cah-she. The northern Indians called it wo-ha).

I replied, *"Yo soy captain; ninguna bakashee por usted* (I am captain; no beef for you.)."

My back being turned to the wagon, I did not see Chisum leave camp, but one of the boys rode up and informed me and I signaled the chief to remain where he was. I rode back to meet Mr. Chisum. He was very angry and wanted to go to the chief and I asked him not to interfere and to go back.

I called Bill Henry who was nearby and told him to tell the boys if they saw Mr. Chisum and me ride back to the chief to surround the Indians and if I fired a shot not to let an Indian escape nor an Indian horse get back to the agency; that if Mr. Chisum interfered I would shoot the chief.

Henry went off in a gallop and "Old John" being thoroughly convinced by this time, turned his horse and started back to the wagon, which had gone up close to the herd. I returned to the chief who sat on his horse with a sullen look on his face and I pointing in the direction of the reservation said, *"vallese bakashee nada."*

He grunted and offered me his hand, which I refused to take, knowing that if I did so every one of his warriors would offer their hands and he and every buck would want to shake hands with every man of us and thus get to the big boss, which I did not want to occur.

He wheeled his paint mustang and took the back trail at a fast gait and every buck formed in single file and followed him. We had no more trouble with them and when we got the lead cattle to within a mile of the reservation Frank Baker and I were sent ahead to see that the Indians were kept back so as not to stampede the herd.

Godfroy, the agent, had a confab with Solomon, the chief, through the interpreter, who gave orders and our way was cleared.

Here I was shown the Indian whom I shot and wounded at Pope's Crossing in September. He was convalescing, but as poor as a snake, my bullet having struck him in the back, passing through the right nipple. I told him I shot him and killed one and a horse.

Several stood by him who said they were there and all seemed pleased to see me and shook hands and asked for *"el otro?"* (the other man?). I told them he was with the herd and they said, *"bueno,"* and rode to meet the herd.

We watered at Lost River and started over the long trail of sixty miles over the "white desert" to San Augustine Springs, where Shedd's ranch was located. It took us nearly thirty-six hours to reach there with the lead cattle and the tail drags were forty-four hours in getting in.

When the lead cattle got to within five miles of San Augustine, they were held back and allowed to go in slow, the drag end was twenty miles behind, which meant a line of cattle twenty miles long.

The remuda had been sent in to water and back twelve miles the evening of the second day to enable the line men to change mounts and send their jaded ones to water.

This drive was the worst of the whole trip but we did not lose a single head. Chisum said it was the first drive he ever made over it that he did not lose cattle, both from exhaustion and cattle thieves who would cut the line between the riders, who were often necessarily several miles apart, and get away with them as they were never followed on account of scarcity of men. These thieves were generally Mexicans, but sometimes Indians and white men.

When we reached the Rio Grande we laid over a couple of days to rest and graze, while some of the boys were sent down the river to Dona Ana and vicinity, to pick up stolen cattle he had previously lost.

For some reason or other I was generally made "side boss" on these trips, so taking four men we left early in the morning and began to round up at Dona Ana in the afternoon and we had picked up nearly fifty head, nearly all work oxen, and started back with them when we were followed and attacked by a bunch of Mexicans.

We had seen them coming and rode back to a gully where we dismounted. They could see us and came at us on a charge, yelling and shooting.

Our first volley scattered them and drove them back. It seems that some soldiers from Fort Selden were with the Mexicans and two of them got hurt or were killed, for the next day an officer and ten men came to us while we were crossing the river to inquire into the occurrence.

He was shown the cattle we had brought in, all bearing the same brand and earmark as the balance of the herd and informed that they were stolen cattle belonging to Mr. Chisum, with whom he had been conversing.

He said that after the fight it had been reported to the post commander that it was cattle thieves who had taken the oxen and the Mexicans had followed to recover them when they were attacked and seven killed and two soldiers badly wounded. The soldiers had no right to be with them, but were courting some Mexican girls and were induced by the Mexicans to go with them, not thinking of having a fight.

I quit the outfit when we reached the San Simon in Arizona, thirty-five miles from our destination, which was Croton Springs, in Sulphur Springs valley, and where I again worked for Chisum in 1878, "circling and signing" and guarding his range from the point of Pinal Mountains on the north to about where Pierce is now on the south, from the Dragoon Mountains on the west, to the Chiricahua Mountains on the east.

It would require too much space to relate the incidents that transpired in connection with our lives the short time I worked there, but all will be told in detail in a book I hope to have published in 1924.

In the latter years I served as a special ranger in Companies D and F, Texas Frontier Battalion, and U.S. deputy marshal and also deputy sheriff and other official positions on the frontier. This service was from 1881 to 1889.

I have met most of the so-called outlaws and bad men who ranged in Texas, New Mexico and Arizona from 1865 to 1890 and never knew but one but what had some good traits about him.

On the other hand I have known some so-called good men and officers with some very bad traits about them.

I married in San Antonio in 1885 and have two boys and a girl dead and three daughters living. They are, Mrs. William E. Lea, of Sanderson, Texas; Mrs. A.M. Preston who was with her husband in France and Mrs. Robert C. Courtney of Del Rio, Texas.

Now at the age of sixty-eight years I am still hale and hearty and square with my fellow men, but owe much to God for keeping me and mine.

# The Poet of the Range

C.C. WALSH OF SAN ANGELO, TEXAS, is known all over the southwest and western parts of Texas as the poet of the range. When he meets a man whose character impresses him he studies the man and the man's character.

Idiosyncrasies of his speech, peculiarities of expression, distinguishing facial features – all of these are within the purview of the studies of Col. Walsh, the banker and student of men. Then he writes the man he has studied into a poem and poems he has written will preserve a race of men rapidly passing from the range and from existence.

The west Texas cowman's folk life is a hobby with him. He believes the Texas cowman to be one of the noblest American type. Their brogue, their mannerisms, their ideals and their shortcomings are his study book and he has faithfully incorporated them into poems, one of which follows:

## The Old "Square Dance" of the Western Range

*Imagination – onc't I had!*
*I hain't got none no more.*
*It wuzn't like we used t' dance*
*Out on th' old dirt floor—*
*With cowboys thar in highheeled boots,*
*A kickin' up, my law!*
*While that old fiddle played, I think,*
*'Twas "Turkey in th' straw."*
*That old square dance we used t' see—*
*With fiddle er guitar,*
*Accordeum an' tambourine,*
*While folks f rum near an' far*

*Cum driftin' in fur miles around,*
*Th' tops of all th' herds,*
*All laughin', happy, bright an' gay*
*An' full o' pleasant words.*
*The glow of health, an' pride of strength,*
*That grace, which nature gives,*
*Unto them rugged boys an' ghels*
*Who clost to Nature lives,*
*Wuz somthin' grand to look upon*
*When tha cum on th' floor—*
*An' danced th' graceful minuet*
*Which all seemed to adore.*
*The old square dance of Airley Days*
*Wuz unsuggestive, Bill,*
*Thar wuz no vulgar stunts pulled off—*
*But, like the laughin' rill,*
*Which flows through pleasaint shady dells,*
*An' sparkles in th' sun,*
*Mid innercence an' purity,*
*Tha danced each merry run.*
*Bill, sumtimes, when I shet my eyes,*
*It all comes back onc't more.*
*I see ole "Uncle Jimmie" Jones*
*A comin' thru th' door.*
*His violin within its case,*
*Which he removes with care;*
*I see him rosum up his bow*
*With artist's skill most rare.*
*Ole Uncle Jimmie, praise his name,*
*An' rest his soul in peace;*
*Wuz known all over the Western Range;*
*His fame shall never cease.*
*Th' music, which he played, I know,*
*May have been cor-do-roy;*
*But it wuz jist th' kind, which pleased*
*A country ghel an' boy—*
*His rep-er-tore wuz circumscribed—*
*In keepin' with his skill.*
*But everything he tried to play,*

*Wuz done with right good will.*
*That "Ar-kan-saw-yer Traveler" chune*
*Wuld allus head th' list—*
*No cowboy dance would be complete*
*Ef this one chune wuz missed.*
*It mattered little what tha danc'd—*
*The Ole Virginia Reel,*
*A polka, Schottisch er a waltz—*
*It was th' same old spiel.*
*In sets o' four, in sets o' eight,*
*A one-step er a two,*
*That "Ar-kan-saw-yer" chune wuz play'd*
*Th' blessed evening through.*
*'Mong other chunes were "Money Musk,"*
*"My Sailor's on the Sea,"*
*Er—" The Old Fat Gal," an' "Rye Straw,"*
*"The Fisher's Hornpipe"—Gee!*

*Of course— with "Turkey in the Straw,"*
*Er "Bonapart's Retreat,"*
*Th' "Ole Gray Eagle" soarin' high,*
*We got thar with both feet.*
*Thar also wuz another man*
*Who made himself a name*
*Which may sumtime be posted up—*
*Within "Th' Hall of Fame"*
*It wuz Ole "Windy Billy" Smith,*
*A waitin' with a grin—*
*"Official caller" at the dance—*
*In whom there wuz no sin.*
*Yuh couldn't call him hansum, Bill*
*He wuz no cherum fair,*
*He had a long beak fur a nose*
*With carrot reddish hair,*
*His eyes wur like two small black beans,*
*His mouth was one long slit,*
*Then he wuz kinder lantern jaw'd,*
*An' stuttered quite a bit.*
*But when he stood up fur t' call*

Th' changes in the dance,
His stutterin' 'ud disappear;
Th' creases in his pants
Caused by them short bow laigs of his'n
Wuld make you laff an' grin
Until th' herd commenced to mill!
As "Windy" would begin.
Th' fiddle now is chunin' up—
As Jimmy draws his bow;
While he begins to plink and plonk
Th' folks git in a row.

Then as he plonks and plinks and plunks,
An' tightens up his strings,
The boys and ghels form into squares
An' sich delight it brings.
Ole "Uncle Jimmy's" now chuned up—
He draws his bow at last.
Ole "Windy Billy" takes his stan'
He'd sail'd before th' mast.
His voice rings out upon th' air
Like sum clear bugle call,
While all now liss'n fur th' words
Which opens up th' ball.
Gents: Hang your hats out on a limb,
This one thing I demand.
Honor yer pardners—right an' left.
How pompous his command!
Heel an' Toe —lock horns with yearlin's.
Now chase 'em round an' round,
That fiddle's goin' mighty fine—
Now both feet on the ground.
Gents to the center— How are you?
Man! Hear that fiddle play.
Th' ladies do-ce—how de de?
Now hip! hurrah!! hurray!!!
Right hands across—chase yer squirrels.
Th' gents will do-ce-do.
Now swing six— when you reach th' line—

*My! see them yearlin's go.
"Do-ce— ladies— Th"culls' cut back,
Just see that 'dogie' trail.
Everybody dance —now you go—
See that one steer 'turn tail'—
Salute—pardners—promenade all—
Steve cut th' pigeon wing.
Swing on the corners—mill th' herd.
'Dock' dance th' Highland Fling.
Tie yer hats fast to yer saddles,
Now, ride to beat th' wind.
Every gent salute yer heifer—
Show how th' baboon grinned
All th' ladies to th' center;
Cow punchers, stake yer pen —
Play that tune a little louder—
Now russel 'em like men.
Hog-tie pardners, swing on corners—
Swing across —now swing through.
Elbow twist an' double L swing
Do-ce-do, tight as glue
All big steers do th' buck buck an' wing,'
Young steers 'double shuffle'
Honor pardner—all-a-men left—
'Big Boy' do that scuffle.
Eight pretty Herefords, form a ring,
'Slough foot' in th' center.
Twist th' grapevine round his horns—
Let no Mavericks enter.
All hands up a rarin' to go
Jake don't brand that sleeper.
All promenade around th' pen—
Catch your heifer – keep her.
Boys chase that 'rustler' f rum th' camp—
Th' hon'ry 'ball o' hair.'
The ghels all form a ladies chain—
Of 'Bowleg Pete' take care—

Now then— reverse men— try yer hand,*

*Corral 'em in th' trap;*
*Then swaller fork, an' do-ce-do,*
*Uncinch that broken strap—*
*Walk th' huckleberry shuffle—*
*Do th' Chinese cling—*
*Long Simpson, lead th' trail herd,*
*An' git 'em in a ring—*
*Gents purr round yer purty pussies.*
*Now rope 'em— balance all,*
*Some dance 'clogs' an' sum dance th' 'Tucker'—*
*Ride in an' top th' hall.*
*All hands up, an' circle around,*
*Don't let th' herd stampede.*
*Corral 'em on th' open ground*
*Then drift 'em in t' feed.*
*Do-ce, ladies Salute your gents.*
*Lock horns – now – arm in arm —*
*Start up th' trail – drift —two – two by two—*
*Refreshments have their charm."*
*'Twas thus we'd dance th' night away—*
*In those old days of yore—*
*Sumtimes we'd set a number out*
*An' then, our minds 'ud soar*
*Away out in th' realms o' space—*
*Whar smilin' cupids dwell;*
*Er sumtimes wander near th' brook*
*Down in th' moonlight dell.*
*Then as we wandered, hand in hand—*
*Sumtimes our eyes 'ud meet—*
*We'd feel a twich of th' heart*
*Which was so awful sweet—*
*We culdn't tell you how it felt—*
*Fur it jist felt so good,*
*It culdn't be described to you*
*Jist like I wish'd it culd.*
*Alas! them good ole days air gone—*
*Gone air them good ole times—*
*When "Windy Billy" call'd th' dance*
*In good ole-fashioned rhymes.*

*When dear ole "Uncle Jimmie" Jones*
*Sat with his trusty bow,*
*An' played upon his violin*
*Th' chunes, which made us glow.*
*For both ole "Uncle Jimmie" Jones*
*An' "Windy Billy" Smith*
*Have drifted up th' Silent Trail,*
*A huntin' fur thair kith—*
*Which have been losted frum th' herd,*
*Upon th' range so wide;*
*But tha will find 'em I am sure,*
*Across th' Great Divide.*
*I look back on th' yesterday,*
*With pleasure an' with pride,*
*While calling up familiar names*
*With whom I used to ride,*
*In going to a country dance*
*With sum sweetheart o' mine,*
*When – Oh! such pleasant times we had*
*In days of "Auld Lang Syne."*

# One Trip Up the Trail

*by B.D. Lindsey, San Antonio, Texas*

I WAS BORN IN UNION PARISH, LOUISIANA, Jan. 21, 1856, and came to Texas when I was 17 years old, with my uncle, who located near Waco.

I assisted him on the farm for a while, then went south intending to become a cowboy. I had bunked with Ad Lindsey that winter, and he had been "up the trail" and I had caught the fever from him. In the early days of Feb. 1874, in company with Neally Cone and Bill Foster, I left Waco and traveled south on the Austin road.

We had provided ourselves with a good supply of brandy peaches, a concoction sold in those days. That evening late we landed at the Westbrook Ranch on Cow Bayou. Mrs. Westbrook kindly consented for us to stay overnight and directed us to – the barn.

Just about that time Mr. Westbrook appeared on the scene. I shall never forget him. He was a small sized man, wiry, spare build, about 30 years of age. With a firm look in his eye and a steady voice he said. "Boys, I see that you are drinking and I had rather you would ride on."

We did. We crossed over the bayou and stayed overnight. The next night we stayed with a Swede farmer six miles north of Austin. There were very few houses along the road in those days.

We reached Austin the next day, remaining there only a few hours, then pulled on for San Marcos. When we got to the Blanco River our money was getting scarce so we sought employment.

My first job was planting corn two days for Billie Owens, who now lives at Sabinal, Texas. My next work was for a Mr. Cochran, who owned a farm on the cattle trail. He paid me seventy-five cents per day.

Herds were passing daily, and one rainy day I saddled my horse and drifted with a passing herd. In conversation with one of the boys he asked me if I had ever been up the trail, and when I informed him that I had not, he said I should claim that I had as I would be paid better wages. I kept this information for future use, and when I learned that a herd was being gathered in the neighborhood, to be in charge of Sam Driskill, I made up my mind to go with that herd. I hailed Mr. Driskill as he was passing one day and asked him for a job.

The first question he fired at me was, "Have you ever been up the trail?" "Yep," I replied, right off the reel. Two days later he sent for me and put me and Eberly Peters, who now lives at San Marcos, herding about 400 mixed cattle. We were both green hands, but we came in with all the cattle for two days. We held them bunched as though they were in a corral. The third day we moved out to the Perry Day Ranch, near where the town of Kyle is now situated.

When we stopped at noon my troubles began.

I was left in company with wiser ones, and my idea was to not let any get away, so I kept butting them in. John Rutledge, one of the boys, cussed me for being a fool, and proceeded to give me my first lesson in handling cattle.

When I went to the chuck wagon, Pres Horton, a typical cow-puncher, constituted himself a court of inquiry and began plying me with questions. He asked me if I had ever been up the trail, and who I drove for. I told him I went up the trail the year before, and drove for Chisholm.

I had the idea that Chisholm owned all the cattle in Texas. Then Horton asked me where I drove to, and I told him Wichita.

Next he asked me where I crossed the Brazos, and I said Fort Graham, and that I crossed the Red River at Red River Station. When he wanted to know what river Wichita was located on, I had to study for a moment, then said "Arkansas."

By this time I was growing nervous. He was also stumped, for he could not figure out how it was that I was so well posted. The fact of the matter is Ad Lindsey, who had been over the route, told me these things, and I had not forgotten.

For a little while Horton let up on me, but finally came back with the question: "Where does the bridge cross the river at Wichita?" This was a stunner, but I said, "Kinder toward the lower edge of town." He had me, as there was no bridge there at that time.

Of course, I thought it was back to the farm for me, but Sam Driskill, the boss, who had heard the whole discussion, came to my rescue and said, "Kid, I had discovered you were a green hand in this business, but I see you are willing, and I had rather have one willing hand than one too lazy to perform his duties."

I was much relieved and right there I determined to give the best service I was capable of giving. We remained at the Day Ranch about two weeks, and then moved on to the Baggett Ranch, near where Temple is now, for our next and last stop.

We completed our herd there and started on our long journey. Jess Driskill and Dock Day were the owners of the herd.

Jess Driskill built the Driskill Hotel at Austin.

An incident occurred at the Baggett Ranch, which while a little personal, I think is worthy of mention, as it will show how green and foolish I was.

A downeaster, whose name I have forgotten, had been employed. He was about thirty years old and weighed 230 pounds. Aside from being a greenhorn he was really too heavy for trail work, and the bunch wanted to get rid of him, and set about to do this very thing, while I was made the "goat."

The boys began to carry news to him of talks I had made about him, and from him they brought yarns to me. Of course neither of us had said anything about the other.

We all carried the old style cap-and-ball navy pistols, as was the custom in those days. One evening while I was holding the cattle, the evening relief came out and this big 230-pounder made straight toward me, saying that I had talked about him long enough and he was going to put a stop to it. I had been told by the other boys that the trouble was coming, and to open up on him when it started, which I proceeded to do.

I shot at him six times as he was coming toward me, aiming at his paunch, but he did not fall.

Now mind you, the boys had previously extracted the bullets from my pistol, and I was shooting only wads, but I did not know it. The wads set his clothing afire, and also the sage grass, and it took us several hours to put out the prairie fire.

The "wounded" man ran off, left his horse, went to camp, got his time and quit, just what the bunch wanted him to do. The boys told me that I would be arrested when we got to Fort Worth, and advised me to go to the boss and get a horse and leave the herd, scout along in the neighborhood for a few days, and fall in again.

I took it all in like a sucker, until I asked Sam Driskill for the horse. Sam told me then it was all a put-up job, and to pay no attention to them. From that time on I got along very well.

When we arrived at Hays, Kansas, 500 beeves were cut out and left there or driven to Ellsworth and held for a time. John Driskill was left in charge of the beeves. He now lives at Sabinal, Texas. There were twenty-three men in our outfit, but I can remember only the following: Orland Driskill, Sam Driskill, Dallas Driskill, Tol Driskill, Pres Horton, Charlie Raymond, Eberly Peters, John Rutledge, Tom Evans, Mills, one of the cooks, and Bill Hicks, my guard mate.

# A Trip to Kansas in 1870

*by W.R. Massengale, Rio Frio, Texas*

I WENT WITH A DROVE OF 700 BIG STEERS, about the first of April. We put the road brand on them at the Strickland Ranch, a few miles east of Helena, on the Yorktown road.

The first night it came a little rain and wind and hail and the cattle not being used to herding out we had one of the worst stampedes I was ever in up to this time. We only had a small opening to hold them on and it was very thick brush all over that country so in less than twenty minutes they were cut up in five bunches and running as if they had tin cans tied to their tails.

We crossed the San Marcos River below San Marcos town; there we met with John Campbell. He was bossing a herd for Choate & Bennett, and we camped close together that night. He penned his cattle. We herded out that night and had a bad thunderstorm and hard rain, but we held our "old mossy heads," all right till about one o'clock.

It quit raining but the lightning kept up and the whole herd went to grazing and scattered all over the country, so Mr. Drake sent word to all hands to come in and let them alone. W.H. Mayfield was owner of the herd.

Just as we were all getting together a Mexican rode up and asked for Spencer (one of our men). Spencer asked what he wanted and the Mexican told him that his brother, Ran, was dead, so we all turned and went to Campbell's camp. *(Editor's note: The original text is unclear as to who died.)*

We found Spencer sitting against a tree, his head drooped down just like he was asleep. We got down and took him to a nearby house and laid him out. A young man by the name of Fly had his head on Spencer's legs and was struck also, but did not die until next day.

We crossed just below Austin where we had to rope two and drag them up the bank and roll them off in the river. It was about half-bank full. One of them got half way across and turned back, so when he came where we were we turned him back, and I turned my horse over to Vicento Carvajal and got the old scalawag by the tail – well if you never saw an old steer scared in swimming water you have no idea how fast one can swim.

After we got our cattle broken in I think we had the best herd on the trail. We had a very good time. At Austin was the last ferryboat so we had to cross all the streams without a boat.

At Belton we took the "New Chisum Trail," went by the way of Fort Worth, which was a small village of one or two small business houses, a blacksmith shop and I think a school house and about twenty families.

The Indians were bad in that section and we had a double watch on every night, which made it hard for us. Some nights the cattle would run the first watch and maybe we would be up all night. I have gone three days and nights without sleep, on the same horse, and with very little to eat.

We crossed the Red River about the 20th of May at Red River Station. It was up swimming and there were at least twenty herds balled up there waiting for the river to run down. It was a bad place to hold cattle, so many herds close together, so the boss, Mr. Drake, held a council with us all; some wanted to drive back a few miles and wait.

We crossed the Wichita the next day. From the time we crossed Red River we never saw a house till we got to Wichita. We soon began to have a little trouble with the Indians.

They would come and want a beef or two, but we would send them on to the next fellow, so we did not have to give them any at all, but they would stampede the cattle at night. We got into the buffalo country, and they gave us a little trouble.

Once just as we were getting our herd on the trail, a little after sunrise, a man from the herd just ahead of us loped back and told us that the buffaloes were coming, so we held our herd up. I went to the top of a little hill and I saw a black string. It looked as though it was coming straight to our herd.

I went back and we rounded our cattle up so we could hold them if the buffaloes did strike them but they passed just ahead of us. Our cattle got a little nervous, but we held them all right. It took the buffaloes two hours to pass us. Sometimes they would be one behind the other, and then they would come in bunches of 300 or 400.

I don't know how many to guess there was, but I think there must have been at least 50,000. Another time a bunch of about 300 ran through our herd while they were grazing.

We had some bad storms while we were on that long stretch across the plains. We crossed the Arkansas River at Fort Wichita about the 15th of June. About the 20th of June we stopped on a little creek called Beaver Creek. There Mr. Mayfield met us, and the hands all went back but myself and a Mr. Mimms, Charley Angermiller and the cook, Bill Payne. We stayed in that camp till about the first of September, and had a good time.

In October we started back to Texas. When we got to Red River there were at least 100 families waiting to cross coming to Texas and it looked like we were not going to get across at all, so I told Mimms and Angermiller if they would let me, I would come alone. They said all right, so I came on.

I got down to Belton and "swapped" horses with a man and gave twenty-five dollars "to boot," and got a dandy saddle, and sure "went yonder."

I had written to my wife to write me at Austin so when I got to Austin I got some very interesting news. I stayed in Austin that night, but the next morning by sun up I was on the road home. The next day at three o'clock I landed at home, 110 miles from Austin.

It was Sunday and there were several ladies there. Two of them had young babies, so after a kiss and a general handshake I wanted to see my baby (which had been born during my absence) and there were three all on one bed and all the same size, so they told me to take my choice.

After looking at them all I took a little redheaded girl baby, and that same red-headed baby is living at Rio Frio, Texas, and is 45 years old.

# Andrew G. Jones

I WAS A MEMBER OF ROBERT BALLENTYNE'S company of minute men, organized for the protection of the frontier. We had to scout twenty days in each month, and our pay was twenty dollars per month.

We furnished our own grub and mounts, while the state supplied us with guns and ammunition, and gave orders how we should take care of our horses. When in camp we had to stake and sideline each animal and put out a guard.

A Mexican named Manuel, who had been an Indian captive for fifteen years, was our trailer and guide, and he was a good one. He knew just how to follow all signs and trails, and he thoroughly hated an Indian.

One day we struck an Indian trail on Mason Creek and followed it to where the San Antonio road crosses Privilege Creek. Here the trail led up the creek, and we found a Mexican that had been killed by the Indians.

The Mexican was at work building a fence when he was attacked, and when he was struck with a rifle ball he ran and took refuge in an old chimney, which was standing where a frontier cabin once stood, and there he died. We found his body in this chimney in a sitting posture, with his pistol in hand ready to shoot.

From there we went on and came to a house, which the Indians had pillaged. They carried off a number of articles and trinkets, some of which we picked up as we hastily followed the trail.

We then found where they had stopped and painted themselves, preparatory to an attack on Jim and John Scott, who were clearing land, but they probably discovered our approach and fled, scattering in several directions, so that we could not successfully follow their trail.

We then went to the Bladen Mitchell Ranch and decided to go over to the Casey Ranch on the Hondo and try to intercept the Indians as they came out of the country.

We patrolled that region, two men each twenty miles apart scouting and observing signs, but without success. Then we crossed over to West

Prong of the Medina, and here we found a bunch of wild beef steers. Our captain told us to kill them and we shot eight of the big fellows, and as wild as cattle ever got.

Taking a supply of the beef we went on to head of the Frio, Tom Click and I patrolling. We found a place where the Indians had left fourteen Indian saddles, and also where they had made a great many arrows and mended moccasins. We stayed there four days expecting the Indians to come and get their saddles, but as they did not show up we burned the rudely made saddles and left there.

I remember when the Indians killed Mr. and Mrs. Moore on North Prong of the Medina River. We took their trail the next day and followed it across the mountains. They went into a dense cedar brake where it was impossible for more than one or two men to go together.

F.L. Hicks was with us on this scout and when we came to the dense cedar brakes our captain said it was unsafe to go in, and several of the men turned back, but Mr. Hicks said to me: "Andy, let's go in; we can whip every red rascal in there." So we went.

It was a risky thing to do, but Mr. Hicks was a man absolutely without fear, and when duty called he was always ready to respond. It is said that Indians will not kill a crazy man, so I guess they thought we were crazy for entering that big thicket.

The next scout we made we hired Old Man Smith with his three yoke of steers and went to the Frio Water Hole, where we built a good pen, and then we went to Bull Head on the Nueces and gathered 400 steers, which we intended to bring to Bandera and sell to Schmidtke & Hay for two dollars per head.

We appointed Sam Jones as our boss on this mavericking expedition. While on the Nueces we captured two government horses on the range with halters on. They had escaped from some post months or years before and had become wild. We brought the steers into the pen as we gathered them, and one night they stampeded and seventeen of them were killed by running against cedar stumps, which had been left in the pen.

About ten miles this side of the water hole was another pen, which was called Post Oak, and we brought our steers to it. Four men had to stay with the wagon, and as we were coming to the Post Oak pen, Jim Brown, Jim Gobble, Lum Champion and myself intended to reach a spring at the head of the hollow.

There were some Indians there, but I suppose they heard the wagon and hid out, as we did not see them. Near the spring I picked up a pair of moccasins and a small mirror, which had been dropped by them.

Leaving Champion and Gobble with the wagon, Jim Brown and I scouted around the spring to try to locate the Indians, but without success. We found where they had killed a cow just a short time before and taken some of the beef.

They were afoot, evidently coming down into the settlements on a horse-stealing expedition. When we reported our discoveries to the captain he said we could not leave the cattle to follow the Indians, but to guard against attack.

That night old Manuel and I stood guard around the horses, and at different times during the night the horses showed signs of alarm and we made ready to secure an Indian scalp, but they did not come.

We delivered our steers in due time and received two dollars per head for them, and also received fifty dollars for the two government horses we had captured, and we thought we were making money.

Somebody reported that we had gathered the 400 steers, and our arms were ordered to be returned and we all got fired from the Ranger service.

When I was a boy on my father's ranch the government kept a lot of camels at Camp Verde.

One day we hobbled three or four of our horses and turned them loose near the house, and fourteen of those old camels came lumbering along. The horses took fright at the sight of them, and we did not see those horses again for many days. My brother and I penned the camels, all of them being gentle except one.

We roped the wild one, but never wanted to rope another, for the old humpbacked villain slobbered all over us, and that slobber made us deathly sick.

We had a jolly time with those camels when we got rid of the foul, sickening slobber, and as we often rode broncos and wild steers we rode those camels too. The camel has a swinging pace and is easy to ride when you catch the motion of its gait. They could easily travel 100 miles in one day.

The Indians seemed to be afraid of the camels and, of course, never attempted to steal any of them.

# In Conclusion

*by J. Marvin Hunter, Editor and Author*

IT HAS BEEN A PLEASING TASK to compile this wonderful book, and I feel that something should be said of the efforts of Mr. George Saunders to "round up" all of the old boys and get their history in print so that the coming generations may read of the hardships and dangers they encountered and the splendid achievements of his comrades of days gone by.

For years Mr. Saunders endeavored to interest men in the publication of this kind of a book. At the Old Trail Drivers' convention held at San Antonio in 1917 the first steps were taken in this direction when the cowboys there present each volunteered to write a sketch of his life and send to Mr. Saunders for publication in the Trail Drivers' Book.

Some of them sent in the sketches in due time but some of them failed to respond promptly, and then the "roundup" started. Letters were sent out, phone and telegraph requests were made, and finally a sufficient number had been corralled to make an interesting book.

Arrangements were made to have it printed. An editor was employed to compile the sketches and get them in shape, and the editor and printer were going to get them out for Mr. Saunders. Suddenly the editor "went all to pieces" with a nervous breakdown, and the printer closed shop and departed for parts unknown, taking along all of the manuscripts and letters that had been sent in.

But nothing daunted, Mr. Saunders, set about again to roundup the old boys, and after two years' effort the first volume of *The Trail Drivers of Texas* was brought out, but it was incomplete, although it contained 500 pages.

The old trail drivers were delighted with the book and decided to have an additional volume. It was my happy privilege to write, compile and edit the first volume, at the behest of Mr. Saunders, and when it was decided to get out a second volume he insisted that I take charge of the work.

I have been handicapped in several ways, chiefly because I never was a cowboy, never put a rope on anything larger than a milk calf, never rode a yearling, forked a bronco or adorned my boot with a pair of "cornbread" spurs, and only by accident am I entitled to membership in the Old Trail Drivers' Association.

Sometime in the remote past, my father, John Warren Hunter, helped to keep up the drags with a herd going north, and thereby made me a son of a trail driver. My father was born in Alabama, but came to Texas when he was about nine years old.

His father was a Methodist preacher, and settled near Sulphur Bluff, in Hopkins County, where he was living when the Civil War broke out. My father, being about fifteen years old at the time, was employed as a teamster to haul cotton to Brownsville, the only port open to the Confederacy.

He spent the term of the war on the Rio Grande, where he became well known for certain daring feats. After the war he spent awhile in Lavaca County and returned to his home in Hopkins County to find that home broken up, his father dead and his brothers and sisters scattered to different parts of the country.

He went to Tennessee where he was happily married to my mother, Mary Ann Calhoun, and went to Arkansas where he farmed for a season, but he longed to get back to Texas, and returned in 1878, and became a schoolteacher.

For many years he taught school in Gillespie, Mason, Menard and McCulloch counties, being one of the pioneer teachers of that section. In 1891 he quit the school room to take up newspaper work, having purchased the *Menardville Record*, later moving the plant to Mason and establishing the *Mason Herald*.

He was one of the fearless editors of that time and the *Herald* became known as an outspoken weekly. Oftentimes he had to back up his assertions with muscle and brawn, but he was of Irish descent and really enjoyed a fisticuff, and when the match had been pulled off he was ready to shake hands and make friends.

He removed to San Angelo in 1907, and for several years was connected with the *San Angelo Standard*. His death occurred Jan. 12, 1915.

For many years prior to his death he had been engaged in collecting historical data and manuscript pertaining to the early history of Texas, and became recognized as one of the leading historians of the state.

Naturally I became interested in this kind of work and have tried to follow the same line, with the result that I fell right in when Mr. Saunders announced that he was going to print a book of reminiscence sketches of the early cowmen. I realized then that it would be a wonderful contribution to the historical annals of Texas, and that the time was ripe for its publication, as the older fellows are passing off the stage of action at an alarming rate and that within a few years not many would be left to tell the tale.

I realized then which fact has been made apparent since, that I was not qualified for the task that has been assigned me, but I have done my best, and that is all anyone can do. It has been a great pleasure to perform this task under the direction of Mr. Saunders, for he has been very considerate and patient, and left matters very much in my hands.

The Old Time Trail Drivers, as well as the youth of Texas, owe him a debt that can never be paid for thus rescuing from oblivion and preserving this important link in the chain of Texas history.

# Index

Abilene, Kan., 16, 20, 22, 23, 24, 25, 54, 55, 79, 80, 82, 95, 99, 105, 115, 116, 154, 155, 161, 180, 202, 218, 261, 263, 264, 294, 295, 298, 304, 311, 317, 320, 321, 330, 345, 363, 366, 385, 386, 387
Abilene, Texas, 244, 248
Adams, Bill, 354
Adams, Cood & Mart, 354, 355, 357
Adams, James, 354
Adams, John, 354
Adams, Mart, 354, 357
Alamo Plaza, 340
Albany, Texas, 38, 221, 318
Alice, Texas, 141, 144
Allen Ranch, 323
Allen, Bob, 249
Alley, Billy, 252
Alpine, Texas, 284
Amite County, Miss., 152
Ammons Ranch, 310
Ammons, Rocky, 310
Anderson, L.B., 152, 170
Anderson, W.P., 19, 385
Angermiller, Charley, 414
Apache Indians, 274, 397
Arapahoe Indians, 303
Arkansas City, Kan., 248, 322
Arkansas River, 19, 25, 49, 51, 55, 78, 89, 99, 100, 120, 138, 141, 142, 159, 160, 177, 215, 217, 218, 221, 304, 317, 322, 363, 364, 368, 380, 414
Arlington, John, 139
Arnold, Bill, 49
Atascosa County State Bank, 343
Atascosa County, Texas, 99, 171, 249, 251, 255, 270, 300, 340, 343, 346
Atascosa River, 310
Atascosa, Texas, 249, 270
Atkins, Mr. __, 341
Austin County, Texas, 228, 238
Austin Male College, 315
Austin, Texas, 47, 48, 54, 61, 76, 78, 87, 99, 103, 114, 148, 157, 158, 176, 195, 201, 217, 221, 226, 229, 261, 289, 294, 321, 323, 328, 347, 348, 351, 408, 410, 412, 413, 414
Awalt, Johanna, 232

Ayers, Pink, 349
Baggett Ranch, 410
Baker, Frank, 397, 398
Baker, O.J., 182
Baldo, Charlie, 326
Ballentyne, Robert, 415
Bandera County, Texas, 132
Bandera, Texas, 132, 133, 252, 282, 355, 416
Barnum & Bailey Circus, 143
Bartlett, Texas, 139
Bass, Sam, 85, 138, 195
Bastrop, Texas, 179, 181, 223, 348
Bates County, Mo., 353
Battle of Manassas, 325
Baxter Springs, Kan., 19, 20, 23, 59, 154, 159, 261, 332, 386
Baylor, John R., 124, 273
Baylor, Tom P., 122, 124
Beal, H.C., 240, 242
Bear River, 22
Bee County, Texas, 344
Bee, Ham P., 124
Beeville, Texas, 310
Belcher, John, 295
Belchers, 338
Bell County, Texas, 135, 249, 323
Bell Fourche, Wyo., 124
Bell, George, 247, 260
Bell, W.C., 207, 209
Belle Fourche River, 225
Belle Fourche, Wyo., 225
Belle Hotel, St. Louis, 330
Bellville, Texas, 228, 238, 239
Belton, Texas, 22, 87, 177, 217, 220, 249, 294, 413, 414
Benavides, Juan, 252
Bennett Ranch, 208
Bennett, Bill, 250
Bennett, Pink, 263
Bennett, William J., 102
Benton, Texas, 253
Berry, John, 207
Best, Jack, 346
Bexar County, Texas, 126, 129, 387, 392
Big Bow, Kiowa Chief, 337
Big Horn Ranch, 39
Bill Shope Ranch, 323

Billings, Jimmie, 330
Billy the Kid, 34, 35, 37, 397
Black Hills, S.D., 138, 225, 324, 380
Black, Gus, 111, 255, 306, 307
Blackburn, George, 99
Bladen Mitchell Ranch, 415
Blair, Wiley, 338
Blanco City, 241
Blanco County, Texas, 203
Blanco Creek, Texas, 344
Blanco River, 61, 354, 408
Blanco, Texas, 90
Bland, Billie, 170
Blank, Capt., 167
Blanks and Withers Ranch, 184
Blanks, Dr. John G., 83, 158
Blocker Ranch, 118
Blocker, Ab, 338
Blocker, Davis & Driscoll, 124
Blocker, J.R., 15, 118, 119, 154, 161, 162, 197, 247, 338
Bloomington, Ill., 330
Blue Mountains, 323
Bluntzer, Nick, 310
Bob Stafford Ranch, 286
Boon, Nestor, 354
Booth, Helmar Jenkins, 280
Borroum & Choate, 100
Borroum, B.A., 95, 99, 265
Bosler Ranch, 75, 76
Bosque County, Texas, 211
Bosque Grande Ranch, 395
Bosque River, 24, 316, 388
Bowles, Tom, 116
Boyce, Charles, 107, 108
Bradley, Sheriff William, 35
Brady City, Texas, 38, 224
Braners, Mr., 327
Brazel, Wayne, 35
Brazoria, Texas, 179
Brazos River, 38, 58, 61, 78, 87, 90, 99, 217, 221, 222, 270, 301, 316, 368, 374, 409
Brazos, Texas, 58, 317
Brewster County, Texas, 286
Brite, S.B., 57
Brock, George W., 183, 196
Brodbent, C.S., 311
Brooks County, Texas, 346
Brown County, Texas, 90
Brown, A.B., 100
Brown, Ganahl, 282

Brown, Jim, 416, 417
Brown, John & Joe, 354
Brown, John Henry, 362
Brown, Os, 98
Brown, Robert, 349
Brownsville, Texas, 50, 226, 267, 419
Buckalew, Sandy, 125
Buda, Texas, 289
Buffalo, Kan., 357
Bunton, Desha, 159
Bunton, John, 217
Burckley, Jack, 255
Burk, Sheriff James, 267
Burke, Billie, 38, 39
Burkett, T.J., Sr., 378
Burks, Mrs. A., 210
Burks, W.F., 210
Burleson County, Texas, 238
Burleson, Ed, 207, 209, 354
Burnet County, Texas, 93, 135
Burnett, Crawford, 315, 318
Burnett, Tally, 255
Burns, John, 244
Burns, Pat, 155
Burrows, G.O., 101
Burton, Texas, 232, 237
Bush Ranch, 324
Bush, Gov., 307
Butler, Baylor & Rose, 95
Butler, Pleasant Burnell, 292
Butler, W.G., 263, 293, 294, 295, 345
'Butter Weed', 338
Byler, Frank, 158
Byler, J.N., 95
Cabaniss, Mr. __, 340
Cache Creek, 335, 337
Caldwell County, Kan., 65, 321
Caldwell County, Texas, 50, 51, 52, 57, 78, 92, 118, 119, 120, 158, 181, 183, 190, 217, 223, 321, 340, 357, 387, 388
Caldwell, Kan., 66, 103, 169, 177, 244, 311, 330, 363
Calhoun, Mary Ann, 419
Cameron County, Texas, 388
Camp, John, 251, 252
Camp, Rosser & Carroll, 252
Campbell, Billy, 51, 80, 81, 82, 217, 252
Campbell, John, 412
Canadian River, 54, 57, 64, 65, 117, 130, 155, 193, 205, 214, 222, 245,

270, 304, 330
Carlyle, Jimmy, 35
Carrizo Springs, Texas, 250, 297, 395
Carroll, C.F., 251
Carroll, Columbus, 295
Carroll, Jake, 80
Carson, Kit, 25
Carter, T.J., 228
Casey Ranch, 415
Castro colonists, 110, 325
Castroville, Texas, 47, 132, 133, 256, 257, 282, 283
*Cattle Trail* (newspaper), 20, 386
Chambers, Ed, 256
Champion, Lum, 416
Chapman, Bud, 250
Chapman, Joe, 253
Chappa, Lebora, 251
Charco Largo, 341
Charles Goodnight Ranch, 38
Charles Lehmberg Ranch, 148
Cherokee Indian, 19, 20, 385
Cherryvale, Kan., 244
Cheyenne Indians, 250, 251, 303
Cheyenne, Wyo., 22, 39, 55, 56, 87, 89, 114, 137, 138, 142, 150, 160, 219, 225, 251, 252, 324
Chickasaw Indians, 100
Chicksaw Nation, 141
Chihuahua, Mexico, 276, 326
Childress, "Billy", 185, 188, 250
Childress, San, 185
Chisholm Trail, 19, 20, 24, 36, 51, 61, 95, 99, 103, 117, 119, 141, 148, 154, 180, 181, 191, 192, 196, 204, 217, 250, 255, 257, 262, 294, 301, 316, 320, 335, 367, 382, 385, 386, 388
Chisholm, Jesse, 385
Chisholm, John, 19, 20, 24, 25
Chissum, John, 20, 231
Chisum, John, 388, 395
Choate & Bennett, 99, 100, 261, 263, 265, 412
Choate, D.C., 100
Choate, Dunk, 261
Choate, Monroe, 95, 99, 261
Choate, W.M., 99
Choctaw Indians, 100, 294, 332
Chug River, 154
Cibolo Creek, 240
Cibolo River, 92, 93, 153, 261

Cimarron River, 141, 169
Civil War, 19, 24, 25, 58, 92, 95, 103, 104, 111, 127, 133, 146, 153, 164, 212, 227, 228, 237, 254, 259, 260, 277, 293, 314, 321, 333, 341, 344, 353, 362, 364, 391, 419
Clark & Woodward, 295
Clark, Asa, 38, 39
Clark, Jasper, 210
Clarksville, Texas, 56, 353
Classen Brothers, 289
Clayton, N.M., 65, 66
Clear Fork River, 189, 329, 374
Cleburne, Texas, 85, 177, 262, 294, 328
Click, Tom, 416
Coahuila (Mexican territory), 362
Cochrane, Frank, 323
Coe, Phil, 155
Coffeyville Trail, 257
Coffeyville, Kan., 20, 148, 386
Cold Water Creek, 204
Coleman & Stokely, 295
Coleman County, Texas, 58, 97, 113, 114, 289
Coleman Ranch, 344
Coleman, Thomas A., 352
Collins, F., 284
Collins, Joe, 251
Collins, Joel, 88, 138, 195, 261
Collins, Joel & Joe, 195
Collins, N.G., 267
Collins, Young, 345
Colorado City, Texas, 91
Colorado County, Texas, 124, 226, 254, 320
Colorado River, 22, 25, 54, 58, 59, 61, 78, 87, 90, 98, 99, 120, 129, 148, 175, 183, 195, 204, 217, 221, 224, 232, 236, 245, 251, 289, 316, 317, 320, 323, 328, 348
Columbus, Texas, 80, 90, 150, 159, 179, 222, 286, 317, 320, 323
Comal County, Texas, 387
Comanche Indians, 42, 90, 136, 137, 143, 177, 185, 209, 245, 246, 247, 273, 295, 303, 309, 336, 369
Combs, D.S., 285
Comfort, Texas, 97
Commerce St., San Antonio, 340
Company Ranch, 138
Concho River, 58, 59, 90, 131, 175,

177, 245, 251, 348, 370, 388, 389, 393
Cone, Neally, 408
Confederacy, 25, 50, 51, 61, 78, 127, 133, 200, 218, 347, 353, 361, 362, 391, 419
Connolly, Jeff, 157
Conover Ranch, 336
Conover, __, 336
Cooke County, 253
Coolidge, Kan., 43, 90
Cooper, Capt., 355
Coorpender, Bill, 155
Copeland, Joe, 99
Corley, Billy, 59
Corn Ranch, 364
Corpus Christi, Texas, 38, 216, 244, 267, 338, 385
Cottonwood Ranch, 274
Cotulla, Texas, 51
County, Denton, 388
Courtney, Mrs. Robert C., 400
Cow Creek, 39, 333
Cow Creek Station, 99
Cox, Isaac W., 58
Cox, Jim, 295
Craig, J.M., 232, 238
Craig, Sam, 240, 241, 242
Craig, Walter A., 241
Crenshaw, Nick, 328
Crow Ranch, 39, 40
Crutchfield, James, 98
Cruze Ranch, 61
Cruze, Joseph S., 61
Cruze, S.J., 62
Cude, N.W., 181
Cude, R.D., 182
Cuero, Manuel, 287
Culberson County, Texas, 332
Culberson, Hon. C.A., 144
Cureton, Capt. Jack, 58, 362
Cureton, John C., 58
Cureton, W.E., 58
Curtis & Cochran, 238, 239, 240
Custer, Gen. George Armstrong, 40, 250
Dallas County, Texas, 212
Dallas, Texas, 20, 95, 180, 301, 323, 351, 386
Dalrymple, James, 97
Dan Trent Ranch, 230
Daugherty, J.M., 332

Daugherty, Texas, 332
Daughtery, G.W., 209
Davis Ranch, 256
Davis, Allison, 98
Davis, J.H.P., 150
Davis, Tip, 98
Day Ranch, 410
Day, Dock, 285, 410
De Witt County, 235
Deadwood, S.D., 225
Deer Trail, Colo., 160, 380
Del Rio, Texas, 99, 101, 281, 400
Delaney, Frank, 153
Delaware River, 274
Deming, N.M., 391
Denison, Texas, 45, 46, 78, 264, 337, 338
Dennis, Capt. Tom, 295
Denton County, Texas, 332
Denver, Colo., 47, 150
Devil's River, 98, 245, 311
Dewee Ranch, 171
Dewees, Bill, 251
Dewees, John & Tom, 154, 170
Dewitt County, Texas, 391
DeWoodey, T.V., 315
Dickens, Texas, 310
Dignowity Hill, 327
Dillon Ranch, 72
Dillon, Mr. __, 76
Dimmit County, Texas, 392, 395
Dixon, H.M., 20, 386
Dixon, Mitchell, 297
Dixon, Shady, 354
Doak, John, 252
Doan, C.F., 335
Doan, J., 335, 337
Doan, Robert E., 335
Doan's Store, 20, 90, 119, 120, 136, 160, 185, 204, 222, 225, 270, 317, 388
Dobbins, John, 333
Dobie, J.M., 57
Dobie, Jim, 247
Dodge City Trail, 378
Dodge City, Kan., 20, 34, 36, 41, 43, 44, 68, 87, 88, 90, 93, 100, 105, 114, 120, 138, 141, 142, 154, 168, 185, 186, 194, 197, 204, 222, 225, 244, 250, 251, 270, 271, 280, 283, 295, 298, 310, 323, 326, 335, 357, 379, 386, 387, 388, 389

Dodge, Kan., 90
Donald Lawson & Co., 80
Dougherty, Bill, 250
Drake, Mr., 412, 413
Draper, York, 87
Drewry, Don, 231
Driscoll & Day, 221
Driskill, Dallas, 411
Driskill, Jess, 410
Driskill, John, 411
Driskill, Orland, 411
Driskill, Sam, 409, 410, 411
Driskill, Tol, 411
Druce Rachel Ranch, 100
Dubose, __, 338
Dumant, John, 204
Duncan, Ben, 306
Duncan, Uncle Ben, 255
Durango, Colo., 323
Duval County, Texas, 144
Dyer, Foster, 228
Eagle Pass, Texas, 98, 226, 281, 306
Eagle's Nest, 290
Eckert, Billy & Ed, 240, 241
Eddlemans, 338
Eddy County, N.M., 314, 318
Edwards & Ervin, 327
Edwards, Tobe, 98
Eggle, Joe, 251
Eisenhauer, Louis, 130
El Paso County, Texas, 274, 318
El Paso, Texas, 19, 245, 276
El Reno, Okla., 336
Ellis County, Texas, 212
Ellis, Joe, 155
Ellis, Noah, 51, 217, 220, 338
Ellison & Dewees, 93, 286
Ellison & Sheril, 286
Ellison & Sherill, 357
Ellison Ranch, 158
Ellison, Col. James F., 50, 57, 85, 93, 122, 124, 154, 158, 170, 191, 194, 221, 222, 223, 224, 225, 357, 358
Ellison, Jake, 115
Ellison, N.P., 191
Ellison, W.M., 191, 196
Ellsworth, Kan., 51, 106, 321
Emporia, Kan., 45
Enderle, Louis, 287, 288
English, Capt., 208, 209
English, Ed, 250
English, Lem, 250

English, Levi, 207
Eustace, A.N., 196
Evans, Tom, 411
Evans-Snider-Buel Co., 149, 150
Everts, Sam, 98
Ewing and Ingrams of California, 176
Fant, D.R., 68, 154, 204, 266, 380
Fawcett, Harry, 270
Fayette County, Texas, 183, 228, 347
Felder, W.F., 191
Fentress, Rany, 93
Ferrier, John, 99
Field, Sheriff Allie, 158
Fields, Major, 340
Figure 2 Ranch, 332
Finch, Riley, 316
Finche, Ischam, 315
Fisher, Tom, 160
Flint Hills, Kan., 322
Florence, Kan., 330
Flores, Pedro, 252
Folts, J.E., 320
Fort Arbuckle, 177, 321
Fort Belknap, 58
Fort Bend, 20
Fort Clark, 281
Fort Cobb, 25
Fort Concho, 58, 392, 393
Fort Dodge, 85, 198, 224
Fort Duncan, 393
Fort Ewell, 250
Fort Fetterman, 142, 154, 219
Fort Gibson, 78, 95, 305, 332
Fort Graham, 99, 409
Fort Griffin, 38, 83, 90, 157, 177, 197, 221, 225, 356
Fort Harker, 20
Fort Hays, 20, 52
Fort Laramie, 56, 69, 142
Fort Lyon, 20
Fort McKavett, 97, 288
Fort McPherson, 170
Fort Reno, 89, 250
Fort Riley, 20
Fort Robertson, 138
Fort Scott, 19, 333, 334
Fort Sill, 55, 85, 91, 95, 148, 155, 247, 251, 254, 330, 335, 336, 337
Fort Stanton, 59
Fort Steele, 83
Fort Stockton, 90, 252, 393
Fort Sumner, 25, 59, 64, 252, 374,

377, 389
Fort Wallace, 20, 254
Fort Worth & Denver Railroad, 270
Fort Worth Trail, 378
Fort Worth, Texas, 22, 78, 85, 87, 99, 102, 117, 129, 168, 169, 172, 176, 177, 180, 183, 202, 212, 221, 249, 262, 264, 276, 279, 294, 295, 317, 321, 323, 328, 410, 413
Fort Yuma, 348
Fort Zarah, 19, 25
Foster & Allen, 261
Foster, Bill, 408
Foster, W.B., 327
Franks, Dan, 252
Franks, L.A., 207
Fraser, Bill, 289
Fredericksburg, Texas, 38, 78, 90
Frio County, Texas, 97, 102, 112, 133, 207, 287, 306
Frio Ranch, 355
Frio River, 176, 282, 354
Fry, William L., 269
Fuller, Rufe, 119
Fullerton, John & Bill, 315
Gage, J.B. Mrs., 351
Gainesville, Texas, 95, 100, 115, 177, 254, 294, 295, 321, 338, 363
Gallagher, Barney "Buckshot", 395
Gallatin County, Ill., 327
Galveston, Texas, 80, 103, 179, 181, 200, 216, 314, 317
Gamel, John, 58, 148, 388
Garner, T.J., 321
Garrett, Pat, 35
Gatling, Billie, 378
George, Major, 327
Georgetown, Texas, 54, 152, 177, 217, 221, 261
Gerdes, George, 134, 280
Geronimo, 274
Gildea, A.M. (Gus), 391
Gildea, J.E., 391
Gillespie County, Texas, 50, 135, 242, 326, 419
Gillespie, Jack, 364
Gipson, Daniel P., 378, 379
Glenn, George, 320
Goat Creek, 288, 345
Gobble, Jim, 416
Goliad County, Texas, 88, 107, 166, 258, 260, 267, 268, 270, 292, 344,

345, 385, 388
Gonzales County, Texas, 107, 180, 181, 182, 191, 196, 258, 301, 315, 318
Gonzales Prairie, 107
Gonzales, Texas, 99, 200, 249, 251, 257, 261, 294, 295, 317, 318, 321, 323, 344, 388
Goode, Bill, 159
Goodnight & Loving Trail, 20, 24, 25
Goodnight Trail, 385, 389
Goodnight, Charles, 20, 24, 368, 374, 377, 386, 388
Goodnight, Texas, 24, 368
Goodwin, Texas, 22, 23
Gordon County, Ga., 135
Gore, Mrs. Lou, 345
Gosling, Hal, 47
Gran Tinnon Ranch, 274
Granada, Colo., 25
Grand River, 19
Grant, N.M., 252
Grant, President Ulysses S., 303
Gray, Billie, 170
Grayson County, Texas, 141
Great Bend, Kan., 20, 51, 94, 100, 154, 177, 221, 386
Greeley, Colo., 39
Greeley, Horace, 340
Green, Jim, 230, 231
Green, William, 22, 23
Grimes, W.B.G., 250, 299, 364
*Gruene Cowboy* (book), 13, 14
Gruene, Ernst, 13
Gruene, H.D., 13, 22
Guadalupe County, Texas, 152, 153, 244, 344
Guadalupe River, 92, 99, 129, 161, 236, 237, 240, 245, 256, 327, 328
Gulf Coast, 312
Gulf Railroad, 342
H&D. Ranch, 251
Haby, Nic, 281
Haddocks, Frank, 137
Hale, Sam, 238, 239
Hall, __, 176
Hall, Capt., 204
Hall, Emory, 345
Hall, N.H., 274
Hamilton, Mary, 379
Hampton, Wade, 327, 328
Handy, Paul, 97

Hankins, J.M., 92
Hannibal, Mo., 269
Hardeman, Monroe, 114, 186
Hardeman, W.B., 122
Hardin, Wesley, 116
Hargis, Willis, 185
Harkey, Levi J., 309
Harlan, Forest, 62
Harmon, Bill, 310
Harmon, C.T., 310
Harmon, Mrs. C.T. (Julie), 309
Harmon, Sam, 284
Harrell, Monte, 301, 302, 304
Harrington, S.B., 349
Harris, Jack, 43, 101, 315, 317
Harrow & Packer, 330
Hartmann, Alf, 130
Haskell County, Texas, 144
Hawker, Tom, 121
Hawkeye Land & Cattle Co., 133
Hay, Len, 250
Haymond, Texas, 286
Haynes, Charles, 200
Haynes, George, 78
Haynes, John James, 200
Hays City, Kan., 82, 410
Hays County, Texas, 23, 61, 87, 89, 182, 190, 285, 297, 361
Head & Bishop, 68
Head, Dick, 68, 83, 114, 154
Head, Jerry, 218
Headquarters Ranch, 395
Hearne, Texas, 85
Hedgepeth, Charlie, 114
Hennant, King, 38, 39
Henson, W.T., 256
Heven, John, 280
Hez Williams Ranch, 161
Hickok, Wild Bill, 116, 155, 330
Hicks, Bill, 411
Hicks, F.L., 416
Hilderbrandt, Bud, 250
Hill, George, 51, 83, 113, 218
Hilliard, E.F., 191, 192
Hindes, George F., 250, 251, 340
Hindes, Texas, 340, 342
Hindman, George, 35
Hinds & Hooker, 59
*History of Texas* by John Henry Brown, 362
Hohmeyer, Charles, 238
Holden Ranch, 154

Holstein, Sim, 249
Holt Live Stock Co., 63
Holt, Jim, 235, 237
Hondo River, 415
Hondo, Texas, 59, 133, 134, 171, 255, 289, 300, 348
Hons, Dr. __, 238, 240
Hood & Hughes, 321
Hopkins County, Texas, 419
Horn, Dick, 250
Horsehead Crossing, 58, 389, 392, 393
Horton, Pres, 409, 411
Houston Packing Company, 271
Houston, Samuel Dunn, 63, 66, 68
Houston, Texas, 179, 182, 226, 250, 323
Howard County, Mo., 353
Howell, George, 115
Hudspeth County, Texas, 332
Hughes, Will, 270
Hugo, Colo., 65, 67, 162, 323
Hullum, Joe, 118
Humboldt, Kan., 323
Hunt, Hub, 257
Hunter, J. Marvin, 6, 13, 418
Hunter, John Warren, 419
Hunter, Lem, 363, 364
Huntsville, Texas, 314, 315
Hutcheson Ranch, 161
Immigrants' Trail, 348
Independence Ranch, 252
Indian Bend Ranch, 250
Indian Territory, 19, 22, 45, 46, 51, 85, 87, 90, 91, 94, 103, 106, 107, 114, 115, 119, 123, 124, 130, 144, 148, 155, 161, 163, 169, 172, 193, 197, 204, 212, 256, 257, 262, 268, 282, 294, 301, 303, 305, 311, 317, 318, 320, 330, 332, 335, 363, 378, 379, 386, 388, 389
Indianola, Texas, 216
Irvin, W.C., 153, 154
IS Ranch, 141, 144
Isbell, Branch, 213
J.C. Loving Ranch, 367
Jack County, Texas, 253
Jackman, Col. S.D., 361
Jackman, W.T. (Bill), 124, 159, 160, 161, 222, 224, 353
Jackson County, 105
Jackson, Ace, 191

Jackson, Nat, 244
James, Coleman, 321
Jary, W.E., 276
Jayhawkers, 138, 332, 333
Jeff Davis County, Texas, 90
Jefferson, John & Dud, 153
Jefferson, John & Fenner, 155
Jefferson, Texas, 363
Jennings, Bob, 118
Jennings, W.H., 118, 119
Jim Wells County, Texas, 144
John Adams Ranch, 255, 256
John Chisholm Cherokee Trail, 20
John Chissum Trail, 20
Johns, Bob, 135
Johns, C.R., 354
Johnson County, Texas, 212
Johnson, A.B., 315
Johnson, Capt. A.J. & Martha, 350
Johnson, Col. T.H., 363
Johnson, Delia, 350
Johnson, Gen. Albert Sidney, 325
Johnson, Gus, 83
Johnson, President, 391
Johnson, President Andrew, 147
Johnson, R.B. (Bob), 320
Johnson, Slim, 44
Johnson, Tom, 80, 81, 229
Johnson, Tom & Sam, 78
Johnson, V.A., 255, 256
Johnson, W.A., 318
Jones Ranch, 120, 344
Jones, A.C., 344
Jones, Andrew G., 415
Jones, Arthur, 239
Jones, Coleman, 50
Jones, Emanuel, 51
Jones, J.J., 120
Jones, Russ, 185
Jones, Sam, 416
Jordan, Bud, 345
Jourdanton, Texas, 343
Judge L. Moore Ranch, 183
Julesburg, Colo., 89, 138, 185, 187, 188, 219, 323
Junction City, Kan., 20, 201, 270, 305, 386
Juvanel, Cul, 48
Kansas City, 23, 45, 76, 101, 103, 169, 252, 283, 289, 321, 323, 364
Kansas Pacific Railroad, 80, 180, 182
Kansas Trail, 132, 210, 216

Karnes County, Texas, 99, 155, 168, 169, 292, 294, 296, 345
Kaufman, Ed, 134, 282, 283
Kaw Indians, 100
Kaw Nation, 321
Kaw Reservation, 99
Kaynaird, __, 332
Keeney, Wiley & Hurst, 274
Keith, Gus, 235
Kenton, Okla., 38
Kerrville, Texas, 270, 282, 288, 289
Keys, Mr. __, 334
Kilgore Ranch, 171
Kimble County, 388
Kincaid, W.D., 286
King & Kenedy, 267
King Ranch, 69, 226, 295
King, Capt., 157
Kinney County, Texas, 111
Kiowa Indians, 137, 246, 303, 336, 337
Klappenbach Ranch, 280
Knight, George, 360, 361
Knowles, Joe, 196
Kokernot, John, 274
Konda, Gus, 153
Krempkau, William B., 325
Kuykendall, Sauls & Burns, 244
Kyle, Felix, 354
Kyle, Ferg & Curran, 354
Kyle, Texas, 87, 159, 160, 161, 225, 244, 248, 256, 289, 409
L L Ranch, 323
L.X. Ranch, 121
La Junta, Colo., 39, 120
La Luz, N.M., 275
La Parita Ranch, 251
LaGrange, Texas, 236, 348
Lamb, Drew, 99
Lampasas County, Texas, 118
Lane, Givens, 357
Lane, Givings, 119
Lansford, Bud, 346
Laredo, Texas, 144, 245, 251, 267
Larkin, Mr. & Mrs., 314
Las Moras Ranch, 240
LaSalle County, Texas, 57, 184
Lauderdal County, Miss., 340
Lavaca County, Texas, 106, 107, 419
Lawhon, Luther A., 19, 163
Lawrence County, Miss., 314
Lay, John & Tom, 155, 171

Lea, Mrs. William E., 400
Leakey, George, 98
Lee County, Texas, 229, 238
Lee, Gen. Robert E., 19, 353, 391
Leedy, Hank, 322
Leona Ranch, 97
Leona River, 102, 207, 208
Lewis & Blunzer, 251
Lewis, C.C., 310
Lewis, Hugh, 235
Lewis, Joe, 196, 197
LFD Ranch, 157
Lincecum, Brace, 22
Lindsey, Ad, 408, 409
Lindsey, B.D., 408
LIT Ranch, 270
Littlefield, George W., 157
Live Oak County, Texas, 168, 204, 228, 310, 391, 392
Live Stock Commission Co., 276
Llano County, Texas, 49, 50, 200, 201, 347, 349, 351
Llano River, 245, 315, 317, 356
Llano, Texas, 348
Lloyd, Eli P., 349, 350
Lockhart, Texas, 22, 23, 50, 54, 69, 76, 78, 80, 92, 113, 114, 117, 157, 158, 183, 189, 191, 195, 211, 217, 220, 229, 261, 321, 323, 340, 385
Lomax, John J., 27
Long, Jim & Tobe, 92
Longview, Texas, 225
Lopez, Benito, 294
Lopez, Manuel, 289
Lott, Miss Clip, 268
Lours, Dave, 335
Loveland, Colo., 321, 324
Loving, Oliver, 25, 58, 368, 369, 370, 371, 374, 375, 376, 377, 388
Low, Pinkney, 153, 154
Lowe, Jim, 341
Luling, Texas, 111, 117
Luna Valley, Ariz., 274, 275
Lynn, Capt., 295
Lytle & McDaniel, 111, 133, 255, 306
Lytle & Schreiner, 306, 307
Lytle, Capt. John, 133, 154, 255, 307, 338
M.A. Withers Ranch, 189, 195
Maberry, Col. Seth, 154, 244
Maberry, Seth, 252
Maden, John, 267

Madison County, Texas, 85
Magdalena, N.M., 275
Magee, Alex, 160
Major Wolcott Ranch, 170
Malone, Jas. L., 354
Manewell, Neal, 248
Markwardt, Ad, 130
Martin Ranch, 208
Martin, Arch, 349, 350
Martin, Jim, 155
Martinez, Edmundo, 196
*Mason County Herald*, 419
Mason County, Texas, 114, 148, 315, 326, 355, 419
Mason, Texas, 38, 58, 90
Massengale, W.R., 412
Matthews, Willie, 65
Maverick (definition), 164, 165
Maverick, Sam, 164
Mayes, Bill, 155
Mayfield, W.H., 412
McBride, William, 305
McCaleb, J.L., 297
McCarty, Jesse, 99, 157
McClellan, J.D., 228, 229
McClellan, J.T., 230
McCoy, Joe G., 20, 80, 386
McCoy, John, 24
McCulloch County Land & Cattle Company, 49
McCulloch County, Texas, 49, 114, 347, 388, 419
McCurley, Jack, 250
McCutcheon & West, 106
McCutcheon, Willis, 106
McDaniel, Tom, 255
McDonald Ranch, 330
McKenzie Crossing, 290
McLean, Billie, 155
McMullen County, Texas, 113, 341, 346
McQueen, Albert, 191
McRae, Dick, 287
Medina County, Texas, 110, 111, 132, 133, 280, 282, 283, 284, 341
Medina River, 132, 255, 416
Mellard, R.T., 314
Menard County, Texas, 240, 388, 392, 419
Menges, Joe, 130
Meridian, Miss., 58, 316, 340
Mescalero Indians, 393, 396, 397

Meyers, Al, 327, 328, 329, 330
Meyers, Col. Jack, 50, 321
Meyers, J.J., 20, 386
Middlebrack, Jake, 107
Miles, Col. John D., 303
Miller & Lux, 60
Miller, T.B., 155
Millett & Irvin, 154
Millett & Irvin Ranch, 170
Millett & Lane, 274
Millett Brothers, 221
Millett Ranch, 120, 221, 222
Millett, Alonzo, 154
Millett, E.B., 154
Millett, Eugene, 154
Millett, Hie, 154
Mills, __, 411
Mills, G.W., 184, 189
Mills, Henry P., 189
Mississippi River, 80, 152, 181, 269, 292, 348
Mitchell & Pressnall, 252
Mitchell, Bladen, 132, 133, 154
Mitchell, L.W., 285
Mock, Isaiah, 249
Mohle, G.H., 54, 218
Mongomery, Black Bill, 54
Monier, Mr., 325, 326
Monoy & Wilbert, 327
Monroe County, Mo., 78
Montague County, Texas, 85, 141, 321
Montgomery, Bill, 52, 55, 83, 218, 220, 221
Montgomery, J.W., 118, 218
Monument Rock, Kan., 329
Moore, Jack, 328, 329, 330
Moore, Judge L., 183
Moore, Sam, 224
Moreland, Anderson, 269
Morgan, Haynes, 155
Morgan, John, 330
Morris, Julia, 327
Morris, Ysidro, 346
Morrow Ranch, 48
Moss Mercantile Co., 350, 351
Moss, James R., 347, 349, 350
Moss, W.B., 349, 350
Moyer, Babe, 345
Mulhall, Zack, 330
Murchison, William, 22, 49
Murphy, J.W., 250

Murray, Wash, 51
Muscatine, Iowa, 133
Myers, Col. Jack, 22, 92, 217
Nail, Col. G.W., 328, 329
Nance, Maj. E., 354
Nations, Andrew, 228
Nations, Bob, 228, 229
Navasota, Texas, 314
Naylor, John, 345
Ned, Jim, 58
Nelson, Col., 330
Nenecatchie Mountains, 290
Neosho County, Mo., 249
Neutral Strip, Okla., 332, 334
New Braunfels, Texas, 13, 256, 289
New England Livestock Co., 38
New Iberia, La., 285
New Orleans, La., 80, 103, 111, 180, 181, 216, 249, 314, 317, 391, 392
Newman & Davis, 276
Nickols, Mit, 155
Ninnesquaw River, 170
Ninnesquaw River, 100, 130
Niobrara Ranch, 76
Noonan Ranch, 257, 282
Northern Pacific Railroad, 143
NOX Ranch, 176
Nueces County, Texas, 157, 158, 210
Nueces River, 45, 92, 97, 98, 124, 229, 245, 293, 311, 341
Nunn, J.W., 229
O'Connor Ranch, 244
Oakville, Texas, 274
Oatman, John, 347
Obar, Dr. John, 230
Odell, Jim, 137, 138
Odem, Tobe, 232
Oden, Dean, 207, 209
Oden, Volley, 251
Ogallala, Nebr., 40, 45, 68, 69, 72, 75, 76, 85, 89, 90, 114, 124, 138, 142, 148, 154, 186, 187, 191, 194, 195, 197, 204, 222, 223, 224, 225, 244, 252, 286, 296, 323, 357, 358, 361, 387
Ogden, Utah, 23, 220, 321
Oklahoma City, Okla., 34
Old Love Ranch, 363
Old Time Trail Drivers' Association, 1, 6, 13, 15, 17, 19, 48, 283, 310, 382, 385, 387, 389, 419, 420
Old Trail Drivers' Convention, 394

Old Yellow Bear, 173
Oliver, Frank, 276
Oliver, John, 153
Olney, Richard, 351
Osage Indians, 79, 100, 177, 294, 295, 298, 342, 364
Overland Drive, 311
Overland Immigrant Trail, 56
Owens, Billie, 61, 408
Owens, Pete, 61
Ozment, N.G., 347
P.D. Armour & Co., 315, 317
Packer, William, 330
Packsaddle Mountain, 50, 347, 349
Painted Cave, 291
Palo Pinto County, Texas, 58, 59, 362
Palo Pinto, Texas, 25, 58, 59, 362, 363
Panhandle Ranch, 154, 223
Panhandle, Texas, 20, 386
Parker County, Texas, 253, 364
Parker, Quanah, 135, 136, 336, 378, 379
Paschal, John, 99, 100
Paul's Valley, 172, 336, 363
Payne, Bill, 414
Pearl River, 314
Pearsall National Bank, 343
Pearsall, Texas, 102, 255, 340, 343
Pease River, 38, 119, 120, 135, 197
Peck & Evans, 321
Pecos County, Texas, 252
Pecos Land & Cattle Company, 252
Pecos River, 24, 25, 58, 63, 64, 65, 67, 90, 91, 98, 157, 245, 348, 368, 369, 370, 374, 389, 393, 394
Pedernales River, 288
Peeler, Tom, 170
Pena, Jesus, 252
Penick, Taylor, 49
Perry Day Ranch, 409
Perry, Mr. __, 340
Perryman & Lytle, 132
Perryman, Bill, 111, 256
Persons, Ed, 52
Pete, Tim, 335
Peters, Eberly, 409, 411
Pettus Ranch, 260
Pettus, W.A. "Buck", 267, 268
Phillips, Dan, 217
Pierce, "Shanghai", 250
Pierce, A.H., 103

Pierce, Shanghai, 261
Pine Bluff, Wyo., 252
Pittsfield, Ill., 269
Platte River, 25, 39, 55, 57, 69, 72, 83, 85, 89, 90, 138, 142, 170, 187, 191, 219, 223, 318, 380
Platte Rivers, 296
Pleasanton, Texas, 57, 83, 207, 346
Plumer, J., 328
Polk, Cal, 121
Polk, F.M., 117
Pope County, Ark., 391
Pope, C.W., 196
Porter, Dave, 346
Post, Texas, 362
Potter, Jack, 38, 42, 47, 265, 266
Powder River, 39, 142, 252, 324
Pressnall, Jesse, 44, 83, 154, 252
Preston, Mrs. A.M., 400
Price, Gen. Sterling, 353, 361
Prinz, Philip, 130
Pryor, Col. Ike T., 145, 146, 148, 150
Pryor, Dave & Ike, 49
Pucket & Rogers, 95
Pueblo, Colo., 90, 134, 280, 283, 389
Pumphrey, Beal, 48
Pumphrey, J.B., 48
Pusey, W.M., 328
Putman, Harve, 201, 202
Putman, John, 318
Quigley, Sheriff, 47
Quihi, Texas, 280, 284
R2 Ranch, 378
Rabb, Lee, 267
Rachal, Chris, 310
Ragsdale, Uncle Bob, 255, 256
Ranch, Tortilla, 251
Randolph County, Mo., 102
Rattlesnake Canyon, 274
Ray, J., 351
Raymond, Charlie, 411
Read, Jim, 345
Reame, Joe, 251
Red Cloud Agency, 68, 71, 76, 154, 224, 244
Red Fork Ranch, 141
Red River, 19, 20, 22, 25, 51, 52, 53, 54, 59, 78, 85, 87, 90, 93, 94, 95, 99, 100, 103, 104, 107, 117, 119, 120, 135, 136, 141, 143, 157, 158, 161, 169, 172, 177, 180, 181, 185, 192, 193, 196, 202, 204, 212, 217,

221, 222, 225, 251, 254, 256, 262, 264, 270, 282, 294, 301, 305, 306, 317, 320, 321, 332, 335, 338, 348, 363, 378, 385, 387, 388, 409, 413, 414
Red River Canyon, 329
Red River County, Texas, 353
Red River Station, 22, 87, 95, 99, 100, 103, 117, 155, 172, 262, 295, 297, 306, 323, 329, 367, 388, 409, 413
Redus Ranch, 255, 300
Redus, George, John & Bill, 255
Redus, Mr. __, 342
Reed, Charlie, 170
Reed, J.D., 266
Reed, Jim, 330
Reeves, Rachel, 268
Reeves, W.M., 268
Refugio County, Texas, 268, 346
Reynolds, Coleman, Matthis & Fulton, 267
Reynolds, Hiram, 345
Reynolds, John, 345
Rhodes, Frank, 155
Rice, John, 356
Richie Brothers, 324
Richland Springs, Texas, 309, 310
Richmond, Texas, 150
Ricks, Sarah Ann, 292
Ricks, Uncle Billy, 293
Riggs, John, 23
Rio Frio, Texas, 412, 414
Rio Grande, 46, 59, 102, 103, 118, 144, 226, 245, 251, 275, 290, 311, 388, 391, 398, 419
Rio Medina, Texas, 110, 132
Ripps, M.J., 287, 289, 291
Roberts, Charlie, 118
Robertson, J.C., 124
Robuck, E.A. (Berry), 50
Robuck, Emmet, 50
Robuck, Terrell (Tully), 50
Rock Creek, 99
Rockwall County, Texas, 363
Rocky Ammons Ranch, 310
Rocky Ford, Colo., 323
Rocky Mountains, 23, 38, 154, 161, 170, 219, 380
Rogers, Billy, 364
Roland, Barney "Pard", 196
Roosevelt Ave., San Antonio, 327
Roswell, N.M., 392

Round Rock, Texas, 48, 85, 129, 176, 323, 328
Rout, Gov., 187
Rowden, Jim, 93
Rung, Louis, 240
Runge Ranch, 235, 237
Runnels County, Texas, 250
Rust, C.H., 174
Rutledge, E.B., 99
Rutledge, John, 409, 411
Rye, Edgar, 175
Saathoff, Eames, 134
Saathoff, Ehme, 282
Saathoff, J.M., 282
Saathoff, John, 134
Sabinal, Texas, 408, 411
Sabine River, 362
Sacramento River, 274
Saffold, Gen. William, 154
Saline River, 81
Salt Lake City, Utah, 22, 150, 321
Saltillo, Mexico, 326
*San Angelo Standard*, 419
San Angelo, Texas, 58, 85, 86, 90, 97, 174, 177, 401, 419
*San Antonio Express*, 347
San Antonio Railroad, 342
San Antonio River, 287, 292, 293
San Antonio, Texas, 19, 24, 38, 41, 43, 44, 47, 61, 62, 63, 64, 68, 92, 93, 103, 104, 106, 111, 113, 114, 121, 124, 125, 126, 127, 128, 129, 130, 131, 134, 135, 150, 151, 153, 163, 164, 165, 168, 176, 179, 200, 229, 238, 251, 255, 256, 258, 267, 268, 270, 271, 276, 279, 281, 285, 286, 287, 289, 290, 291, 301, 310, 311, 315, 316, 321, 323, 325, 326, 327, 340, 352, 354, 355, 362, 382, 385, 387, 390, 392, 394, 399, 408, 418
San Carlos, Ariz., 395
San Felipe, Texas, 290
San Fernando Cathedral, 325
San Luis Potosi, Mexico, 326
San Marcial, N.M., 275
San Marcos River, 93, 118, 328, 412
San Marcos, Texas, 27, 85, 92, 115, 124, 159, 161, 176, 238, 240, 285, 289, 293, 353, 354, 361, 408, 409, 412
San Miguel Creek, 340

San Miguel, Texas, 92, 133, 341, 342
San Patricio County, Texas, 100, 310, 388
San Saba County, Texas, 135, 309, 318, 326
San Saba River, 271
San Saba, Texas, 309
Sanderson, Texas, 400
Sandies Creek, 315
Sandrock Springs, Texas, 232
Sandtown, Texas, 226, 228, 238
Sansom, Capt. John, 273
Santa Fe Railroad, 16, 59, 317
Satanta, Chief of the Kiowas, 336
Saunders, George W., 7, 13, 14, 16, 34, 44, 47, 100, 155, 206, 244, 245, 246, 247, 248, 258, 276, 283, 289, 291, 308, 310, 385, 418, 420
Schelcher, J.W., 287
Schmidtke & Hay, 416
Schorp & Spettel, 132
Schorp & Spettel Property, 112
Schorp, Louis, 110, 112, 132, 282
Schweers, Johanna, 284
Schweers-Kern Commission Co., 134
Scott County, Miss., 292
Scott, G.W., 97
Scott, Jim & John, 415
Scroggin, Jack, 99
Scurry County, Texas, 232
Seals, Mr. __, 341
Sears, Will, 119
Seguin, Texas, 114, 115, 152, 154, 170, 244, 289, 327, 328, 344
Seven Crook Ranch, 69
Seven D Ranch, 98
Seven Rivers Ranch, 395
Seven Rivers, N.M., 274
Shackleford County, Texas, 59, 318
Shadley, Bill, 135
Shadley, Bob, 138
Shawnee Creek, 138
Shawnee Indians, 336
Shedd Ranch, 398
Sheehan, John, 289
Sheeley, Capt. Joe, 47
Shelby, Joe, 361, 391
Shepard, Della, 318
Sheridan, Phil, 354
Sherill, Jas. H., 357
Sherman, Texas, 100, 141, 144, 323, 338
Sherrill, Jim, 154
Shiner, Joe, 252, 287, 288, 289
Short & Saunders, 289
Shreveport, La., 78, 180, 353, 363
Sinton, Texas, 309
Sioux Indians, 154, 250, 251
Sitting Bull, 40, 250
Skull, Sally, 267
Slaughter Ranch, 234, 235
Slaughter, C.C., 20, 232, 362, 363, 386
Slaughter, Elizabeth, 382
Slaughter, Gen. J.E., 391
Slaughter, J.B., 362
Slaughter, John, 250, 395
Slaughter, Mr. & Mrs. W.B., 382
Slaughter, P.E., 362, 363
Slaughter, Sarah Jane & Rev. George Webb, 362
Slaughter, William Baxter, 362
Smith & Elliott, 326
Smith & Leedy, 321
Smith & Wimberly Ranch, 50
Smith, Cap & Doc, 155
Smith, Capt. Bill, 276
Smith, Henry, 130
Smith, John, 38, 39
Smith, Old "Dog Face", 44, 45, 416
Smith, Tom, 255
Snively, Capt., 58
Snyder, John, 323
Socorro, N.M., 275
Solomon River, 317
Somerset, Ky., 189
Southern Pacific Railroad, 252, 317
Southern Pacific Railway, 226, 282, 290
Sowell, Leroy, 155
Speed, Jim, 255, 306
Spettel, Joe F., 110
Spettel, John, 110
Spotted Agency, 323
Springfield, Ill., 269, 326
St. Louis, 317, 330
St. Louis, Mo., 80, 353
St. Mary, 267
Stafford & Selmer, 293
Stafford Brothers, 124
Stafford, Bob, 159, 222, 286
Stanefor, Billy, 233, 234
Steele, Henry D., 113
Steen, George N., 115

434 | The Gruene Cowboy

Stephens & Worsham, 367, 378, 379
Stevenson, Taylor, 98
Stewart, Mac, 51, 52, 321
Stewart, Monroe, 99
Stoddard, Latman & Howard, 252
Stone, Capt., 366
Stonewall County, 49
Storey, E.M., 191, 192
Story, Capt. G., 354
Strait, John, 99
Strickland Ranch, 412
Studebaker wagon, 281, 320
Sturm Hill, 280, 284
Suggs Brothers, 144
Sullivan & Skidmore, 295
Summer County, Kan., 311
Sumner, John, 99
Sutton, Fred E., 24, 34
Swearingen, Tobe, 186
Swilling, Thomas W., 392, 394
Tabor & Rodabush, 83
Tafolla, Little Pete, 289
Tarno, "Old Man" Charlie, 238
Tascosa, Texas, 20, 389
Tat Huling Ranch, 274
Taylor, Dan, 53, 124, 154, 207, 208, 209
Taylor, Dan & George, 301
Taylor, Jim, 108
Taylor, L.D., 301
Taylor, Texas, 46, 48, 90, 118, 135, 157, 195, 244
Taylor, Tom, 85
Temple, Texas, 410
Terrell, Tom, 155
Texas Cattle Raisers' Association, 58, 149, 312
Texas Rangers, 260, 268, 321
*The Chisholm Trail* by John A. Lomax, 382
The Old "Square Dance" of the Western Range, 401
The Old Chisholm Trail (poem), 382
Thomas, Mike H., 352
Thompson River, 324
Thompson, Billie, 155
Tigre Ranch, 57
Todd, Col., 327, 328, 329, 330
Todd, W.M., 327
Tom Green County, Texas, 86, 286, 318
Tom, Dud, 153, 155

Tom, Dudley, 171
Tom, John Ranch, 171
*Tombstone Epitaph* (newspaper), 30
Tombstone, Ariz., 30
Tonkaway Indians, 362, 364
Toyah Land & Cattle Company, 90
*Trail Drivers of Texas* (book), 6, 13, 15, 385, 387, 389, 418
Travis County, Texas, 347
Trinidad, Colo., 38, 396
Trinity River, 22, 78, 99, 100, 102, 212, 262, 301, 314, 315, 317, 329
Trotters Landing, Miss., 327
True-Heart Ranch, 287
Tucker & Duncan, 256
Tula Rosa, N.M., 348
Tularosa, N.M., 275, 393, 396, 397
Tusler Ranch, 68
Tuttle & Chapman, 251
Tuttle, Cal, 118
Underwood, Nath, 393, 394
Union Pacific Railroad, 41, 85, 195, 317
Union Parish, La., 408
Union, Texas, 310
Upton, Jim, 296
Uvalde County, Texas, 111, 185, 326
Uvalde Railroad, 342
Uvalde, Texas, 46, 85, 97, 98, 103, 124, 176, 282, 290, 321, 322, 354, 355, 388
Val Verde County, Texas, 311
Valley Mills, Texas, 294
Vance, John, 132
Vick, Whit, 153, 155, 170
Victoria, Texas, 106, 108, 244, 267, 276, 295
Victorian, 289
W.K. McCoy & Bros., 79, 80
Waco, Texas, 78, 87, 217, 262, 300, 301, 328, 408
Waelder, Texas, 180, 301, 378
Walbarger County, Texas, 378
Walker County, Texas, 85, 314
Wallace, Bigfoot, 273
Walsh, Col. C., 401
Warner Ranch, 348
Warren, Dr. D.B., 59
Washington County, Texas, 61, 226, 227, 228, 229, 230, 232, 238, 242
Washington, D.C., 303
Washita River, 88, 114, 130, 155, 172,

186, 222, 263, 330, 363
Waterloo, Iowa, 285
Watson & Co., 135
Watts, Jim & Dock, 255
Weatherford, Texas, 337, 377
Webb County, Texas, 144
Webb, Alex, 135, 136, 138
Webberville, Texas, 195, 221
Wellington, Kan., 311
Wells, John B., 135, 139, 318
Wesson, Stock, 240, 241, 242
West, George W., 106, 204, 228
West, Sol, 105, 106
Westbrook Ranch, 408
Wetmore, Texas, 289
Wharton County, Texas, 159
Wheat, Mr. __, 341
Whitaker, S.H., 78
White Lake, N.M., 97, 98
White, Bill, 345
Wichita Falls, Texas, 135, 185, 270, 330, 338
Wichita River, 38
Wichita, Kan., 20, 79, 99, 103, 118, 129, 130, 135, 136, 138, 177, 180, 217, 218, 249, 250, 257, 289, 311, 317, 321, 335, 342, 363, 386, 387, 388, 409, 413, 414
Wilcox, George, 63
Wild Horse Jerry, 45, 46
Wilder, Tony, 328
Williams, Bill, 244, 273, 330
Williams, Frank, 207, 208, 209
Williams, H.G., 244, 248
Williams, Hez, 159
Williams, Judge J., 346
Williams, Miles, 248
Williams, Miss Nelia, 346

Williamson County, Texas, 152
Wilson County, Texas, 261, 387
Wilson Ranch, 283, 295
Wilson, Bill, 25, 204, 205, 368, 370, 371
Wilson, Sallie L., 315, 318
Wilson, Sam & John, 170
Wimberly Ranch, 50, 51
Winchester rifle, 70, 136, 137, 205, 322, 323, 338, 349, 350, 356
Withers, G.B. (Gus), 57, 83, 120, 121, 184, 187, 196
Withers, Mark A., 52, 57, 78, 113, 114, 120, 121, 183, 184, 188, 195, 196, 197, 199, 218, 220, 221
Wolf, Wash, 366
Wolfington, Lee, 124
Woodland, A.A., 157
Woods, Dr. P.C., 354
Woods, Jack, 75, 76
Woods, S.H., 141
Woodward & Oge, 306
Woofter, Newt, 255
Wooler, Steve, 130
Wootan, Dick, 25
Word, Charley, 338
Worsham, __, 338
Worth, Lt., 102
Wright, W.C., 249
Wrightsboro, Texas, 315, 317
Wyoming Ranch, 143
Yell County, Ark., 309
Young County Ranch, 367
Young County, Texas, 362, 367
Young, John, 346
Youngford, Texas, 327
Zook & Odem, 252